The Crisis Manag

Responding to the era of crises in which we now live, *The Crisis Manager* offers wise counsel for anticipating and responding to crises as well as taking the steps required to reduce the impact of these events. Spotlighting the reality of crisis at levels ranging from local to global, author Otto Lerbinger helps readers understand the approaches and ways of thinking required for successful crisis management in today's world. As no organization or individual is immune from crisis, he guides managers to make good decisions under conditions of high uncertainty, and to consider the interests not only of stockholders but also of a wide variety of stakeholders.

With a focus on the threat of crises to an organization's most valuable asset— its reputation—*The Crisis Manager* covers:

- Preparation for crisis, including crisis communication planning
- Physical crises—natural, biological, and technological
- "Human climate" crises, stemming from targeted attacks on an organization's policies, actions, or physical holdings
- Crises due to management failure, including mismanagement, skewed values, deception, and misconduct

New to this second edition are the use of social media in crisis management, and chapters on image restoration strategies and crises stemming from mismanagement, as well as a comprehensive updating of the entire work. Real-world case studies provide examples of what worked and what did not work, and the reasons why.

Written for present and future crisis managers in all types of businesses and organizations, this resource will be required reading for managers at all levels, as it prepares them for their crucial roles as decision makers.

Otto Lerbinger is Professor Emeritus at Boston University, specializing in corporate public affairs and applying the social sciences to management and communication. He holds a PhD in Economics and Social Science at the Massachusetts Institute of Technology.

Routledge Communication Series
Jennings Bryant/Dolf Zillmann, Series Editors

Selected titles in Public Relations (advisory editor James E. Grunig) include:

Strategic Public Relations Management
Planning and Managing Effective Communication Programs,
Second Edition
Austin/Pinkleton

Gaining Influence in Public Relations
The Role of Resistance in Practice
Berger/Reber

Public Relations Theory II
Botan/Hazleton

Crisis Communications
A Casebook Approach, Fourth Edition
Fearn-Banks

Crisis Management by Apology
Corporate Response to Allegations of Wrongdoing
Hearit

Applied Public Relations
Cases in Stakeholder Management, Second Edition
McKee/Lamb

The Global Public Relations Handbook
Theory, Research, and Practice, Revised and Expanded Edition
Sriramesh/Verčič

The Crisis Manager

Facing Disasters, Conflicts, and Failures

Second Edition

Otto Lerbinger

Routledge
Taylor & Francis Group

NEW YORK AND LONDON

Second edition published 2012
by Routledge
711 Third Avenue, New York, NY 10017

Simultaneously published in the UK
by Routledge
2 Park Square, Milton Park, Abingdon, Oxon OX14 4RN

Routledge is an imprint of the Taylor & Francis Group, an informa business

First edition published by Lawrence Erlbaum Associates, Inc. 1997

Library of Congress Cataloging in Publication Data
Lerbinger, Otto.
  The crisis manager / by Otto Lerbinger.—2nd ed.
  p. cm.—(Routledge communication series; 2)
  Rev. ed. of: The crisis manager: facing risk and responsibility. 1997.
  Includes bibliographical references and index.
  1. Crisis management. 2. Conflict management. I. Title.
  HD49.L468 2011
  658.4'056—dc23
  2011018811

ISBN: 978–0–415–89228–5
ISBN: 978–0–415–89231–5
ISBN: 978–0–203–22213–3

Typeset in Baskerville & Gillsans
by Swales & Willis Ltd, Exeter, Devon

Printed and bound in the United States of America on acid-free paper
by Edwards Brothers, Inc.

Contents

Preface to the Second Edition   xi

PART I
Preparing for an Era of Crises   I

The Connection Between Risk and Crisis Management 2

1 Understanding Crises   5

Proliferation and Severity of Crises 6
Recognizing a Crisis 8
Characteristics of a Crisis—How Managers Are Affected 10
Crisis as Opportunity 14
The Inevitable Involvement of the Media 15
Potential for Public Exposure of Crises Grows 15
Classifying a Crisis 17
Conclusions 22
Appendix to Chapter 1: Guidelines for Analyzing Crises 23

2 Risk Management: Preparing for the Worst   25

The State of Crisis Preparedness 26
Examples of Crisis Preparedness 28
Surveys on State of Crisis Preparedness 29
Components of Crisis Preparedness 30
Essentials of a Contingency Plan 33
Keep a Log—and Learn from Failures 42
Conclusions 44

3 Crisis Communication   45

The Media Can Damage Reputations 45
Crises of Communication Failure 46
Essentials of Crisis Communication 51

Guidelines for Crisis Communication 53
Conclusions 59

4   Image Restoration Strategies in Crisis Communication   61

Defensive and Accommodative Strategies 62
The Art of Apology 63
Analyzing Crisis Types—Marcus and Goodman Study 66
Two Illustrative Cases: Firestone/Ford and Archbishop Cardinal Bernard Law 67
Conclusions 74

PART II
Crises of the Physical Environment   77

Similarities and Differences 77
Coping with Risk 78

5   Natural Crises   85

Major Natural Disasters 85
Hazard Management Strategies 90
Overview of FEMA's Emergency Management Strategies 90
Mitigation: Reinforce the Physical Infrastructure 91
Preparedness 92
Quick Response—Activate Contingency Plans 98
Relief and Recovery Efforts 99
Conclusions 105
Appendix to Chapter 5: Major Issues in Relief Efforts 106

6   Biological Crises   111

Characteristics of Biological Diseases 111
Major Cases of Biological Crises 114
Strategies for Dealing with Biological Crises 124
Conclusions 130

7   Technological Crises   131

The Rapid Pace of Growth of Technology 132
Relevance of Risk Analysis 133
Three Recent Technological Crises 134
Hazard Management Strategies for Managing Technological Crises 141
The Future for Dangerous Technologies 150
Conclusions 151
Appendix to Chapter 7: Nanotechnology 152

PART III
Crises of the Human Climate   155

Application of Issues Management 156

8 **Confrontation Crises**   159

The Dynamics of Confrontations 160
Case Studies 164
Managing Confrontation Crises 174
Conclusions 183

9 **Crises of Malevolence**   185

Terrorism 185
Varieties of Malevolent Acts 187
Strategies for Countering Acts of Malevolence 200
Conclusions 206

PART IV
Crises of Management Failure   207

Damaged Relationships 208
Central Role of Ethics 209
Measuring Degree of Success 212

10 **Crises of Mismanagement**   215

Cases of Mismanagement 216
Strategies for Responding to Crises of Mismanagement 226
Conclusions 233

11 **Crises of Skewed Management Values**   235

Cases of Skewed Values 236
Strategies for Managing Crises of Skewed Values 246
Conclusions 250

12 **Crises of Deception**   253

Cases of Management Deception 254
Response Strategies to Crises of Management Failure 270
Conclusions 277
Appendix to Chapter 12: Risk as Seen by Behavioral Economics 278

13   Crises of Management Misconduct   281

Major Cases of Misconduct 283
Strategies for Handling Management Misconduct 292
Conclusions 297

PART V
Conclusions   299

14   Learning from Crises   301

Lessons Learned from Crises 303
Organizational Renewal in the Aftermath of a Crisis 310
Don't Waste a Crisis! 313

Notes   315
Index   365

Preface to the Second Edition

We are living in an era of crises, as daily news headlines remind us. Crises have become an unavoidable part of our private and organizational lives. Our attentiveness to messages on our cell phones and eagerness to remain in contact with friends on Facebook or Twitter reflect not only our desire for connectiveness but also our need to avoid unsettling "surprises." Over the centuries of manning watchtowers and listening to "Cassandras" to warn us of approaching enemies and dangers, we share the characteristic of animals always on the alert. With more things changing in our environment and more alarms sounded, we recognize the imperative of guarding against crises.

This book's first edition described this crisis awareness in the following paragraphs:

As crises become more numerous, visible and calamitous, organizations have no choice but to accept them as an inescapable reality that must be factored into their planning and decision-making. This book is written for present and future crisis managers—men and women who will be drawn into that inevitable occurrence and whose performance will determine their organization's future as well as their own. It is also written for all managers because the lessons learned in crisis management add to their qualifications as policy makers and decision makers.

The stability and predictability sought by managers in their dealings with the marketplace and socio-political environment are less and less attainable. There are now so many discontinuities in the business environment that an extrapolation of past trends can no longer be trusted to predict the future. Managers must learn to make decisions under conditions of high uncertainty and to consider the interests not only of stockholders but of a wide network of stakeholders—people who are affected by a company's decisions and actions and who, in turn, can affect the success of the company.

The imperatives of crisis management are still relevant today. But the dangers have become more urgent and the prescriptions more difficult. As the second decade of the 21st century begins, crises have become more numerous and more widespread and hazardous. In addition to businesses, nonprofits have also succumbed to crisis-producing conduct and, not surprisingly, government continues to be rife with corruption and scandals. No organization or person is immune from crises.

Furthermore, the frantic pace of globalization has spread crises throughout the world. Some are biological crises, like SARS; others are management failures, like Sanlu's baby formula scandal. As crises cross borders, they become more dangerous because they affect more institutions and people. The best illustration is the 2008 financial crisis, which, although starting in the United States, has threatened the economic stability of financial institutions worldwide and caused widespread hardship. Recovery from such a crisis requires the joint effort of the private and public sectors of many nations. One consequence is that the free-market system enjoyed by business will be constrained as governments impose more regulations.

Several forces and trends create greater uncertainties and possible dangers. New technologies, such as bioengineering, while holding much promise for feeding growing world populations, continue to face opposition because their underlying science contains many uncertainties that might pose dangers. Another development is that new diseases, such as H1N1, seemingly spring up from nature spontaneously. They must be added to natural disasters as a threat to life. Because people constantly travel throughout the world, diseases are readily transmitted globally. This edition of the book includes a new chapter on biological crises as one of the crises of the physical environment.

Climate change is another force that has widespread consequences. It causes weather-related disasters, threatens the permanency of some land areas, and endangers the health and lives of all living creatures. Some areas of the world, not only Bangladesh and Greenland but also regions like Florida, face inundation. And even as the world land mass shrinks, world population is expected to increase from the current 6.5 billion to an estimated 9 billion by 2050, creating the potential for conflict as the availability of many resources, such as wheat, rice, oil and water, declines.

A case can also be made that the morality and trust that hold organizations, communities, and nations together are eroding. This is evidenced in the growth of deception and misconduct in business, government, and social institutions.

These trends and forces create an enormous challenge for the world's leaders and managers. Big and rapid changes create conditions that produce crises. A feature of crises is that they require new approaches and new ways of thinking. Crisis managers have learned that they must go beyond "single-loop" learning, which simply finds better ways of doing what the organization is already doing, and engage in "double-loop" learning which requires them to examine what can be done to change what is happening. This requires managers to supplement their existing practices with strategies that help them understand and respond to the new forces. More monitoring of the socio-political environment and communicating with diverse stakeholders, which are major aspects of crisis management, will be required. Along with these added activities, organizations may have to reconsider their goals and values, including the audiences they serve and the environments in which they operate. Even now, large companies such as General Electric Co. and Duke Energy Corp. are expressing support for a climate bill that would curb the use of fossil fuels.[1]

This reconsideration of basic premises under conditions of high uncertainty requires an integrated approach to managerial decision-making. Organizations must ask themselves: Does management concentrate so heavily on market and economic factors that it ignores political repercussions and social consequences of decisions? Is management so self-centered that it fails to consider the interests and concerns of employees, customers, local citizens, and other stakeholders? Does management have such a bias toward short-term profitmaking that it ignores what happens to its reputation and, therefore, to its long-term profitability and chances of survival? By withholding important information from its customers and other stakeholders, does it deliberately or unwittingly practice deception? Is it so amoral or immoral that it commits misdeeds that are unethical or illegal? The answers to these questions reflect the essence of crisis management.

* * *

This book is organized into four parts. Part I deals with the critical subject of "Preparing for an Era of Crises." Chapter 1 discusses the meaning and nature of crises and the economic, political, social and cultural conditions that have given rise to an era of crises. This book views crises as a threat to an organization's most valuable asset—its reputation. The implications of major crisis attributes—uncertainty, suddenness, and time compression—are discussed. Because crises require speedy decision-making, all that can be decided in advance should be anticipated, which is the subject of contingency planning— preparing for the worst—in Chapter 2.

Careful and responsible crisis communication is an indispensable activity in all crises because continued operations and safeguarding of one's reputation are at stake. Chapter 3 discusses the basics of crisis communication. A major development is that crisis specialists no longer restrict themselves to communications through the traditional print and broadcast media. They increasingly employ the new media of email, blogs, Facebook, Twitter, YouTube, MySpace and other applications in the Internet. More attention is also given to communication with specific groups, such as employees and government agencies. This edition of the book has also added a new chapter (Chapter 4) that discusses new image restoration strategies and the art of apology that are needed in dealing with aggrieved individuals and angry people.

Part II in the first edition included chapters of all seven types of crises. This typology was the core of the book. Its intention was to enable a manager to identify the type of crisis faced and then to choose the most effective response to it, much as a physician prescribes appropriate remedies to an illness that has been diagnosed.

In this revised edition, the different types of crises are divided into three parts: those dealing with the physical environment (Part II), those dealing with crises of the human climate (Part III), and those dealing with management failure (Part IV). The sequence generally moves from crises over which humankind and management have little control to those over which they have much control. The first two groups refer primarily to external forces and the third primarily to internal causes.

The crises of the physical environment in Part II include natural crises, which are universally recognized, and two others: biological crises (a new chapter—6) and technological crises. Biological crises share the characteristic of natural disasters in that they seemingly spontaneously spring up from nature and threaten life. They also require some of the same responses as natural disasters. Chapter 7 on technological crises deals with humankind's application of the physical sciences to advanced technologies—aerospace, nuclear, biotechnology, and nanotechnology—rather than routine industrial accidents.

Part III, Crises of the Human Climate,[2] deals with individuals and groups that seek change in a target organization's policies and actions—or, sometimes, want to harm an organization. Chapter 8 discusses a variety of confrontations by labor unions, environmental groups, animal groups, and others—confrontations that are often considered normal in our democratic society. Conflict resolution strategies have been developed to resolve contentious issues. When confronting groups use radical tactics, they escalate to crises of malevolence, which are discussed in Chapter 9. Malevolence, moreover, includes violent groups that engage in terrorism and other means to achieve their goals, which includes the desire to harm institutions and people.

Part IV, Crises of Management Failure, includes four chapters: crises of mismanagement (Chapter 10), crises of skewed management values (Chapter 11), crises of deception (Chapter 12), and crises of management misconduct (Chapter 13). Chapter 10 is new in this edition, added because so many crises are simply the result of negligence and misguided or poor management. It serves as an overview of some basic management principles, which when violated expose incompetence or negligence. Chapter 12 highlights two major crises of deception in this decade: Enron Corp. and the financial system. Deception is made easy when billions of dollars, Euros and other currencies can be transferred to anywhere in the world in a matter of seconds. Some deceptions became outright fraud and therefore serve as examples of misconduct in Chapter 13. This chapter includes a discussion of Madoff's Ponzi scheme and other forms of misconduct, such as bribery and corruption.

Each of the typology chapters (Parts II, III, and IV) defines the distinguishing features of a particular type of crisis, provides illustrative cases, and, most important, discusses management response strategies and tactics most relevant to each type of crisis. Some crises may fall entirely under one type, such as an earthquake, which clearly qualifies as a natural crisis. Other crises will primarily be of one type but contain elements of one or more other types. All crises contain elements of management failure. For example, Hurricane Katrina was unquestionably a natural disaster, but it was also a case of management failure because governments on all levels inadequately prepared for such a catastrophic disaster nor effectively responded to it.

The response strategies of each chapter draw on a wide range of disciplines: hazard management, risk assessment, engineering, social psychology, sociology, political science, economics, public relations, and general management. This interdisciplinary nature of crisis management presents a learning challenge to all managers and explains why group decision-making is often desirable.

The purpose of three chapters in the first edition of the book, titled "Improving Management Performance," was to discuss the integrative concepts of these disciplines. The first chapter was on "risk management and communication;" the second on "ethics: a moral code for executives," and the third on "issues management and stakeholder relationships."

In this revised edition these integrative concepts are discussed in the context of where they apply. For example, risk management is mainly applied to technological crises. Managers learn to overcome the arrogance of expert knowledge by understanding that people are subjective in their assessment of risks, which explains why risk communication has become a specialized field. Ethics is included in the introduction to crises of management failure in Part IV, but it has general application throughout the book. Managers must learn how the basics of a sense of right and wrong behavior must be incorporated into their organizational cultures and overseen by their governing boards. Issues management is mainly applied to crises of confrontation and malevolence. The broader insights of issues management are also applied to improving surveillance of early warning signs of crises.

This revised edition includes more references to the growing management literature on crises; for example, on repairing relationships within and between organizations. Reference to the newly recognized field of behavioral economics—which shows the danger of assuming that people act rationally—is also included in Chapter 12 on deception.

Part V, "Conclusions," summarizes the management and communication lessons learned from crises and shows how crisis management contributes to the practice of everyday management. A crisis manager is one who can assimilate and synthesize many kinds of information, who is able to work with a wide variety of individuals and groups both inside and outside the organization, and who can take a long-term as well as a short-term time perspective. As the many crises presented in this book are examined and reflected upon, the crisis manager becomes aware of the dangers inherent in existing management thinking and acting. The hope is that by seeing the limitations of these approaches, managers will be ready to accept new modes of thinking and behaving that will reduce the likelihood of crises and, more generally, improve the quality of decision-making.

Various groups of professionals will find selected chapters of particular interest to them. Public relations professionals will find the chapters on crisis communication and image restoration strategies (Chapters 3 and 4) especially helpful. Executives and engineers in the chemical industry and bioengineering will find Chapter 7 on technological crises particularly relevant in determining public reaction to new technologies or devising better safety and security measures. The accounting profession will recognize the need for renewed efforts to provide greater transparency of financial information to prevent bankruptcies and panic. The book's overriding purpose is to inspire all managers to enlarge their perspectives and response repertoires to include those of the crisis manager.

Part I

Preparing for an Era of Crises

The word *crisis* is embedded in our vocabulary. People are increasingly saying, "I have a crisis," rather than "I have a problem." They seem to realize that today's problems are graver and more difficult to cope with. The media reflect this situation as shown by a Nexis search of the word crisis that yields almost one thousand entries for just one week.

Crises are more omnipresent because humankind has been pushing out on all kinds of boundaries. Geographically, missionaries have gone to all corners of the world. So have enterprises that obtain resources from all over the world and seek to sell their products and services in world markets. Their supply chains are long and distribution centers span the Earth. World population is growing rapidly putting a strain on resources of all kinds, including food. The British economist, Thomas Malthus, appears more frequently in journals because he warned that population growth would outstrip the production of food.

Another push has come from population shifts as people move to more hospitable and beneficial regions, often causing problems of assimilation and coexistence of differing cultures. Communication channels have extended to all corners of the Earth, making it easy to obtain almost any kind of information, but also making it difficult to conceal problems and wrongdoing. Marshall McLuhan's global village has truly materialized. Change produces strains that can easily erupt into crises. Just as plates on faults of the Earth's crust cause earthquakes, tension points caused by human interaction can flare up.

Awareness of crises has grown as science discovers new mysteries both in outer space and the inner space of cells. Astronomers have shown what a small part of the universe Earth is, and environmentalists warn how fragile it is. We are warned that asteroids from outer space can collide with Earth and decimate living creatures, as happened to the dinosaurs. Physicists, using colossal facilities with such awesome names as "heavy ion relativistic collider," seek to discover the smallest unit of matter and how the Earth was created by the "big bang" millions of years ago. In the meantime, medical researchers and psychologists are using MRIs to penetrate the intricacies of the brain. They are discovering that humans are not as rational as commonly thought and are instead "wired" to respond emotionally to crises just as their evolutionary predecessors did.

Science and technology are opening up new areas that create both uncertainty and vulnerability.

Human beings may become overwhelmed by the changes and accompanying risks they encounter. They may recognize entropy—a trend toward disorganization—or sense that chaos is near. Some people may respond by engaging in risk aversion, blotting out unpleasant stimuli. This reaction carries the same danger as the psychological state of repression. Awareness of the actual disturbance disappears, but it nevertheless manifests itself in unhealthy and dysfunctional attitudes and behavior. Rational problem solving is impeded. People may engage in rational concentration on the important task at hand and simply ignore, at least temporarily, "peripheral" matters. Economists have long used the magic wand of *peribus paribus*—let other things remain the same—to do this. They also limit their cognitive burden by thrusting some variables under the heading of externalities. These solutions, however, do not work during a crisis, because a crisis is a holistic event that combines a wide variety of variables. One of the purposes of risk management—and contingency planning—is to try to identify the operative variables.

The purpose of Part I of this book is to understand the nature of crises, how to prepare for them, and how to limit the damage. Chapter 1 describes the types of crises organizations and the people in them are likely to face; also the stress caused by the key characteristics of crises—uncertainty, suddenness, and time compression. Chapter 2 discusses how the surprise accompanying crises can be reduced through risk management planning—deciding in advance what the most likely threats are and how they can be averted or minimized. The essentials of a contingency plan, which deals with specific crisis situations, are outlined so that organizations can prepare for the worst. Chapters 3 and 4 deal with an unavoidable aspect of a crisis—how it is reported by the both traditional and social media. The aim of an organization is to preserve its reputation and ability to continue to function effectively.

The Connection Between Risk and Crisis Management

Crisis management begins with risk management planning—asking about all the "what ifs" that might occur to an organization and the dangers it faces in its socio-political and human environment. Crisis management overlaps with risk management in focusing on the following concerns and activities:

- Reducing vulnerability to natural disasters;
- Engaging in surveillance for biological diseases;
- Considering such "upstream" measures as alternative technologies to lessen the chances of a technological disaster;
- Evaluating an organization's vulnerability to confrontation;
- Establishing surveillance systems to warn of possible malevolent acts;

- Reevaluating optimistic risk analysis premises to ward off crises of skewed values and crises of deception; and
- Intensifying detection and control systems to discourage management misconduct.

The objective of these concerns and activities is reducing the risk faced by an organization. These risks may take the form of loss of sales, reduction in a company's share value, destruction of human capital, an intensified regulatory environment, and loss of reputation. Like risk managers, crisis managers identify these risks, assess them, and seek to mitigate them. Some differences in degree exist, however, between the two types of managers. Risk managers are better trained to assess risks involving mathematical calculations—they know about "quants." Crisis managers know what to do when vulnerabilities turn into actual crises. They know how to communicate with the media, deal with government authorities, and limit damage to an organization's other stakeholders. They know how to protect and repair an organization's reputation. The best crisis managers—those with a knowledge of management—also know what changes are needed in corporate governance, organizational culture, and information technology.

Three Obstacles Facing Risk Recognition

The joint message of risk and crisis management is that managers must have the courage to acknowledge the risks they face and to deal with them straightforwardly. They must overcome several kinds of mindsets that obstruct the honest analysis of risk: fatalistic attitudes, belief in a "naturalistic syndrome," ego defenses, fear of disrupting group relationships, and unwillingness to impede the achievement of immediate goals.

A fatalistic attitude asserts that what will happen is bound to happen. It is most clearly manifested in attitudes toward natural crises. Public authorities and the public often feel that certain disruptions and disasters wrought by nature are inevitable and must simply be endured. Closely related is the naturalistic syndrome, which makes people accept the forces and consequences of nature and dissuades them from intervening. For example, a woman in New England voted against fluoridated water in the belief that "nobody should fool around with God's water." And there are still some economists and businesspeople who want to let business cycles follow their natural course, believing that thereby sick businesses will be weeded out and healthy ones allowed to survive. For this reason, some free market advocates opposed the plan by the Federal Reserve Bank and the Treasury Department to bail out major banks and financial institutions when the financial system was on the brink of collapse. The main trouble with such mindsets is that the possibility of human intervention is forfeited.

Blindness or resistance to risk is further explained by ego defenses, which ward off unpleasant and threatening information and events, as well as "affiliative constraints" that disrupt group relationships. Regarding the latter, Irving Janis warns:

> Whenever a crisis arises, policymakers are likely to seek a solution that will avert threats to important values in a way that will not adversely affect their relationships with "important people" within the organization, especially those to whom they are accountable, and that will not be opposed by subordinates who are expected to implement the new policy decision.[3]

A final reason for the unwillingness to face risks is the reluctance to interfere with the achievement of immediate goals. As seen with the procrastination on the O-ring of the *Challenger* spaceship, fatal flaws in design were tolerated so that the organization could move forward unimpeded. As discussed in contingency planning and crises of skewed values, management must be willing to consider "worst-case scenarios" in its risk assessments. It must encourage engineers and line managers to give greater weight to safety factors and not treat negative evaluations as disruptive of team loyalty or akin to whistle blowing.

Looking Toward the Future

Comprehensive crisis management looks beyond the immediate crisis event and preceding contingency planning with the aim of reducing the incidence of future crises and strengthening an organization's ability to cope with those that do occur. Many of these efforts involve improved communications during a crisis; others involve the post-crisis phase of rebuilding.

The positive side of crises is that they prepare an organization for change. The Chinese symbol for crisis is taken earnestly, for it signifies opportunity as well as danger. The trauma of a crisis provides the stimulus and motivation for rebuilding, improving, and even transforming the organization. Its members develop a readiness for change. Resistance is reduced because change is legitimized. For this reason many a leader has maneuvered an organization into a crisis state even when there was no real crisis. By such devices as rearranging and reinterpreting statistics, license is obtained to undertake draconian measures.

Certainly when a crisis erupts, top management should seize the opportunity to restructure company thinking. Management must determine what organizational changes are needed, e.g., strengthening corporate governance, setting up new units, revising managerial roles, improving control systems, and instilling a new organizational culture. These have been among the response and renewal strategies discussed in conjunction with the various crisis types discussed in this book.

Chapter 1

Understanding Crises

Each year the news media report on natural disasters, biological diseases, technological mishaps, human conflicts, and management failures. When these events are severe and threaten vital values, they are classified as crises. Unfortunately, they seem to be happening more frequently and threatening to become more catastrophic. Humankind and no type of organization are immune from them.

In recent years, crises of management failure were the most numerous and widespread. Leading the list was the financial crisis of 2008, which started in the United States and caused the collapse of Bear Stearns, Lehman Brothers and several smaller banks, such as IndyMac. It was accompanied by the scandal of Bernard Madoff whose illegal Ponzi scheme accounted for losses of over $50 billion. These were accompanied by a cascade of stories about food poisoning from beef, tomatoes, jalapenos, pancake mix, bottled water, and melamine-tainted eggs. A meat company, Topps Meat Co., which had been in business more than 60 years, was forced out of business in early 2008.

The more familiar type of crisis, natural disasters, continued to menace people. Major ones were the May 2008 earthquake in Sichuan, China, which killed over 80,000 people and left over 5 million homeless; the Indian Ocean tsunami in 2004 which killed almost 230,000 people and displaced 1.7 million; and Hurricane Katrina in 2005 which caused widespread destruction to the city of New Orleans and its environs. Another kind of crisis, malevolence, manifested itself on a global scale by terrorism and on a local level by violence in the workplace and schools. The Virginia Tech massacre in 2007 dramatically demonstrated that no type of organization was immune to violent acts.

Managers in all kinds of organizations are slowly—all too slowly—recognizing the likelihood that at some time they will face a crisis. They must be ready, at an instant, to serve as crisis managers. They must acquire a crisis mentality that recognizes unwanted uncertainty and risk and a readiness instantly to respond to an erupting crisis.

Proliferation and Severity of Crises

The environment surrounding people and organizations is becoming increasingly complex and unstable. Too many things are changing: all products, not only high-tech, have shorter life cycles; new technologies such as bioengineering and nano-technology embody risks that are increasingly difficult to calculate; government regulation, deregulation and reregulation continue to change the rules of the marketplace; competition is intensifying and has become global; consumerism, civil rights, animal rights, and other social movements require greater and quicker social responsiveness; concern about global warming is causing the substitution of the heralded goal of economic growth with the goal of sustainable growth. When these challenges overwhelm the ability of managers to cope with them, a crisis occurs. Their aim is to restore predictability and stability in the environment so they can concentrate on regular operations to achieve organizational goals.

Trends That Promote Crises

Pressures of the Free-Market System

Managers are taking larger risks to meet the incessant pressure from stockholders to meet quarterly profit goals. Furthermore, incentive systems, especially in the financial industry, have the perverse effect of encouraging risk-taking. Executives are rewarded with bonuses when they meet or surpass profit expectations and increase stockholder value. In the banking industry, mortgage originators earn a flow of commissions by processing a greater number of mortgages. They do so without risk to themselves because mortgages are "securitized" and passed on to other financial institutions. They rationalize that they can avoid short-term and long-term risks and thereby avert a crisis.

This mentality expresses faith in the automatic functioning of the free-market system, heralded in the U.K. by Margaret Thatcher and Ronald Reagan in the United States. With the slogan "Get Government Off Our Backs," they convinced citizens that economic growth and prosperity would follow. It did, but not for everyone and not without spawning a series of financial crises. In the mid-1980s some banks, notably Continental Illinois, faced runs on their deposits. By the end of the 1980s savings and loan associations collapsed by the dozens. In December 2001, Enron, the United States' seventh largest corporation, filed for bankruptcy. And to top them all, the financial crisis of 2008 threatened the economies of the United States, Europe, and many other nations. The free-market system is now on trial, threatened by government regulations intended to avert future financial and economic crises.

Globalization

Globalization fosters crises in a variety of ways. On a human level, international travel accelerated the spread of SARS in 2002 as travelers from China flew to international airport hubs in Toronto, New York and London, and then to dozens of further destinations. The same dispersion occurred with "toxic securities" sold by U.S. investment and commercial banks that infected financial institutions in Europe and elsewhere. Bank failure virtually bankrupt Iceland.

Increasingly, firms in one country are linking with suppliers and customers through a complex nexus of strategically critical interfirm relationships.[4] As supply chains become more distant and longer, they become vulnerable to all kinds of disruptions. Some are caused by natural disasters. The earthquake in Taiwan in 2004, for example, destroyed factories and seriously disrupted the supply of motherboards, chipsets, and an array of other vital computer parts. When breaks occurred in three vital undersea Internet cables that connect South Asia to the outside world, India's call centers and companies dependent upon them discovered their vulnerability. Some call centers were forced to shut down for hours, if not days.[5] A 2007 study by Accenture, a global management consulting firm, found that 73 percent of the executives interviewed had experienced a serious supply-chain disruption in the past five years. Boeing's embarrassing two-year delay in rolling out its Dreamliner jet has been attributed to its aggressive strategy of outsourcing parts of the plane, such as the tail section, to hundreds of suppliers.[6]

The usual recommendation for avoiding disruptions is to build redundancies, but such efforts are often delayed in a world of cost-cutting. Corporations are advised to seek resilience through planning, flexibility and creative management of risk.[7] Some companies have decided to "go back to the future" by reviving "vertical integration"—a strategy whereby a company controls materials, manufacturing and distribution. Boeing is partly doing this, having bought a factory and a 50 percent stake in a joint venture that makes parts for the troubled airliner. It also bought a factory in Charleston, South Carolina, that makes the rear fuselage sections for the Dreamliner.[8]

Nonprofits No Longer Immune

Nonprofit organizations are not immune to crises, especially scandals. In 2007, a new CEO of the American Red Cross was forced out six months after taking the job when he admitted to an inappropriate personal relationship with an employee.[9] Even universities are no longer immune. The dean of the University of San Diego's business school resigned after being arrested for trying to buy cocaine. His misconduct was ironically at odds with the school's description of its M.B.A. curriculum as being "focused on developing socially responsible leaders who make thoughtful decisions that impact their organization and the world at large."[10] The value of reputation can't be overstated says Angel Cabrera, president of the Thunderbird School of Global Management. "All we've got as business schools is our reputation."[11]

Severity of a Crisis

Crises are described by the amount of damage caused immediately and over periods of time: a few days, weeks, months, years, or permanently. Expert judgment is required to assess the impact of a crisis. The media typically describe the severity of a crisis by reporting on the number of deaths and injuries, loss of property, and other financial losses such as drop in sales. Other consequences should also be added. A comprehensive study, covering public-profit, private-nonprofit, and private-profit organizations, listed these:

- major restructuring of an organization;
- severe budget cutbacks/shortfall;
- intense scrutiny from regulators;
- potentially damaging civil litigation;
- re-election/reappointment of CEO;
- forced resignation of executive;
- public protests;
- intense scrutiny by regulators;
- major relocation of operations;
- political controversy.[12]

The severity of a crisis increases when not only parts of an organization are affected but the entire system. Accordingly, Thierry C. Pauchant and Ian I. Mitroff in *Transforming the Crisis-Prone Organization* define a crisis as "a disruption that physically affects a system as a whole, and threatens its basic assumptions, its subjective sense of self, its existential core."[13] By the system as a whole they mean an entire plant, organization, or industry, rather than a self-contained part of that system. Three Mile Island and Chernobyl, for example, threatened the environment and undermined the future of the entire nuclear power industry. Pauchant and Mitroff recognize that managers must become aware of the faulty foundations of their basic assumptions if they are to avert a severe crisis.

Recognizing a Crisis

A manager knows when a crisis hits. It may be visibly apparent in an explosion or tidal wave, or it may be known when a phone rings that reports an accident or incident. The news media may be the first to report an event and ask for details, such as when a customer becomes ill after eating in a company's restaurant. A cable news show, eager to be the first to disclose an incident, may report on insider trading by a company's top executive. A staff member may discover that its products are attacked on Facebook or a blog. In all these situations, a manager must immediately decide whether the situation merits a crisis designation. If he or she senses "big trouble," then it's a crisis. It's a serious crisis if the organization's very existence is imperiled. The crisis then demands full attention as normal activities are placed on autopilot or suspended.

Formal Definitions

Formal definitions of a crisis help a manager to recognize when he or she faces a crisis. Definitions contain a combination of these elements:

- the event is sudden, unexpected and unwanted;
- decisions must be made swiftly;
- it is a low-probability, high-impact event;
- it has ambiguity of cause, effect and means of resolution;
- it interrupts the normal operations of an organization;
- it hinders high-priority goals and threatens an enterprise's profitability, growth, and survival;
- it may cause irreparableness and degeneration of a situation if no action is taken;
- it creates significant psychological stress.[14]

This book's definition emphasizes a common denominator of most crises—that an organization's reputation is endangered. Thus, this book's definition is that a crisis is an event that brings, or has the potential for bringing, an organization into disrepute and imperils its future profitability, growth, and, possibly, its very survival. This definition explains why crisis communication is sometimes mistakenly confused with the larger scope of crisis management. Reputation is an intangible asset that increases an organization's financial value and the price of its products and service. Loss of reputation is a very serious matter. When a crisis occurs, the worth of an entire organization and its future prospects goes through a process of swift reassessment by its investors, other stakeholders, and the public. As Warren Buffett stated, "It takes 20 years to build a reputation and five minutes to ruin it. If you think about that, you'll do things differently."[15]

Reputation represents people's awareness of a person or organization, favorable attitudes toward it, and positive attributes associated with it. All the past contacts of an organization with its various constituents contribute to its reputation, as do advertising and other communication campaigns. Reputation is included in the bookkeeping account called Goodwill, which is listed as one of the intangible assets on an organization's financial statement. The value of Goodwill is reflected in the higher price a buyer is willing to pay beyond the value of its physical assets.

Reputation can be eroded in a matter of hours through a crisis event. A study by Charles J. Fombrun, executive director of the Reputation Institute, and Naomi A. Gardberg shows the decline in the post-crisis market value of several companies that have faced highly publicized crises. After product tampering of Tylenol in 1982, Johnson & Johnson lost $1 billion (14 percent), and again in 1985 after a second tampering event, $1 billion. In the first week after the *Exxon Valdez* oil spill, Exxon Corp.'s value dropped $3 billion (5 percent). And after scientists hinted at a link between cell phones and brain cancer in 1995, Motorola suffered a $6 billion (16 percent) drop.[16] As Fombrun and Gardberg explain, "Clearly these market losses incorporate investors' expectations of future cleanup, legal and reparation costs. They also factor in anticipated losses from weakened perceptions among current and potential customers, employees and communities."[17]

Characteristics of a Crisis—How Managers Are Affected

The mental and emotional state of a manager facing a crisis situation further describes a crisis. He or she may experience uncertainty, confusion, and even chaos, which is accompanied by a sense of "loss of control" and even panic. Three aspects of a crisis are particularly responsible: suddenness, uncertainty, and time compression.

Suddenness

A crisis always appears to arise suddenly, as emphasized by Bart J. Mind-szenthy, T.A.G. Watson, and William J. Koch's book, *No Surprises: The Crisis Communications Management System.*[18] Other authors also refer to suddenness. James E. Lukaszewski, a corporate communications counselor, states, "Crises generally happen explosively in an instant,"[19] and Chris Nelson, senior vice president/director, North American issues & crisis management network at Ketchum, states, "Today, an issue can go from zero to 60 overnight."[20] In the famous Tylenol case, Johnson & Johnson could not foresee when some malevolent person would taint its Tylenol capsules with cyanide. Neither could Pepsi Cola foretell when someone spotted a syringe in a can and blamed Pepsi for its presence. These crisis events seemed to occur instantaneously.

The suddenness or unpredictability of a crisis, however, should not be overstated. Antecedents must be considered. There may have been an incremental build-up of problems or the presence of a dangerous or risky condition, such as the neglect of safety measures by BP in the Texas refinery that led to an explosion in 2005. Such crises, called "smouldering crises," build up over time until an accident occurs. As the Institute for Crisis Management explains, "They are the kind of issues and problems that could be spotted and fixed before they ever get big enough and out of control."[21]

When this build-up is gradual and small, managers deny signs of an approaching crisis, much as a frog placed in water that is very gradually heated is unaware that it is about to be cooked to death. Denial is a common behavior when a person or organization wants to avoid unpleasant experiences.[22]

Managers erect defense mechanisms against receiving unpleasant information that threatens their core assumptions.

When a crisis follows this slow, cumulative pattern, the danger is that a manager may be unaware that the accumulated total of the increments has reached a crisis threshold. A manager may have had weak and sporadic early warning signals that consciously or unconsciously were ignored. It is human nature that when everything seems to be going well, there's no incentive to look for trouble. That task is left to outsiders—a government official, a whistle-blower, a public interest group, or the media. To avoid surprise and maintain control, organizations need monitoring systems to keep apprised of developments.

One of these monitoring systems is issues management. Many organizations have instituted systems to identify warning signals of controversial issues that have the potential of turning into crises. These systems include the four-step process of issue scanning and monitoring, issue prioritization, issue analysis, and strategy formulation. From a crisis management viewpoint it is important to establish a threshold for each issue—under the steps of prioritization and analysis—that would alert management to take action.[23]

A growing difficulty is that the complexity of issues is increasing, says Kanina Blanchard, director of global issues & industry affairs for The Dow Chemical Company. One of the issues that will need to be watched, he says, is biodiversity, which has long-term consequences. Another complication with issues, as Chris Nelson of Ketchum notes, is that organizations such as Earth First! and People for the Ethical Treatment of Animals (PETA) "aren't always looking for solutions. Their goal is to keep issues alive."[24]

Uncertainty

Management rationalizations for ignoring unpleasant information come easily because of a second characteristic of a crisis: it deals with uncertainties—and, sometimes, unknowns. Especially when an organization's environment is complex and unstable, managers may have difficulty in obtaining sufficient information about environmental factors and in predicting external changes.[25] When this happens, managers tend to lose their normal mental reflexes or framework in thinking about a problem, as Patrick Lagadec excellently describes in his *Preventing Chaos in a Crisis: Strategies for Prevention, Control, and Damage Limitation.*[26] He explains how established boundaries are crossed into the unknown as a wide variety of inside voices and external agencies and stakeholders become involved—also how rules of the game are ignored as uncertainty corrupts normalcy.

To ascertain uncertainty is difficult, but some attempts to predict the likelihood of certain kinds of crises can be made by estimating statistical probabilities, giving attention to those occurring most frequently. Such reckoning, however, carries the danger that managers will give insufficient attention to low-probability events. The likelihood of a Chernobyl nuclear disaster or of an

Exxon sea captain crashing his supertanker onto a well-marked reef is figured to be highly remote.

Executive attention to these low-probability events tends to be minimized in favor of activities related to obtaining short-term "bottom line" results. Only when a crisis occurs does management learn the hard way that low-probability, high-impact events must be taken seriously. Managers then recognize that environmental monitoring activities and risk assessment are a first-line of defense against the surprise element of a crisis. They are compelled to replace defense mechanisms and a siege mentality with an attitude of openness to information about the organization's internal and external environments.

It is easy to understand that a person wants to deny unpleasant information, especially when it deals with remote possibilities expressed in statistical probabilities. But procrastination only multiplies the causes and conditions that produce crises. Managers should not wait to recognize the reality of an impending crisis until after unwanted events reach a critical threshold as a result of an accident, confrontation, legal suit, or public disclosure.

Time Compression

The seeming suddenness of a crisis amid great uncertainty aggravates already difficult decision-making with the urgent need to make decisions rapidly lest a situation further deteriorate. This time compression adds to the enormous stress and anxiety that a crisis causes among managers at all levels. Management is now put to the test. Can it, within a restricted time frame, limit the damage caused by the crisis and regain control under conditions of high risk and uncertainty? Can it control the media's bias toward bad news and sensational news? Every affected manager becomes a military commander under battle conditions. Anxiety, which is a generalized fear of the unknown, prevails.

When decisions are made under stress, pressure on individuals is extraordinary as they are pushed to the limits of their capacity and organizational systems are strained. Although psychologists say that a moderate degree of stress enhances problem-solving ability, too much of it distorts a person's sense of reality and contaminates sound decision-making. Lagadec lists several specific effects of high stress and anxiety:

- judgment may be affected, sometimes creating a tendency to consider ideas that would normally be dismissed;
- individuals' personality traits become exaggerated (for example, an anxious person becomes very anxious);
- a siege mentality may set in with those in charge withdrawing, doing nothing, saying nothing, and becoming inert;
- the search begins for a scapegoat;
- instability sets in and decision makers may adopt the latest opinions they have heard; and

- management turns defensive, declaring in reflex fashion that "everything is under control."[27]

Three psychological theories—cognitive, psychoanalytic, and trauma—shed further light on the stress aspects of a crisis. Cognitive theory sees crises as "highly uncertain, complex, and emotional events," during which people are limited in their information-processing capability.[28] Consequently, "crises arise or spiral out or control because executives, managers, or operators have responded irrationally and enacted errors of bias and other shortcomings in their information processing and decision making."[29] Because of these cognitive limitations, individuals require organization-based solutions.

Psychoanalytic theories suggest that personality disorders, mental health and defense mechanisms contribute to an organizational crisis, as illustrated by the *Challenger* explosion.[30] Excessive optimism and system pressures may have inhibited some concerned parties from prohibiting the liftoff. As for trauma, the third psychological factor, a variety of crises show that some people are traumatized and require psychological counseling. Christine M. Pearson and Judith A. Clair explain that a crisis can undermine a person's beliefs—that "bad things can't happen to me," that "doing the right thing will yield good things"—and replace a sense of worth and control with a feeling that they are "weak, helpless, and needy."[31] Too much stress distorts a person's sense of reality and contaminates sound decision-making. A person may feel so tired, depressed, and angry that it is difficult to get things done.

Restoring Equilibrium

In summary, the impact of these crisis characteristics is that a person's or organization's equilibrium is disturbed—something has gone wrong that can cause unwanted and undesirable consequences. Having been disturbed, a metaphorical stable rocking chair moves back and forth treacherously. An unstable situation has been created in which the "system" is not at rest and, at the extreme, might cause chaos and suffering. There is a sense of "loss of control."

To reestablish control and restore equilibrium requires that the forces that caused the crisis and upset the equilibrium be removed. Using the rocking chair metaphor again, a window through which winds came might be closed or the chair might be relocated so that people wouldn't stumble on it. A second way to respond to a crisis is to alter the forces themselves. This is what organizations do when they lobby to change the outcome of issues that affect them. Third, an organization may change the way it functions and relates to these forces. It might, for example, appoint a new leader, which is a common practice when a crisis is caused not by outside forces but by poor organizational policies and practices, or negligence and other forms of mismanagement. Such a new leader could use the crisis as a justification for making changes in the organization.

Sometimes an existing leader will contrive a crisis, e.g., a financial deficit, so that opposition to change is reduced or removed.

Crisis as Opportunity

As the Chinese symbol for a crisis indicates, a crisis denotes both danger and opportunity. Danger is fully recognized by managers, but a greater understanding is needed of when a crisis becomes an opportunity. The value of perceiving a crisis as an opportunity is that it encourages reflection and learning. Joel Brockner and Erika Hayes James explore the idea that crises have the potential to be a catalyst for positive organizational change.[32] They distinguish between two types of managers:

(1)   managers who perceive only threats argue that they sense more control and less uncertainty and can accordingly undertake such actions as cost-cutting, budget tightening, and other restrictive activities; and

(2)   managers who recognize opportunities and are more likely to change their mindsets and behaviors to accommodate a situation.

The second type is better able to make necessary changes in an organization.

Managers who are not solely outcome- and process-focused are more likely to recognize opportunities. Organizations that tolerate and legitimate organizational failure create a learning climate and enable managers to develop competence by acquiring new skills and mastering new situations. A learning orientation elicits more adaptive responses to adverse conditions.

A manager's perception of a crisis as an opportunity is influenced by an individual's and organization's values. People engage in self-regulation, which is the process of trying to match behaviors and self-concepts with appropriate goals and standards. In doing so they can be promotion-focused or prevention-focused. The former is favored because it encourages the opportunity orientation; it is a "playing to win" form of self-regulation, not a "playing to not lose" one.[33] Opportunities are also more likely to be seen when they appear attainable. Trying to build a new infrastructure in the large area of tsunami-ravaged Asia is not as readily attainable as rebuilding in and around New Orleans.

Another factor that influences the perception of opportunities is the personality and perceptions of managers. Those individuals with a strong sense of self-efficacy are more likely to see opportunities. This orientation also prevails when crises are perceived as less severe or less public, and crises for which an organization is less perceived as being responsible. An organization's belief system can also foster positive views on the part of employees, such having an optimistic ("can-do") attitude.[34]

The Inevitable Involvement of the Media

It often seems that an event becomes a crisis only when it receives a "bad press." Therefore, an immediate concern of a crisis manager is how the news media and, nowadays, the social media, describe and treat the crisis event. The media serve as a "multiplier," for they can grossly amplify the damage of a crisis. At risk is the reputation of an organization and its managers, their legal liability, and likelihood of government intervention. For this reason, most counseling firms that offer crisis management services mainly refer to their crisis communication capability.

In their concern to safeguard the reputation and credibility of their companies, therefore, managers must become sensitive to the role of the news media and social networking, which indisputably have the power to build or destroy reputations, and doubly so during a crisis. The news media are attracted to crises because they are part of the five C's that define news: catastrophes, crises, conflict, crime, and corruption. Bad news sells and the public expects the media to serve as "watchdogs" to alert them to impending dangers.

What events the social media—blogs, Facebook, Twitter—choose to cover and how the potential cadres of reporters treat an event is a source of further uncertainty.

Potential for Public Exposure of Crises Grows

The proliferation of crises is likely to increase because organizations now operate in an information society in which people are "wired together" on a 24/7 basis in one gigantic global village. What happens in Cairo, Egypt, is reported immediately on CNN and Al Jazerra. Terrorist killings in Mumbai, India, first appeared on Facebook. With so many onlookers, accidents and disasters cannot be concealed. A head-in-the-sand approach is no longer plausible.

Aerial photography, which allows citizens to comb city streets for shops, restaurants and other locations, is a further source of exposure. Microsoft's Virtual Earth and Google's Google Maps and Google Earth vie to offer the best aerial views of the Earth. Although their interest is in tapping into a pool of advertising by local businesses, the services can be used by the media or any other watchdog, as well as by ordinary people, to observe and report on questionable behavior.[35]

Government sources provide another source of exposure of organizational misdeeds. Various regulations require organizations to disclose ever-increasing amounts and kinds of information to the public and, thereby, to the news media. Reams of other information that are filed each year with the federal government are, with some exceptions, readily available to the public through the Freedom of Information Act. Congressional hearings, especially following crises, lead to further demands for information and disclosures, and when lawsuits are filed more information is made public.

One of the newest and most far-reaching requirements is that companies producing or storing certain hazardous substances must report the type and amount of such material to the Environmental Protection Agency, which in turn makes it available to the media and the public. This is mandated by the Emergency Planning and Community-Right-to-Know Act of 1986 (Title III) of the Superfund Amendments and Reauthorization Act, known by the acronym SARA.

Research by public accountability groups provides the public and the media with another source of information. Groups like the Interfaith Center on Corporate Responsibility and the Council on Economic Priorities are especially active in gathering and disseminating information about the practices of U.S. corporations. By confronting corporations and other organizations, public interest groups attract media attention and can trigger a crisis.

Whistle-blowing is initiated by individuals who are close enough to a situation to know what is going on. They may be bothered by their consciences or motivated by self-gain through rewards offered by the government or private foundations. They are sometimes roused into action by public interest groups and spokespersons, notably Ralph Nader, who have urged conscientious employees to "blow the whistle" on their employers. Because employees in the private sector work under "at will" contracts, the federal government and some states have provided protection to such employees.

Growth of Crisis Industry

Public relations professionals are always involved in crisis management because a crisis endangers an organization's reputation. They provide information to the media and respond to blogs with an eye toward how the reputation of the troubled organization will be affected. They also know the importance of communicating with all stakeholders of an organization: stockholders, employees, government officials, the local community, suppliers, dealers, and others. Besides handling crisis communications, public relations professionals help prevent crises by identifying issues that might erupt into crises and by helping to inculcate organizational ethics and a regard for social responsibility. They also participate in contingency planning and devise strategies to enable an organization to repair its reputation and damaged relationships.

Most PR firms list crisis communication/management as one of their services. In June 2008 Burson-Marsteller opened an Issues & Crisis Group in Washington, D.C., with a staff comprised of former White House, congressional, and political employees to counsel companies on crisis communications, corporate social responsibility (CSR), litigation, and hostile media environments. In 2009 a new practice was launched within the group that focuses on product-related issues and crises, such as recalls, regulatory communications, and stakeholder engagement.[36] A regional firm, Wilson Group Communications in Columbus, Ohio, offers crisis management counseling and training, including media training workshops, mock disasters, and crisis planning.[37] Some firms combine security services with crisis management because of current concern about national security.

The programs of some professional associations reflect an interest in crisis management. For example, the New York Society of Security Analysts held a conference on "Anatomy of a Corporate Crisis: Managing Distress." Speakers included corporate turnaround executives who talked about finding value in a distress situation; bankruptcy attorneys on bankruptcy protection and creditors' and debtors' leverage and rights; and lenders and investors on strategies and views that help companies look for danger signs in a company's financial statements and operations.[38]

Classifying a Crisis

Crisis managers can more easily decide on the most appropriate and effective response to a crisis by immediately classifying it according to its type based on its symptoms. This approach is similar to that used by the American Medical Association (AMA) in its *Family Medical Guide*.[39] The reader is told to track down the significance of a particular symptom, either on its own or in combination with other symptoms, to a logical conclusion, i.e., what should be done about it? For example, a person with a temperature of about 100 degrees Fahrenheit has the symptom of a fever. Further symptoms are then examined to determine the remedy. If a person has a headache and/or aching bones and joints, a viral infection is suspected. The remedies that should be considered are immunization along with antibacterial, antibiotic, and antifungal drugs.[40]

The AMA approach can be applied to organizational crises. A mass demonstration (the symptom) in front of company headquarters would be classified as a confrontation type of crisis. Appropriate questions can then be asked (as with a fever) about who the demonstrators are, what organizations, if any, they represent, what their grievances or demands are, whether they are using lawful or unlawful tactics, whether they have attracted media attention, and so on (see Chapter 8). The crisis manager can then decide whether to seek police intervention, answer the demonstrators by holding a press conference, meeting with their leaders, negotiating, or otherwise engaging in conflict resolution.

To help in such diagnoses, crisis consultants and crisis books list a wide assortment of crisis types from which to choose. W. Timothy Coombs synthesized various typologies into the following list:

- natural disasters;
- malevolence;
- technical breakdowns;
- human breakdowns;
- challenges;
- megadamage;

- organizational misdeeds;
- workplace violence;
- rumors.[41]

Most of these types are helpful in determining what action to take. Others, however, are best classified as a subset of a crisis type in that they provide a further explanation of why a certain type of crisis occurred, or indicate the magnitude of a crisis. For example, in this book workplace violence is understood as an act of malevolence with various possible causes: frustration, rage, or a feeling that wrong was committed. Human breakdowns, or errors, are associated with practically all types of crises; e.g., the human error explanation of the Three Mile Island accident, which otherwise is best understood as a technological crisis. Megadamage, such as the *Exxon Valdez* oil spill, tells us that a large area was affected by the spill, but not the cause of the spill. Experts are bound to disagree on the utility of different typologies. The ultimate test is whether the diagnosis and naming of a typology sheds light on the kinds of questions that should be asked and whether the process points to appropriate responses and recovery.

In this book, crises are classified into three major parts: crises of the physical world, crises of the human climate, and crises of management failure. Each part contains several specific types of crises, which are the key basis of classification.

Crises of the Physical World: Nature and Technology

Natural Disasters

Natural disasters and catastrophes still dominate many definitions of a crisis. These include earthquakes, tornadoes, landslides, tidal waves, storms, floods, droughts that menace life, property, and the environment. The big disasters in recent years have been the Indian Ocean tsunami in 2004, Hurricane Katrina, which devastated New Orleans in 2005, and the earthquake in China in 2008. They attest to the continuing vulnerability of humankind to what have been called "acts of God." Such a description, however, increasingly does not hold public authorities blameless. People in stricken areas ask why communities were not better prepared, why not enough advance warning was given, and why emergency response was slow or inadequate.

World population growth and the search for natural resources has extended to less hospitable and geographical areas, resulting in high concentrations of people, buildings, and waste near places where floods, storms, volcanic eruptions, and earthquakes occur. More reports are published about unsustainable ecological trends. Most troubling are rapid population growth and the ecological damage caused by "the developing world's rush to enjoy First World living standards."[42] This theme was graphically reiterated by Pope Benedict in a speech to a youth rally in Sydney, Australia, in July 2008, when he said,

"Reluctantly we come to acknowledge that there are also scars which mark the surface of our earth, erosion, deforestation, the squandering of the world's mineral and ocean resources in order to fuel an insatiable consumption."[43]

Global warming has become the major global issue that threatens the health of people and the sustainability of coastal regions. An increasing number of scientists warn of the depletion of the ozone and the greenhouse effect. At first called alarmists and resisted by the business community, scientists have amassed overwhelming evidence that global warming is in fact taking place. The arguments are summarized in Al Gore's film, *An Inconvenient Truth*, and supported by such evidence as receding glaciers, the melting of icebergs in the Arctic, the shrinking of Greenland, and the decline of the penguin population in the Antarctica.

Eminent groups of scientists now declare the reality of global warming and most assert that it is caused by human activity. Global warming raises the incidence of natural disasters. More hurricanes are expected in the Gulf region as the waters of the South Atlantic become warmer and generate higher velocities of hurricanes. So many hurricanes followed Hurricane Katrina in 2005 that the National Hurricane Center ran out of names and had to turn to Greek letters. Hurricanes are expected to become more destructive, with a doubling of storms in the higher 4 and 5 categories on the Saffir-Simpson scale usually employed by meteorologists.[44] Low-lying coastal regions, such as in Bangladesh, may become uninhabitable within the century, and major shifts in suitable agricultural areas will occur. The positive benefits are that agricultural regions in northern areas, such as Canada, will expand and Arctic waters will remain open to navigation year round. The negative effects of global warming are that the melting of the glaciers will not solve the looming problem of a world shortage of water, which could cause whole swaths of the Middle East and Asia to run dry within 40 years.[45]

Global warming is also a reminder that, along with globalization of economies, the threat to the environment has increasingly become more global. "What were once local problems of pollution have now merged into a huge general threat to the planet's delicately balanced ecosystem," writes the *Guardian*.[46] Some writers foresee catastrophe. In *Collapse: How Societies Choose to Fail or Succeed*, Jared Diamond reports 12 unsustainable ecological trends, including global warming and rapid population growth, and hopes that the problems will not be resolved "in unpleasant ways not of our choice, such as warfare, genocide, starvation, disease epidemics, and collapses of society.[47]

In recent years more attention is being given to another kind of natural crisis: the biological crisis as illustrated by the continuing scourge of AIDS, the spread of SARS, the onset of the Mexican flu, and the fear of new diseases from future mutations for which vaccines do not exist. *— ebola —*

Technology

In developed societies, the source of hazards has shifted drastically from nature to technology.[48] As technology has become more complex and closely linked, the chances of malfunctioning multiply and the consequences become bigger and more profound. Charles Perrow, a management expert on technologies, presents the case that the potential for technological failure and recovery from failure is so great that some technologies, such as nuclear power, should be totally abandoned, and others, like marine transport, should be restricted.[49]

Perrow identifies two features of modern technology that make it so risky. One is its complexity, not only in the technological components but in sub-systems and larger systems; the other is the tight coupling of these sub-systems, so that malfunctioning in one sub-system will trigger unpredictable reactions in other sub-systems in the entire interrelated system.[50]

Crises of the Human Climate: Confrontation and Malevolence

Crises are caused in the human realm because people's expectations continue to rise globally and when their satisfaction is curtailed or frustrated they turn to aggressive acts. More broadly, the social and political environment has also heated up. Government has been playing an increasing role in the economy as measured by the rise in the number and kinds of regulations.[51] These regulations no longer deal with problems in specific industries but deal with such issues as minority rights or the environment that cut across all industries and institutions. They encourage further social action.

Following the pattern of technology, the human and social environment has also become more complex, interrelated, and tightly coupled, with the result of being more conflict-prone. As people have become better informed and educated, they demand safer and more reliable products, a lower-risk work environment, equal job opportunities, pay equity, and many other rights. Swayed by the mass media, satellite communication, and computer networks, people have joined social action groups which often resort to confrontations and, sometimes, to acts of malevolence.

These groups are intent on pressing their demands and exposing corporate and government wrongdoing. They focus on a wide variety of real or imagined grievances and make new demands based on changed values and new expectations of business behavior. These groups vie with one another to gain media attention and to promote their causes. The *Public Interest Profiles* manual of the Foundation for Public Affairs classifies 250 of the most influential public interest groups concerned with problems in such areas as civil/human rights, community improvements, consumer/health, corporate/governmental accountability, the economic system, energy/environment, and public policy.[52] Corporations are consequently confronted by these adversary groups on a variety of issues. Some confrontations escalate into crises because these groups have learned that the use of crisis-provoking tactics are effective in attracting media and, therefore, management attention.

Another source of crises are the malevolent acts of governments, groups, and individuals. Extremist persons and groups use terrorism and other forms of violence to force compliance with their demands or to punish a perceived source of evil. The demands may be purely selfish, as with extortionist plots. Often the targets appear to be chosen at random; other times the most visible and vulnerable target is chosen. Not only do these crises of malevolence add to a company's risk of doing business but they create enormous uncertainty. Management's ability to monitor violence-prone groups and to predict their actions is exceedingly limited.

Many companies have faced expropriation of property by hostile regimes, extortionist attempts by criminals, computer break-ins and contamination by computer viruses, malicious rumors about a company or its products, and product tampering. Furthermore, world tensions and ideological conflicts have resulted in terrorist acts not just against government targets but against private organizations.

Crises of Management Failure: Mismanagement, Skewed Values, Deception, and Misconduct

The rising incidence of natural and biological disasters and the cumulative burden of pressures from the social and political environment has placed an enormous burden on managers. But their own behavior is the cause of a third type of crisis, called crises of management failure, which has grown enormously in the past few decades.

Powerful market and financial pressures have tempted managers to engage in questionable behavior, such as illegal overseas and political payments, fraud, embezzlement, and other unethical practices. Pressure has further been heightened by government regulations, increased global competition, and hostile takeovers. Managers have been taking greater risks to score high profits and to survive. They have been willing to risk their reputations and, more broadly, public confidence in business. Too little value is apparently assigned to these intangible values, partly because short-term goals prevail over a long-term time perspective. The seeds are thereby sown for more government intervention in the economy as the loss of public confidence in business removes the protective shield that allows business to manage itself. In a world that is changing so rapidly, everything, including public goodwill, is likely to be seen as transient. Such tunnel vision has created many crises of management failure and exacerbated other kinds, such as confrontations with social action groups.

In addition to ordinary mismanagement, three subtypes of management failure prevail. The first deals with skewed values, when managers are excessively concerned with the "bottom line" and interests of stockholders and themselves at the expense of other stakeholder interests. The *Exxon Valdez* oil spill remains a prime example of the sacrifice of environmental values. The second type deals with deception, as exemplified by Enron and the 2008 financial crisis. The third type deals with unethical, illegal, and even criminal specific acts of management misconduct. Bernard Madoff's Ponzi scheme and bribes paid by Siemens to obtain business are recent examples of misconduct.

Conclusions

The incidence and severity of crises is rising with the complexity of technology and society. Fewer crises remain unpublicized as the number of society's watchdogs increases. Wise managements, therefore, are devoting increasing attention to an understanding of crises—their causes and dynamics, vulnerability to them, ways of reducing their incidence and, if they do occur, lessening the damage they cause to lives, property, and that precious intangible asset called reputation. It is the purpose of this book to support the endeavor to make crisis management a part of every manager's responsibility and capability.

If risk management and contingency planning have been conscientiously applied, the following criteria of a successful crisis outcome will have been met:

(1) early detection of signals of a crisis so that appropriate responses are brought to bear;
(2) incident is contained within the organization and there are no injuries or deaths;
(3) business is maintained as usual during and after the crisis;
(4) learning occurs: policies and procedures of an organization are changed as a result of the crisis and lessons are applied to future incidents;
(5) reputation is improved by the organization's effectiveness in managing the crisis;
(6) resources are available from the organization or external stakeholders; and
(7) evidence is ample of timely, accurate decisions grounded in facts.[53]

Management needs to develop a crisis mentality that recognizes that:

(1) a crisis can happen any time;
(2) risk must be factored into business planning and decision-making;
(3) monitoring and feedback systems must be developed to provide a warning system;
(4) relationship building with stakeholders should take place as part of building a strong crisis infrastructure; and
(5) a crisis manager function should be established, as a full- or part-time position depending on the size of an organization and its vulnerability to crises.

In addition, this book endeavors to make crisis management a part of every manager's responsibility and capability.

Appendix to Chapter 1: Guidelines for Analyzing Crises

A crisis must be seen from the perspective of a particular person or organization that is seen as the cause of a crisis event. For chroniclers of crises, the following outline of what should be observed and reported upon is helpful:

1. Describe crisis event

   - The 4 W's (who, what, where, when?)
   - Who or what precipitated the event?
   - Typology of event
   - Profile of affected organization and its key managers

2. Impact of crisis

   - Deaths, injuries, property damage
   - Financial costs: sales, stock value
   - Lawsuits
   - Organizational reputation
   - Broader effects, e.g., environmental and "social costs"
   - Media and Internet coverage of event
   - Extensiveness
   - Accuracy and fairness
   - Context/perspective
   - Assessment of cause and organization's handling of crisis

3. Context of crisis

   - Related economic, social, and political issues
   - Legal and regulatory
   - Recent experience of actors involved
   - Public opinion

4. Response

   - Was contingency plan, if any, implemented?
   - Immediate action taken
   - Crisis communication efforts
   - Other action taken, e.g., curtailing advertising

5. Post-Crisis

   - Aftermath communications
   - Rebuilding efforts
   - Changes in societal institutions
   - Evaluation of organization's strategy, actions, and communications

Chapter 2

Risk Management: Preparing for the Worst

More and more managers are coming to realize that crisis events that impact their operations and reputations will inevitably occur. They want to prepare for those occasions by applying risk management. The basic idea of risk management is to identify risks, analyze them, and figure out how to deal with them. Some companies are viewing risk management from the perspective of "enterprise risk management" (ERM), which relates risk to strategy in individual business organizations.[54] The Conference Board defines ERM as "an in-depth, proactive approach to preventing, mitigating, and otherwise dealing with all the relevant risks to an organization—strategic, operational, financial, legal, and so on."[55] The highest priority objective is to ensure that risk issues are considered in decision-making and avoiding surprise and "predictable" failures. Too often "known unknowns" remain buried within "silos" because of poor risk-management processes. Douglas W. Hubbard, the author of *The Failure of Risk Management*, calls it a comprehensive approach to risk for the firm.[56]

More generally, companies that adopt risk management view it as a central discipline that assists them in making better-informed decisions in a wide variety of areas. Hubbard mentions 12 areas. Three are included in the chapters of this book: physical security, information security, and business recovery from natural catastrophes. Three are entirely excluded: investment volatility, political risks in foreign government, and getting vendors or customers to share risks. Six other areas are partially discussed: e.g., regulatory compliance in terms of needed government oversight in cases of management failure; actions of competitors when malevolent or unethical actions are committed; workplace safety when violations lead to confrontations; various forms of insurance as a way to lessen the need for crisis management; and product liability as a danger of product defects. The final area—any other uncertainty that could result in a significant loss—is the same in risk management and crisis management.[57] In short, the scope of risk management is broader than crisis management.

Risk management and crisis management are both dedicated to risk mitigation: alleviating or moderating a risk—to lessen it in some way.[58] Like risk management, the ultimate objective of the contingency planning aspect of crisis management is to reduce the total risk to an organization. Risk management, however, relates "to the total risk to the firm for a given expected return" and includes the transfer of risks, e.g., through insurance or contracts.[59] Hubbard has a delightfully short definition of risk management: "being smart about taking chances." His long definition is: "The identification, assessment, and prioritization of risks followed by coordinated and economical application of resources to minimize, monitor, and control the probability and/or impact of unfortunate events."[60]

The same definition could be used for contingency planning. Despite his narrower focus, Kenneth N. Myers in his book, *Total Contingency Planning for Disasters,* refers to the planning of a "development strategy and methodology that balances the low probability of a disaster with the need to take reasonable steps to (1) take preventive measures to minimize the likelihood of a disaster, (2) provide an organized response if a disaster does happens, and (3) ensure business continuity during a disaster recovery period."[61] He calls contingency planning the "dismal science," much like economics, because "no one likes to look into the abyss." His book provides a complete sample of a contingency plan for a company called Bestabrand Foods. The policy statement appearing at the beginning restates the idea of contingency planning:

> The contingency plan policy of the Bestabrand Foods Division is to: 1) assure an organized and effective response to an isolated disaster that would render telephone communications, remote data communications and/or DEC/VAX computer equipment inaccessible or inoperative, or normal work locations inaccessible; and 2) ensure business continuity for business functions dependent on computer technology, until normal processing capability is restored.[62]

Despite reference to now outdated technology, the statement reinforces the importance of crisis preparation, which is integral to risk management and contingency planning.

The State of Crisis Preparedness

Crisis preparedness is a form of risk management. It pertains to the first of three phases of a crisis: pre-crisis, the crisis event, and post-crisis. The pre-crisis phase—the calm days before a crisis occurs—is when the crisis manager attempts to ascertain the kinds of crises his or her organization is most likely to experience, determine the likelihood of their occurrence, and do as much advance preparation as possible to deal with each contingency. Phase 2, the crisis event, is the most dramatic, volatile and precarious, because the time compression aspect of a crisis requires that decisions be made swiftly under conditions of high uncertainty. Management seeks to contain the damage, not only of the crisis event itself but the media's reporting of it to the public. In Phase 3, post-crisis, management attempts a recovery by making changes in its organizational structure, corporate governance policies, corporate culture, and control mechanisms. It also seeks to rebuild and strengthen its reputation.

The 2008 financial crisis has stimulated interest in risk management, says a survey of "quants"[63] and risk professionals by 7City Learning. Its report says there is increased focus on risk management in the wake of the financial crisis: 55 percent of respondents said they were being consulted more on risk management issues, and 35 percent of these professionals are being consulted much more often.[64] These findings support the observation of Hubbard that risk management is a "new and rapidly growing trend in management methods. . . ."[65] When a crisis manager defines risk as "something bad that could happen," he or she should be able to provide cases that can convince management of the importance of contingency planning.[66] One of these illustrative cases is Domino's Pizza.

Domino's Delayed Response to Video Prank

Domino's Pizza's delayed response to a video prank illustrates the urgent need for contingency planning in face of the rapid pace of the social media. Domino's is a 49-year-old American brand with 8,700 stores in 60 countries around the world, making more than one million deliveries a day. A video showing an employee sticking cheese up his nose and then putting it on a sandwich was made by a fellow employee and posted on YouTube.[67] Serving as the narrator, the employee commented, "In about five minutes it'll be sent on delivery where somebody will be eating these, yes, eating them, and little did they know that cheese was in his nose and that there was some lethal gas that ended up on their salami. Now that's how we roll at Dominos."[68]

Unfortunately, Domino's was still playing by the rules of the traditional media. Domino's spokesman, Tim McIntyre, was alerted to the video by a consumer affairs blog, *The Consumerist*, 45 minutes after it was posted on the Monday after Easter Day. This monitoring function was effective, but it wasn't until the following day that company executives decided what to do about it. Their decision was not to respond aggressively, hoping the controversy would quiet down. They waited until Domino's CEO and president Patrick Doyle returned from Florida on Wednesday to respond to the YouTube video.

The first 24 hours weren't wasted, said McIntyre, because they communicated to their entire U.S. franchise system, found the employees who created the video, fired them, turned them over to the police, and had the health department in the store.[69] Domino's also communicated with *The Consumerist*, whose audiences it considered the most relevant at the time. By the evening of the following day, Domino's social media team reported, "There's starting to be some chatter on Twitter."[70] The team had been assembled about a month before and was building a plan to introduced Domino's to Facebook, Twitter and other relevant social media sites.

By midday on Wednesday, the YouTube post had hit one million views. That day Domino's posted a video on YouTube featuring Doyle's response. McIntyre admitted, Domino's didn't do it fast enough, commenting that "yet nobody has been able to answer: How can you do something that's never been done before, but not fast enough?"[71] That comment acknowledged that the basic idea of contingency planning was not being recognized.

Richard Nicolazzo, president of the Boston public relations firm of Nicolazzo & Associates, severely criticized the 48-hour delay and recommended the "old-fashioned idea" of Boy Scouts of America's motto "Be Prepared." It again proves, he said, "that major companies are not spending enough time on contingency crisis communications planning."[72] McIntyre showed that he misjudged the power of the social media when he at first told the website ragan. com, "Right now, it (the video) is on web sites and blogs. It's not on ABC, CNN or USA Today."[73]

In just a few days, Domino's reputation was damaged. An online survey by YouGov (conducted every day for hundreds of brands) showed its quality rating among consumers drop from positive to negative. McIntyre mused, "Even people who've been with us as loyal customers for 10, 15, 20 years, people are second-guessing their relationship with Domino's, and that's not fair."[74] Paul Gallagher, managing director and head of the U.S. crisis practice at Burson-Marsteller called the experience a "nightmare" and said, "It's the toughest situation for a company to face in terms of a digital crisis."[75]

McIntyre's counsel to others is sound when he says, "Do as much as you can to quickly address the multiple sides of an issue." He adds, "You can't just take a hard line. If anybody believes that there is a notebook or a manual that you can pull off the shelf and say, 'When X happens, do Y,' then they're deluding themselves." The goal of contingency planning, however, is to do as much as possible to disprove this notion.

⚘ Examples of Crisis Preparedness

An example of crisis preparedness and contingency planning is found in the construction industry which, besides being concerned about the best and proper design and construction of a project, also includes a solid health and safety plan as well as training. Crisis plans focus on field evacuation and safety protocol to ensure workers are out of harm's way. All necessary emergency contact numbers are made easily accessible at the jobsite trailer. Speaking to the public and the press is also part of the plan. Messages should address evacuation procedures, response to fire hazards, responses to building collapse, worker injury, and potential fallout of debris to surrounding areas. In the event of a crisis, the advice given is that communication should be limited until a senior manger or owner can present information in a professional manner. Whatever is said should be simple and brief and be limited to such staid remarks as, "We are working on getting this crisis under control and will be back to you with further information at the proper time."[76]

Ocean Spray demonstrates the value of risk management and, specifically, contingency planning. After identifying the possibility of a hurricane striking its grapefruit-processing operations in Florida as a plausible risk, the company took two steps: it secured sections of buildings most vulnerable to high winds and purchased back-up portable generators for a modest cost. Its preparedness paid off. During the wild 2004 hurricane season, its plants were hit by two of the four major hurricanes, which were so severe that they damaged the majority of the state's grapefruit crop. Before the hurricanes arrived, Ocean Spray took the precaution of lowering the freezer temperature (in case of power outage) of its refrigerated products and brought the portable generators on site. Despite loss of service for 48 hours, freezers remained cold and its facilities sustained only superficial damage. The auxiliary power proved critical. Its experience demonstrated the value of ERM and contingency planning by ensuring its ability to sustain continuous operations.[77]

The need for crisis management is often recognized in the aftermath of a crisis. For example, the Virginia Tech shootings heightened the awareness for readiness by colleges and universities. Boston University president Robert Brown sent the following email to the faculty and staff:

> In light of the deadly tragedy at Virginia Tech University, we are reviewing Boston University's emergency response plans and communication systems to ensure that they are the best available. A group of University safety and security experts is evaluating our procedures so that the University can respond to emergencies and communication with all members of our community swiftly and effectively.[78]

One idea has already been acted upon at Virginia Tech: Twitter will be another way to reach students because so many of them carry cell phones with them.

Surveys on State of Crisis Preparedness

Unfortunately, various studies suggest that few organizations have crisis plans, and even those that do, do not take them seriously. A study of Fortune 500 companies conducted by the University of Southern California's Center for Crisis Management showed that 95 percent were completely unprepared.[79] Another survey by PricewaterhouseCoopers' Management Barometer of 104 chief financial officers and managing directors found that although nearly half of respondent companies faced a major crisis that impacted one or more business units between 2004 and 2007, one-third were not concerned about their company's preparedness for a major crisis. More than 60 percent felt confident that key business processes such as legal and insurance services, financial management, and accounting and reporting were sufficiently well-prepared in the event of a major crisis.[80] In other words, they place their faith in traditional risk management.

Even more discouraging findings were reported by Forrester Research Inc. Although it found that 70 percent of 189 tech leaders surveyed said their companies were "prepared" or "very prepared" for a disaster, their practices did not support that optimistic claim. Twenty-seven percent of the companies didn't have backup data centers and 48 percent of those that did were located within 50 miles of the primary facility, which wouldn't necessarily help a company survive a natural disaster. Another unfortunate finding is that 40 percent only practice disaster-recovery procedures once a year and 23 percent don't test their plans at all.[81] Realistic drills help evaluate the adequacy of a contingency plan.[82] A study by the Harvard School of Public Health found that even though fear of a possible H1N1 swine flu epidemic gripped the United States, two out of three U.S. businesses were unprepared to deal with the effects of a flu pandemic.[83]

These findings again show management's resistance to invest in programs that deal with low-probability events. To change this attitude, the challenge for crisis managers is to present scenarios that the probability for some crises is higher than management imagines and that the consequences of a crisis can be catastrophic.

Components of Crisis Preparedness

Crisis preparedness has several components: executive willingness to recognize risks, involvement of the board of directors, engaging in scenario planning, and building a supporting crisis preparedness infrastructure.

Executive Willingness to Recognize Risks

Crisis preparedness starts with executive perceptions about risk and risk-taking. These perceptions are part of an organization's cultural beliefs about their vulnerability to risks and the extent to which executives should incorporate risk management into their function. Executives, however, may resist this extension of responsibility by a variety of defense mechanisms. Among them are such rationalizations as "our size will protect us," "our employees are so dedicated that we can trust them without questions," and "if a major crisis happens, someone will rescue us."[84] Management must not be lulled into complacency by these reassuring assumptions, for they will allocate resources for crisis preparation only if they admit that their organizations are vulnerable to crises.

Management should conduct ongoing analyses of their operations and management structures from a risk perspective. The process is similar to that of a safety manager in a manufacturing plant who tours the premises for any signs of dangerous conditions.[85] With such an orientation, a manager would also assess an organization's awareness of its risk vulnerability and the availability of structures and procedures that would help should a crisis occur. The goal is to design and implement an organizational system that is capable of coping with crises. Unfortunately, managers who are totally performance oriented tend to resist such introspection because, as Abraham Carmeli and John Schaubroeck warn, they don't want to take time out to conduct ongoing analyses of their operations and management structure, nor to proactively monitor potential difficulties.[86]

Board Involvement

To begin the crisis preparedness process on the enterprise level, an organization's board of directors, as well as its top management, must value the importance of risk management. This has been happening, as a survey by the Conference Board and Mercer Oliver Wyman found: 91 percent of board members and senior management were either positively disposed toward accepting ERM or were actively preparing, developing, or implementing it. Some drivers of board involvement noted are compliance with corporate governance requirements (66 percent); a desire to gain a greater understanding of strategic and operating risks (60 percent); and the expectation that their companies can expect moderate increases in external and internal risks over the next five years.[87] Another survey, by FM Global and Harris Interactive, lends support to ERM. It found that 600 financial executives around the world who work with companies with at least $500 million in annual revenue assigned risk management a moderate to high corporate priority for 96 percent of North America-based companies.[88]

Some boards of directors create a special risk-management committee that engages in regular scenario planning with the aim of anticipating and averting trouble. The board of Reynolds American Inc., for example, held a mock board meeting when the directors and executives of the tobacco maker simulated the death of chairman and CEO in a plane crash. The two-hour simulation exposed gaps in the company's emergency succession plan. They found it easier to air such issues without the intense emotion of an actual loss.[89]

Boards are including more of their members in risk management. At a roundtable discussion of the role of risk management held by the National Association of Corporate Directors, 24 chairmen of audit committees who attended agreed that "the whole board needed to be engaged" in monitoring risk. Another method of involvement was used by Jack Krol, a former DuPont Co. CEO, when he joined the Tyco board in 2002. He created a risk-assessment process of visiting each business unit once a year, along with one or two fellow directors, to review a 10-item checklist of risks and proposed remedies. They then discussed their findings with the full board.[90] Included in the list were the presence of early warning surveillance systems, such as inspections of safety-related facilities, and compliance with laws and regulations.

When a crisis occurs, some boards become involved. At New Century Financial Corp., independent board members, who usually restrict themselves to providing oversight and monitoring of a company, assumed a hands-on role. Their experience yielded these helpful tips: (a) create a subcommittee to focus on the crisis; (b) collect information from managers directly; don't rely solely on the CEO; (c) hire board-only advisers; (d) serve as executives' sounding board.[91]

Building a Supporting Crisis Preparedness Infrastructure

Certain features of an organization sensitize it to its vulnerability to crises and provide "shock absorbers" for a crisis event. Among these features are:

- A culture among employees to be on the lookout for any potentially dangerous or disruptive events. Such cultural beliefs are likely to exist when senior executives recognize and value and need for crisis management. An organizational culture should also reflect an environmental ethos and, in general, embody a code of ethics.
- Strong two-way relationships with stakeholders encourage their participation in risk management and can help soften negative reactions to a crisis event. Some feedback mechanisms are employee grievance systems and customer complaint systems, which explore satisfaction with an organization's policies, products, and behavior. Stakeholders can also be including in crisis planning
- An open management style that encourages the dissemination of information and the use of a team approach to a crisis event. Instead of focusing exclusively on the training of individual managers, a collective concern about adverse events should be encouraged so that accountability is both individual and collective.
- Innovations in computer technology and telecommunications information preparedness provide further support. Stuart Z. Goldstein, vice president of corporate communication of New York's National Securities Clearing House, includes three components in such a technology infrastructure: (1) an integrated database that makes internal information available across all public affairs/corporation communications disciplines; (2) on-line access to external databases; and (3) a diagnostic database that tracks and helps analyze opinion data on key stakeholders over a wide range of issues.[92] Such infrastructure enables an organization quickly to assess a crisis event and to get its story out and define the situation before the media or others do.

Crisis preparedness is a holistic concept that involves the entire organization from the board of directors down to rank-and-file employees, and outward to the organization's entire stakeholders.

Essentials of a Contingency Plan

Contingency planning applies risk management to specific situations where things could go wrong. Its purpose is to recognize and address as many uncertainties and risks as possible so that management can maintain control over its affairs when a crisis strikes.[93] It focuses on preparation for anything that could happen—to do as much in advance as possible to deal with each contingency. Specifically, the objectives of a contingency plan are to:

- remove ambiguity during a crisis by outlining response actions, communication procedures, and responsibilities;
- provide guidance for personnel who manage major crisis events;
- offer guidelines for company spokespersons who communicate with the media and key audiences during a crisis;
- indicate what additional emergency and public affairs resources and personnel are available in the organization.

A contingency plan might start with such a statement of objectives and then proceed to describe the following steps.

Identify Areas of Vulnerability

Each organization and industry must identify all potential contingencies and areas of vulnerability. Some organizations, such as the Institute for Crisis Management, help prepare vulnerability assessment reports.[94] Chemical companies, for example, are highly vulnerable because they typically use some risky technologies. Their manufacturing processes and products could pose a threat to life, health, property or the environment, or may cause great public concern. In addition, larger firms tend to be more vulnerable to such risks as product liability suits, government action, and public confrontation. Interestingly, the Institute for Crisis Management, which covers business crises, listed the following five industries as the most crisis-prone in 2008: banking, food industry, security brokers/investment co., petroleum industry, and insurance industry.[95]

Specific Vulnerabilities

A planning team representing all divisions of an organization should meet and begin by identifying every possible disaster or other crisis event that could occur. They can start by examining definitions of a crisis and listing the types of crises and major problems that the organization and industry have encountered. Several sources and research procedures are helpful:

1. Lists of crisis types should be consulted to stimulate thinking. The previous chapter and Parts II, III, and IV of this book serve that purpose, as well as lists of crises in other books.[96]

2. Organizational resources should be examined. Inspect the news clipping files of the public relations department for reference to past emergencies and incidents. Database searches, such as Lexis/Nexis, reveal even more similar information. Talk to senior managers, operating managers, and staff department heads, including legal, security forces, human resources, safety engineers, and members of the crisis planning team. Include everyone. If there is a labor union, talk to its leaders. Visit plants, facilities, divisions and departments, and scrutinize them for areas of potential vulnerability.
3. Go outside the organization and talk with local government officials, police and fire department heads, community leaders, and responsible public interest groups. Also contact trade associations and other companies in your industry for news reports and other information on past crises. Business insurance consultants are another valuable source of potential risks.

In talking with managers, ask especially about "worst case" scenarios. Encourage them to imagine the worst possible thing that could happen to their organization, particularly in their sphere of responsibility. Ian Mitroff in *Why Some Companies Emerge Stronger and Better From a Crisis* warns that this task is extremely difficult because it requires managers to change their frames of reference.[97] Listen to the type of event mentioned, what their assessment of the probability of its occurrence is, what factors make it serious, what groups of people would be affected, how company operations would be impacted, and how the organization would respond to the crisis. Try to relate what they say to external events, issues, and trends that might have served as the context and perhaps aggravated a situation.

This review should include "historical" references—major catastrophes in the last century—and not just events that have happened in the past decade.[98] The end result of this worst scenario approach is to prepare a list of the mostly likely crises that could occur in an organization's various areas of operation. Furthermore, by studying the patterns associated with past crises, critical lessons can be discerned that managers can put into practice so that the potential for crises is lowered.

When the list of possible crises is completed, each entry should be prioritized by level of severity: minor, serious, and major. A minor incident might be one confined to organization premises and causing only minor injuries, damage and impact on third parties and the environment. The media may have limited interest. A serious incident is one that might occur outside as well as within organization premises but is controlled or contained. While having only moderate impact, it involves authorities outside the organization and creates moderate media interest. A major incident is one in which control or containment is not yet secured, results in a fatality or more than three injuries, involves the authorities, and has actual or potential public significance and receives media attention.[99]

A "Pre-Mortem" is a good way to expose faulty or optimistic thinking in crisis preparation plans. After a plan has been made by a group of people, bring them together for a special exercise. Tell them to imagine that a year has passed and that when the plan was implemented it was a disaster. Give them about 45 minutes to write down on a sheet of paper what happened. Why did the plan turn out to be a disaster?[100]

Vulnerability Based on Organization's "Public Nature"

In addition to considering an organization's specific vulnerabilities, the planning team should appraise the organization's vulnerability based on its public nature. Judging the public nature of an organization requires legal, economic, and political perspectives, as discussed later. Experience shows that the greater the perceived public nature of an organization the higher and more severe people's expectations and judgments are. In general, people expect organizations imbued with a public nature to follow the government model, one aspect of which is the "public's right to know" about all activities except those threatening national security.

Omitting government enterprises such as the Tennessee Valley Authority, public utilities are perceived by the public as possessing a public nature. In the absence of competition, a utility is treated as a natural monopoly by government and franchises are awarded to them that provide the exclusive right to supply given services within a specified geographical boundary. Competition is thus precluded but, in return, utilities must submit to government regulation of rates, services, and other matters. Although certain other industries and companies are not technically public utilities, they may be treated as if they were. These businesses are often called "public corporations" following the rationale of Adolf A. Berle and Gardner Means in their classic, *The Modern Corporation and Private Property*:

> The economic power in the hands of the few persons who control a giant corporation is a tremendous force which can harm or benefit a multitude of individuals, affect whole districts, shift the currents of trade, bring ruin to one community and prosperity to another. The organizations which they control have passed far beyond the realm of private enterprise—they have become more nearly social institutions.[101]

During and after the 2008 financial crisis, many economists concluded that if a bank or other financial institution is "too big to fail," it should be broken up into smaller units or, like a public utility, be subjected to greater regulation.

The courts long ago upheld the primacy of the public interest over property rights, as shown in the 1971 case of Munn v. People. Here the United States Supreme Court introduced the doctrine that when private property is "affected with a public interest, it ceases to be *juris privati* only." The Court added that property becomes clothed with a public interest and subject to public regulation "when used in a manner to make it of public consequence, and affect the community at large."

Using this reasoning, the Court applied the principle of eminent-domain in the Fort Trumbell neighborhood of New London, Connecticut, after Pfizer Inc. announced plans to build an adjacent research facility. The city then decided to develop a 90-acre site including a waterfront hotel, conference center and new residences—all in the name of revitalizing the area.[102] In this case of Kelo v. New London, the Court ruled that the state may seize private property on behalf of private developers, so long as this serves some broadly defined public purpose.[103]

Some specific reasons why a company might be vulnerable because of its public nature are listed here:

- A company or industry receives a government favor or uses public resources. Banks, broadcasting stations, the atomic energy industry, and extractive industries, and logging and grazing on government lands may be so perceived. Banks use money and credit instruments that are based on people's trust in government support of the monetary system; broadcasting stations use air waves that are public property and must be allocated to specific users to have value; the atomic energy industry uses a public investment of billions of dollars of previous research and development; oil and mining companies, especially if foreign owned, are seen as using up limited natural resources that belong to the people.
- A product or service is a biological or cultural necessity. It is one which is required by practically everyone in a given community or region, such as hospital services, milk deliveries, daily newspapers, and local transportation. One way to determine the existence of necessity is to examine the history of industrial disputes and to note which received public attention and were treated as "emergency disputes." If there are no substitutes or alternatives sources, and if the demand cannot be postponed, public opinion will be quick to react to such things as a shortage, excessive prices, and poor quality.
- An industry lacks competition. There is no "invisible hand" that automatically tends to regulate the industry in the public interest. Under such circumstances, the public tolerates the mechanism of government regulation.

Companies seen as "public corporations" are likely the most visible and prominent in an industry. As is well known, big companies are the usual targets of government and social action groups and get the most media attention.

Establish Crisis Thresholds and Assign Crisis Alert Responsibility

Once potential crises have been identified, a "crisis threshold" should be established for every recognized contingency, i.e., a concrete signal or set of indicators that a crisis is on hand or imminent unless emergency measures are taken to avert it. A clear-cut signal is most evident in the case of accidents—plane crashes killing a certain number of crew and passengers, or an industrial fire or explosion injuring employees, damaging property, and harming the environment.

The lack of a well-defined crisis threshold—sometimes reflected in the use of the ambiguous word "incident" instead of "accident"[104]—was directly responsible for the critical delay in warning local residents in Bhopal, India, in what was described as "the worst industrial accident ever" when lethal gas spread to the local community. Confusion about the crisis threshold caused the delay in warning the local community of the leak. In contrast, in 2008 when the National Weather Service decided that Hurricane Ike was definitely headed for Houston, Texas, it issued an unequivocal evacuation warning: "Persons not heeding evacuation orders in single-family, one- or two-storey homes may face certain death."[105]

Many crises do not follow the pattern of natural disasters, but instead evolve from a series of weaker signals, which appear before the climax that triggers a crisis is reached. Unfortunately, these early signals may not be noticed because no deliberate effort is made to search for them or because a serious problem cannot be inferred from events, issues and trends outside the organization. For example, there may have been numerous consumer complaints about a product, an expression of concern by an employee about some wrongdoing, or a government inquiry, but these indicators may not have been noticed because no one was assigned the responsibility. Another reason for lack of problem recognition says Charles Perrow, is that a certain situation is hard to imagine, i.e., no "heuristic"—a simple way of organizing information—is available.[106] Responsibility for monitoring signals must either become part of an employee's job or developed into separate positions, such as a consumer complaint manager, an auditor, or ethics officer.

Regardless of which pattern a crisis follows, specific individuals should be designated who have the responsibility to alert the crisis management team when thresholds are reached. Organizations should also instill active awareness and vigilance in their workforce so that potential crisis triggers can be recognized and brought to the attention of leaders.[107] Anyone in an organization can sound an alarm for a well-recognizable emergency such as a fire, and employees in different workstations can be instructed to sound an alert when a process malfunctions and becomes dangerous. They or their supervisors should know that the crisis communication center should be called. For less obvious events, special training and authority may have to be given to designated individuals, e.g., a member of an audit committee.

For whoever is given the responsibility to judge that a crisis threshold has been reached, instructions must be clearly known as to the person(s) to be notified. It is a good idea to load the cell phones of appropriate employees with the names and phone numbers of individuals who should be notified. As backup, the old-fashioned way might be used of providing critical employees with wallet-sized cards listing the names of individuals to be notified along with their cell phone, office and home telephone numbers. The "commander" of the crisis management team is the first to be notified and it is often that person who notifies others.

Organize and Train a Crisis Management Team

Every organization must organize a central, top-level crisis management team and, for multi-plant companies, similar local teams. The core members are the chief executive officer or other senior operating officer, the senior public relations or communications officer, the general counsel, and, in the case of large, multi-division companies, the head of the affected operating company. In addition, depending on the nature of the industry and crisis, the following may be included: the chief financial officer, director of security, director of environmental affairs, director of engineering, director of human resources, and director of marketing.[108] It is imperative that the team includes members with strong communication skills and this should be an essential quality of the team leader.[109]

   Johnson & Johnson's team during the famous Tylenol crisis was chaired by James E. Burke, the company chairman, and included the company president, the relevant group chairman, an executive committee member, chairman of Johnson & Johnson subsidiary, McNeil Consumer Products (which manufactured Tylenol), the general counsel, and the vice president for public relations. Crisis task forces should also be established for various types of emergency situations, such as fire or natural disasters, and specific tasks assigned to each member of the team. In crises involving breach of privacy, the manager of information technology must be included.

Designate Crisis Communication Center

Some organizations establish dedicated crisis control or communication centers, resembling "war rooms," where the activities of the crisis management team are coordinated. British Airways maintains a crisis control center at Heathrow airport on continual 24-hour standby and an in-house legal department ready to advise on all crisis issues. It offers its in-house department to other airlines, which buy its services in times of crisis.[110]

   The communications center should meet physical and equipment requirements: the size of the center should be 25 percent larger than the space required to accommodate the expected number of media representatives, and a separate room should be set aside for private interviews. Besides tables and chairs, there should be broadband connections for laptop computers, copying equipment, faxes, writing materials (pads, pencils, and pens), staplers, scissors, general reference books, telephones (in the event mobile phones don't work), telephone directories, video and audio tape equipment, coat racks, and bulletin boards. Telephone switch-ins should also be installed from the public relations department to the crisis communications center. Press kits should be stored digitally, along with stock photos and background information. If high website usage is expected, extra servers might be made available. As Melanie Magara commented after the Northern Illinois University shooting, "You don't want your site to crash in the midst of a crisis, especially since increased cell phone calls can cause those channels of communication to become overloaded."[111]

The entire organization should be made aware of the functions and relationships of the crisis management team and its various task forces. At the same time, all employees should be advised to refer inquiries from the press about an emergency to the crisis communications center. Those likely to be asked questions by the media must receive media relations training and take part in rehearsal sessions, preferably with the participation of journalists. If emergency teams are part of a contingency plan, the readiness of the team and supporting equipment must be monitored.

Games, simulations, and exercises are increasingly used to prepare managers for crises. Many of these training programs are modeled after the Crisis Management Exercise Program used by the U.S. State Department to prepare diplomats for disasters. Crisis simulation also serves to spot the most obvious flaws in an emergency plan, such as dependence on key staff who turn out to be ill or on vacation, or having a crisis control center that is too close to the likely cause of the catastrophe. Ideally, a crisis exercise should be done by independent experts, working with company staff, who are prepared to be both critical of current systems and informed on alternatives.[112]

Make Advance Arrangements

A contingency plan may include a variety of advance arrangements that improve the capability of responding to a crisis. Sometimes referred to as emergency plans, they might include such matters as prearranging redundant facilities and the logistics of renting cots and hotel rooms to accommodate needed employees, and the renting of ferries and other transportation for employees who would be relocated. Plans might also include the stocking of food and other supplies in buildings that might be used for emergency shelter.

Obtain Advance Approvals for Contingency Plan Measures

If approvals are required from governmental authorities to execute portions of the contingency plan, they should be obtained in advance. If this is not possible, clearance procedures should be carefully outlined, together with names, addresses and telephone numbers (including emergency numbers) of all involved individuals. Organizational clearance and approval procedures should similarly be reviewed, outlined, and kept up-to-date. Lack of clarity about approval for the use of chemical dispersants was one of the difficulties encountered by Exxon during the *Valdez* spill.

List and Prioritize Publics That Must Be Informed

Every public relations department should have a list of all publics—key stakeholders, constituencies, audiences—that are affected by the organization and who have an effect on it. These should be reviewed from a crisis perspective and those listed in the contingency plan who (a) must immediately be notified in order to protect life and property, and (b) should be informed as soon as the emergency allows, e.g., employees not at the crisis location, suppliers, and distributors.

Lessons from TWA Flight 800

The July 17 1996, crash of TWA flight 800 illustrates how an emotionally charged situation can cause companies to lose control of their contingency plans when government authorities get involved. Two hundred and thirty passengers were aboard the Paris-bound flight when it burst into flames and fell into the sea off the coast of Long Island. A meeting organized by Contingency Planning Exchange, Inc. identified some of the communication problems encountered. Melvin Reeves, director of disaster service for the American Red Cross of Greater New York mentioned the importance of knowing who has to be notified and what trained responders are available.

Another participant, Lt. Commander John McCarthy of the United States Coast Guard, observed that "you will find yourself working with agencies you never thought you would."[113] One example was the New York State Emergency Management Office which in turn worked with over 21 agencies to investigate the explosion, clean up the beaches, counsel grief-stricken families and, basically, to make some order out of chaos. New York Mayor Rudolph Giuliani, who was involved in the crisis, was concerned about notifying victims' families, the potential of environmental damage and keeping the public informed. Having a high-ranking official on hand to answer questions and provide direction is particularly important, said Bradford Billet, deputy director of the Mayor's Office of Emergency Management. TWA was remiss in initially having only a head ticket agent at JFK Airport to deal with the incoming rush of families wanting answers.

Increasingly, participation in crisis planning includes local authorities. The community has "right to know" about dangers to it from industrial products and processes. Some plans are provided by the government. For example, the U.S. Environmental Protection Agency prepared the Chemical Emergency Preparedness Plan, which is designed to help state and local governmental authorities respond to the emission of toxic chemicals. Its two-part plan assists communities in obtaining information on toxic chemicals in developing and improving their emergency planning.[114]

Contingency plans must also be responsive to business interruption losses. As stated by Hugh Loader, president of the European Association of Risk Managers, the worst thing that can happen to an industry is "losing your customers."[115] If a company is a manufacturer, it should have several alternative suppliers rather than just one that could be shut down by unforeseen events.

Prepare a Crisis Media List and Background Press Materials

An up-to-date list of media outlets is a basic requirement. The traditional news media of newspapers and broadcasters remain on the list, but in the new media environment they must be augmented by social media. This trend is international, as shown in an analysis of 120 corporate websites in the United States, Europe, and Asia.[116] It is part of the trend over the last decade, which has made the Internet a key tool for sharing knowledge, ideas or corporation information.

As the Domino's Pizza case illustrated, a major crisis event is often first discovered and reported in the social media. When US Airways Flight 1549 splashed into the Hudson River, it was Twitter that provided the first photo for the world to see. Twitter is included as one of the tools of microblogging, along with blogs, social networking sites (My Space and Facebook), and photo/video sharing sites (Flickr and YouTube).[117] For example, the U.S. Coast Guard uses social media to distribute public information, and Twitter specifically for instant updates. Its practice is to use images, videos and YouTube for distributing stories about rescues, responding to oil spills and conveying information abut law enforcement activities.[118]

Media lists should include names of public relations contacts and their telephone numbers (cellular, business, home), fax numbers, and email addresses. Some organizations keep a list of experts and others whom the media can consult for technical details and for verification of various kinds of data. Other times organizations use these "high credibility" persons as the source of background and supplementary information. It is a good idea to keep these individuals updated on company policies and activities. This information should be stored in a computer file ready for last-minute updating.

In the new world of the rapid pace of social media, organizations have established "online newsrooms"—also known as "Net relations," "Webbed public relations," and "Internet PR."[119] They are used as central headquarters to store everything that the media might want. They are becoming more important as many newspapers shrink their newsrooms and more and more "mobile journalists" (known as "mojos") work from their homes. They often carry "backpacks" that include a laptop computer, cellphone, video camera, and audio recorder.[120] A survey on the Online Newsroom conducted in April 2009 by the TEK found that 90 percent of reporters will visit an online newsroom for breaking news and company statements during a crisis.[121] The survey found that journalists look for the following information (along with some of the "best in online newsrooms"):

- PR contacts and their cellphone numbers;
- News releases, preferably organized by type of news;
- Background information about your organization, including company history and a timeline—and don't forget the company address (Pitney Bowes's Fast Facts sheet at http://news.pb.com);
- Product information/press kits (CIGNA has multiple press kits at http://newsroom.cigna.com);
- High-resolution photographs, along with logos, available on downloadable images (the Walgreens Press Room provides logos along with downloadable images at http://news.walgreens.com);
- FAQs about your organization;
- Events calendar;
- Financial information;
- Past news coverage;
- Video (Disneyland Resort Online Newsroom at http://www.disneyland-news.com);
- Audio (Ford Motor Company at http://media.ford.com);
- Links to your social media endeavors;
- RSS feeds (AAA Chicago Newsroom at http://media.aaachicago.com);
- Company blogs;
- Twitter feed. Note, however, that only 61 percent of journalists said they want to receive pitches/story ideas from a company Twitter account.[122]

Designate and Train Spokespersons

A roster of persons who are likely to be called upon as spokespersons for an organization during a crisis should be prepared and these persons trained to deal with the news media. For any given situation the status of the spokesperson should match the seriousness of the incident. A local manager, for example, would be inappropriate for a crisis with national implications.

As will be seen throughout the book, and summarized in the next chapter, "Crisis Communiation," the plan is activated during a crisis and its benefits seen both during the crisis and in the aftermath.

Keep a Log—and Learn from Failures

Crisis managers should keep a log of all information received, procedures undertaken, and steps decided upon, despite the extra burden during a time of stress. Everyone involved in crisis management should write down what he or she does and thinks. This discipline forces a manager to become more objective about events and even facilitates the formulation of responses. Those handling communications should keep a log of all media contacts—both inquiries and initiatives—by simply recording the date and time of the contact, the name of the publication, radio or TV station, the name and phone number of the reporter or other contact, and the subject of the inquiry and response given.

During a crisis, log information can be shared among individuals and teams and allow the smooth transfer of responsibility among them during different shifts. It is ultimately helpful in evaluating how well the crisis was handled and finding oversights and deficiencies. This post-crisis analysis helps improve future crisis performance and suggest post-crisis rebuilding efforts. Some companies debrief their employees after a crisis event for the purpose of reevaluating their procedures and asking how they could be improved. The aim is to make the contingency plan more comprehensive and realistic. Consider whether more training and drills are necessary. Fine-tune the plans and procedures. These reviews are a reminder that a crisis contingency plan is never completed; it must constantly be updated and renewed. All plans should show the date of last revision.

In their article on organizational crisis preparedness, Carmeli and Schaubroeck argue that the process of learning from failures is critical to an organization's crisis preparedness.[123] Such a process, they say, is more likely in organizations with a psychology of safety and high level of tolerance toward failures—an attitude that might be resisted by managers who are afraid it might interfere with the "image of the prototypically optimistic, forward-thinking, effective leader."[124] Also, as Daniel Kahneman, known as the father of behavioral economics, suggests, decision makers are reluctant to go back and look at their past mistakes because it's against their interests. "Nobody likes to expose themselves. So any systematic attempt to collect the way decisions are made, which is really essential for any organization to improve, is generally sabotaged within the organization."[125] Yet, although organizations that have previously experienced a crisis event tend to have a higher level of preparedness than those that haven't, their crisis preparation is enhanced when they try to learn from failures.

The distinction between single-loop learning and double-loop learning applies to the process of learning from failures. The former detects an undesirable state of affairs, such as low temperature (e.g., a thermostat) in a room, but it doesn't explain what might account for the low temperature. Double-loop learning would address the root causes of the low temperature, such as an open window or lack of insulation. As stated by Carmeli and Schaubroeck, "Second-order problem-solving behaviour is a response that not only corrects the immediate failure in order to ensure the continuity of the operation or the provision of a service, but also addresses the failure in a wider sense by either correcting its causes or alerting others to its occurrence."[126] Besides resolving current difficulties, double-loop learning may point to possibilities of taking advantage of new opportunities.

The fast-food restaurant Jack-in-the Box belatedly learned the value of learning. After deaths and illnesses resulting from under-cooked hamburgers caused a loss in business and reputation, Jack-in-the-Box called in an outside expert (a microbiologist) to specify every point in its workflow in which bacterial contamination could occur, beginning with its suppliers.[127] It engaged in double-loop learning in that it sought to identify the error and modify it by changing its underlying norms, policies, and objectives, e.g., increasing the cooking time for hamburgers.[128] It rejected the solution of engaging only in damage control, e.g., convincing prospective customers of its food safety. At its subsequent annual meeting it announced a budget allocation for the purpose of "correcting" the organization and to assist the victims of food poisoning.[129]

An organization's leadership is closely scrutinized during a crisis and sometimes challenged. Many questions may arise. Events such as an aircraft explosion, oil spill, or scandal may lead members of an organization to question their organization's cultural beliefs. Also questioned may be the type of technology used, e.g., nuclear power and chemical, as well as management procedures, policies, practices, and routines. Eventually old practices and relationships may be replaced. In organizations dealing with risky technologies, caution, perhaps in the form of extra protection, may be needed for an organization to see itself as "crisis-prepared."

Conclusions

Risk management has become an unavoidable management function because the most likely future scenario is one in which crises will continue to erupt. Nature, technology, and human beings all conspire to present management with complex challenges that must be responded to in ever-smaller time frames. Some crises will be of management's own making. Yet, surveys show that many organizations are so involved with current operations that they postpone making decisions on possible future disruptions. Boards of directors and top managements must accept responsibility for putting risk management on their organizations' agendas.

Contingency planning is an expression of risk management. It accepts the fact that most organizations will face a crisis sooner or later and that preparations must be made. Knowing the kinds of crises that have occurred, what caused them, how they were handled, and the lessons that could be learned from them should help managers to cope with future crises. Contingency planning is a learning process as well as a rehearsal for unwanted but inevitable events.

Chapter 3

Crisis Communication

Crisis communication determines whether a crisis event becomes even more serious than it is, for how the traditional and new media report on a crisis event largely determines how it will be perceived and treated by an organization's stakeholders and the general public. The traditional media can also create a crisis by investigative reporting, and the new media may report information unobserved by the traditional media. For example, Sony was engulfed in a crisis in 2006 as bloggers reported instances when its batteries in Dell computers caught fire.[130] The story spread fast exponentially through the online world. This also happened in 2005 when a series of blog postings titled "Dell Hell" by an influential blogger, Jeff Jarvis, was shared with thousands. He detailed his nightmarish experience with Dell's customer service department.[131]

Not every unfavorable media story, however, is a crisis. Negative stories can more accurately be considered "media attacks" rather than a crisis, says James E. Lukaszewski in his book, *Crisis Communication Plan Components and Models*.[132] His examples include a *Wall Street Journal* article about diversity that mentions a company unfavorably; a chairman of a company who apparently insulted three Latinas while presenting them with awards; a raid by local, state and federal authorities that found drug dealing in a TCG store; worker layoffs; a truck accident in a neighborhood that critically injured a child; and the death of a volunteer worker caught in gang war crossfire during a community involvement program. These situations generally require the types of communication responses discussed in this chapter or direct communications with the stakeholders affected.

The Media Can Damage Reputations

The danger of unfavorable stories by the media, both traditional and new, is that they can potentially damage the reputation of an organization and cause a variety of employee relations, consumer relations, and community relations problems. How quickly and effectively crisis communication is employed will affect the severity of damage and whether the event reaches the magnitude of a crisis. In the Dell case, the company set a precedent when it responded in the new media that caused the riff rather than issuing a statement of apology in the traditional media or ignoring the online chatter.[133]

The luxury of consulting with all organizational executives about how to tackle an unfavorable news report is gone, as the experience of Domino's Pizza discussed in the previous chapter illustrated. The critical response time is no longer the first 24 hours. It's now the first 24 minutes because of the instantaneous reporting by the social media and 24-hour cable news. Karen Doyne, managing director of Burson Marsteller's crisis and issues management group, commented: "One of the major yardsticks in crisis communications is meeting public expectations. And public expectations are rising all the time, particularly because of technology. First it was the 24-hour news networks. Then it was the Internet. And now, people demand information immediately and on a continual basis."[134]

Because every crisis creates an information gap, an organization has a better chance of affecting dissemination of a potentially negative story when it speedily fills the void. Silence by an affected organization works against it because the media and the public believe it has something to hide. Moreover, the first hours or, in quick-moving crises, minutes after a crisis event, are of critical importance for an organization to gain control over the reporting of the event—not only in describing what happened but in framing the event.

Doyne suggests the following actions:

- Constantly monitor not only the media but also the blogosphere, where many modern crises are born.
- Make a statement during the very first news cycle of a crisis, including what you know, what you don't know, and what you plan to do.
- Give a clear plan of how a crisis is being fixed and what steps you will take to ensure it doesn't happen again. Reach out to key stakeholder groups after a crisis to mend any broken relations.[135]

Crises of Communication Failure

The above advice was not heeded after the Russian submarine *Kursk* sank, when the Catholic Church faced a sexual scandal, and when Arla Foods became embroiled in a Danish newspaper's depiction of Mohammad.

Silence After the Sinking of the Russian Submarine Kursk[136]

Silence is dangerous. On August 12, 2000, the Russian attack submarine *Kursk* sank during a naval exercise in the Barents Sea approximately 100 miles off the coast of Murmansk, Russia, with a loss of 118 sailors, including 49 officers[137] It was caused by an unexplained explosion or series of explosions. The Russian Navy made several futile attempts to rescue the surviving submariners who were tapping inside the sunken vessel. Offers of help from nearby British and

Norwegian NATO ships monitoring the maneuvers were rejected for several days, until it was too late.

The *Kursk* sinking can be seen from several perspectives. It was an accident that had a touch of skewed values because the Navy was more concerned about saving its honor than about saving sailors' lives. But its significance is that the Navy and government engaged in abysmally poor crisis communication.[138] Russian officials did not report the incident until two days later, Monday, August 14. Reflecting the tradition of secrecy of the former Soviet Union, the information provided was untruthful. It blamed NATO ships for the sinking and claimed that sailors never survived the blast and certainly did not tap on the submarine's hull to indicate that they were alive.

Russian officials were found wrong, however. A note found in the pocket of a recovered submariner proved that at least 23 of the 118 men survived the initial explosion. This was a human-interest story favored by journalists. The Russian and world media reported on the anger of the thousands of friends and family members of the perished sailors as their bodies were retrieved. All over the world people were hearing of accounts of the sailors' last few hours as written in retrieved messages that were released to the public.[139] Russian and world media gave extensive coverage to the sinking of the *Kursk*. Russian newspapers such as *Komsomolskaya Pravda*, *Rossiykaya Gazeeta*, *Nezavisimay Gazeta*, and *Segondnya* also severely criticized the Russians' refusal of offers of foreign assistance.

At least an equally large crisis communication failure was the absence of Russian president Vladimir V. Putin, who had stayed at his vacation hideaway on the Black Sea and made no statement to the public or the families of the sailors. He didn't speak out publicly until Wednesday, August 16, four days after the incident. By August 18, CNN reported, "The growing public outcry has forced President Vladimir Putin to cut short his holiday in the Black Sea, where he remained silent on the unfolding drama in the Barents Sea, and return to Moscow."[140] Although he announced an official day of mourning for August 23, the gesture did not assuage the relatives' feelings because many were awaiting the burials of their loved ones.[141]

The Sexual Scandal of the Catholic Church[142]

The Catholic Church sexual abuse scandal demonstrated how a long-smouldering crisis was ignited by sudden media attention. The Catholic Church ignored or minimized an issue that lay dormant for over a decade despite intermittent media stories. In the mid-1980s, Louisiana writer Jason Berry reported extensively on the widespread problem of sexual abuse by priests and was interviewed by radio and television outlets around the country.[143] His book, *Lead Us Not Into Temptation: Catholic Priests and the Sexual Abuse of Children*, was published in 1992. But the scandal failed to arouse public consciousness. Neither did a July 1996 story in the *Boston Globe* about Catholic priest John J. Geoghan. In December 1995 he was charged with molestation in the Greater Boston area of Waltham,

Massachusetts, after a parishioner sued, saying Geoghan had molested her three sons.[144] Again the Catholic Church made no response.

A Small Newspaper Triggers the Story

Finally, in March 2001 a small Boston newspaper, the *Boston Phoenix*, succeeded in triggering the crisis when Kristen Lombardo published a 7,000-word block-buster story.[145] In addition to reviewing Geoghan's abuse, she exposed how the local Church hierarchy, including Cardinal Bernard F. Law, was complicit in allowing the abuse to continue. Diocesan authorities had simply transferred errant priests to another parish, after they received psychological counseling. It became clear that the Church hierarchy plainly cared more for the institution of the Church than the welfare of its children.

The exposure in the small newspaper persuaded Boston's two major news-papers, the *Globe* and the *Herald*, to put the story on their agendas and to report on the scandal every day. It has become a common pattern for the main media to follow suit after a small newspaper or blog reports on sensitive matters and takes on powerful individuals or entities.

Other factors also explain what happened. The time was right. Public atti-tudes toward disclosure of sexual conduct had changed, adding to the explosive power of the expose. The Monica Lewinsky scandal broke the journalistic taboo of not writing about sexual issues. Another factor is that a handful of people—journalists and victims—can push an idea past *The Tipping Point*, as explained in Malcolm Gladwell's book. Helping to do this is that religion no longer com-mands automatic respect or adherence by secular authorities.[146] And, finally, the unbelievably unresponsive attitude and behavior of the Church was at fault. Belatedly, the Vatican convened American bishops who promised to place the issue on the agenda of an upcoming Dallas conference on June 13–14, 2002, and to produce corrective action.[147] The bishops voted to bar from the ministry any priest found to be involved in sexual abuse of a minor in the past, present or future. They did not, however, agree with the victims that such priests be defrocked so that they could not exercise the power that comes with calling themselves "a priest," a title that has always been held in great deal of respect, particularly with kids.[148]

When the news broke in Boston that several priests were being charged with illicit sexual behavior towards minors, the story was watched by neigh-boring dioceses, which waited along with the rest of the world. Susan Gibbs, spokesperson for the Archdiocese of Washington, said, "When it started, it was a single diocesan issue and no one had any more information than what the media had. Then, it just spun randomly, took on a life of its own and moved into a direction that 'no one knew where it was going.'"[149] The U.S. Council of Bishops responded by posting directives and Q&As on its website, but the onslaught from the media overwhelmed various communication officers. "It's difficult to be effective when you're getting hundreds of calls a day. It's difficult to find people who can talk on the issue."[150] For their part, the various dioceses cooperated by sending one another emails and information alerts about breaking news.

The Archdiocese of Washington had dealt with the issue on its own turf back in 1995 when three priests were charged with sexual abuse toward minors. "We got in front of the issue," says Gibbs. "We were up front with it and we took the hit. It really is the best way to deal with it."[151] Indeed, the Archdiocese was responsive to the victims and arranged for them to have confidential interviews with a reporter from the *Washington Post*. The ensuing long-term benefits were enhanced relationships among the Church, the press, the victims, and members. So when the recent scandal revisited Washington with yet another priest's admissions of inappropriate conduct, relationships were in place. The diocese looked to the 1995 case as a model. The press was contacted and Archbishop Theodore McCarrick broke the news to area Catholics via a letter read by priests during Palm Sunday Mass.

Complexity of a Decentralized Church

This crisis cannot be discussed, however, without recognizing the several levels of what is meant by "the Church." The statements of Pope Benedict represent the highest level of the Church, namely, the Vatican. Despite the prominent role of the Pope, the daily operations of the Church are decentralized and carried out on a local level. The Church is likely the most multi-layered, multi-lingual multicultural group in the world, held together by a core set of values and beliefs. In another organizational environment some tenets might not hold as solidly.

When people ask, "Why can't the Vatican just tell the dioceses to report abuse to the authorities?" Gibbs explains, "there are millions of different local laws governing these issues. . . . It's impossible to come up with a specific policy that would be applicable everywhere." Gibbs elaborates: "We have core teachings, which are global, but the way we operate as a Church is often local." The Pope teaches the theology, but the application of the teachings is up to the dioceses. "Child abuse, for example, is sinful and illegal, obviously, but it's up to the individual dioceses to live that out." Therein, she says, lies the potential for breakdown. "It is a decentralized structure and that has definitely been problematic."[152]

The Boston diocese suffered the initial brunt of the crisis. Cardinal Law became the paramount spokesperson and decision maker. He largely limited his efforts to image restoration, as discussed in the next chapter. The next highest level was the Pope, who now had to guarantee that Law's statements supported the necessary responses to this communication crisis.

Although the media relations and communications aspects of the crisis are most prominent, it is also a massive crisis of management failure. It is partly a crisis of skewed values because the Church appeared to care more for the welfare of its priests and the authority of the Church than the welfare of the molested children—the victims. It is also a case of deception, because the Church withheld information about errant priests from law enforcement authorities and its own parishioners. Finally, it is a crisis of misconduct in that the Church seemingly condoned the misconduct of offending priests by not applying existing policies.

Arla Foods: Innocent Bystanders Can Be Harmed by Editorial Position of Media

Arla Foods, a Danish dairy company with significant Middle East markets, became the victim of the decision by the newspaper *Jyllands-Posten* to publish cartoons depicting the prophet Muhammad unfavorably. One cartoon depicted Muhammad in a turban shaped like a bomb. Another showed a turbaned figure in heaven telling ascending suicide bombers to stop because "we've run out of virgins," which is purported reward for Islamic martyrs.[153] The newspaper's aim was to demonstrate Denmark's devotion to freedom of the press.

The immediate Muslim reaction was by its local leaders in Denmark. They sent a protesting letter to the newspaper and to the Danish culture minister, neither of which replied. Their request to meet Prime Minister Anders Fogh Rasmussen was also declined, but he replied as follows:

> The freedom of expression has a wide scope and the Danish government has no means of influencing the press. However, Danish legislation prohibits acts of expressions of a blasphemous or discriminatory nature. The offended party may bring such acts or expressions to court, and it is for the courts to decide in individual cases.[154]

Dissatisfied with this response, Danish Muslims took their case to the Middle East, where the issue escalated into a crisis. Retaliatory boycotts against Danish products were initiated in Saudi Arabia where supermarkets displayed signs indicating that Danish products had been removed. The boycott spread throughout the Middle East.

Arla Foods became an innocent victim of association as events quickly evolved. It had to decide how to respond: whether to distance itself from the controversy (as New Zealand companies had) or to publicize its position. If the latter, it had to decide whether to support the Danish view of upholding freedom of the press or to disassociate itself from the views of the Danish newspaper and government, and thus possibly antagonize Danish public opinion. Arla Foods chose the option of publicizing its position. On January 27, 2006, it published the Danish government's press release in Saudi papers, explicitly stating that the ads were paid for by Arla Foods. It said the press release, "reiterates that Denmark respects all religions," but added, ". . . underlined that freedom of expression is a vital and indispensable element of Danish society and that the

Danish government cannot influence what an independent newspaper chooses to bring."[155]

Although pleasing the Danes, the advertisement backfired in the Middle East. Seeing a worsening of the boycott and fearing that it might have to withdraw completely from those markets, Arla applied the option of disassociating itself from the cartoon. It did so in mid-March when it launched a new advertising campaign in 25 Arab newspapers and asked consumers to reconsider their attitude toward Arla.

Advertising to consumers was the wrong approach, said some New Zealand companies with sales in the Middle East. Their view was that Arla should have avoided direct public comment as far as possible and instead have communicated through diplomatic channels and relationships and business-to-business methods, such as using Muslim "gatekeepers" in the distribution channels and emphasizing messages about quality and adherence to religious halal methods. These intermediaries would be expected to reassure retailers. It worked for them and might have for Arla.

Essentials of Crisis Communication

Crisis communication begins with the first public statement made by a spokesperson about a crisis event, says Lukaszewski. It "sets the tone, priorities, and the tempo of the response process" and hopefully the secondary damage that might be caused.[156] He recommends establishing an "order and priority sequence" as follows:

- Limit the problem, end the problem, or at least control the problem.
- Communicate with those most directly affected, i.e., victims, families and relatives. This act helps reduce media interest and coverage while also building the trust of employees, the community, public, and regulatory officials.
- Communicate with the news media and other channels of external communication, and "the self-appointed."[157]

Strategic thinking is an important part of crisis communication. The overriding concern is to control damage to an organization's reputation. A supplementary objective is to use the occasion of media attention as an opportunity to publicize oneself, i.e., to tell the public about the organization's mission, values, and operations. Management has to consider what basic goals and values are at stake. In the case of an explosion of an underground pipeline owned by Calnev Pipeline Company in San Bernardino, California, management recognized that the government could withdraw the company's pipeline rights, which would put it out of business; or require it to relocate the pipeline, which would be costly. It was necessary to remind the public of the pipeline's importance to the local economies.[158]

When a crisis strikes, the benefits and shortcomings of the contingency plan are tested. As always, the plan must now be applied to the particulars of the situation and additional judgments made. The occurrence of a crisis must be confirmed, the crisis management team must be mobilized, and damage control efforts undertaken. Public relations activities focus on media relations and relationships with the organization's stakeholders.

Apply Basic Rules of Media Relations

As many case studies in this book demonstrate, crisis communication is based on the basic rules of media relations developed by public relations professionals. Chester Burger's article on "How to Meet the Press" has become a classic in describing these "rules of the game."[159] Some rules pertain to a general attitude by spokespersons that reflect concern for the public. His first rule, "Talk from the viewpoint of the public's interest, not the company's," is a reminder that the press and the public want to know how a crisis event affects them and, if relevant, what they can do about it. His second rule, "Speak in personal terms whenever possible," should be extended to include statements of compassion for injured people or animals.

Several other rules pertain to the handling of interviews with reporters: "If you do not want some statement quoted, do not make it," and "If a question contains offensive language or simply words you do not like, do not repeat them, even to deny them." Burger also advises: "Do not argue with the reporter or lose your cool." In dealing with the message itself, Burger says, "State the most important fact at the beginning," "Do not exaggerate the facts," and "If the reporter asks a direct question, he is entitled to an equally direct answer." But do not go beyond the question.[160]

Burger's last two rules are the most important in crisis communication: "If an executive does not know the answer to a question, he should simply say, 'I don't know, but I'll find out for you,'" and "Tell the truth, even if it hurts." Stonewalling and otherwise holding back on information about a crisis is the most common mistake made by executives.

A crisis can dramatically change the relationship between an organization and the media. During a crisis, the job of the media relations practitioner changes from "Let's get the word out" to "Let's control the flow of information."[161] To increase the chances of fair treatment during a crisis, Greg Efthimiou, a manager at Accenture, advises PR professionals to build relationships during the "steady state" of media relations. He quotes an energy company executive, "During the steady state, it's important to be proactive and develop relationships with the media so when you have a crisis, you already have the credibility established."[162] When a threat is seen as evolving, pre-briefings with reporters might be valuable. This sharing of information is preferable to having a journalist dig deeper and seek alternative—and not always reliable—sources of information.[163]

One question that often arises is whether some reporters should be given preferential treatment. The general rule is that all reporters should be given the same information at the same time. But in returning calls, the wire services should be given priority because they serve all media outlets. However, by opening a website early on, all reporters have access to essential facts as well as company background information. The design of a website can be planned in advance, as well as templates to handle a variety of crisis situations.[164]

Guidelines for Crisis Communication

Crisis communication involves guidelines that go beyond the above media relations principles. The following sum up the key ones:

Ascertain and Face Up to the Reality of a Crisis

Crises do not always declare themselves as such. As discussed under contingency planning, spontaneous events like earthquakes, a power outage or breakdown of the telephone system, and industrial accidents causing many deaths are automatically designated as crises. But many slowly evolving smouldering crises are either overlooked or disregarded, even when a situation gains momentum and signals become clearer, as the Catholic Church scandal demonstrates.

Critical judgment is required in deciding what events determine that a crisis threshold is reached. Preliminary fact-finding is almost always necessary to ascertain the existence of a crisis situation, as shown in food poisoning cases. When a journalist's inquiry or call from a hospital alerts management to a possible crisis, the information must quickly be verified by talking to relevant executives and technical people within the organization, and any outsiders who are in a knowledgeable position. In other cases, as in the Domino's Pizza case discussed in Chapter 2, evidence (the video on Facebook) must be taken at face value to begin the crisis response. If contingency planning had the prescience to include the particular scenario, the planned response can be followed.

Activate Crisis Management Team and Alert Top Management

Whoever detects an accident or problem and judges it to have the potential of reaching a crisis threshold begins the crisis activation process. This person may be an operations executive if the situation is internal or, as in food poisoning cases, an outside hospital representative. These calls should be routed to a single telephone number, usually in the public relations department. From there, members of the crisis management team and top management can be alerted, using digitally stored phone numbers in cell phones or those listed on wallet-sized cards according to the prearranged procedure of the contingency plan.

To speed up the notification process, an automated warning system[165] or telephone tree technique—whereby each successive person calls several others—may be used. Depending on the severity and scope of the crisis, the individuals initially alerted will be the local crisis management team or, with a serious crisis, the headquarters crisis management team. In short, implementation of the contingency plan begins.

Designate Crisis Media Center

Because reporters and television and radio crews will immediately descend on an organization when a serious crisis occurs, a crisis media center must be established. The day after the *Challenger* explosion, for example, between 1,400 and 1,500 members of the press were on hand.[166] A field crisis communication center is established at the site of a crisis event, and the media informed of its location. It must, however, be reasonably accessible. If restricted areas are involved, the field press- room may have to be isolated from these areas and, in the case of an accident, away from the immediate scene.

Communication lines must be maintained between the field and headquarters communications centers. When a crisis occurs, the news media should be notified of the location of the crisis communication center(s) and, if necessary, transportation and sleeping quarters arranged for them. The details of the contingency plan arrangements for the communication center can then be implemented, e.g., press kits prepared and distributed. Arrangements should also be made for providing journalists with refreshments.

Conduct Necessary Fact-Finding

Collect all pertinent information necessary to cope with the crisis and to prepare for the media when they arrive. Be ready to answer the journalist's five W's—Who? What? When? Where? Why?—and How? Expect the news media to ask questions about:

- What happened and, if possible, what caused the crisis?
- How many casualties were incurred (both injured and dead)?
- What damage was caused to property and the surrounding environment?
- Whether any public health or environmental dangers exist?
- How rescue and relief operations are proceeding?
- What consequences—legal, financial, etc.—stem from the crisis?
- Who the heroes and culprits were?
- What witnesses, experts, victims, and others might be interviewed?[167]

Do not overlook some seemingly minor facts. For example, Johnson & Johnson suffered a temporary credibility setback after claiming that no cyanide was kept where Tylenol capsules were manufactured—it was later discovered and they had to admit that cyanide was kept in the laboratory for testing raw materials.

Speak with a Single Voice

Many crisis plans state the desirability of designating a single spokesperson to act as the information source for public officials, the press, and the public. What this means, however, is that management speak with a single voice, even though more than one spokesperson is involved.

The choice of spokespersons depends on the severity of the crisis and its nature. In major crises, a high level officer, preferably the chief executive officer, should serve as chief spokesperson because the CEO personifies the organization. But he or she must be media-savvy and comfortable in dealing with the media. The presence of CEO James Burke, chairman of Johnson & Johnson during the Tylenol crisis, met that qualification. If a crisis is not severe, however, the CEO should not serve as the spokesperson because it might signal to the media that the worst of the crisis has not yet occurred.[168]

As shown in the Firestone/Ford case discussed later in Chapter 4, top executives should express concern for the victims of an accident or product defect and promise corrective action. In the *Exxon Valdez* oil spill, Exxon's chairman, Lawrence G. Rawl, was generally criticized for not making a statement during the initial news conference and not visiting the site of the oil spill until three weeks after the event. His greater involvement and visibility were important because of the magnitude of the environmental damage and because of the photojournalism dimensions of the disaster.

Individuals in staff positions relevant to a specific crisis should be considered for spokesperson roles. When technical complexities exist, as in the aerospace or biotechnology industries, a technical expert may be appropriate, provided the individual is well briefed on the overall situation and reasonably articulate. In other situations, a chief financial officer may be most effective if investors are mainly impacted, or a human resources manager if employees are affected. Backup persons must be available to support the primary spokesperson. The key consideration is that an authoritative source of information must be available at the central media center at all times during the crisis. If there is also a field crisis communications center, communications personnel, briefed about the "single voice" message, should similarly be on duty. All employees should be reminded that all media inquiries must be referred to the crisis media center.

Speaking with a single voice is necessary to maintain control over the accuracy and authenticity of information and to prevent a blunder that could ruin the reputation of the organization. This happened with the Three Mile Island accident in 1979. Both Metropolitan Edison and the Nuclear Regulatory Commission were the prime information sources for the media about what was happening during the accident. They provided very little useful information during the first few days. As described by Lagadek, "... their responses to media queries were confusing, conflicting, and disorganized. On the first day of the accident, no one even knew who was in charge of informing the public. Metropolitan Edison issued statements from three different places, all saying something different about off-site radiation."[169] Consultant Richard Hyde commented: "The absence of a single qualified spokesperson at the site during the initial stages of the accident, armed with a comprehensive crisis communications plan, severely hindered any attempt to get consistently valid information to the public."[170]

Say It Fast, Say It All, Say It Accurately

When the essential facts of a serious crisis have been verified, a statement and news release must be prepared in consultation with senior management and legal counsel. A news conference should be held as soon as possible. A media advisory should be issued notifying the media of the field location, listing the people staffing it and their phone numbers. PR Newswire and Business Wire are helpful services to disseminate the advisory quickly. It may be necessary to counter the ingrained caution of legal advisors who are primarily concerned with the possibility of future litigation. Openness, honesty and accuracy are essential to the organization's reputation, which is always at serious risk in a crisis. Willingness to take bad news to the media is another way of demonstrating openness.

Silence can jeopardize a reputation, as Blackberry learned. From roughly 8:15 p.m., Tuesday, April 17, 2007, through Wednesday morning, an estimated five million users of BlackBerry's wireless email device found themselves without service. An outage knocked out email service for North American and overseas roaming customers. The provider, Research in Motion Ltd. (RIM), failed to explain what had happened, angering some customers. It wasn't until late Wednesday night when RIM issued a statement tracing the disruption to a "non-critical" software update that hadn't been properly tested. Prior to this announcement, a RIM spokesperson reported that finding the full root causes of the outage would take more time. Speculation ensued, with technical experts and analysts believing that the problem almost certainly concerned a disruption in RIM's so-called network operations center in Waterloo, Canada.

In terms of typology, the cause is technological, but the crisis itself was reputational, because of RIM's slow and inadequate communications. What was being questioned was RIM's boast about how reliable its platform was. As the chief information officer for Boston's Beth Israel Deaconess Medical Center, John Halamka said, "I find their reluctance to discuss the event a bit baffling—it undermines their credibility."[171] Some users felt RIM owed them more than a solid explanation; they also wanted compensation.

The advice to "just tell it," raises questions about "what **it** is"—just how much should be disclosed. Journalists must be given "all" the information relevant to a crisis event to help them write completed stories, so unwelcome stories won't drag on for days or even weeks. "What else might they uncover?" is a question that must be considered, especially if they are motivated. The bigger the crisis, the more these barriers will be penetrated. Although ambiguous, the advice is to give out as much information as you can.

Despite the pressure for open communication, unconfirmed or speculative information should never be released. If pressured, just tell journalists that facts are still being collected. The "don't speculate" rule, however, does not mean that an obvious interpretation of an event shouldn't be made; e.g., when everyone on the ground around Cape Canaveral saw the *Challenger* explode, the NASA spokesperson shouldn't have referred to "an apparent explosion."[172]

By tradition, certain other types of information should be withheld, e.g., the names of victims until next-of-kin have been informed. Airlines make it a practice to release the passenger list following an accident. But in the case of Sioux City forced-landing of United Flight 232, United initially refused. Journalists were told about the complexity of the passenger manifest—that there are actually three: one by the reservations office, one at check-in, and the third from the "ticket lift" at the gate.[173]

Do not interfere with the legitimate activities of journalists, but always escort them and camera crews everywhere on the emergency site. These virtues will usually be rewarded by more balanced treatment in media reports. If unreasonable requests are made, explain why they have to be turned down. Although control over the movements of journalists and camera crew members is essential, positive efforts should be made by the public relations staff to provide assistance to the media.

Communication must be prompt, because events move rapidly in an emergency and critical decisions must be made quickly. The news media are also likely to become impatient if information is slow in coming; they will attempt to find other sources and, sometimes, cast suspicion on the non-cooperative source. At Three Mile Island, reporters tracked down plant employees by taking their automobile registration numbers and finding the addresses from the State Motor Vehicle Department files. During a crisis, media—both traditional and new—should be monitored. If errors or inaccuracies are found in media statements, prompt action should be taken to correct them.

Consider preemptive strategies

Metabolife International produced a popular diet pill, Metabolife 345, which reportedly produced dangerous side effects. After Arnold Diaz, a reporter for the ABC television news magazine program 20/20, interviewed the company's CEO, Michael Ellis, for a program on September 9, 1999, which Ellis considered unfair, he decided to launch a preemptive attack. Prior to the October 15 appearance of the program, Ellis spent $1.5 million on full-page newspaper ads and radio programs to air his concerns that the 20/20 program would be unfair and to publicize a site (www.newsinterview.com) on which an unedited 70-minute videotaped interview of Ellis and Randy Smith, the company's medical director, would appear.

Was this effort effective in offsetting the negative program? After the October 15 program, Ellis judged the program not to have been "terribly unfair." But he defended his publicity campaign by saying it was "effective in holding 20/20's feet to the fire to some degree." His publicist, Michael Sitrick, said the website attracted more than 1 million users in its first 15 hours. The company's pre-program publicity campaign helped to make the 20/20 broadcast the highest rated one that night among women ages 18 to 49. One effect of the broadcast was that more people would now know about the pill's side effects and some embarrassing personal information, namely, that in 1988 Ellis was charged with illegally making methamphetamine, or speed.[174]

Communicate Directly with Key Stakeholders

Information must also be disseminated as quickly as possible to various involved government agencies and the organization's employees, stockholders, dealers, suppliers, and customers. The airline industry, for example, would notify the National Transportation Safety Board (NTSB) and the Federal Aviation Administration (FAA). It is important to demonstrate cooperation with all local, state, and federal safety authorities investigating the cause of an accident or other crisis event.

Employees are another prime public for several reasons. First, they might have been directly involved in the crisis, such as an accident, or affected by it because of implications about their personal safety or the safety of company products used by consumers. Second, their morale and pride in the organization may be undermined if they feel their employer is responsible for the crisis. Third, they are likely to be asked questions by their neighbors and the media about what happened and what they think about their employer. Employees should be told to refer all media inquiries to the crisis spokesperson. For these and other reasons, an organization should use its existing channels of communications to inform employees and, when necessary, special bulletins, websites, social media, and meetings. They should also be notified of what was said at news conferences. Employees will want to know how their jobs are affected and what the company is doing to remedy problems caused by the crisis.

Especially in cases of product flaws or product tampering, customers and dealers, patients and doctors need to be kept informed. In a classic example of rapid response, Johnson & Johnson had sent out half a million warning mailgrams to distributors, doctors, and health care practitioners by mid-afternoon of the day on which the first deaths from contaminated Tylenol were announced. Its domestic employees received two letters to keep them updated and to thank them for their support. The company established a toll-free consumer hotline, which received more than 30,000 calls through November. All letters from consumers regarding Tylenol were answered; 3,000 had been answered between the crisis event in September and late November 1982.

In dealing with suppliers, special attention should be given to informing trade publications because the "trade press are among the most aggressive, negative, and competitive in terms of disclosing or revealing information," states Lukaszewski.[175] He also suggests that customer service and purchasing departments should coordinate communications to customers and suppliers.

Conclusions

An important aspect of a crisis is how to communicate during and after a crisis. The damage caused by a crisis is multiplied if an organization's reputation is impaired, so communication efforts to preserve it must be undertaken. This intangible asset, which takes years to build, can literally be wiped out in a matter of hours or days if a crisis is perceived as exposing grievous management flaws or shown as being mishandled.

Crises become public because people are affected and the media seek out crises as important news. Attempts to conceal the occurrence of a crisis or important details about it no longer work, as seen in the *Kursk* submarine accident. Nor is it wise to delay facing up to a smoldering crisis, such as the Catholic Church's sexual scandal. Basic problems are thereby compounded when the crisis becomes public. How well crisis communication is handled determines how much damage is done to an organization, especially its reputation. This is why the subject of crisis management is often equated with crisis communication.

Sometimes the actions of a medium, as the Danish newspaper *Jyllands-Posten*, cause a crisis and implicate other organizations identified with it. When this happens, as it did to Arla Foods, they have no choice but to publicly state whether they support the medium's position. Again, crisis communication becomes the most prominent feature.

Crisis communication applies the principles of media relations, which is a central function of public relations, to specific situations. In addition to applying the basics, crisis communicators have developed insights about the most effective actions and communications to undertake during a crisis. These are summarized under the eight guidelines of crisis communication above.

Chapter 4

Image Restoration Strategies in Crisis Communication

In recent years, crisis communication has been supplemented with image restoration strategies, which some communication scholars consider the "dominant paradigm."[176] These strategies focus on statements made by leaders and spokespersons in organizations in the aftermath of a crisis event, especially if accused of wrongdoing, to repair their image and preserve their reputations. More generally, the subject is part of impression management whereby people want to present themselves in a favorable light, believing that they will then be treated more favorably.

Keith Hearit, author of *Crisis Management by Apology*, relates image repair strategies to the study of apologia, which is primarily concerned with individuals accused of wrongdoing who seek to clear their names. He distinguishes apologia, which means "defense" or "speech in defense," from apology, which commonly means to acknowledge and express regret for a fault without defense.[177] The difference mirrors the distinction between the defensive and accommodative strategies discussed later.

Most public relations problems faced by individuals and organizations, he says, result from organizational misbehavior. To defend their actions, organizations use five typical responses:

- denial ("We Didn't Do It");
- counterattack;
- differentiation ("It's Not Really Our Fault");
- apology ("We promise not to do it again");
- legal ("Talk to our lawyers".)[178]

Their goal is "the repair of an image-based social relationship, not through forgiveness but instead through public acknowledgment."[179] Hearit appears cynical about these efforts, saying they "are best characterized as a rhetoric of failure." The apologia constitute a ritualistic form of communication, "one in which an organization enters into a public confessional, taps into well-established themes of guilt and restoration, and, in so doing, completes the story and gets the individual or organization off the front page."[180]

Much of the literature on image restorative strategies describes additional strategies and relates each to situations where they are appropriate. W. L. Benoit developed a list of 14 image restoration strategies, which he later reduced to these five: denial, evasion of responsibility, reduction of offensiveness, corrective action, and mortification.[181] In his "The Language of Apologetic Speech," Hearit also elaborates on the "many strategies that apologists have to draw from in formulating their responses." Included in "image repair strategies," are denial, bolstering, differentiation, and transcendence.[182] These strategies are used when an organization faces allegations of wrongdoing, which is roughly synonymous with crises of management failure, especially misconduct.

Defensive and Accommodative Strategies

In deciding how to respond to allegations of wrongdoing, an organization must first decide whether to be defensive or accommodative, i.e., whether or not to accept responsibility for a crisis. In a defensive stance, responsibility for the crisis in one form or another is denied—it defends itself against blame. In an accommodative stance, an organization takes responsibility for the crisis and seeks amends with those adversely affected, i.e., the victims. Lawyers typically dominate in making this decision, although public relations people will emphasize the impact on an organization's reputation and relationship with its stakeholders.

Following this framework, W. T. Coombs positions a specific crisis on a continuum of whether an organization has "weak" or "strong" responsibility for it.[183] The defensive stance is appropriate for the weak end and the accommodative stance for the strong end. Using a family of five types of crises—rumors, natural disasters, malevolence, accidents, and misdeeds—Coombs positions them on the continuum, with rumors on the weak responsibility end and misdeeds on the strong responsibility end.[184] His list of image repair strategies are similarly positioned on this continuum, starting with denial on the weak responsibility end. In the following list, he explains each and suggests their use when crises contain certain features:[185]

- Denial: denying that the action was taken or shifting blame to someone else. Appropriate when evidence of a crisis is lacking; not appropriate when crisis damage is severe.
- Attacking the accuser, perhaps with threats, such as a lawsuit, assuming the accuser can be identified.
- Excuse or evasion of responsibility: claiming that one's action was an accident, that one acted with good intentions; arguing that one's action is a reasonable reaction to an action committed against one; or that the action stemmed from lack of information—which is called defeasibility.
- Justification and minimization: attempt to reduce an act's offensiveness; using tactic of differentiation by arguing that the act was not as harmful or

offensive as it might appear; attacking the accuser's credibility. Use only when crisis damage is minimal.

- Ingratiation: praising a stakeholder or oneself, e.g., by reminding stakeholders of good deeds done for them in the past. Suitable for organizations with solid reputations and a history of good deeds.
- Mortification: admitting wrongdoing and asking for forgiveness.
- Corrective action: promise to fix the damage caused and to take steps to prevent action from occurring again; suitable for misdeeds and for accidents, especially for an organization with a history of accidents.
- Full apology: suitable for organizational misdeeds.

The Art of Apology

The art of apology is an important rhetorical approach to crisis management and conflict resolution. Several books, such as Hearit's *Crisis Management by Apology*[186] and Dr. Aaron Lazare's *On Apology*,[187] discuss the importance of this approach and how effectively to respond to situations where an apology is required. People who see themselves as victims of what someone has said or done feel entitled to an apology.

As stated by Lazare, dean of the University of Massachusetts medical school, an apology "is an ongoing commitment by the offending party to change his or her behavior. It is a particular way of resolving conflicts other than by arguing over who is bigger and better. It is a powerful and constructive form of conflict resolution."[188] He states, "One of the most profound human interactions is the offering and accepting of apologies. Apologies have the power to heal humiliations and grudges, remove the desire for vengeance, and generate forgiveness on the part of the offended parties."[189] Implicit in these descriptions is that an apology is a response to a situation of an ethical nature. Hearit's book examines how individuals, organizations, and institutions seek to respond to criticism of an ethical nature.

As Barbara Kellerman states in her *Harvard Business Review* article, "When Should a Leader Apologize and When Not?," making apologies has become not only acceptable but routine: "Apologies are a tactic leaders now frequently use in an attempt to put behind them, at minimal cost, the errors of their ways."[190] Dennis Logue, management professor at Dartmouth College, believes an apology "will buy them one more chance. If they don't deliver after that, then they're in some serious difficulty."[191] Or, as Hearit states, "A good apology completes the cycle . . . It's like the third act of a morality play—evil has been punished. It's wonderfully powerful theater."[192] When the Japanese dairy company Snow Brand produced a batch of milk that sickened more than 14,000 customers, the company sent 2,000 employees into victims' homes to personally, bow, scrape, apologize, and pay cash compensation to each of the victims.[193]

JetBlue demonstrated the full measure of an apology. It had angered passengers who waited ten hours on a runway on Valentine's Day 2007. A winter storm had crippled air travel in the Northeast, with its service at John F. Kennedy International Airport taking the brunt of the operational meltdown.[194] JetBlue had built a culture to "bring humanity back to air travel" and to care for its passengers end to end. Now that reputation was in tatters. A defensive stance was out of the question, even though the weather was the cause. The bitter fact was that the airline's passengers were stranded on the runway.[195]

CEO David Neeleman used the apology strategy, saying, "We are sorry and embarrassed. But most of all, we are deeply sorry. . . . We subjected our customers to unacceptable delays, flight cancellations, lost baggage, and other major inconveniences. . . . Words cannot express how truly sorry we are for the anxiety, frustration and inconvenience that we caused."[196] The words of the apology itself were more than adequate. But in the light of its own culture, JetBlue needed to do more. Neeleman listed some immediate corrective steps to regain customer confidence. Its grand move, however, was to publish a new JetBlue Airways Customer Bill of Rights—its official commitment of how it would handle operational interruptions going forward, including details of compensation. A further act might have been for Neeleman to resign as CEO, which he said wouldn't do. But within four months he did; he was replaced by Dave Barger who came from an airline family.

Apologies by British Bankers for the Financial Crisis

In the aftermath of the financial crisis of 2008, questions about whether bankers should be advised to apologize were raised in the British media. In a newspaper article, Jonathan Russell stated, "Given the public appetite for bankers' blood, they know their appearance is likely to be as much about humiliation as explanation for their part in the financial crisis."[197] Michael Fallon, a Member of Parliament (MP), confirmed this view by saying, "We would certainly expect a large dose of humility from them."[198] The article pointed out that Britain is not famous for its public apologies. One notable exception was in 2008 when British Airways chief executive Willie Walsh stood up amid the confusion of the opening week of Heathrow's Terminal 5, apologized and accepted responsibility for what had gone wrong.

What do British experts on apologizing say? Piers Pottinger, one of the U.K.'s most experienced PR practitioners, explained: "Politicians and businessmen have this in common: they do not like apologising. It shows weakness." A lawyer, David Berkely, says, "For it to make sense, an apology has to be grounded in a sense of responsibility. Sometimes it is important, even cathartic, to empathize with people and express genuine feelings of sorrow, but what is more courageous is to take responsibility." A performance psychologist, Karl Morris, who has worked with some of the U.K.'s biggest companies, says, if made correctly, an apology can save careers as well as reputations. "It needs to be a specific apology, about what we call a conspicuous flaw. What you need to do is to say, 'On this issue I got it wrong,' rather than saying: 'I am useless. I'm not fit to run the company.' The converse is if people will not admit to flaws, everyone thinks they're stupid."[199]

In fact, the former bosses of bailed-out banks Royal Bank of Scotland (RBS) and HBOS offered their "profound" apologies before the MPs of the Treasury Select Committee. They explained they had misjudged the extent of the financial turmoil that engulfed both banks. However, any sympathy that might have been obtained was erased by subsequent actions. Shortly after the meeting, RBS announced a cut of around 2 percent of its 106,000 U.K. workforce.[200] Furthermore, the media had reported that ex-HBOS chairman Lord Stevenson and ex-HBOS chief executive Andy Homby, along with two other bankers, were paid £7.6 million a year between them. A columnist for the tabloid *The Daily Star* was particularly severe in his judgment, as his story's headline indicated: "Sorry . . . But We're Keeping Our Dosh & Sacking 2,300."[201] The "dosh" referred to the £7.6 million collective pay of the four bankers who appeared before the committee. The suggestion was that their high salaries were unwarranted because the bankers admitted not having a single banking qualification between them. In a society that is still known for its class system, attitudes might be colored by the fact that the bank heads held titles: the RBS boss was Sir Fred Goodwin, the ex-RBS chief was Sir Tom McKillop, the ex-HBOS chairman was Lord Stevenson, and a fourth banker was Sir James Crosby.[202]

Apologies by U.S. Bankers

An aspect of an apology is contrition and humility, which public appearances by bankers should reflect. Appropriately, when eight Wall Street bankers went to Washington in February they gave the impression of being modest and conciliatory. Avoiding the blunder of auto executives who flew from Detroit to D.C. in their private jets, the bankers kept their corporate planes parked at home. They trumpeted their (relatively) modest pay expectations for the year. They sat politely during the occasional tirade by a member of the House Financial Services Committee. Bank of America CEO Kenneth Lewis even demoted himself from "Captain of the Universe" to "corporal." But as *USA Today* commented, "It is not enough that the leaders of the banking world came in humility. They should be made to explain both their actions of the past and their ideas for the future."[203]

The rehearsed humility, however, was betrayed by the lavish expenditures of some bankers. Lawmakers noted that AIG had spent more than $440,000 for a gathering at a posh California resort—including $200,000 for rooms and $23,000 for spa treatments—a week after the government bailout.[204] Citigroup's plan to buy a $42 million corporate jet in the midst of the banking crisis was a public relations blunder. CEO Vikram Pandit, Lewis Kaden, a Citigroup vice chairman, and other top managers debated over how best to handle the matter. After President Barack Obama called the planned purchase "outrageous" and Treasury officials pressured Citigroup executives, the order was scrapped.[205]

An apology is weakened by other actions taken around the time of an apology. In the U.K. two of the bankers appearing before the committee were said to have "sacked and gagged" a worker who tried to warn them of the impending disaster. The reference was to the predecessor of Mr. Homby, the head of HBOS, who allegedly dismissed a senior official who raised fear that the bank was growing too quickly and putting itself in danger. The whistle-blower was Paul Moore, the former head of group regulatory risk at HBOS and the official directly responsible for assessing the correct balance between risk and safety. Mr. Moore claimed that "anyone whose eyes were not blinded by money, power and pride" would have realized problems were building up for HBOS and other banks. "I told them that their sales culture was significantly out of balance with their systems and controls," Moore said. He was made to agree to a " gagging order," which prevented him from speaking out.

Analyzing Crisis Types—Marcus and Goodman Study

As Coombs suggests, much judgment is needed to determine the appropriate strategy for a specific crisis, which includes specifying its type. Some crisis types, however, are ambiguous. For example, accidents have many causes, so they can more helpfully be classified under several crisis types—with some based on technology and others on mismanagement, such as human negligence. An article by Alfred A. Marcus and Robert S. Goodman describes some of the complexities in judging responsibility in accidents, as well as scandals and product safety.

Marcus and Goodman examined how announcements by corporate managements of three types of crises were interpreted by its stakeholders, including shareholders, customers, employees, and suppliers.[206] The criterion was how investors responded to different strategies, based on the effect on stock market prices. Prices would tend to be high when the interests of investors were favored and low when the interests of victims were favored. The objective was to determine whether a defensive or accommodative strategy worked best.

The three types of crises were described and related to victims as follows:

- Accidents are discrete one-time, "undesirable or unfortunate happenings that occur unexpectedly and without design."[207] Accidents produce victims and therefore favor the use of a defensive strategy.
- Scandals are "disgraceful or discreditable occurrences that compromise the perpetrators' reputations."[208] They result in less identifiable victims. A scandal is usually not a discrete event; it has obscure origins and no immediate victims. Scandals are caused by human and organizational lapses and inadequacies. Typical factors are greed and corruption, government failure and inability to prevent wrongdoing, failure of companies to police their employees, and an environment in which excuses abound like "everyone is doing it" and "it is possible to get way with it." An

accommodative strategy is therefore most appropriate because of the culpability of the perpetrator.

• Product safety incidents: no unique event creates mass suffering by a single stroke; instead there are repeated events or revelations, such as in Ford's safety problems with its Pinto vehicles. Neither the defensive or accommodative strategy was favored.

Elaborating on the strategies of defensiveness and accommodation, the authors defined defensive statements as "those in which a manager insisted that problems did not exist, tried to alleviate doubts about their and the firm's ability to generate future revenues, and took actions designed to resume normal operations rapidly."[209] They mention that in Union Carbide's Bhopal, India, gas leak, corporate leaders consistently denied wrongdoing, suggesting that sabotage likely occurred.[210]

Accommodative statements are "those in which managers accepted responsibility, admitted to the existence of problems, and attempted to take actions to remedy a situation."[211] The authors give the examples of Lee Iacocca's apology for the Chrysler executives who were indicted for rigging cars with disengaged odometers and Frank Lorenzo of Continental Airlines who took out advertisements saying he was sorry for misplaced baggage, delays, and reservations errors that plagued the airline. In his apology, Lee Iacocca said, "Our big concern is for our customers, the people who had enough faith in Chrysler to buy a vehicle from us. We did do something to have them question their faith in us. Did we screw up? You bet we did."[212]

The study by Marcus and Goodman concluded that investors reacted more positively to a defensive statement in an accident because they expected significantly better stock market returns. The opposite was true with scandals: investors responded more positively and expected better returns to an accommodative statement. There was no significant difference in investor responses to either defensive or accommodative statements with product safety and health incidents. The authors point out that the causes of such incidents are usually not as complex as the root causes of accidents and incidents evolve relatively slowly. A company can usually at least limit product recalls and attach warnings to them. Ford's decision to be defensive in response to Pinto crashes resulted in reputational damage and the payment of large award to the victims. The article supports the defensive strategy when a crisis produces identifiable victims.

Two Illustrative Cases: Firestone/Ford and Archbishop Cardinal Bernard Law

Firestone/Ford Tire Recall

On August 9, 2001, Firestone Inc., the U.S. subsidiary of Japan's Bridgestone Corp., announced a voluntary recall of 6.5 million tires, mainly on Ford

Explorers, a recall that would eventually cost $350 million. The tires had been implicated in deadly vehicle rollovers, reaching 62 deaths by August 15 and 148 by December 6.[213] Firestone's vice president John Lampe (who later during the crisis was named president) blamed Ford's Explorer vehicles, noting that the problem with tires occurred mainly on "one size tire on one application." At the time he did not name Ford's Explorer because Firestone did not want to jeopardize its position as the main source of tires for the Explorer. Besides, there were family connections between Ford and Firestone. (The mother of Ford's president, William Clay Ford, is the granddaughter of Harvey S. Firestone.)

Just as adamantly, Ford blamed the accidents on Firestone tire tread separations, saying, "We've built Explorers with brands of tires other than Firestones and had absolutely no problems."[214] Ford denied fault in the design of the Ford Explorer's suspension and technical specification for the tires, as some consumer groups claimed, although it changed the design in its 2002 model, making it wider and lower, and, therefore, safer. The denial strategy backfired, as their subsequent adoption of the accommodation strategy acknowledged.

Switching from Defensive to Accommodative Strategy

Both companies were using the image repair strategy of denial. The tire recall and lawsuits for deaths and injuries would be costly. Yet, Firestone couldn't seem to explain the cause of tread separations. They blamed each other and applied the strategy of differentiation—for Firestone, it was a "vehicle problem," and for Ford, "a tire problem." Denial and differentiation supported their defensive strategy. News stories of tread separations, deaths, and mutual blaming continued virtually every day for over a month. The companies' different recommendations about tire pressure—26 vs. 30 psi—received a lot of media attention. In the meanwhile, corporate reputations and product brands were getting battered. Stories on the Internet by consumer groups like the Tire Action Group exasperated the problem. For example, a *BusinessWeek* article summarized the problem for Ford: "Ford, A Crisis of confidence."[215]

They began to realize that their initial decision to adopt a defensive stance was a massive mistake. An accommodative stance was needed. This was not just a communication problem. They had ignored the public perception that they gave greater weight to company profits than to customer safety concerns. As a headline in the *Los Angeles Times* stated, "Ford and Firestone failed to recognize that consumers were their key stakeholders."[216] They had exercised a transaction mentality when what was needed was a relationship mentality that accepts their responsibility for product stewardship. As Stephen Greyser, a Harvard Business School professor, said: They may have underestimated the importance of consumer confidence in terms of the reputation of the company."[217]

The legal department, which examined warranty claims, seemed to view the consumer as a plaintiff—an enemy—and the sales department viewed the consumer as an annoying claimant. The company appeared to make no effort to integrate the obtained information with any research on consumer satisfaction with the tire or, more generally, with a company consumer relations program. This was a crisis of skewed management values. The companies had to assert consumer-friendly corporate cultures and revise their crisis management approaches accordingly.

Early Warning Signals Ignored

The big mistake made by both companies is that they ignored early warning signals. In late 1998 Ford heard of problems with Firestone tires on Explorer SUVs in Venezuela, and in 1999 it replaced Firestone tires on Ford vehicles in Persian Gulf countries after reports of tread failures. They assumed the problem was not related to the United States, using the rationale (or excuse) that temperatures in those countries were hotter than in the United States.[218]

Another early warning signal was ignored. A lone researcher, Sam Boyden, at State Farm Mutual Automobile Insurance Co. spotted the pattern of tread separations on Firestone tires and forwarded the information to the National Highway Traffic Safety Administration in 1998. But the government agency, resigned to fatalities, didn't think the number of deaths (only 22 at the first reporting) was high enough to take action. Taking this cue, neither Firestone nor Ford took further action. That decision illustrates the relevance of issues management to crisis management. The issue of tire tread separation was duly reported but, as later events proved, was inadequately analyzed. Skewed values may have influenced the analysis in that the long-term effect on company reputation was sacrificed in favor of short-term profits.

The tread separation problem was also a classical case of not recognizing the existence of a smoldering crisis that was accelerating. In February 2000, Anna Werner of Houston's KHOU-TV reported on the pattern of accidents connected with tread separation in Firestone tires on Ford Explorers. Instead of taking this as a sign that a crisis point had been reached, Firestone engaged in more denial. After all, the news item was only from a local station; it could be contained. That decision changed, however, when the national newspaper *USA Today* carried the story on August 7. Two days later, Firestone announced the recall. Ford also later admitted that the story was the trigger that sounded the alarm bells at the company.

The media had again demonstrated its role as society's watchdog. Whether liked or not, they judge the behavior of organizations. Because they serve as society's unofficial designators of a crisis, their judgment of a particular event affects how an organization and its management are perceived by the public. During every major crisis, an organization must endure a trial by media. A major part of damage control, therefore, is to temper the media's criticism of management so that an organization's reputation is kept intact. Because this is the task of public relations, it plays a major role in crisis management.

Firestone Violated the Criteria of a Sincere Apology

In her *Harvard Business Review* article, Barbara Kellerman provided criteria of a sincere apology:

- Acknowledging the offense;
- Accepting full responsibility;
- Expressing regret, e.g., saying "I'm sorry" (similar to mortification);
- Providing assurance that the offense won't be repeated; and
- Immediacy—is well-timed.[219]

These criteria were almost completely violated by Firestone's CEO, Masatoshi Ono. Although he gets credit for following the rule that CEOs must speak out in a major crisis, he broke the rule of immediacy. He was not heard from until September 6 at a Congressional hearing, almost a month after the recall. He excused his silence by saying he restricted himself to a low profile in order to let his American senior managers handle the crisis. When he broke his silence, he said, "I also come to accept full and personal responsibility . . . for the events that led to this hearing."[220]

His statement does not meet other criteria of a sincere apology as described by Kellerman: he doesn't acknowledge the offense because he simply refers to "events." He at first says he accepts full responsibility, but later reneges by explaining that he was merely showing a concern for those who had accidents while using Firestone products and that the apology was not an admission of responsibility. He never said he was sorry for the accidents; and he provides no assurance that the offense won't be repeated.[221]

A Bridgestone/Firestone ad on August 16 did no better. Titled, "How to tell if your Firestone Tires are included in the voluntary recall," the ad included the sentence: "We apologize for any inconvenience or distress this recall may have caused you. The safety and confidence of our customers is always the first concern of Bridgestone/Firestone." The apology doesn't express regret for having made "bad tires," and the concern for consumer safety seems insincere.

Foreign Ownership Complicates Communications

The foreign ownership of Firestone complicated crisis communication. First, it endangered the principle of speaking with a single voice. Lampe and Ono contradicted each other, and the CEO of the parent company, Bridgestone, Yooichiro Kaizaki, also confused matters. He remained silent until September 12, when the summoning of Nasser and Ono to testify before the U.S. Congress persuaded him to make a statement. According to one company source, at a packed 90-minute news conference at the Tokyo headquarters of Keidanren, Japan's big business lobby, he said, "An explanation by a Japanese person who doesn't know the situation well could have annoyed U.S. consumers." Kaizaki said, "We managed subsidiaries located in Japan quite carefully but have not applied the same attention to managing overseas subsidiaries. . . . We let the U.S. unit use its own culture. There was an element of mistake in that."[222]

Ford's Communications Were Better

Ford was more active in communicating with its employees as well as its customers, helped by CEO Jacques Nasser (an Armenian with a French name who was raised in Australia), who served as Ford's chief spokesperson. He declared in ads and TV shows, "There are two things we never take lightly: your safety and your trust." He also made the call centers 24-hour operations and boosted their number of employees from the normal 300 to 800. Ford told its employees that nothing was more important than Ford's corporate reputation.[223] Its employee communications included:

- a series of town-hall-style meetings for senior executives to discuss the ongoing Ford/Firestone tire recall with employees;
- live broadcasts of events on company's daily TV network, e.g., Nasser's testimony before Congressional committees;
- presentation materials for managers to use in their operating groups;
- a special edition of the Ford employee newspaper.[224]

In communicating with customers, both Firestone and Ford used full-page newspaper ads to announce recalls. Jacques Nasser, however, reached more customers because he appeared on an advertisement aired during the Monday Night Football. Both made use of their company websites to provide tire recall information.[225] Firestone's site included "An Open Letter to Firestone Recall Customers," signed by John Lampe, president of Firestone. It also included his testimony before Congress, dated September 6. Ford's site included Nasser's September 6 statement before a Congressional committee.[226]

Recovery Efforts

Corrective action is part of image restoration. After the recall, both companies sought to regain public confidence. Christine Karbowiak, Firestone's vice president of public affairs, acknowledged that "customer confidence in Firestone is really low right now, and we need to do something."[227] On September 12, 2000, Firestone hired Ketchum to "restore its tattered image and boost its standing here in the nation's capital, where the company is under attack."[228] Karbowiak explained the switch from Fleishman-Hillard to Ketchum by saying, "Ketchum matches our personality, our overall business, the best. They also have a very strong presence in Washington, which is very important to us."[229]

Firestone had a huge deficit of consumer trust and confidence to overcome. Its image restoration required further corrective action beyond the tire recall. It included:

- getting rid of that ineffectual Masatoshi Ono on October 10. His apology at the Congressional hearing was ritualistic and interpreted as lacking sincerity;
- admitting that it had made some "bad tires." Lawyers probably argued over that statement for hours, even though consumers and the media were convinced of that fact. It was refreshing that the obvious was finally admitted and it was a step—albeit a very small one—in the direction of regaining credibility. The Dayton, Ohio plant where the defective tires were manufactured had a history of poor labor relations. Tire quality might have been jeopardized when replacement workers were hired during a labor dispute;
- Bridgestone's chairman, Yoichiro Kaizaki, clarifiying the future of Firestone and the relationship with the parent company. At a press conference he said, "Bridgestone absolutely will rebuild Firestone, and we want to regain the trust of our customers as quickly as possible." In a candid admission, he also acknowledged that the parent company should have exercised more control over U.S. operations and ensured that Firestone met parent company standards;
- Firestone starting to restructure its staff, beginning with the appointment of John Lampe as the new chairman and CEO of Firestone. He was given more autonomy than ever for an American management team to run U.S. operations and its crisis-control efforts without having to seek constant approval from Tokyo;[230]
- strengthening customer relationships. Improve the quality control program and hire more inspectors; maintain a database of tire customers, which shows that you care and allows you to communicate important product information and to alert customers of any product inspection or recall. If there isn't already a consumer relations unit, start one, and preferably have it report to someone outside of sales. It gives consumers a voice, e.g., by placing a consumer advocate on the board or establishing a consumer advisory council that can both initiate issues and respond to company decision. It recognizes the need for some system to establish greater symmetry between profits and consumer needs and rights;
- Firestone seeking to recover sales by planning to make use of its dealers and its connection with racing to regain consumer confidence. Taking out an ad showing that your tires are used on race-cars should fortify your corporate image.

What is most interesting about the Firestone/Ford case is the ineptness with which crisis communication was handled by both companies. They violated the crisis rule of "say it fast, say it all," with the consequence that news stories of tire separations and deaths continued virtually every day for over a month, and corporate images were getting more and more tarnished.

Archbishop Cardinal Bernard Law's Image Restoration Strategies

When a crisis event occurs because of media exposure, media relations becomes the appropriate response to minimize the damage done and to restore the image of the accused. Law followed this approach, focusing on image restoration techniques discussed earlier. Law carefully crafted a message delivered at a press conference, which provides an excellent test of whether image restoration strategies in the form of an apology works.

The Apology

Cardinal Law asked his flock to forgive him for the pedophilia scandal. He told a crowd of nearly 3,000 Catholics at the Boston World Trade Center,

> "I stand before you recognizing the trust many of you had in me has been broken, and it has been broken because of decisions for which I was responsible. . . . With all my heart, I am sorry for that." He added,
> "You have my commitment that I will do the best I can to find the course, the path to take us where we need to be. . . . I take what you have said to heart. I will ponder it in prayer and with the thoughtful consideration of others and, please God, we can go forward from here."[231]

Following the criteria of what constitutes an effective apology, Law avoided an outright denial of wrongdoing and openly acknowledged his failure. But he evaded taking personal responsibility—which is another criterion of an effective apology—by ambiguously saying "judgments were made" about the errant priest and that he lacked information (using the strategy of defeasibility) about the nature of pedophilia. He said he had trusted the professional opinion of therapists and doctors. His apology rested heavily on the strategy of mortification, which is defined as admitting wrongdoing and asking for forgiveness. It is similar to the act of contrition in confessionals. To strengthen and complete his apology, Law promised to take corrective action. Besides hedging on taking personal responsibility, Law's apology further falls short of an effective apology because he avoids mention of compensation for the victims. Nor had he shown enough empathy with the victims by never saying "I'm sorry"—words that convey greater emotional power than "I apologize."

Law fell slightly short of using the best available image restoration strategies to the fullest extent because of two limiting factors: his audience and the context he faced. Relevant audiences were the general public, his "flock," "liberal Catholics of Boston," and, highly important, the victims and their families. Regarding the context, Law's "relational history" with his audience was a factor, especially his response to coverage of an abusive priest nearly a decade before. Considering the public's impression of Law as an arrogant and intolerant individual, the finding that the audience questioned the sincerity of his apology seems logical. Because the impression of sincerity is the ultimate test of an effective apology, it is not surprising that the public rejected Law's response. A poll by *The Boston Globe* and WBZ-TV showed 48 percent of Catholics in Boston wanted Cardinal Law to resign.[232]

Only *The Boston Globe* was impressed with Law's "extraordinary apology." Perhaps because they live in the world of rhetoric, Globe reporters and editors responded favorably to Law's "heartfelt" apology and his "contrite" and "humble" demeanor. Hearing him admit that he was wrong and asking for forgiveness appeared to complete the apology for the media. Although Law gets credit for making the apology personally and not through intermediaries, it should be noted that he was depending on the media to persuade his flock. The news media, however, have limited influence on public opinion.

The Limits of Image Restoration Strategies

By referring to his previous policy initiatives in addressing the sexual abuse of minors by the clergy, Law used the strategy of "bolstering." But the policy initiative did not prevent him from making wrong decisions. His values were skewed because of the authoritarian nature of the Catholic Church and its exemplification in Law's own personality and behavior. The lack of openness and unwillingness to disclose information amount to deception and explains the public's suspicion of Law's insincerity and the erosion of trust. Because Law had for over a decade turned a deaf ear to complaints by parishioners in his own diocese and ignored media stories of errant priests, he too can be accused of misconduct.

A crisis of this magnitude and scope cannot be solved through communications and apologies alone. Other responses appropriate to crises of management failure must be used. Ultimately, the limitation of image restoration strategies is their focus on image when the problem is more profound. To confirm the sincerity of his apology, Law would have to announce his willingness to resign. Often in a corporate environment, the resignation of the CEO assuages injury and the crisis is abated, as was demonstrated in the Enron scandal. But Law resisted mounting pressure to resign, even from some behind the pulpit. But as Law said in a *Boston Herald* article, an "Archbishop is not a corporate executive. He's not a politician. It's a role of pastor. It's a role of teacher. It's a role of a father. When there are problems in the family, you don't walk away. You work them out together with God's help." Image restoration techniques work in simpler situations. This problem deals with an intractable Church and its embodiment in Law's character, which was highly flawed.

Conclusions

Comprehensive crisis management looks beyond the immediate crisis event and preceding contingency planning with the aim of reducing the incidence of future crises and strengthening an organization's ability to cope with those that do occur. Many of these efforts involve improved communications during a crisis; others involve the post-crisis phase of rebuilding.

Crises prepare an organization for change. The Chinese symbol for crisis is taken earnestly, for it signifies opportunity as well as danger. A crisis can provide the stimulus and motivation for rebuilding, improving, and even transforming the organization. The trauma of a crisis prepares members of an organization for change. Resistance is reduced because change is legitimized. For this reason many a leader has maneuvered an organization into a crisis state even when there was no real crisis. By using such devices as rearranging and reinterpreting statistics, license is obtained to undertake draconian measures.

When a crisis occurs spontaneously, top management should seize the opportunity to restructure company thinking. Management must determine what organizational changes are needed, e.g., strengthening corporate governance, setting up new units, revising managerial roles, improving control systems, and instilling a new organizational culture. These have been among the renewal strategies discussed in conjunction with the various crisis types. These and other strategies are summarized in the final chapter.

Part II

Crises of the Physical Environment

Part II discusses three types of crises of the physical environment: natural disasters, biological crises, and technological crises. Natural disasters are probably humankind's earliest type of crisis because floods, earthquakes, volcanic eruptions have always been with us and set the stage for the evolution of crisis management. Biological crises also have a long history, e.g., the Black Plague in the Middle Ages, but they are receiving renewed attention because of the onset of AIDS, SARS, and other communicable diseases, and because globalization is accelerating their geographic spread. These diseases too spring from nature and share similarities with natural disasters. Technological crises relate to the physical environment because they result from the human application of science and technology to the manufacture of products and construction of buildings and other facilities that become part of the physical environment.

Similarities and Differences

The strategies used to deal with each of these three types of crises draw on the basic principles of emergency management associated with natural disasters, but there are significant differences among them. Natural disasters and technological crises harm people and damage property whereas biological crises affect only people and other living organisms. For this reason, biological crises have been likened to the neutron bomb.

A second difference is that the degree of human intervention in preventing a crisis is lowest with natural disasters and highest with technological crises. While efforts can be undertaken to avoid or decrease the occurrence of a technological crisis, the same cannot be done with a natural crisis. Humans cannot prevent a hurricane, tsunami or earthquake from happening. All they can hope to do is to predict when it will happen and attempt to lessen the damage caused through mitigation and preparatory efforts. That is why natural crises are considered "acts of God." They are generally uncontrollable and the public tends to accept them fatalistically. Technological disasters, on the other hand, are seen as "man-made" and subject to human manipulation. Biological crises fall somewhere in between: Their origin cannot be controlled but their spread and severity depends on the success of early human intervention.

These distinctions in the possible degree of human intervention are crucial in terms of risk perception, public opinion, and legal status. God may be questioned, but not blamed, for a natural disaster or the inception of a biological crisis. But human entities—business, government, and nonprofits—will not only be blamed but sued for a seemingly avoidable and controllable technological disaster. The human tendency to blame someone is very strong, strengthened by the hope that assistance and compensation may be provided.

Among other differences is that some natural disturbances lend themselves to high predictability. The chances are high that hurricanes will continue to strike the southeastern coast of the United States, that Bangladesh will experience more floods, and that earthquakes will erupt in vulnerable locations in the Pacific and Indian Oceans. Another difference is that natural disturbances and biological crises show no respect for political boundaries or private property lines, while technological crisis events generally occur within an organization's property and most are contained within them.

Some technological crises, however, are so enormous that they also extend beyond normal boundaries. The Chernobyl nuclear explosion of 1986 affected much of eastern Europe, and the *Exxon Valdez* oil spill damaged much of Prince William Sound. Furthermore, if the definition of a technological crisis is extended to include the impact on the wider environment—impacts such as acid rain, seepage of toxins into groundwater, destruction of the Earth's ozone layer and the greenhouse effect—the geographical and environmental scope of technological crises is more extensive than that of natural and biological crises.

Coping with Risk

Role of Risk Analysis

Pressures for management to avoid or downplay risks are enormous and must be recognized before affirmative attitudes to face up to risks can take hold. Fortunately, the increasing recognition and role of risk analysis gives greater weight to risk factors in management decision-making. Managers must go further, however, than scientists, engineers and other technical people who calculate risks; they must also examine what risks are publicly acceptable and compatible with social, political, and economic concerns. For these reasons, public attitudes toward science and technology must be considered as well as the public's perception of risk.

Management must engage in the growing activity of risk communication. Although most technology-based industries, like chemicals and pharmaceuticals, have long engaged in risk analysis, it is only relatively recently that sufficient attention has been given to risk communication. Providing the greatest impetus has been the Emergency Planning and Community-Right-to-Know Act, Title III of the Superfund Amendments and Reauthorization Act (SARA). This legislation has been a major impetus in encouraging or forcing business to engage in risk communications with its employee and local communities.[233]

Specifically, the law requires governors to appoint local planning committees, which must draw up plans addressing the following:

- identification of facilities that make or store hazardous chemicals;
- routes used to transport hazardous substances;
- procedures emergency-response personnel should follow after a hazardous substance is released;
- methods to determine whether a release has occurred;
- a description of emergency equipment in the community and at industrial facilities;
- evacuation plans; and
- training programs.

Companies covered under Title III must meet four requirements:

(1) Distribute material safety data sheets (MSDSs) to the state commission, the local committee and the local fire department. (The public may request MSDSs from local committees.)
(2) Let the public know the amount (in ranges) of the hazardous chemicals kept on their plant sites.
(3) Report on emissions—the amounts of specified chemicals they release into the air, land and water.
(4) Have emergency-response plans in place.

The law has changed the relationships between industries that use hazardous substances and the communities in which they operate, making companies more "vulnerable to controversy and problems with communities."[234] Companies must now let the public know the amount (in ranges) of the hazardous chemicals kept on their plant sites. Persons with home computers can, for a small charge, obtain Title III information on disks.

A handful of companies responded to the law by recognizing the need for full commitment to risk communication. They follow the principle that a limited program of dissemination of information might inadvertently end up creating public alarm and fall far short of truly communicating essential risk information. For this reason, even before Title III's July 1, 1989, deadline for providing information, Dow Chemical developed several brochures for employees and the community explaining the law, the company's programs to reduce waste, and its emissions, and how these programs compare to health standards.[235] It also held day-long seminars for its business customers and established a computer database in its Midland, Michigan, plant and made it available to the public.

Public Perception of Risk

Underlying general public attitudes toward science and technology is the public's perception of risk. People seem to believe that they can live in a zero defect, no risk society yet enjoy the fruits of an industrial society. When they do consider risks, they typically overestimate the risks imposed by business and industry and underestimate the risk of daily life, such as driving to work and having radon in the home.

Business tends to blame the media for the public's faulty risk perceptions. Besides media influence, there are other reasons why people are becoming more afraid of more things, states Paul Slovic, an expert on risk perception. He cites these:

- People have witnessed several spectacular catastrophes—Bhopal, Chernobyl, *Challenger*—that stick to the mind, and some feel that the chances of further catastrophes is greater now than in the past.
- Powerful new technologies are unfamiliar and scary, just as the steam engine and gasoline engine were in their day.
- People have become more frustrated; on the one hand they are urged to wear seat belts and to exercise to reduce risks, yet other risks are imposed on them involuntarily.
- The benefits of some technologies seem too small to justify their potential costs. For example, if food is assumed to be safe, they see no benefit in irradiating it.
- As litigation pits expert against expert, the public is left questioning all the facts.
- Special-interest groups force issues to public attention.[236]

Perceived Risks

The above influences account for the public's assessment of risk. These perceived risks tend to be qualitative rather than the quantitative ones discussed by scientists. As stated by Irving Lerch, "We are not frightened by the probabilities of danger . . . but by more personal and irrational fears."[237] At public meetings, citizens often become angry when asked to accept a risk estimated at fewer than one-in-a-million increased cancer deaths. Yet they will smoke during breaks, drive home without wearing seat belts, and ignore geological radon in their homes—risks that are far greater.[238] No wonder scientists, government policymakers and business managers conclude that the public is unable to understand the scientific aspects of risk.

Factors influencing risk perception are often called outrage factors because they arouse community anger and resistance toward a variety of issues. These include the citing of hazardous waste facilities, industrial facility permits and expansions, and a variety of environmental and public health concerns. The following list provides an overview of risk perception factors that influence public outrage and acceptability of risk:

More acceptable	Less acceptable
Risk assumed voluntarily	Risk borne involuntarily
Effect immediate	Effect delayed
No alternatives available	Many alternatives available
Risk known with certainty	Risk not known
Exposure is an essential	Exposure is a luxury
Encountered occupationally	Encountered non-occupationally
Common hazard	"Dread" hazard
Affects average people	Affects especially sensitive people
Will be used as intended	Likely to be misused
Consequences reversible	Consequences irreversible[239]

Additional factors account for increasing or decreasing public concern with risk situations:

Increasing concern	Decreasing concern
Fatalities and injuries grouped in time and space	Fatalities and injuries scattered at random
Unfamiliar	Familiar
Mechanisms or process not understood	Mechanisms or process understood
Children specifically at risk	Children not specifically at risk
Risk to future generations	No risk to future generations
Identifiable victims	Statistical victims
Much media attention	Little media attention
Major and sometimes minor accidents	No major or minor accidents
Inequitable distribution of risks and benefits	Equitable distribution of risks and benefits
Unclear benefits	Clear benefits[240]

Principles of Risk Perception

The above lists of characteristics that make risk more or less acceptable or that cause increasing or decreasing concern lead to several principles that those concerned with risk must consider:

People do not perceive danger in the familiar. People avoid questioning the safety of their neighborhood, job, or way of life. Familiar objects such as cars and, for some, cigarettes, are hard to fear. On the other hand, nuclear power is easy to fear, partly because the sites have been located far from urban centers and regulations have restricted public visiting to nuclear installations.

A favorable cost-benefit calculation makes risks more acceptable. Nuclear power does not cause as much fear in less developed countries because the economic importance of these plants overshadows their risks. Similarly, the defense establishment was careless in its environmental stewardship because winning the Cold War was the overwhelming benefit.

A NIMBY (not in my back yard) attitude prevails when community residents feel that social cost burdens are concentrated in their community for the broader benefit of society—or, selfishly, if people do not want to bear any social costs even though they benefit. This fairness aspect is illustrated when poor people feel that they are targeted for landfills because they lack political muscle. The NIMBY syndrome has often manifested itself with nuclear power installations as well as other kinds of power plants. For example, a Harris poll showed that while 56 percent of the public opposed a nuclear plant near their homes, so did 55 percent oppose a coal-fired plant.[241]

In calculating the costs associated with risks, organizations must also factor so-called "higher order" impacts—those beyond an immediate impact, such as the number of people killed in an accident—that include secondary effects like subsequent costs of lawsuits and damaged company reputation. The Ford Motor Co. learned this lesson during its dispute with Firestone on the tire recall.

Risks one believes one controls are feared less. People who engage in the recreational activities of skydiving, bungee-jumping, skiing, and skateboarding willingly assume a high risk because they feel they control the situation. Similarly, even though living next to a nuclear power plant is less dangerous than riding a bicycle around the block once a week, the risk in the former is denied. The fear of nuclear power is exaggerated, says Dr. Robert L. DuPont, a practicing psychiatrist and president of the nonprofit Institute for Behavior & Health in Washington, D.C., because the risk is seen as controlled by "big utilities" and "remote bureaucracies" such as the Nuclear Regulatory Commission.[242]

The public fears unknown risks, "dread risks," and "high-signal accidents" more. Unknown risks are new risks that are not yet known to science and are not observable. Those who are exposed do not know at the time of exposure because their effect is delayed. As with unfamiliar risks, these are feared more. Nuclear power is considered one of the "unknown risks," i.e., defined as "hazards judged to be unobservable, unknown, new, and delayed in their manifestation of harm."[243] Chemical technologies and biotechnology also illustrate this unknown risk.

Also feared more are "dread risks." These are defined as possessing the properties of "perceived lack of control, dread, catastrophic potential, fatal consequences, and the inequitable distribution of risks and benefits."[244] Combining features of both unknown and dread risks are "high-signal accidents" which, even if small, people amplify into huge proportions, for they are seen as a sign or harbinger of further and possibly catastrophic mishaps. The high-signal aspect of an accident aggravates the "control" problem for an organization if the industry to which it belongs, such as nuclear power, is so perceived.

Three Mile Island not only devastated the utility that owned and operated the plant but imposed enormous costs on the nuclear industry and on society. Some of the costs to the industry were stricter regulation, reduced operation of reactors worldwide, and greater public opposition to nuclear power. Society suffered because of greater reliance on more expensive non-nuclear energy sources.

Other factors that affect community outrage are that risks that seem fair are more acceptable than those that seem unfair; risks that seem ethically objectionable will seem more risky than those that do not; natural risks seem more acceptable than artificial risks; and hazards that show up as one big event are feared more than those that occur in separate, individual events scattered over time and space.[245]

New threats

A science-fiction type of threat to the physical environment is the grim envisioned future that asteroids and other space objects may hit the Earth from large-scale asteroid or comet collisions. This has occurred in the Earth's history and is blamed for the extinction of the dinosaur. In his article, "The Sky Is Falling," Gregg Easterbrook cites evidence that it has happened before.[246] He refers to Dallas Abbott, a Columbia University geophysicist, who said that in 536 A.D., a space object about 300 meters in diameter hit the Gulf of Carpentaria, north of Australia and released as much energy as 1,000 nuclear bombs. Dust and gases thrown into the atmosphere would have blocked sunlight, temporarily cooling the planet. Only a century ago, in 1908, a small asteroid or comet that detonated as it approached the ground caused a huge explosion above Tunguska, Siberia. It devastated an area of several hundred square miles. Had the explosion occurred above London or Paris, the cities would no longer exist. The Russian Space Agency considers the possibility of asteroid Apothis hitting Earth around 2036 so seriously that it is planning efforts to deflect it. Apothis would be a "country buster" capable of destroying an area almost the size of France.[247]

The standard assumption a generation ago was that a dangerous object would strike Earth perhaps once in a million years. But by the mid-1990s, that probability was moved to every 300,000 years and now one steroid specialist thinks there is a one-in-10 chance per century of a dangerous space-object strike.[248] In an optimistic note, however, futurist and author Ray Kurzweil predicts that occasional large and destructive visitors from space will almost certainly be destroyed before they destroy us.[249]

Chapter 5

Natural Crises

Natural crises—which are typically called disasters—deal with environmental phenomena such as earthquakes, volcanic eruptions, tornadoes and hurricanes, floods, landslides, tidal waves, storms, and droughts that menace life, property, and the environment itself. Disaster experts call these events natural *hazards*.[250] They become natural *disasters* when they cause human death and injury or destroy natural and physical capital on which people rely for their livelihood and quality of life.[251] As humankind's earliest type of crisis, they establish the models and tools of analysis for the study of other crises. Natural disasters are the most frequently reported crises.

Climate change is more and more suspected as increasing the frequency and intensity of weather-related natural disasters. Moreover, climate change may put people at risk by affecting access to water, coastal flooding, disease and hunger, and, more generally leaving them with a more degraded environment.[252] Several sources have supported this view. The Centre for Research on the Epidemiology of Disasters believes that climate-related hazards have become major triggers for the majority of disasters.[253] Referring to the 2010 flood in Queensland, Australia, Frank Pegan, the chair of the Investor Group on Climate Change, which represents $600 billion of funds under management in Australia and New Zealand, says, "While the devastating floods are an extreme weather incident, we know that a consequence of a climate-change world is the increased frequency of such events."[254] The reinsurance firm's Munich RE report, "Weather Extremes, Climate Change, Cancun 2010," states that by the end of September, the year 2010 geared up to be the warmest year since records began 130 years ago. The company also states that the number of major weather-related natural catastrophes, such as floods, has tripled since 1980, and the number of windstorms has more than doubled.[255] If these dire predictions materialize, we can expect the topic of natural disasters to become an even larger part of crisis management.

Major Natural Disasters

The five most damaging natural crises in the first decade of the 21st century have been the Indian Ocean tsunami on December 26, 2004; Hurricane

Katrina which struck New Orleans on August 28, 2005; the earthquakes in Sichuan, China on May 12, 2008, and Haiti on January 12, 2010; the wildfires in Victoria, Australia, on January 28, 2009; and flood in Queensland, Australia, about a year later.

The 2004 Indian Ocean Tsunami

The world's most powerful earthquake in 40 years, centered off northern Indonesia, on December 26, 2004, sent tidal waves, called tsunami, crashing into Asian shorelines in 12 Indian Ocean nations from Thailand to India, Sri Lanka and the Maldives, killing 227,000 and displacing 1.7 million people.[256] The *Global Journalist* called it "arguably the world's most devastating natural disaster."[257]

The floods, sometimes reaching more than a kilometer inland, displaced more than half a million people from their homes in the coastal villages along the south and east of the northern Indonesian island of Sumatra. More than 158 people died in Phuket, Thailand's popular tourist southern island, as a wave four meters in height swept beaches. "For all the huge advances in the control of our lives through science and technology, an earthquake on this scale is truly humbling as well as profoundly tragic," said British Foreign Secretary Jack Straw.[258]

The tsunami was caused by an underwater earthquake, which sent huge waves to regions of South Asia. The term *tsunami* is Japanese, formed from the characters for harbor and wave. It is adopted around the world to refer to widespread effects.[259] The earthquake, at a magnitude of 8.9 struck at 7:59 a.m. about 10 kilometers (six miles) off Sumatra.

Hurricane Katrina

Hurricane Katrina was the worst natural disaster to befall a city and region in the United States. It made landfall at New Orleans on Sunday, August 28, 2005, killing 1,500 and flooding three-fourths of the city. It is comparable only to the hurricane that flooded Galvaston, Texas, in 1900, killing 8,000. Wider damage and disruptions to regions around New Orleans also occurred, ruining 160,000 or more homes in Louisiana and causing $25 billion or more in insured property losses and $40–60 billion in private insured losses. In addition, economic losses were estimated at $125 billion or more.[260] The already inadequate infrastructure in New Orleans—roads, water supply, sewage, electricity, hospitals, schools—was destroyed or severely damaged.

Widespread Environmental and Cultural Damage

Environmental damage was considerable in the coastal marshes near New Orleans that contain marine life and wildlife and exhibit natural beauty. They had already been weakened by many rigs and pipelines for oil and natural gas. A million acres of wetlands along the gulf coast, which environmental planners said would be a first line of defense against storm, were destroyed. Coastal Louisiana's commercial fishery infrastructure, which produces a third of the nation's commercial seafood—about a billion pounds of fish, crab, and oysters annually—was badly damaged and in some cases destroyed.[261] Louisiana's thriving sports-fishing industry, valued at more than $1 billion a year, also suffered. Shipping on the Mississippi, which funnels through the Port of New Orleans, the largest port in the United States, was disrupted. The city's acclaimed tourist industry was uprooted. As noted by Joel Kotkin, author of *The City: A Global History*,[262] New Orleans's dominant industry "lies not in creating its future but selling its past, much of which now sits underwater."[263] Recovery was to become a slow process.

China's Lunar New Year Snow Storm and Sichuan Earthquake

Double trouble hit China in 2008. The worst weather conditions in 50 years struck central and southern China in mid-January 2008 just as about 178 million Chinese were on their way home to celebrate the Lunar New Year.[264] Most were stranded in railway stations. Trains stopped running because electricity lines had fallen and coal deliveries to power stations were disrupted. The ordeal lasted for more than two weeks, causing dozens of deaths, damaging buildings, and forcing roads and airports to close. In tropical Guangzhou, near Hong Kong, 200,000 people slept in temporary shelters after trains and air flights were canceled.

China's second disaster in 2008 was a massive earthquake that struck Sichuan province in southwestern China at 2:28 p.m. on Monday, May 12, which measured a magnitude of 7.9, so strong that it was felt as far away as Bangkok.[265] It was the country's worst natural disaster in three decades. Residents in earthquake-affected areas were warned by a senior Chinese seismologist that aftershocks could be just as devastating as the main tremor because they could bring down already damaged buildings.[266]

The earthquake killed over 80,000 people, left over 5 million homeless, and damaged homes, school buildings, roads, and other infrastructure. The damage was widespread and severe. Collapsed schools —often caused by shoddy construction—received much media attention. One of the worst scenarios was at Beichuan, where a middle school completed in 1998 collapsed and killed 1,000 of its 2,793 students. In a goodwill gesture, Premier Wen Jiabao paid a surprise visit to the school on the first day of the new semester.[267]

Earthquake Haiti

In the afternoon of Tuesday, January 12, 2010, a magnitude 7 earthquake, the most powerful to hit Haiti since at least 1770, struck the capital city of

Port-au-Prince.[268] Haiti authorities reported that 220,000 people (later estimated at 316,000) were killed and 300,000 were wounded; about 105,000 houses were flattened and 208,000 were damaged; 1,300 schools and 50 hospitals crumbled or couldn't be used; the presidential palace and most ministries were destroyed.[269] Nearly 1.3 million Haitians were left homeless, more than 750,000 of them in metropolitan Port-au-Prince.[270] Haiti's already weak infrastructure was almost completely destroyed. Electric power was unavailable, the airport control tower was inoperative, seaport facilities had collapsed, and roads were filled with debris and bodies. The cellular-phone network, however, suffered only minor damage. Nevertheless, response groups in Haiti couldn't reach one another and relatives in diaspora communities in New York City, Boston and elsewhere had difficulty finding out who had survived and the extent of the damage.

The devastating effects of Haiti's earthquake exposed an abysmally dysfunctional country. Haiti has the lowest per capita income in the Western Hemisphere and the weakest political and social infrastructure. Although nothing can be done to avert an earthquake, no effort was ever made to make buildings quake-proof. When crises result in "chaos," this was it. Port-au-Prince's governmental institutions were extremely weak and corrupt. Their initial response was virtually nil. There was no police force or fire department to respond to the chaos that ensued, partly because civil authorities were also victims of the quake. Although Haiti is reputed to have 10,000 non-government organizations (NGOs)—some call it the "Republic of NGOs"—they were too scattered and weak to respond effectively. The city and the surrounding communities were virtually isolated. Survivors had to fend for themselves in the immediate aftermath.

Headlines like "Time Running Out for Haiti Survivors" reflected Haiti's desperate struggle.[271] Water, food, medical supplies, and shelter were all in short supply. It was a race against time to try to save those trapped under buildings and to mend the injured. People can survive about three days without water and about five or six days without food, or for the injured, without dressing tissue wounds. This would be an extreme test of response and relief efforts.

Fire and Water in Australia, Russia and Pakistan

Australia's "Black Saturday"

Drought has become a chronic problem in the state of Victoria, Australia, and along with it, the dread of wildfires. On January 28, 2009, Victoria experienced the most severe heatwave in its history and by February 7 the temperature reached 115.5 degrees Fahrenheit (46.4 degrees Celsius) Melbourne and 120 degrees elsewhere. Six hundred fires started that day, the worst seen in decades. The death toll reached 173. Some people were effectively cremated in their homes and others found unburned in positions that suggested they had simply dropped dead while running from the flames. Fire plans are a distinctive feature of Australian life and in light of the continuing extreme heat conditions were being reconsidered.[272]

Two-thirds of Queensland Flooded

A major flood inundated Queensland state in Australia, covering an area equal to the combined size of France and Germany. In this area, 86 communities were inundated or cut off by floodwaters; 17,500 homes and more than 3,000 businesses were affected.[273] The weather pattern is blamed on one of the strongest, if not the most severe La Nina weather events since records began.[274] The city of Rockhampton was entirely engulfed by water and residents in another city, Toowoomba, faced a horrific flash flood—which some called an inland tsunami—that found them clinging desperately to trees, signposts, and power poles to save their lives. Residents were warned against poisonous snakes, such as the Eastern Brown, which can grow more than six feet and are considered the second most venomous snake in the world, and to stay away from Fitzroy River, which harbors crocodiles.[275]

Much of Brisbane, the capital of Queensland and Australia's third largest city, was flooded, affecting 20,000 homes.[276] The economic impact of the Queensland flood was considerable. Senior economist Bob Cunneen of AMP Capital says it will cost approximately A$6 billion and 0.5 percent of nominal gross domestic product, much of it attributed to lower coal and food production.[277]

Russia's Summer of 2010 Wildfires

Stoked by the hottest summer-time temperatures ever recorded in Russia, wildfires burned through forests and dried-out swamps in the central part of Russia, killing about two dozen people and rendering more than 2,000 homeless. The Ministry of Emergency Situations said the 779 wildfires included 42 peat-bog fires whose flames burrow into the ground. More than 10,000 firefighters and 2,158 pieces of firefighting equipment, including 43 planes, were deployed.[278] Because thousands of acres of wheat were scorched, world wheat prices were expected to rise.

Pakistan's Devastating Flood

On July 28–30, 2010 Pakistan suffered its worst flooding in more than 100 years. Flood waters gushed from the Indus River, which divide the country north-to-south, and inundated villages, towns, and whole districts. It started in the mountainous north and spread to southern and western provinces of Sindh and Baluchista. The toll was measured in loss of human life, livestock, crops and food stores, and destroyed homes and irrigation systems. More than

20 million people were affected by the flood, leaving some 900,000 homeless who faced the risk of diarrhea, malaria, and other diseases.[279]

Hazard Management Strategies

Hazard management is the purposeful activity by which society informs itself about hazards, decides what to do about them, and implements measures to control them or to mitigate their consequences.[280] The strategies for managing natural disasters are developed from the general principles of risk management dealing with mitigation and preparatory measures as developed by the Federal Emergency Management Agency (FEMA).

Overview of FEMA's Emergency Management Strategies

In the United States, FEMA is the government's major disaster coordinating agency. It provides immediate disaster relief as well as funds to repair roads and bridges and critical repairs to public and private buildings, and makes loans up to $10,000 for individuals in distress. FEMA was drastically overhauled after being severely criticized for its poor response to Hurricane Andrew in 1992.

President Clinton hired a professional disaster expert, James Lee Witt, who formerly was chief of the Arkansas Office of Emergency Services, to head FEMA. Positive views of him were formed by his visits to flood sites and willingness to talk with victims, officials, relief workers, and the media. He further reinforced his public image by "wearing jeans, ostrich-skin cowboy boots and a belt with a big brass buckle" when examining flood damage in the Midwest.[281] All the progress made during the Clinton administration was undone, however, when FEMA retrogressed into the political mode during the Bush administration. It was no longer a cabinet-level agency but was "demoted" to become a "rather a small cog in the mammoth Department of Homeland Security."[282] Its budget was cut and people without training in disaster planning or management were put in charge.

FEMA remains credited for developing the four stages of hazard management, which is widely recognized for planning and analyzing natural disasters. Its four parts consist of:

1. mitigation—efforts to reduce harm to human life and property if a crisis occurs
2. preparedness—efforts to improve the capability of responding
3. response—activities undertaken immediately before, during, and directly after a crisis event in order to reduce damage
4. recovery—activities to stabilize the stricken area and allow it to return to normalcy.[283]

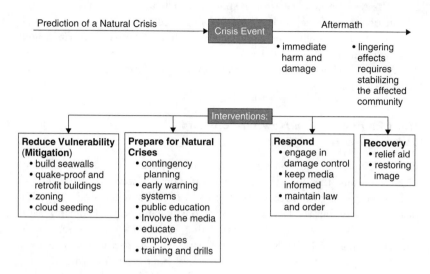

Figure 5.1 Hazard management of natural crises.

Mitigation: Reinforce the Physical Infrastructure

Mitigation seeks to reduce the impact of disasters by doing everything possible before a crisis event to protect life, limit damage, and strengthen a vulnerable community's ability to bounce back quickly. The major questions are whether any planning was done, whether worst-case scenarios were considered, and whether efforts were undertaken to reduce exposure to hazards and minimize their effects. The solutions may lie in simple things such as educating children on what to do in emergencies, or planting trees on unstable hillsides to prevent landslides. More complex solutions include advocating for such measures as earthquake-safe construction and responsible urban planning.[284] The United States Geological Survey jointly with the World Bank estimated that natural disaster-related economic losses worldwide could have been reduced by $2,880 billion had $40 billion been invested in mitigation and prevention.[285]

In his *Handbook of Emergency Management*, William L. Waugh categorizes four types of mitigation efforts:

1. "Hard" engineering or structural responses, such as building offshore breakwaters and seawalls to reduce the force of tidal surges and inland flooding, or retrofitting vulnerable buildings.
2. "Soft" engineering or environmental responses, such as sand fill to build up beach areas or planting of beach grasses and other vegetation to reduce the movement of sand and to maintain natural slope.

3. "Passive" or nonstructural responses which are principally regulatory, involving land use, such as using zoning regulation to limit development close to the shoreline and land use policies that will curb post-storm rebuilding in vulnerable coastal areas.
4. Meteorological responses, such as cloud seeding to reduce the threat of a hurricane.[286]

Hard Engineering in New Orleans and Soft Engineering in China

Hard engineering, the first mitigation effort, is particularly relevant to New Orleans because the city is largely situated in a bowl as low as 10 feet below sea level. Levees along the Mississippi River and Lake Pontchatrain were built to protect the city, but the levees were built to withstand only a Category 3 hurricane, not the more severe Category 4 that occurred. One flaw in FEMA's emergency planning for New Orleans was that worst-case scenarios were not seriously considered. The levees were not built high enough and strong enough, even though predictions warned of the likelihood of a Category 4 or 5 hurricane.

The value of hard engineering could be learned from Holland, where the 1953 flood killed nearly 1,900 people. It embarked on a 40-year, $8 billion project, called Delta Works, which is a network of sluices, dams, levees, and barriers. The project includes the Maeslant barrier, an enormous moveable sea wall completed in 1997, which can close off the North Sea from the main shipping lane into Rotterdam.[287] The massive infrastructure project includes levees and locks that are expected to protect the country from any predicted storm and the slowly rising sea level caused by global warming.

The importance of land use policies and building codes is particularly important in the earthquake-prone areas of China. It was widely recognized that damage from earthquakes could be reduced through strict building codes for new construction and retrofitting of existing structures, a lesson learned from California earthquakes. New Orleans and countries struck with the tsunami could also benefit from better-designed land use policies and stricter building codes. In beach areas of Thailand, for example, buildings were too close to the water. The other mitigation effort mentioned by Waugh, meteorological responses, has not been used in recent years.

Preparedness

Preparedness refers to: (1) strengthening physical and institutional human preparedness; (2) creating early warning systems; and (3) engaging in public education.

Physical Preparedness—Wal-Mart's Infrastructure Serves as a Model

New Orleans could have served as a model for the application of FEMA's emergency management strategies, but it disgracefully showed that it had no established procedures for directing people and materials and no inventory of available transportation, such as rescue boats and helicopters.[288] In contrast, Wal-Mart serves as a model for FEMA and other rescue operation organizations. When Jason Jackson, Wal-Mart's director of business continuity, went to the company's emergency command center on August 24, he learned that Katrina was reclassified as a more dangerous tropical depression. He consequently followed the company's specific contingency planning protocol for responding to disasters. Two days later he was joined by 50 Wal-Mart managers and support personnel, including trucking experts and loss-prevention specialists. Before the storm made landfall on the Gulf Coast on August 28, Wal-Mart warehouses were delivering emergency supplies, such as generators, dry ice and bottled water to designated staging areas, enabling company stores to reopen quickly if disaster struck.

Wal-Mart's advantage over FEMA was that it has its own trucks, distribution centers and dozens of stores in most areas of the country. When 600 law-enforcement officers from around the state met to start rescue operations, they had no supplies. But they called Wal-Mart the day after the hurricane hit and two days later they were supplied with two truckloads of flashlights, batteries, meals ready to eat, protective gear, and ammunition.[289] Jackson was well qualified to tackle the disaster, because he has an undergraduate degree in emergency management and a master's degree in security management.

Activating Early Warning Systems

Although the occurrence of a natural hazard cannot be controlled, it increasingly can be predicted. If surveillance systems operate successfully, people can be alerted so that precautions can be taken. The mass media are an essential component in disseminating warnings, and increasingly the digital media of Twitter and YouTube are supplementing and sometimes taking over that function.

Nevertheless, local radio remains the preeminent medium for emergency information, not only because messages can be heard on battery-assisted radios but because of its ability to broadcast information as soon as something happens.[290] During Hurricane Andrew in 1989, the military's establishment of Radio Recovery was especially helpful because television sets were damaged when homes were destroyed and power lines downed. Where power outages are not a problem, local television can serve the same purpose, with the added advantage of visual presentation. With the proliferation of cell phones and the social media, the dependence on local broadcasting has been lessened, but as seen in New Orleans, Sichuan, and Victoria, they still play a vital role.

In New Orleans and countries struck by the Asian tsunami, victims of natural disasters can rightfully blame authorities for not sounding an early warning. Hurricane Katrina was predicted days in advance of its arrival. Two days before landfall, Houston TV stations started wall-to-wall hurricane coverage. Dan Keeney, president of DPK Public Relations, used Twitter dispatches to keep his clients informed of the storm's progress. One of them read, "Helicopter shots show police escorting ambulances into Galveston to evacuate critical patients. Northbound lanes stopped."[291] The big uncertainty was which path the hurricane would take as it made landfall—whether it would hit New Orleans and whether any of the levees would be breached.

The answer soon became clear. At 8:14 a.m. Monday, August 29, the New Orleans office of the National Weather Service (NWS) issued a flash flood warning, which said, "a levee breach occurred along the industrial canal at Tennessee Street, 3 to 8 feet of water is expected due to the breach."[292] It obtained the information from ham-radio transmission by the Orleans Levee Board, a city-state agency. After the NWS lost communications, the NWS office in Mobile, Alabama, repeated the message at 10:52 a.m. Another early source of information was Governor Kathleen B. Blanco who helplessly said on NBC at 7:33 a.m. on Monday, "I believe the water has breached the levee systems, and is—is coming in."[293] Officials with the U.S. Army Corp. of Engineers were also aware of one canal breach early Monday, but "massive logistical problems with communications in the hours after the storm hit" created some confusion.[294]

The news media gave confusing and contradictory reports about whether the levees in New Orleans were breached. Although CBS and National Public Radio correctly reported the breaking of the Industrial Canal and flooding on Monday, *World News Tonight* wrongly said, "In New Orleans, entire neighborhoods are under water, but the levees held." Local correspondent Jeffrey Kaufman said, "It was simply the volume of rain that left many areas under water. . . . This was not the apocalyptic hurricane that many had feared."[295] Finally, on Monday Helinet Helicopter Services began feeding the first aerial images of New Orleans to the major networks, and they became aware of the awful extent of destruction.

Amazingly, Secretary of Homeland Security Michael Chertoff's source of news was not a dedicated government warning system, but the mass media. He said that on Tuesday morning, August 30, he picked up newspapers and saw the headline, "New Orleans Dodged The Bullet," and concluded that the levee began to break overnight Monday to Tuesday. But it was later learned that major levee breaks occurred starting the morning of Monday, August 29. The head of Homeland Security and the media were woefully misinformed.

In the Indian Ocean, no international system to track tsunamis existed. An early warning of gigantic waves, as officials in Thailand and Indonesia conceded, "could have saved lives." This view is increasingly justified as meteorological and technological advances permit early indications of impending dangers. Victims of natural disasters often blame authorities for not sounding an early warning. But countries in the region could not afford the sophisticated equipment to build an early warning system.[296] Although Indonesia and other Southeast Asian countries spent millions of dollars to install sirens and implement other programs, they could not be expected to deploy sirens in all the areas where they are needed. This limitation was recognized after a smaller tsunami (of 7.7 magnitude) struck the remote Nentawai Islands of Indonesia on October 25, 2010, killing more than 300 people.[297] A more realistic option for rural communities is to focus on public education, e.g., urging villagers to run for higher ground whenever they feel an earthquake.

In China, although there were signs of a severe winter everywhere in January 2008, travelers were never told about the prolonged bad weather. Even the China Meteorological Administration issued faulty weather alerts. When the weather situation was already dire on January 25, it activated only a level-three (the lowest) severe weather emergency plan. Two days later, after 17 days of snowstorms, it raised the alert to level two in the morning and level one in the evening. The railway ministry did no better. It waited until January 28 to activate emergency plans, which addressed the sharp increase in passengers during the Lunar New Year holiday. Activating other emergency plans were deemed unnecessary.[298]

Nor were the major media helpful. On January 11, the second day of the extreme weather, CCTV evening news reported snowfalls. After remaining quiet from January 14 to 16, it erroneously stated on January 18 that most transport in the snow-affected area had resumed. It wasn't until January 26 when massive electricity blackouts and a huge backlog of angry travelers became stranded that the evening news reported the disaster in its main headline news. The next day, the State Council convened an emergency meeting, chaired by Premier Wen Jiabao, to deal with the shortage of coal and electricity.

During the subsequent earthquake, the Chinese government learned to relax its restrictions on the media, realizing that information would flow through the Internet and mobile phones. During the earthquake, a college student in Sichuan province, some 60 miles from the epicenter recorded the upheaval and posted it online after ducking for cover in his dormitory. Micro-blogging, text messaging, and online videos resulted in some extremely swift on-the-ground reports, as well as the viral spreading of rumors.[299] This disclosure helped prompt greater transparency from the state-run media, Xinhua, which pumped out a steady flow of reports. Not surprisingly, some reports continued with their support of government. For example a comment on one scene was, "When you see Hu Jintao or Wen Jiabao with their arms around an eight-year-old, it tends to soften people's images. It just does."[300]

Preparation Through Public Education and the Media

Public education, often with the help of the media, is a sound preparatory strategy. People and organizations must know how to respond to early warnings and, when these don't exist, they must rely on their own knowledge of how to respond to danger signals. Had hospitality personnel in resort communities in Asia been trained to recognize the signs of a tsunami, they could have warned visitors. Public education programs might also have given people the simple advice that when a tsunami appears, "run like the wind, away from the sea."[301]

Public officials must give people essential information about existing plans and how they can prepare for emergencies. Four types of activities are relevant:

1. Well before any crisis occurs, make the public aware of community emergency planning and the legitimacy of the emergency management agency. Credibility can be established by pointing to technical training and access to special equipment by the manager and his or her staff. When an accident does occur, mitigation efforts are aided by making emergency service workers easily identifiable by such devices as pocket plaques, arm bands, distinctive uniforms, and clearly marked vehicles.

2. Build and maintain public communication channels. The public should be alerted to specific hazards and protective steps, initially by print publications, such as brochures distributed by direct mail. Brochures on a variety of emergency topics can be obtained from local governments and several federal agencies—the National Weather Service, the Forest Service, the U.S. Geological Survey, and FEMA. Public service announcements and radio and television interviews with emergency service personnel can reinforce brochures.

3. Exchanges of information should be encouraged and staff members should serve as listening posts and information disseminators in their own neighborhoods. A "hazard information" hotline should be set up, well advertised, and staffed by operators trained to handle inquires. This line can be expanded into a rumor control or warning confirmation line during times of disaster. Speakers should also be made available to community and neighborhood groups and citizen advisory committees and volunteer groups established.

4. Involve the public in emergency planning. Effective planning must be based on accurate data on the pre-crisis situation but must also make provision for an effective information flow during and after the crisis. As was previously discussed, planning should take into account the behavior of people during an emergency; e.g., families will refuse to leave a danger zone until all of their family members have been accounted for. Once a plan has been established, it should be widely disseminated and the public trained to recognize warnings and all-clear signals and to identify emergency personnel.

The public should be informed that a potential hazard is not always immediately detectable, for example, many toxic gases are invisible and odorless, and radiation is not noticed by the human senses. Instructions should be detailed and concrete. General advice, such as "Prepare your family to be ready to leave your home," is neither helpful nor informative. Clearly defined evacuation steps should be listed. Experts say evacuation plans should be simple. Russell Dyhes, co-director of the University of Delaware's Disaster Research Center, advises building around the natural rhythms of life: "Just tell the people to get out of the area and head north," for example. "People adapt . . . . They'll evacuate safely just like they do during a hurricane."[302] Evacuation planning should also consider the return of people.[303]

Cooperation with the media is an integral part of pre-disaster planning and emergency operations. Thus the following provisions for cooperating with the media should be undertaken:

- Establish specific contacts with local newspapers and radio and television news departments. Encourage publishers, editors and news directors to become involved in the general planning process and to develop their own disaster plans for emergency power supply, transportation, food and other essentials. They should also know that FCC regulations allow a station to broadcast beyond its normal hours during emergencies.
- Evaluate the media's capacity to survive a disaster. Contingency media plans should include provisions for emergency generators and portable broadcasting equipment which can be used to convert repeat radio towers into low-powered local stations. Emergency personnel should also know where to reach news staff and technicians at all times. With the wider use of cellphones, public safety officials have complained about disruption of emergency radio communication by police, firefighters and first responders. Sprint Nextel's network has especially been a problem because its broadcast spectrum is interwoven with one used by police and firefighters.[304]
- Since disasters can occur at any time, determine audience listening and viewing preferences so that the most effective media can be deployed in an emergency. Attention must also be given language preferences of audiences, e.g., to reach Hispanics through Spanish-speaking stations. Diffusion of information throughout an entire population is seldom accomplished by the mass media alone. The social media may originate news of a disaster or they may further disseminate mass media information.

Experience during the Australian bushfire showed that it was desirable to make fire information available on real time via Twitter. Relying on land telephone lines, or listening to the radio, or watching TV was unsatisfactory. Some reported that emergency calls were never answered and fire crews said that calls for backups never came. A radio station of the Australian Broadcasting Corporation became a kind of emergency information service, but a number of its broadcasts were based on official reports that were inaccurate or obsolete by crucial minutes, or even hours. The fire that hit the town of Marysville, near Melbourne, was so fast that no one had good information about what was happening. It experienced a colossal firewall, 300 feet high.[305]

Quick Response—Activate Contingency Plans

A quick response is necessary to help save lives and minimize damage. The implementation of a sound contingency plan helps enormously in making decisions about the evacuation of people, search and rescue operations, provision of emergency medical services, law enforcement, and crisis communication. A quick appraisal of a specific disaster's magnitude and characteristics must be made to allow existing plans to be modified and, if necessary, expanded, to cope with existing and arising problems. Pakistan's government was severely criticized for its slow and wholly inadequate response to the Indus River flood.

China Quickens Response Time

In contrast to its slow response to the snowstorm, the Chinese government's response to the earthquake was exemplary—and far better than the U.S. response in New Orleans. It showed the positive side of an authoritarian regime. President Hu Jintao convened a special meeting of the ruling Communist Party's powerful Politburo Standing Committee to discuss the disaster and said relief and rescue work would be the government's top priority. Symbolically, he left Beijing for the affected area within hours of the quake and was seen on top of debris talking to stricken victims.[306] China quickly mobilized one of the largest relief operations in its modern history, using the military as it did in response to snowstorms early in the year. It included the largest airlift in the history of the two-million-member People's Liberation Army, which ran the campaign. Nearly 100,000 military personnel were deployed.[307] In addition, firefighters came from Shanghai, using cranes, saws and jacks to dig into the ruins of buildings such as the Yink Dian Hotel.

Evacuation Bungled in New Orleans and Hampered in Australia

When Hurricane Katrina struck there was "poor coordination among federal, state and local officials in the days immediately before and after the hurricane."[308] FEMA has become synonymous with the government's bungled response. Previous preparatory plans were ignored. A "Southeast Louisiana Catastrophic Hurricane Plan" had been written IEM Inc., a Baton Rouge, Louisiana, consulting firm hired by FEMA and awarded $800,000. It had warned that "a substantial portion" of city residents wouldn't be able to evacuate, and that "a major limiting factor in executing this plan would be the shortage of transportation facilities."[309] Jefferson Parish, a community that did follow the plan, reported that most people were evacuated and those who didn't had food and water for the first couple of days.

The evacuation, which Mayor Ray Nagin claimed he had ordered, was abysmally handled. Most people with cars managed to leave, but most poor people had no vehicles and were left stranded. Buses that could have evacuated them were abandoned and later found flooded. Outsourcing caused serious delays. FEMA had outsourced so much of the response plan that it took the agency several days to hire the contractors and several more days for the contractors to move on the response. As Witt explained, after he left as head of FEMA, "It's my experience that any time you add more layers to bureaucrats into emergency plans, it's a hindrance."[310]

Because wildfires are a common occurrence in parts of Australia, people have been asked to choose one of two options: "leave early or stay and fight the fire." Until "Black Saturday" the popular choice was to stay, partly because of "a streak of self-reliance in the Australian character." Fire plans include removing flammable items from around the house, storing as much water as possible, and being ready to put out flames as a fire front draws near. Public information ads taught people to wear long sleeves and trousers and to avoid all synthetic materials, which ignite much faster in radiant heat. Such heat can be so intense that it can ignite mattresses and curtains through closed windows. The "stay or go" policy was now questioned. People are told that the safest option is simply to leave.

Relief and Recovery Efforts

Relief efforts in the aftermath of a disaster provide people with the essentials to maintain life: water, food, shelter, and medical care. Every hour and day counts, so rapid response is necessary. These efforts are undertaken by government bodies, nonprofit organizations and NGOs, and by people helping one another. The subject of relief is so large that besides the description of immediate relief efforts, some of the broader policy issues and other complexities are discussed in the appendix.

Relief in China

An outstanding feature of earthquake relief efforts in China was the high priority given to debris clearance to facilitate evacuation and to bring heavy equipment into stricken areas to help in rescue operations. Temporary shelter was an urgent need. The Chinese government applied Communist Party organizational strategy to the problem of housing the estimated five million homeless people.[311] People's Liberation Army soldiers created red, white and blue tents stretching for kilometers. The area was anchored with a new town center, overflowing with free food and water, plus ample medical attention from Red Cross

Society of China volunteers. The center contained a post office and even cell phone cards from China Mobile Ltd.[312]

A notable feature is that the Chinese government tried to keep communities together, a feature recommended by disaster experts. China also exploited its economic miracle by building low-cost, fast production $460 Styrofoam houses (161-square-foot structures with front and back windows, as well as electricity, with public kitchen and bathrooms facilities at the end of each block). This design is usually used for construction workers. Private companies also participated; e.g., a chemical company in Shifang cleared a field it owns to set down a new tent village designed for the households of 300 employees who were displaced by the quake.[313]

Recovery efforts begin after the immediate requirements of a disaster are addressed. The problems encountered and the progress made are discussed in the experiences of New Orleans and Asian nations in the aftermath of the tsunami. Restoring tourism was important to both areas because it is a major source of jobs and income.

New Orleans Bounces Back Slowly

The American Red Cross, which is generally in the forefront of relief efforts, initially performed slowly and poorly in New Orleans. It was the Salvation Army that provided water, hot meals, groceries and other basic goods, plus $50, to some of the city's poorest people. It had the biggest presence among the nonprofit groups and churches helping out at East Biloxi's Yankee Stadium. The Salvation Army's military-style structure enhances its effectiveness. The organization is designed for rapid mobilization and places a premium on training people in advance to deal with disasters. It can draw on more than 65,000 employees in the United States, nearly double the paid staff of the Red Cross. The Red Cross belatedly dispatched 163,000 staff and volunteers to shelters and aid centers, but some of its procedures were criticized; e.g., only people living at the Baton Rouge shelter could apply for emergency financial aid.[314]

Wal-Mart was a major player in relief efforts. CEO Lee Scott told his troops to pull out all the stops.[315] Among its accomplishments: it became the biggest corporate benefactor of the Bush-Clinton Katrina Fund, pledging $15 million in cash; it gave $1 million each to the Salvation Army and the American Red Cross; it offered workers displaced by the floods as much as $1,000 in emergency assistance and guaranteed them replacement jobs at any store in the country. It also shipped more than 100 truckloads of merchandise to evacuation centers in Texas, Louisiana, Mississippi and Arkansas; offered residents of affected areas a seven-day emergency supply of prescription drugs free; and donated at least a dozen Wal-Mart buildings for use as shelters, food banks, staging areas and police command centers. In a full-page ad "The power of us all working together is stronger than any storm," it informed the public that every Wal-Mart store and SAM's Club location had established an emergency contact service. Those in need could post messages about their situation, or search for news of family and friends affected by the hurricane.[316]

Other companies also rallied, mainly to provide relief to their employees. Marriott Corp., with 2,800 employees at 15 hotels in New Orleans, paid its workers through the end of the month and housed its own refugees in the ballroom of the Houston Airport Marriott.[317] Hilton Hotels Corp., which has 11 New Orleans-area hotels, arranged for five trucks of emergency supplies to rendezvous in Baton Rouge after the storm to relieve hotels.[318]

In dealing with recovery, almost five years after Hurricane Katrina, New Orleans is beginning to "stop thinking about rebuilding the city we were and start dreaming about the city we want to become," said Mayor Mitch Landrieu.[319] Referring to "The New Orleans Index at Five," a project of the Brookings Institution and the Greater New Orleans Community Data Center, he said the New Orleans region was poised to rebuild communities that are safer, more sustainable and more economically robust than before the storm. The index cites the emergence of influential civic groups, increased entrepreneurship, and sizable federal and philanthropic investments since the flood.

Progress was measured by the metro area's return of more than 90 percent of its population and recovery of almost 85 percent of its jobs.[320] Wages and median household income have improved and poverty declined. Some is due, however, to altered demographics as the city and metro area now have a smaller share of low-income persons, nonwhite households, and households with children, because many of these were displaced or chose to relocate after Katrina. Notable progress has been made in remaking the public school system, reducing the high crime and racial disparities, and lessening economic dependence on industries that are losing steam, such as shipbuilding. Fewer schools are deemed failing and the number of fourth- and eight-graders showing proficiency in reading and math is increasing.

Long-term recovery was slowed by the debate over the extent to which New Orleans should be rebuilt. Some officials thought that areas below sea level, such as Ward 9, should be bulldozed and made into park areas. To restore the area for homes, a precondition would be the strengthening and heightening of the levees. After the Galveston Hurricane in 1900 the Army Corps of Engineers built a seawall that now stretches more than 10 miles and stands 17 feet high.[321] A similar effort in New Orleans would require building supersize levees to 25 feet or higher and would require property to be seized as engineers widen the base of the dirt structure by 100 feet or more.[322] Furthermore, protective gates would be required where the canals empty into Lake Pontchartrain.

Ideological and environmental considerations also slowed renewal planning. While some saw the plight of New Orleans as a perfect argument for a gigantic government planning effort, others favored a free market approach. Policy issues about energy and natural resource management also had to be settled. Knowing that wetlands served as one line of defense against hurricanes, some favored the restoration of these natural buffer zones. A Yale University ecologist said, "I'm hoping that one lesson to come out of this is that talk about rolling back protection for wetlands will end." A related issue was placing a limit on development in the most vulnerable areas and to stop offering federal insurance to building on coastal dunes, barrier islands, and other vulnerable spots.[323]

Amidst discussions about a variety of rebuilding plans—the building of a light-rail system, new schools, a mile-long riverfront park, museums and other cultural facilities—people were reminded that the most important factor was maintaining the character of the city.[324] As Jacob Wagner, a professor of urban planning at the University of Missouri at Kansas City, noted, "The spirit of New Orleans is all about the people. . . . If the people come back and rebuild, the spirit will survive. If they don't fragmentation of local culture could occur. Maintaining the local character of the city must be part of the discussion about how to rebuild."[325]

Massive Relief and Restoration of Tourism After the Tsunami

The tsunami precipitated an unprecedented international relief effort, mostly by the private sector. Jan Egeland, the United Nations' main official dealing with the disaster, called the immediate humanitarian response "remarkably, perhaps, singularly, effective, swift and muscular."[326] Australia led the list, followed by Germany, the EU and Japan, all of which exceeded U.S. government pledges, although when private donations are added, the United States slightly surpassed Japan.

The catastrophic tsunami in the Indian Ocean was a heavy blow to the region's $100-billion annual tourism business. In 2004, tourism accounted for 12 percent of GDP in Thailand and 10 percent in Sri Lanka, according to the World Travel and Tourism Council (WTTC).[327] As some tourists were returning to the beaches on Phuket Island in a little more than a week after the disaster, questions of sensitivity to suffering arose: "Americans played beach volleyball down the street from a shopping mall where customers drowned. Women sunbathed topless in areas where rescue workers last week recovered corpses. And bars with exotic dancers in the island's red-light district have reopened."[328] The nagging question was how long a period of mourning was appropriate for tourists and the tourist industry.

Major airlines, such as Cathay Pacific Airways and Thai Airways International, and hotel chains, such as Marriott International Inc. accommodated sensitivities by making it easier for travelers to cancel or postpone their plans.[329] Generally, however, the attitude of "business as usual" prevailed. The Tourism Authority of Thailand was already trying to promote the country as a vacation destination in some Asian markets. While many European governments, such as Denmark, Norway and Sweden, issued advisories to their citizens not to travel to devastated areas, the 20-member Association of Southeast Asian Nations said in a statement after a two-day conference on January 25, "with the support provided by the international community, we are confident that Asian tourism will bounce back and surpass its pre-December 26 levels."[330] Some used the rationale that vacation budgets would help Phuket recover more rapidly.

More than 805 of the island's hotel rooms were ready for business by the end of the year (2004). JW Marriott Phuket Resort & Spa was expecting to be fully operational on December 31. Its pools were cleaned of mud and debris and refilled; its beachfront restaurant was repaired. Marriott's senior vice president for international marketing was building her sales pitch for "Phuket is back" around lots of pictures. She said, "If I can show fully functioning pools and restored grounds, that goes a long way." Company executives realized they risked offending sensitivities and therefore "would not go out with a direct-to-consumer advertising campaign at this point." Instead, they were communicating first with travel-industry professionals and mapped out a sales campaign that would include special calls on leading tour operators and charter groups.[331]

Haiti: Disorganized Relief and Disappointingly Slow Recovery Efforts

In the hours and days after the devastating earthquake, relief was urgent. Television showed pictures of havoc and the desperate plight of people. Aid soon arrived from the United States and countries around the world. However, the only quick access to Port-au-Prince was through the airport. Fortunately one runway was still intact. Within a day the airport was overrun with relief planes and some had to fly around for up to five hours before landing or landing in neighboring Dominican Republic or elsewhere. It wasn't until Friday, three days after the quake, that the U.S. Air Force brought in air-traffic management equipment to handle the traffic.[332]

Despite the arrival of water, food, medical supplies, rescue teams and medical personnel, the big problem was choosing priorities and coordinating distribution of relief supplies. No one seemed to be in charge. Rescue units and their dogs saved a few trapped victims, but their efforts were limited because no heavy equipment was available to remove debris. Makeshift hospitals were set up in open areas such as the national soccer stadium, but supplies were still stuck at the airport. As one volunteer paramedic said, "No gloves, nothing to sew wounds, no antiseptic."[333]

The social media, however, may have been helpful in two ways: (1) by leveraging public participation in the disaster response; and (2) facilitating communications among the responders. Dave Yates and Scott Paquette, the authors of a study of the role of the social media in Haiti during the crisis, say social media can be used "within formal organizations to support open, collaborative knowledge sharing and reuse. When properly employed, the benefits of social media support are faster decision cycles and more complete knowledge resources."[334] The traditional "knowledge management systems," often resulted in information "silos." Now, for the first time, the U.S. government relied extensively on social media to coordinate knowledge and action between cooperating response agencies, which included the U.S. Agency for International Development, the U.S. State Department, and the U.S. armed forces. Among the situations helped by the new knowledge management system were: untangling lined-up jumbo jets at the airport; overcoming shortages of medical supplies; arresting prison escapees; reporting on contaminated wetlands; and facilitating the primary mission of humanitarian aid. The social media, the authors conclude, "allow for the flexibility, adaptability, and boundary spanning functionally demand by response organizations for their information systems."

Nevertheless, two or three days after the quake, many people living in crowded spaces and on streets still had not received water and food was not reaching people. Only a few of the dead that could be found were buried by surviving relatives. Sanitation was abysmally lacking. With lack of water and sanitation, one fear was the outbreak of disease. Haiti was notorious for its inadequate health system and a high prevalence of infectious diseases.[335] Another looming problem was that in April the annual heavy rain was expected and victims were not yet supplied with enough sturdy tents.

Amid the lack of coordination of relief, the U.S. military took major responsibility for relief efforts. But larger numbers of U.S. military personnel and equipment were not expected to arrive until the weekend at a time when every day and even hours counted. Some experienced disaster experts thought that water and food should be air dropped, but the military feared random drops might start a riot, so it insisted that security forces be in place to manage distribution efforts. By the weekend, a few water trucks reached Port-au-Prince from Santa Domingo, but water purification units were not yet operating.

The private sector was helpful. UPS worked with the Dutch express parcel company TNT, which together with Agility, the global logistics company, transported tons of food and supplies daily; Facebook raised $1.5 million for the World Food Program in five days; and Digicel, the largest mobile telecommunications operator in the Caribbean, transferred instant credit through its mobile phone network to two million Haitians.[336]

Health risks became especially urgent as lack of medicines jeopardized the lives of thousands. Partners in Health, a U.S.-based aid group that has been providing health care in Haiti for two decades, warned that as many as 20,000 people in Haiti might be dying daily from infections such as gangrene and sepsis. One piece of good news was that the U.S. medical ship, the *USNS Comfort*, arrived eight days after the quake, carrying 550 medical staff and 1,000 beds.[337]

The status of Haiti's recovery six months after the disaster is captured in a *Los Angeles Times* headline: "Haiti's Ongoing Disaster; Earthquake Recovery Efforts Have Stalled Amid Poor Planning, Slow Delivery of Aid and Corruption."[338] The sorry state of affairs is symbolized by a CNN story which shows children "near starvation in an orphanage just a few miles from an aid warehouse bursting with undelivered food, and bulldozing contractors sitting idle while men were being paid to break up concrete debris with hammers and haul it away in buckets." The article asks, "Isn't anybody in charge there?"

The fear of an outbreak of disease was realized later in the year when a cholera epidemic broke out, which by mid-November had killed 796 people and hospitalized more than 12,000. The epicenter of the outbreak was in the Artibonite region, north of Port-au-Prince, where many displaced earthquake survivors had moved and where little potable water was available. But cholera was expected to reach the city where more than 1.3 million survivors were still living in squalid tent cities.[339] Slow progress in rebuilding, insufficient sanitation and lack of clean water were taking its toll.

Conditions barely improved by the first anniversary of the earthquake. About 1.6 million were still homeless and the unemployment rate was between 70 and 80 percent.[340] As a report by Oxfam, the British aid organization, stated, Haiti's reconstruction efforts have been paralyzed by a lack of leadership from the Haitian government and the international community. "In the short term, it is hard to be optimistic about progress." Too much of the promised donations were still being used to care for people in camps. A new reconstruction agency, the Interim Haiti Recovery Commission, which has the authority to seek, approve and coordinate projects, was hardly off the ground.[341] The good news came mostly in optimistic announcements by Haitian and U.S. officials of a $250 million deal with Sae-A Trading Co., Ltd, of South Korea to develop an industrial park in northern Haiti that would create some 20,000 jobs over seven years.[342]

Haiti desperately needs a shift from relief to reconstruction. Nation-building strategies of various kinds are needed: unified coordination, e.g., getting the thousands of NGOs to work together; straightening out the legal tangle of property ownership; getting permission to clear the mess away; and speeding up improvements in basic infrastructure. Overall, however, the political and community spirit, and activity that are slowly revitalizing New Orleans are not yet found in Haiti.

Conclusions

The first decade of the 21st century started with several devastating natural disasters in the United States and Asia. There is speculation about whether climate change will increase the frequency and intensity of natural disasters, but a longer time frame is needed to confirm this view. In any event, crisis managers in both the public and private sectors must improve their hazard management capabilities.

Disaster planning, response, and recovery require community-wide involvement and the cooperation of both public and private bodies. Because concern for public health and safety is a governmental mandate, government officials must assume ultimate responsibility. They should take the lead in developing policies and programs to deal with major hazards and disasters. At what level this is done remains a complex problem. On the one hand, the local community is the first responder to an accident or disaster, but on the other hand, the national government is expected to provide basic humanitarian services for all of the country's inhabitants.

Disasters are so diffuse and complex that hazard management will always remain fragmented, not only with respect to level of government but also as to which activities are conducted by each of the agencies within federal, state and local governments. Nevertheless, disaster experts agree that coordination and cooperation among these public bodies, as well as with nonprofit and private organizations, is a fundamental requirement.

Hazard management for natural disasters provides the template for all crises of the physical environment. The template includes mitigation, preparation, response and relief/recovery. Biological crises and technological crises apply parts of it. Because the occurrence of natural disasters cannot be controlled, public attention is focused on response and relief efforts. Crisis managers, however, must also examine ways in which mitigation and preparatory efforts can lessen the impact of a natural disaster event and, following the principles of contingency planning, do everything possible to prepare for it.

Appendix to Chapter 5: Major Issues in Relief Efforts

Accepting Foreign Aid

The decision of whether to accept foreign aid must quickly be decided. In weighing the desire for self-sufficiency balanced against the need for resources from abroad, the Chinese government favored the latter. At first, some Chinese officials politely refused some offers of help, for example, from the Czech Republic which offered a team of 15 earthquake search experts and their specially trained dogs.[343] But a few days later the Ministry of Foreign Affairs announced that China would accept offers from foreign emergency-response units to "bring sniffer dogs, fiber-optic probes and other technology to locate survivors."[344]

China learned from Japan's rejection of much foreign help after the 1995 Kobe earthquake that more lives of citizens buried in the rubble could have been saved if foreign assistance had not been resisted and delayed by the Japanese government. It had decided to accept only blankets, water, waterproof sheeting material and tents from the U.S. military stations in Japan, but it rejected other offers such as aircraft, mobile power generators, earth-movers, and rescue dogs. A 60-member French rescue team with six tons of equipment, sniffer dogs, and six doctors and nurses was delayed for three days because of Japanese government bureaucratic obstacles. The rescue doctors from France and the United States were not allowed to treat critically injured patients on grounds they lacked Japanese medical licenses.

As stated by Professor Gerald Curtis, a Japan expert at Columbia University, the quake threw Japan's weaknesses into stark relief. "Its strengths are its people; their self-discipline, order and stiff-upper-lip stoicism. But the bureaucracy could not get its act together. It works when things are smooth and the country can fly on auto-pilot, but when there is turbulence, the leadership isn't there."[345] The bureaucracy was at fault for its slowness in dispatching rescue troops. The governor of Osaka used the "blame the victim" approach when he "reportedly chided victims as crybabies and urged them to do more to help themselves."[346] The government was put to shame by Japan's largest organized crime group, the Yamaguchi-gumi, which handed out food, water and diapers to people in devastated neighborhoods. It reportedly used motor scooters, boats and even a helicopter to move goods into and around the city.[347]

Political Interference in Relief Efforts in Myanmar

The relevance of political factors is notoriously illustrated by Cyclone Nargis, which battered the delta region of the Irrawaddy River in Myanmar (known as Burma) on May 3, 2008. It was hampered by lack of good roads and a paranoid and undemocratic government that was more concerned about maintaining power than helping its victims.[348] The nation's state-run media had failed to issue a timely warning about the storm, even though the country's Department of Meteorology and Hydrology was told of the formation of the cyclone a week in advance.[349]

Some nations make a fetish of being self-sufficient or staunchly maintaining national sovereignty. Myanmar became a prime example of the latter. More than two weeks after the storm Myanmar's military regime continued to let in only dribbles of aid to the country and was still barring most of the foreign aid workers and equipment needed to distribute it, even though the death toll rose to 130,000. It rejected America's request to let its Navy ships deliver aid directly to the delta, nor would it allow Navy ships from France and Britain to do so.[350] A World Food Program spokesman complained that "all of the food aid and equipment that we managed to get in has been confiscated."[351] Furthermore, seeking credit for relief efforts, the army was caught sticking labels with the names of top generals on aid that had been provided by Thailand.[352]

The government's behavior was so egregious that France, which commented it would take half an hour for the French boats and helicopters to reach the disaster area, suggested the new concept of "responsibility to project," which implies that saving human lives might in some extreme circumstances override sovereignty.[353] The regime's priority was to stick to the election timetable and urge the country's citizens to vote for a new constitution that would legitimize and perpetuate the military's grip on power.[354] General Than Shwe, who was invisible for a fortnight, finally toured the cyclone-hit areas and declared three days of national mourning.[355]

Adequacy of Relief Pledges

In the aftermath of the unprecedented international relief efforts to Asian countries stricken by the tsunami, Jan Egeland, the United Nations' main official dealing with the disaster, accused many Western countries of giving only a tiny percentage of their gross national income to the aid effort. "It is beyond me why are we so stingy, really. . . . Even Christmas time should remind many Western countries at least how rich we have become."[356]

After the United States was stung by criticism that its response was inadequate—it was half of what Japan had promised—it boosted relief aid to $35 million and said it would dispatch 15,000 servicemen on almost a dozen warships in the Pacific to the Indian Ocean.[357] The U.S. force consisted of more than 20 naval ships, six big transport aircraft, and nine surveillance and rescue planes.[358] The Navy's relief efforts led to a swell of favorable public opinion in the region and helped to overcome previous anti-American sentiment.

Another complaint about government pledges is that many are not kept. Of the $1.1 billion pledge to help the people of the Iranian city of Bam, destroyed by an earthquake in 2003, only $17.5 million was sent, according to the Iranian government. Honduras and Nicaragua are also still awaiting two-thirds of the $8.7 billion proffered after Hurricane Mitch swept through in 1998.[359]

Private Sector Augments Stingy Government Tsunami Aid

Private sector aid for the tsunami was unprecedented. The United Nations raised about $2.5 billion worldwide from institutional and individual donors, accounting for roughly 50 percent of total money raised.[360] American companies mobilized more than $565 million: about $273 million in cash contributions; $140 million in in-kind donations; and $73 million in customer donations. Among the biggest givers were pharmaceutical Pfizer (donating $10 million in cash and $25 million-worth of drugs), Coca-Cola (donating $10 million), Exxon Mobil ($5 million), Citigroup ($3 million), Bill & Melinda Gates Foundation ($3 million), and Johnson & Johnson (pledged an "initial cash contribution" of $2 million and also donated medical products and other supplies).

Drug makers with offices or plants in the region sent out employees with antibiotics, nutritional supplements, infant formula, baby food and other supplies. Employees from Coca-Cola, Pepsico and Marriott International hotels in the region delivered bottled water, food and other supplies.[361] Coca-Cola, which for years maintained relationships with the Red Cross and other aid agencies in many countries, converted its soft-drink production lines to bottle huge quantities of drinking water and used its own distribution network to deliver it to relief sites.

Corporate Strengths and Weaknesses

Corporations tend to view a disaster as a business challenge: to analyze the situation, figure out where the greatest need is, and respond in a way that reflects the "market" for aid. "Companies ought to align disaster relief with their business models and their core competencies," said Charles Moore, executive director of one of the committees. The fit seemed natural for Caterpillar. Its corporate foundation donated $2.3 million in cash to disaster relief in 2005, up from just under $100,000 in 2004. Its dealer network also donated equipment worth several hundred thousand dollars, said Will Ball, Caterpillar's manager for social responsibility initiatives.[362]

Corporations have discovered defects in their philanthropy. Certainly, many companies supplied essential goods and services that year, and cash donations provided crucial help, he said. Too often, however, there was little communication about what was needed and available, and too many companies donated unneeded goods that clogged runways and storage space. Companies are advised to collaborate with local officials and charities, ideally on a continuing basis, and not only in the midst of a crisis. The strengths of all parties should be recognized. "The private sector is good at tools and technology and preparing for unforeseen things," said Lynn Fritz, chairman of the Fritz Institute, a charity that works with governments, nonprofits and companies to improve responses to natural disasters. "They're extremely good at training. These are enormous attributes for the humanitarian world." He added, however, that companies often do best when they work with humanitarian organizations. Toys "R" Us, for example, has partnerships with Save the Children and similar groups, said Kathleen Waugh, a spokeswoman.[363]

But there were flaws in the system of private-public relief partnerships. No comprehensive list was available of what was needed and by whom, and there was no mechanism to keep track of what corporations had available and where. Unsolicited items by well-meaning donors just piled up, much of which was inappropriate (Western clothing, carbonated beverages). Discussions were held by the corporate and humanitarian sectors to determine how they could best cooperate through some form of partnership, which takes advantage of the strengths of each party. The strength of business was the "wealth of funds and goods and operational expertise;" the strength of the humanitarian sector was decades of experience on the front lines of disasters and in long-term development initiatives.[364]

Lessons Learned

In the aftermath of the 2004 tsunami, industry groups and nonprofit organizations learned how to improve crisis preparedness. Hank McKinnell, chairman of the Business Roundtable and chairman and CEO of Pfizer Inc., said the next response needed to be more coordinated and efficient. One initiative was to determine which areas were in need of what resources. McKinnell said, "Companies will be identifying right now the equipment, supplies and expertise of skilled employees that could be available on short notice at time of disaster."[365] During the tsunami, resources were sometimes simply sent and local relief agencies didn't know what to do with them. Also, massive amounts of used clothing that was donated to Sri Lankan citizens were not used because cultural traditions forbid the wearing of used clothing. It is imperative that everything from vaccines and stockpiles of medicine to piping and generators be sent to areas of greatest need to cut down on wasted time and resources. Another initiative is to improve coordination with agencies such as the Red Cross, UNICEF and CARE, so that there are clear channels of communications and the capabilities of each will be known.

Some of the relief problems encountered in the tsunami were overcome in dealing with the Kashmir earthquake in October 2005. The global cargo industry applied its nuts-and-bolts logistics techniques to emergency-supply chains. Working with American soldiers, Chris Weeks, an executive from express-shipping DHL Corp., improvised a "speedball" method for quickly getting food and shelter to some of the hundreds of thousands of quake survivors. Tents, food and other supplies were stuffed into red polypropylene bags, which DHL had used for years to handle loose cargo. After loading them into Chinook helicopters, they were taken to rough landing strips near survivors where they were kicked out the door. A bag's supplies could keep seven people alive for 10 days.[366]

DHL also applied other management techniques. After the 2003 earthquake in Bam, Iran, relief supplies were flown in by dozens of aid groups and governments and unloaded on runways where they would block other planes from landing. The unloading process was reorganized so that planes were taxied off the runway and offloaded by a professional team which would keep track of precisely what had arrived and where it should be distributed. The idea was to "manage emergency response in the same door-to-door fashion that freight companies use to supply their customers."[367]

Having learned lessons from the Indian Ocean tsunami of 2004, aid groups were ready to respond during the 2009 tsunami. Save the Children had built up warehouses in various locations in Indonesia and trained hundreds of relief workers.[368] Oxfam had already deposited 5,000 tarpaulins and sanitation suppliers with its local relief partners. World Vision quickly dispatched a needs-assessment team to Padang. Individual donations started to pour in at GlobalGiving.com, a website connecting individuals to international grassroots charity projects.

Chapter 6

Biological Crises

Occurrences like AIDS, mad cow disease, SARS, and the H1N1 influenza (swine flu) represent another kind of natural crisis, which can be called biological crises. They arise from diseases that spring spontaneously from nature and spread from one person or animal to another. The pathogenic viruses that originated in animals and jumped to humans, sometimes called "zoonoses," account for 60 percent of all infectious diseases, and 75 percent of all emerging infections, says Larry Brilliant, an epidemiologist and chairman of the National Biosurveillance Advisory Subcommittee.[369] Besides AIDS, SARS, and H1N1, some other better-known diseases are bird flu, West Nile, Monkeypox, and Ebola.

Biological diseases have increasingly become major killers and must be added to natural disasters as a major type of crisis of the physical environment. The outbreak of infectious diseases and the occurrence of natural disasters share the common characteristic of initially appearing as spontaneous occurrences that can cause enormous harm. According to Herb Schreier, M.D. at Children's Hospital in Oakland, California, just three infectious diseases—tuberculosis, malaria and AIDS—caused 160 times as many deaths than natural disasters in 1999.[370]

Scary scenarios about future outbreaks of disease have been portrayed. A recent one is Robin Cook's *Plague: A New Thriller of the Coming Pandemic*. He wrote it "to shake up the complacent public about the high risk of an imminent, serious pandemic."[371] He sees a repeat of the Black Death, which began in the 14th century, killing a quarter to a third of Europe's population, roughly 15 million to 25 million people.[372] The plague in his book unfolds even faster. He says it may have started with avian flu, which although currently contained, killed about 60 percent of people who contracted the illness over the last three years. His own contingency plan is his ski cottage, well-stocked with supplies.

Characteristics of Biological Diseases

Transmission Between Animals and Humans

A major characteristic of biological diseases is the jumping from animals to humans. SARS is known to be transmitted from fowl, and although the exact origin of AIDS is not known, it is suspected as having been transferred from a monkey to a human being. One reason for this jump is that population growth has pushed people into land that historically was the province of animals. Africans in 2008 consumed nearly 700 million wild animals, which totals about two billion kilograms of "bush meat."[373]

Another reason is that modern industrial farming of chickens, pigs, and cattle is cultivating bacteria that medicine is losing the ability to fight. As stated by Ellen Silbergeld, a former professor of epidemiology at the University of Maryland School of Medicine, "industrial agriculture is fostering and dispersing drug-resistant bacteria that impair medicine's ability to protect the public from them."[374] Factory chicken farms routinely feed antibiotics to their flocks to accelerate growth. Silbergeld found that 41 percent of workers whose job it is to catch chickens in the barns to load onto transport trucks had been colonized by *Campylobaacter jejuni*, which, while benefitting chickens, is pathogenic in people and the second leading cause of gastrointestinal disease in the United States.

At pig farms, says Kellogg Schwab, director of the Johns Hopkins Center for Water and Health, the typical manure lagoons "can have trillions of bacteria present, of which 89 percent are resistant to drugs."[375] When Schwab sampled surface and ground water downgradient from a pig farm, she found that it contained from 11 times to 33 times more pathogens than water upgradient from the facility. The agriculture industry disputes the claims made by Silbergeld and Schwab and argues that removing antibiotics would result in more sick animals. Although supporting the use of drugs to treat sick animals, Silbergeld and Schwab believe all antibiotics should be banned from animal feeds.

A long-term danger of feeding antibiotics to chickens and pigs is that bacterial infections, which were once big killers before the advent of antibiotics, would make a come-back. There are worrying signs that bacteria develop increasingly sophisticated mechanisms of resistance to antibiotics. Receiving much attention has been the uncontrollable spread of methicillin-resistant *Staphyloccus aureus* (MRSA), which is estimated to kill more than 18,000 each year in the United States.[376] As Bill Bryson explains in a chapter on "Small World" in his popular *A Short History of Nearly Everything*, "the source of the infection is a mundane family of bacteria called Group A *Streptoccus*, which normally do no more than cause strep throat. Very occasionally, for reasons unknown, some of these bacteria get through the lining of the throat and into the body proper, where they wreak the most devastating havoc."[377]

The most feared type of biological crisis is a pandemic—"the rapid spread of an infectious disease to many countries in different regions, hitting each with more or less the same severity."[378] Often it is a new or novel agent, making its identification difficult. The Great Swine Flu epidemic (sometimes called the Great Spanish Flu epidemic) of 1918–19, killed 30 million people worldwide. Thus, what was called a "plausible scenario" made by a panel of scientific advisers to President Barack Obama about the H1N1 swine flu that appeared in 2009, sounds scary. They estimate that 60 million to 120 million Americans—or 20 to 40 percent of the U.S. population—would contract the flu, and 30,000 to 990,000 people die of the disease.[379]

Fortunately, those estimates did not materialize—at least in the first wave. In early December, the U.S. Centers for Disease Control and Prevention (CDC) reported that approximately 47 million Americans, or about one in six, were sickened with swine flu from April to mid-November and 9,820 of them died.[380] When the fall wave peaked between mid-October and November 14, about 213,000 people were hospitalized, which was about the same number as in a normal flu season. The vast majority of illnesses were among non-elderly adults and children.

AIDS, which is now known have been first discovered in a British sailor who had died of mysterious, untreatable causes in 1959,[381] has ravished the world. In 2007, there were 33.2 million people infected with HIV (the virus that causes AIDS). As more nations provide treatment, the death rates are falling. They peaked in 2005 with 2.2 million deaths.[382] One sign of hope is that public health workers have persuaded millions of people to modify or abandon risky behavior.

Occasionally, new sources of bacterial danger are reported in the media. One is that clouds of dust from drought-stricken plains of North Africa are carrying living bacteria, fungi, and probably viruses and pesticides to the United States and Caribbean. Hundreds of millions of tons of soil are being blown away every year, scientists estimate. One organism, called *aspergillus sydowii*, causes widespread death of seafans on Caribbean coral reefs. A species of *aspergillus* is a major killer of people with AIDS.[383]

Some Similarities and Differences Between Biological Diseases and Natural Disasters

The responses to biological disasters are similar to those of natural disasters. They require mitigation efforts to reduce vulnerability, preparatory measures and early warning systems, and responses that limit harm. However, differences must also be considered for effective planning and response—differences in geography, duration, detection, and extent of harm.

Natural disasters occur in specific geographical areas that are either immediately or quickly defined. We speak of the earthquake in Kobe, Japan, or Sichuan, China, the drought in South Wales, Australia, or a typhoon in Bangladesh. In contrast, a biological disease typically begins in a specific place but easily and rapidly moves to many cities and regions worldwide, because it is transmitted by respiratory means. Globalization accounts for the wide geographic spread of diseases. The transnational shipment of goods and the international movement of people are advantageous to the migration of bacteria. As David P. Fidler states in his book, *SARS, Governance and the Globalization of Disease*, the great cliche of infectious disease control is that germs do not recognize borders.[384]

The duration of a biological crisis lasts for months and years while that of a natural disaster is measured in days and weeks. The Black Death in 14th-century Europe lasted a whole century, the catastrophic influenza of 1918–19 lasted over two years, and HIV/AIDS, which was first detected in 1981, continues to this day. The existence of a natural disaster is self-evident, but the detection and identification of a biological disease is often difficult. The potential extent of harm focuses on people, not property, and is therefore likened to a neutron bomb.

Major Cases of Biological Crises

Three cases describe how biological crises begin, evolve and end. In recent years, the SARS crisis has received the most attention and helped to develop the responses of nations and organizations to crisis management of biological diseases. The swine flu outbreak in Mexico in 2009 was a test of the lessons learned from SARS and an opportunity to explore further problems and solutions. The long, protracted mad cow experience revealed the difficulty of applying a scientific approach to a problem with vast economic and political consequences.

SARS Crisis

Origin

The severe acute respiratory syndrome (SARS) was initially identified as an atypical pneumonia in the province of Guangdong, China, in fall 2002. In November, when the manager of the World Health Organization's (WHO) influenza program attended a routine Beijing meeting on China's flu-vaccination policy, a health worker from Guangdong province reported that several people in his region had succumbed to an unusually severe influenza. Samples obtained by WHO suggested it was a normal virus.[385] By March 4, 2003, however, a death in Hong Kong was reported as being SARS. And on April 2, a WHO advisory warned against travel to Hong Kong and South China. What began with a few cases in China in fall 2002 had by April 16, 2003, tallied to 3,235 cases in 23 countries, with 154 suspected deaths.[386]

SARS is a virus. Viruses aren't themselves alive, but burst into life when they are introduced to a suitable host. About 5,000 types are known and among them they inflict people with hundreds of diseases, ranging from the common cold to such invidious ones as smallpox, rabies, yellow fever, Ebola, polio, and AIDS. Normally, the flu kills about 500,000 people a year around the world.[387] Smallpox killed an estimated 300 million people in the 20th century alone.[388]

Although there are many epidemiological guesses about the origin of SARS, the leading hypothesis is that the SARS virus was transmitted from an animal species to humans somewhere in Guangdong Province, China.[389] The province is known for its "wet markets" where a wide variety of live fauna are offered for sale. Included among them are three suspected sources of SARS: the masked palm civet, the raccoon-dog, and the Chinese ferret badger. Scientifically, the causative agent behind SARS is a novel kind of coronavirus (SARS-CoV).[390] The outbreak of SARS was a big challenge: "How does public health contain the spread of a new virus spread efficiently by respiratory means from person-to-person without any effective diagnostic, therapeutic, or vaccine technologies?"[391] SARS represented the first "infectious disease to emerge into a radically new and different global political environment for public health."[392]

Traditional Secrecy Replaced with Greater Openness.

The SARS epidemic exposed the tendency of authoritarian governments to keep bad news secret. In keeping the outbreak of SARS quiet, China revealed its history of secrecy and a belief that the *laobaixing*—the common folk—are better off not knowing too much. Some likened China's behavior to the Soviet Union's secrecy about Chernobyl and about the doomed submarine *Kursk*. Arthur Kleinman and James L. Watson concluded in their *SARs in China: Prelude to Pandemic?* that China's handling of SARS "reflected archaic modes of governance: mass mobilization, authoritarian control from the center, and the uncompromising use of military and police power."[393]

China went through three stages in disclosing information about the SARS epidemic: (1) suppression of information; (2) acknowledgment of outbreak but denial and cover up of the extent of the epidemic; and (3) China's Communist Party's halt of the systematic deception.[394]

Stage 1: Suppression of Information (November 2002 to early February 2003). Health authorities in Guangdong Province issued a report on cases of atypical pneumonia on January 23, but it was considered a "state secret" under Chinese law.[395] Nonetheless, the outbreak was visible to people and caused panic in the Guangdong. Between November 27, 2002, and early February WHO's Global Outbreak Alert and Response Network (Global Network) picked up information about the influenza outbreak from users of mobile phones and from local Chinese media.

A February 8 mobile phone text message read: "There is a fatal flu in Guangzhou."[396] Demonstrating the reach of this new medium, phone users resent the message 40 million times on that day through email and Internet chat rooms in China and beyond. The message was also picked up and posted by Pro-MED-mail, a leading non-governmental global electronic reporting system for outbreaks of emerging infectious diseases. Furthermore, despite government restrictions, Guangdong journalists printed stories about the outbreak. China's attempts to suppress information did not succeed.

Stage 2: Denial of Acknowledgment. Based on Internet and local media information, WHO on February 10 officially approached the Chinese government for information. On the following day it received a report notifying the agency of

300 cases and five deaths of acute respiratory syndrome influenza in Guangdong Province. China had thus acknowledged the outbreak. On the same day Guangdong health officials held a reassuring press conference saying that "the situation was under control," an assessment that the Chinese government repeated. On February 27, the Chinese Ministry of Health declared the outbreak in Guangdong province was over.[397] These optimistic statements now appear as denial and cover up of the extent of the epidemic

About a week earlier, on February 21, an important event in global public health history occurred. Liu Jianlun, a 64-year-old physician and medical professor from Guangdong Province checked into Room 911 of the Metropole Hotel in Hong Kong. He had been treating patients in Guangdong Province who were suffering from a mysterious respiratory illness. Having become ill himself, Dr. Liu was admitted to a Hong Kong hospital with severe pneumonia on February 22. He died on March 4. During his one-night stay at the hotel, he transmitted the virus to at least 16 other guests and visitors to the same floor of the hotel. They included a resident of Hong Kong, an American businessman, Singaporean nationals, and two Canadian nationals. The Metropole Hotel thus became the epicenter of the virus as it spread from city to city and nation to nation.[398]

Reports of illnesses ensued. Hong Kong's hospital reported an outbreak of flu-like symptoms on March 12. Based on this information, WHO issued a global alert about cases of atypical pneumonia. This was a bold decision because some WHO staff members pondered: "Are we going to panic the world?"[399] It had to find a delicate balance between the obligation to provide information about a potentially lethal disease without causing panic.[400] Reports of further illnesses justified its decision and encouraged it to make a riskier report. On March 15 WHO linked the mysterious syndrome with air travel, a report that carried widespread implications for world business and tourism. It issued a travel advisory and declared SARS a worldwide health threat. It was at this point that WHO called the new illness Severe Acute Respiratory Syndrome, or SARS.[401] Thus March 15 became the governance tipping point in the epidemic.

On March 26, China reported new figures for the November–February outbreak in Guangdong Province: 792 cases and 31 deaths, from an atypical pneumonia, still not calling it SARS. For a month, WHO received no further information from Chinese officials, who continued to say that the outbreak in China was under control. They even issued a booklet "SARS is Nothing to Be Afraid Of."[402]

However, in an unprecedented action, the head of China's Center for Disease Control on April 4 publicly apologized "for failing to inform the public about a sometime fatal respiratory illness that has infected more than 2,000 people worldwide"[403] On April 9, a prominent Chinese doctor and Communist Party member, Jiang Wanyong, publicly accused the Chinese government of covering up the extent of the SARS outbreak in Beijing and expressed incredulity that on April 3 the Chinese health minister said that the outbreak was under control. The situation was heating up.

For a moment it appeared that the central government would cooperate with WHO, especially after Chinese Premier Wen Jiabao warned that SARS could affect China's economy, international image, and social stability.[404] But, as Fidler concluded, this seeming cooperative spirit "was, yet again, a charade."[405] The need for further action on WHO's part became more urgent. It now recognized that cooperation from China was essential for combating the disease and foreign reporters began to chastise WHO for not confronting China over the "coverup."[406] On April 16, Chinese officials seemingly cooperated by allowing WHO representatives to visit military and other hospitals. But government officials engaged in further cover-up by transferring dozens of SARS patients to hospitals that would not be visited by WHO, an incident that was widely reported by the *Washington Post*. Finally, WHO openly criticized China at a news conference for not having received enough information from China.

Stage 3: Sudden Candor. On April 18, the leaders of China's Communist Party declared a nationwide war on SARS and ordered officials to stop the cover-up. The central government admitted in a nationally televised news conference that the number of people with SARS in the nation's capital was almost 10 times the number previously reported.[407] Two days later, the minister of health and the mayor of Beijing were removed from their Party posts. To restrict further spread of SARS, the government on April 21 canceled the traditional week-long May Day holiday and closed movie theaters, discos, Internet bars, public libraries, and churches. It also quarantined thousands of people and dozens of hospitals.

As the Chinese People's Political Consultative Conference, a government advisory body, explained, "If the SARS problem isn't dealt with well, our foreign relations and international standing will be damaged. . . . If this problem grows even bigger, the legitimacy of the government will be questioned. . . . This is no small matter."[408] China couldn't afford to continue in isolation because it was taking in $52 billion in foreign investment a year and churning out billions in exports.

On May 1, WHO reported a cumulative total of 5,865 probable SARS cases with 391 deaths in 27 countries.[409] But progress in combating SARS was made during the month and by the end of May the spread of SARS was effectively controlled. By June 2003, four months after the appearance of this new virus and respiratory disease, SARS was "stopped dead in its tracks."[410] The battle became one of the great success stories in the history of global public health efforts on infectious diseases and WHO was recognized for its leading role in containing SARS. Kleinman and Watson concluded that the Chinese style of intervention worked and was extolled as a means of controlling future epidemics.[411]

Response by Flextronics

Individual companies engaged in the same hesitancy to reveal information as the Chinese government, as the case of Flextronics demonstrates. Flextronics occupies a 150-acre factory complex in Zhuhai, on the western edge of the Pearl River Delta in Guangdong, next door to the former Portuguese colony of Macao.[412] This area is the world's most important manufacturing site and the place where SARS probably originated. Microsoft Corp.'s Xbox game consoles are made there. Its seven plants employ 11,600 workers and produce about $1 billion worth of products a year.

At first the company denied that it had a SARS problem after New York-based China Labor Watch hinted that it did. But on March 28 an assembly-line worker died of a respiratory disease in one of the company's dormitories and a friend of his also became sick. Management realized that the consequences of SARS could be severe. A severe epidemic could disrupt production for many global electronics companies, including Palm, IBM, Dell, Sony Ericsson, and Motorola. After quickly probing the death of the assembly-line worker and his friend, the company issued a statement saying that the two workers had suffered from tuberculosis, not SARS. The company provided copious medical reports and placed the 30 workers in the dead worker's unit in quarantine.

Soon, however, there was more openness. Local doctors and public health officials briefed the plant's staff and official notice boards throughout the factories were covered with information about SARS. That the message had an impact was shown by whereas in March hardly any workers wore masks, in early April a third did. All workers who had been outside the Zhuhai area had to have their temperature taken daily for ten days (which was believed to be the maximum incubation period for the virus).

Conscious of the need to keep customers informed, the company used phone calls, Internet links, and videoconferencing to keep them in the loop. They were assured that products could not be carriers of the virus because the bug survives only a few hours outside the body. It also corrected the rumor that Microsoft would shift production elsewhere.

Crisis Implications for WHO and China

The focus of an epidemic that might escalate into a pandemic is the death and illness toll worldwide. The fear with SARS was it could not be controlled effectively. SARS required a global health response and WHO provided it.

WHO faced a legitimacy crisis: Would its function be recognized and respected by the community of nations? Could it build its reputation of monitoring diseases in the world and sounding an alert early enough before diseases got out of control? WHO's legitimacy was threatened when China kept it at arm's length by restricting information. This lack of cooperation prevented WHO from pursuing its mission and led to rebukes of timidity from other member countries. WHO feared breaking its tradition of not publicly confronting and embarrassing member states during controversies. It also didn't want to create difficulties for NGOs who work with China and with whom WHO has "official relations" in the pursuit of public health purposes."

Despite these hesitations, WHO asserted its legitimacy by announcing a global alert on March 12 and a travel advisory on March 15. Becoming even bolder, on April 16, 2003, WHO publicly rebuked China for its continued lack of cooperation in providing honest information. When WHO's actions were endorsed at the May 2003 annual meeting of the World Health Assembly, which is WHO's highest policy-making body, its legitimacy was assured. Two resolutions were passed that supported WHO's leadership and actions taken during the SARS outbreak. The Assembly "acknowledged the need for intensive and urgent international collaboration and noted WHO's crucial role in leading the world-wide campaign to control and contain SARS."[413] The power exercised by WHO in China remains a striking feature of the SARS saga.

China faced a crisis of credibility and trust because it was more concerned about its own sovereignty and national interests than in the potential danger it could impose on other nations and their citizens. By suppressing vital statistics on the spread of SARS, China portrayed itself as a country willing to sacrifice the life and safety of citizens of other countries and their economies for the sake of maintaining the flow of tourists and businesspeople interested in trade with China. It also endangered its own citizens because of the very real risk that outbreaks within the country's own territory could spiral out of control.[414] By so doing it exposed a dangerous proneness to take risks in order to achieve declared goals. In short, economic growth took precedence over the safety of people. Its rights of sovereignty were supreme and the responsibilities of being a member of the world community were sacrificed.

As SARS forcefully demonstrated, collaboration is necessary on global health and other matters, such as global warming, where nationalism has become dysfunctional. Like Russia and other authoritarian governments, China learned that secrets about important issues can no longer be contained. The Internet has opened all societies. WHO's May 2003 statement summarizes the lessons learned from SARS:

> This is the most important lesson for all nations: In a globalized, electronically connected world, attempts to conceal cases of an infectious disease, for fear of economic and social consequences, must be recognized as a short-term stop-gap measure that carries a very high price—loss of credibility in the eyes of the international community, escalating negative domestic economic impact, damage to health and economics of neighboring countries, and a very real risk that outbreaks within the country's own territory can spiral out of control.[415]

Swine Flu: A Sequel?

Unlike China, Mexico immediately worked with WHO and was remarkably transparent when the swine flu broke out. It had learned and applied the lessons of SARS. There was good surveillance and case detection. It contacted those who were exposed to victims. In addition, the government responded with several actions: ordering the closure of all schools, night clubs, restaurants, and meetings nationwide; ordering the wearing of surgical masks, which the army distributed to people on the streets; using its abundant media to run public-service ads on radio and TV urging people not to use their own remedies and to go quickly to the hospital if taken ill; and starting a vaccination program.[416]

Origin

It's not certain when the swine flu in Mexico occurred. Mexican health officials noticed a huge spike in flu cases in late March and in mid-April 2009, and they began to notice otherwise healthy people dying from the virus. The deadly new type of flu led to 20 deaths in Mexico City and may have infected more than 1,000 people across the country. After U.S. health officials announced a possible swine flu outbreak, officials sounded the alarm on Thursday evening, April 25 by closing schools. On Saturday, President Felipe Calderon issued an emergency decree. Earlier, he had called in the army to distribute four million masks—called *tapabocas*, or cover-your-mouths—throughout the capital and its surrounding suburbs.[417] This action was symbolic and certainly communicated the message of the seriousness of the flu.

As in Guangdong, China, conditions in Mexico were conducive to the emergence of a new infection agent. Flu viruses could mutate rapidly and intensively because intensive animal husbandry procedures placed poultry and swine in close proximity to humans. Pigs are uniquely susceptible to infection with flu viruses of mammalian and avian origin. They serve as intermediaries in the transmission of flu viruses from birds to people. Pigs can serve as hosts in which two (or more) influenza viruses infecting an animal simultaneously can undergo "genetic reassortment"—creating a new organism. This condition was combined with unsanitary conditions, poverty, and grossly inadequate public health of all kinds. Expertise, coordination, and discipline are lacking in Mexico.[418]

Confirming whether sick people have the swine flu is more difficult than for SARS. SARS victims are contagious at a late stage of the disease when symptoms are already evident, making it easier to round up their contacts before they could spread the disease themselves. But victims of Mexican flu are often contagious before they show symptoms.[419]

Diplomatic Row with China

Mexico did not want the flu named "the Mexican flu," even though it originated there. It preferred calling it by the scientific name H1N1, so as not to jeopardize tourism and trade. U.S. Vice President Joe Biden did not help the Mexican cause. Although a U.S. government travel advisory simply stated "avoid all non-essential travel to Mexico," Biden, in an appearance on NBC's "Today Show" on April 30, said that he would advise his own family not to ride a plane, take the subway or put themselves in any confined spaces. The airline and public transit industries were also infuriated. American Public Transportation Association President William W. Millar retorted, "People should continue to ride public transportation. Buses and trains are as safe as any other public area." Secretary of Transportation Ray LaHood advised, "It is safe to fly."[420]

The Mexican government lashed out at China when Chinese health authorities rounded up and quarantined scores of Mexicans flying in on business and holiday trips.[421] Some 40 Mexican nationals in major Chinese cities were also retained for observation, even though tests indicated they did not have the virus.[422] These actions led to a diplomatic row between China and Mexico.[423] Mexico's foreign minister claimed Mexican citizens had been isolated in "unacceptable conditions" in China (which was actually a Hong Kong hotel). Their rooms were sealed off and twice each day nurses left thermometers outside their rooms to monitor their health.

Beijing's firm all-out war mentality is explained by wanting to avoid facing the accusation of a less than thorough response during the SARS epidemic. Furthermore, China feels more vulnerable because its population is highly concentrated. A diplomatic solution was agreed that both countries would send reciprocal chartered flights to bring back their citizens. China also clashed with Canada when 22 University of Montreal students with no apparent flu symptoms were put into isolation shortly after getting off a plane in China. A Foreign Ministry spokesman said the action was "in accordance with pertinent Chinese regulations."[424] Beijing also banned pork from Alberta, Canada, because, as the largest producer of pork in the world and consumer of half of the world's pork products, it felt vulnerable.

Swine Flu Implicates Pork

Calling H1N1 the swine flu became a public relations issue that worried the pork industry out of fear that consumers would stop eating pork. Because pigs were identified as the source of the epidemic, many people wrongly assumed that eating pork was dangerous. Russia banned meat imports from Mexico, as did several states in the United States.[425] As a result of such fears, Virginia's Smithfield Foods, the world's largest pig processor, which has a farm in Mexico, saw the price of its shares fall 12 percent on the New York Stock Exchange.

To correct misconceptions about eating pork, the National Pork Board launched an information campaign. A full-page ad appeared on May 6, 2009, signed by the board's president Steve Weaver. The headline read, "Let's Keep pork—and all the facts—on the table." The copy said, "Simply put, pork is safe. This is a fact supported by the experts." Two of them are then quoted: "You

cannot get H1N1 flu from eating pork. Pork products are perfectly safe"—
Janet Napolitano, U.S. Secretary of Homeland Security, and "You cannot get
this flu from eating pork or pork products"—Centers for Disease Control and
Prevention.[426]

Mad Cow Disease

The advent of mad cow disease was important because it showed how its recognition as a major crisis was staunchly resisted by farm interests and the government. The unwillingness of the government to face up to the issue and deliberately deceive its citizens undermined trust in government. Considering the few
humans whose lives were at risk, the issue demonstrates the psychology of risk:
people are unwilling to take even small and remote "dread" risks when alternatives are available. Consumers gave little thought to the exceptionally high
economic loss and the drastic action of slaughtering millions of cattle.

The scientific name for mad cow disease is Bovine Spongiform Encephalopathy (BSE). Its characteristic mark is found in the brain in the form of
star-shaped microscopic holes, or a condition called astrogliosis. It was first
noticed and studied in sheep that developed a disease known as scrapie (so-
called because sheep begin to behave oddly, rubbing off or "scraping" a good
deal of their wool). The conventional explanation is that BSE was originally a
form of scrapie, which entered the bovine food chain because of the practice of
feeding chopped-up sheep—and later chopped-up cows—to cows as a protein
supplement.[427]

BSE was officially discovered in Great Britain in 1986 by Dr. Colin Whita-
ker, a veterinarian, who reported his findings to the British Ministry of Agriculture, Food and Fisheries (MAFF).[428] It remained an obscure issue until March
20, 1996, when the U.K.'s chief medical officer Sir Kenneth Calman held a
press conference at which he stated that there was a link between the bovine
disease BSE and the human disease Creutzfeldt-Jakob Disease (CJD). The
declared link that eating British beef might cause CJD became the crisis event as it was widely disseminated by the mass media, domestically and
internationally.

The human disease CJD, which was discovered around 1920, had been associated with a naturally occurring degenerative brain disease that usually struck
the elderly. Its classic symptoms are "massive incoordination, seizures, and
dementia."[429] The prime suspect is something called a prion, a form of protein.
CJD strikes about one in a million people.

MAFF's central theme was that there was no evidence that BSE posed any
risk to human health. It attributed the occurrence of BSE in cattle mainly to
the addition of rendered food in the feeding of cattle. In the rendering process
animal parts and carcasses are boiled down and cooked to produce meat and
bone meal that is fed to animals as a food supplement. Rendering also produces
beef by-products for pharmaceuticals, desserts, cookies, gelatin, and gummy

candies. The industry may have become careless when it was deregulated during the administration of Margaret Thatcher.[430]

The initial solution to BSE was mild, but unrealistic. A panel known as the Southwood Committee, formed by MAFF, made three industry-friendly recommendations: only animals with BSE should be destroyed; ruminants should not be fed to cows; and milk from cows shown to have BSE should not be used.[431] But the number of cows infected with BSE did not decrease after this bovine offal ban went into effect in 1989. The recommendation made to MAFF by Dr. Richard Lacey, a clinical microbiologist from the University of Leeds, was that the whole herd where BSE occurred be slaughtered, not just the infected animal. This ultimate solution was unthinkable and rejected.[432]

That the force of denial was strong was evident when, in 1990, the British government launched an ad campaign to convince the public that eating British beef was safe. To prove it, the Minister of MAFF, John Gummer, used the desperate tactic at a press conference of himself eating a hamburger and feeding another to his four-year-old daughter. A new committee, the Spongiform Encephalopathy Advisory Committee (SEAC), was formed to continue research on BSE. At a SEAC session on March 19, 1994, senior members of the British Cabinet tried to suppress any announcement of Varient Creutzfeldt-Jakob Disease (vCJD), but Stephen Dorrell, Secretary of State for Health, insisted that the public be told. The following day, March 20, he spoke in the House of Commons and informed a stunned nation that, despite the government's many previous assertions to the contrary, BSE had probably spread to humans from eating beef.[433] Even then, as late as October 1994, the government claimed that there was no established link between BSE and the human spongiform disease.

Overnight the market for British beef collapsed. Even domestic fast-food suppliers, such as Wendy's, McDonald's, Burger King, and Wimpy's, refused to use domestic beef products [434] Making the crisis worse, the European Union on March 25 banned the worldwide sale of British beef. Denial became more difficult in 1996 when young people started contracting CJD, which was later determined to be a New Varient CJD (nvCJD). Years later, a small but emotional event hastened the day when the mad cow disease was officially recognized by the government. On May 10, 1990, British newspapers reported that a cat died of BSE and speculated that humans might be the next victims.[435] Finally, in 2000, the government capitulated and accepted Lacey's draconian recommendation to cull herds of cattle. When it was over, 4.5 million cattle perished.[436]

Other countries also encountered mad cow problems. Christi Donnelly of the Imperial College of London wrote in the journal *Nature* that at least 1,200 French cattle had been infected with BSE since 1987, and two people in France had died from CJD. In October 2000, the French government announced that beef from at least 11 potentially infected cattle had reached markets. In late November, Germany and Spain reported their first cattle cases.[437] In 2003, when an infected cow was found in Alberta, Canada, the United States shut its borders to Canadian beef, resulting in a loss of as much as $7 billion in revenue.[438]

The British government's handling of the BSE crisis demonstrates that "science cannot readily be separated from its political context by assigning responsibility for providing risk assessment to institutions or groups that are labeled scientific," concludes Patrick van Zuanenberg, author of a book on the relationship between science and politics.[439] He states that BSE represented a failure in science-based policy-making, arguing that science was invoked to try to provide "a justification for, and a masquerade with which to disguise, flawed policy judgments."[440]

Strategies for Dealing with Biological Crises

Pandemic Preparedness

In recent years, the world has become better prepared to deal with pandemic influenza as the need for international cooperation has been recognized. G. John Ikenberry of Princeton University wrote a paper making the case for centralized responses. He argued that America should help construct an "infrastructure of international cooperation . . . creating shared capacities to respond to a wide variety of contingencies."[441]

Pandemic preparedness has taken four forms: (1) improved health infrastructure; (2) production and storage of antiviral drugs; (3) vaccine campaigns; and (4) preparedness by organizations.

Improved Health Infrastructure

Lack of hospitals, shortage of personnel (doctors, nurses and others), and inadequate drugs and medical supplies hamper responses to biological diseases. Many victims of HIV/AIDS don't know that they have the disease because medical facilities to test for it aren't available, and even when detected and drugs are made available, their regular scheduled use is not administered or monitored by health workers. This problem is gradually subsiding with the creation of more medical infrastructure.[442]

The inadequacy of Mexico's health facilities became apparent during the government's inoculation efforts. To prevent onset of disease, a vaccine must be administered during the first couple of days after symptoms appear and adequate doses must be administered properly because improper vaccination can promote viral resistance and intensify an outbreak.[443]Although the public health system is now much better prepared to handle influenza than it was five to ten years ago, an especially deadly strain of flu would likely overwhelm even the most advanced health systems in the United States and other Western countries.[444]

Production and Storage of Antiviral Drugs

Vaccination programs can prevent some diseases from harming people. Greater attention has been given to the production and stockpiling of antiviral drugs during the swine flu epidemic. The Obama administration ordered vaccines early in spring 2009. It wasn't until November, however, that 40 million vaccines were ready. Excessive caution by the government was partly blamed. Public officials wondered, for example, whether the supply of seasonal flu vaccine would be sacrificed by moving quickly to create a vaccine for the new virus.[445]

The main problem, however, was the slow process for making flu shots that uses chicken eggs to grow the raw vaccine material. For this reason, the United States was initially told that vaccine wouldn't be available until September. Europe increasingly employs the faster method of using mammalian cells. Only two plants of Novartis use modern methods.[446] To be prepared for future outbreaks, the United States needs to invest in more modern facilities for manufacturing flu vaccine that enable rapid production.[447] In the U.K., the government planned to make enough vaccine available for the whole population. Its National Health Service would allow people worried about having been infected by the H1N1 virus to be diagnosed and prescribed medicine by phone or online.[448]

As a preparatory measure for swine flu, the United States made several recommendations. One was to stock up on antiviral drugs, such as Tamiflu and Relenza, and to urge increased production of such drugs. Hospitals were told to set aside more isolation rooms and formulate procedures to keep healthcare workers from getting infected. At the beginning of the swine flu epidemic, the CDC in Atlanta was ready to send teams to New York, California, Texas and Mexico, if requested. It could also assist by releasing supplies of Tamiflu, masks gloves, purifying gel, ventilators and other goods from the National Strategic Stockpile. Finally, the CDC was creating test kits for 140 American labs and dozens of international ones to allow them to test for the new flu.

WHO convened an emergency meeting of experts on April 25, but said it needed more information before raising the pandemic alert level.[449]

Vaccine Campaign

To deal with swine flu, President Obama in May 2009 requested a $1.5 billion emergency appropriation, including development of a vaccine. It was ordered but, by the middle of October, the 40 million doses that had been expected by the end of October had been delayed.[450] Some employers pay drug-makers an annual fee to stockpile antivirals, noted Ralph Dunham, president of Marsh Canada, a risk consulting business.[451]

Public cooperation with a vaccine campaign, however, may be limited. A survey of just over 1,000 adults by the Pew Research Center for the People &

the Press showed that 47 percent wouldn't get the vaccine and, of these, 35 percent said they believed the vaccine is too risky or that it hadn't been thoroughly tested. Twenty-three percent said they don't get the flu or just avoid getting shots, and 16 percent said they don't believe in vaccines, or they think vaccines make them sick.[452] Some skeptics of the vaccine are worried about the possible side effect of the Guillain-Barre Syndrome (GBS), a potentially life-threatening neurological disorder. In the 1976 vaccine campaign against swine flu, hundreds of people out of more than 40 million vaccinated contracted GBS.

Preparedness by Organizations

Business and other organizations should prepare for a possible pandemic by engaging in contingency planning. They should thoroughly assess how their operations would be impacted and how they would respond. Disruptions in services and supplies might last for up to 18 months. Retailers would be affected by customer fear of public places, business travel might be restricted and business failures accelerated.[453] Most important, the possible impact on employees must be considered.

In a true pandemic, 30–35 percent of the population might be either sick, or looking after someone who's sick. Commerce Secretary Gary Locke, Health and Human Services Secretary Kathleen Segelius and Homeland Security Secretary Janet Napolitna advised in a news conference that businesses should allow employees flexibility to stay home to recuperate or care for sick relatives. They should think about alternative work arrangements such as telecommuting.[454] In addition, a transit shut or mandatory quarantines would affect employee absenteeism. To prepare, organizations are advised to build redundancy into critical staff positions, cross-train employees in essential job skills, or identify other ways to augment the workforce.[455] Employers should also provide accessible hand sanitizers, anti-bacterial soap, and cleaners and wipes. In the extreme, they should discourage sharing of work-stations, telephones, computer keyboards, staplers, pens and pencils.

Training and simulation exercises increase the chances that contingency plans are properly executed. About 2,725 U.S. financial institutions engaged in a crisis scenario in October 2007 when they were fed scenarios on the spread of a virtual outbreak. Employees with names beginning with certain letters of the alphabet were assumed unable to work and the remaining ones to follow pre-determined procedures. The exercise was modeled after one carried out by The Financial Services Authority (FSA), Britain's financial regulator in late 2006. It resulted in forcing institutions to think much more systematically about human resource policies. For example, even if stocks of flu medicines were in stock, it was discovered that no decision had been made about which employees would be treated. They also planned to redeploy staff from functions such as sales and product development to positions directly serving customers.[456]

Deciding on Ethical Issues in Advance

The allocation of resources involves many ethical issues that should be decided in advance. The University of Toronto's Joint Centre for Bioethics has identified several of these issues in advance of a second wave of the H1N1 influenza pandemic based on views obtained from 500 Canadians through a national telephone survey and nearly 100 more via a series of town hall meetings nationwide.[457] Their findings pertain to:

- Obligation of healthcare workers: 90 percent said healthcare workers (HCWs) should report to work and face all risks, provided safety precautions are in place. HCWs are viewed as having an implicit social contract based on their profession and training to provide care under adverse conditions. HCWs should, however, be provided with free disability insurance and death benefits during a flu crisis, said 85 percent, and 84 percent think HCWs who feel unsafe at work have a right to file a grievance. *The Economist* wrote that local media in Mexico reported several cases of ambulance drivers who refused to transport flu patients.[458]
- Allocation of limited medical resources such as ventilators, vaccines and antivirals: Although most swine flu victims can probably be treated routinely, the seriously ill will need scarce and expensive equipment. Regarding antivirals, 94 percent said HCWs should receive priority in a pandemic and 89 percent believe children should be given second priority. Age alone, however, should not be a proxy for the seriousness of a disease or provide the basis for allocation decisions. The needs of swine flu victims must also compete with those of accident victims.
- Obligation of rich countries to share such resources with those less fortunate: About 91 percent identified saving lives as the most important goal of pandemic influenza preparations, but 44 percent endorsed saving lives solely in Canada as the highest priority and 50 percent endorsed saving lives globally as the highest priority. Further questions are whether countries have the right to close their borders to travelers coming from affected areas and how collaborative efforts can minimize harms, avoid stigmatization, and prevent unnecessary constraints on international travel and trade.
- Government restrictive measures: Government may need to limit such individual freedoms as traveling, freedom of assembly, and privacy in order to protect the public good. Eighty-five percent thought the government should have that power during a pandemic, but it has the reciprocal obligation to provide food, shelter, social support, and other basic needs both during the restriction and afterwards.
- Availability of information: Information should be available through a variety of sources for both professionals and the public. Transparency should be the rule and recipients should know the source of the information.

Public Education

In the United States, the CDC recommends ways the public can prevent the new flu: wash your hands; cough into your sleeve; avoid touching your eyes, nose or mouth; stay home if you're sick, keep sick children out of school, and follow public health advice regarding school closure, avoiding crowds and other social distancing measures.[459] Soap and hand-sanitizer manufacturers and makers of designer face-masks ramped up marketing efforts. Henkel stepped up advertising of Dial soap and encouraged people to wash hands, and Johnson & Johnson, which makes Purell Instant Hand Sanitizer, updated hygiene information on its website Purell.com.[460]

A new 24-page document by the Food and Drug Administration (FDA) proposes advertising guidelines for drug and medical-device makers. It suggests ways to present risk information to consumers and health-care professionals. The FDA says that omission or minimization of risk information is the most frequent violation of its rules. One example is that when an ad says a product requires monthly blood tests it should state so in clear language rather than saying there might be a need for "certain monitoring." It also points out that details about a drug's side effects might give a different "net impression" if it contains upbeat music and "discordant" images of patients benefitting from the medicine.[461]

As with natural disasters, efforts have been made to improve the early detection and reporting of diseases. As the SARS epidemic showed, detection can be impaired in areas where medical facilities don't exist, when government officials are uncooperative, and when people fear to report because of such disincentives as not wanting their livestock culled. In the case of HIV/AIDS, a major reason for not getting tested is being "afraid to find out."

Mad cow surveillance is now possible by subjecting every cow at slaughter to a so-called rapid test. It costs about $20 per carcass and screens for BSE in a few hours rather than days. Creekstone Farms in Arkansas City, Kansas, wanted to use this test, in part to enter the Korean beef market. South Korea bans U.S. beef because Koreans are worried about BSE.[462] The European Union uses the rapid test and between 2001 and 2006 turned up 1,117 cases of mad cow disease in seemingly healthy cattle approved for slaughter. Protecting the beef industry, the U.S. Agriculture Department refused Creekstone's request to use the test, saying that if one company used it consumer demand would drive all companies to use it and thus add to the price of beef. Michael Hansen, a senior scientist at Consumers Union, calls this decision "madness."[463]

The world's pandemic-alert system is still distressingly secretive, reported *The Economist*. The reasons are understandable but short-sighted and potentially harmful. Governments fear that full disclosure could cause locals to panic and hurt tourism and trade. China seems to have learned from its SARS experience. Its greater transparency was evident when, in May 2008, it experienced an outbreak of a less exotic and better understood bug, called enterovirus, which can cause a dangerous form of hand, foot and mouth disease. Despite nervousness that the outbreak occurred just three months before the Olympics, China reported a total of 15,799 cases with 28 deaths centered in the town of Fuyang in the central province of Anhui. The previous year there were 880,000 cases and 17 deaths.[464]

Happily, more nations are favoring transparency and cooperating in international efforts to study diseases and report them. For example, the Indonesian government now allows its genomic data on bird-flu viruses to be accessed by anyone.[465] A new partnership, called The Global Pandemic Initiative, formed in May 2006, is a collaboration between WHO and the CDC, together with IBM, and over a dozen other groups. It is part of a global preparedness program for responding to potential infectious disease outbreaks. Another new group is the Canadian government's Global Public Health Intelligence Network (GPHIN) that searches public databases in seven languages looking for early signs of disease outbreak.

During the SARS and H1N1 epidemics, several nations, such as Japan, used thermal imaging cameras to screen passengers coming in on flights from Mexico, Canada and the United States. France raises awareness of the flu's danger by posting the warning to passengers traveling to Mexico to avoid large crowds and to wash their hands regularly.

WHO Alert Levels

To help national and regional health authorities determine what efforts to undertake in responding to health warnings, WHO has developed a six-level scale. Action is proposed when level 4 is reached because it signals that countries should prepare for more outbreaks. At this level, WHO concentrates on mitigation because preventing spread is no longer possible. A pandemic could be imminent. A 5 alert level indicates the H1N1 virus has caused outbreaks in at least two countries in one region. A 6 alert level indicates a pandemic. Three conditions are necessary for a pandemic to occur: (1) Virus has to cause high mortality; (2) it must spread relatively quickly and easily among people; and (3) its incubation time in a host has to be sufficiently long.[466]

Some authorities believe that WHO's pandemic scale sends the wrong signal to the public. "It can reach its top level in a mild pandemic so it appears to foretell doomsday even if people around the world have only the sniffles."[467] Recognizing the dilemma, the director general of WHO states, "We cannot overreact, and we cannot be complacent either."[468] Trying to balance the genuine danger of a serious outbreak with the risk of overreacting; this is the key communications lesson.

New means of warning citizens are being offered. New America Media (NAM) unveiled an emergency network system that will use ethnic media outlets to deliver important health and emergency alerts to ethnic communities across the country. Ethnic media reps will activate their media outlets to deliver the messages to their millions of readers, viewers, and listeners not usually reached by mainstream media.[469]

The Internet serves as a fast early warning of flu outbreaks. Google has a Flu Trend site that displays its findings on flu-related keywords. It found a strong correlation between when people searched flu keywords and when they have had flu-like symptoms. Its analysis uses a seven-tier scale of flu activity ranging from "minimal" to "intense." The site includes CDC flu prevention messages, a flu vaccination locator, and links to flu-related news items. A user of the Internet is Harvard Medical School's Children's Hospital, which has a site called HealthMap that reviews 24,000 websites for disease-related terms. A world map then shows the results with colored markers for dengue fever, avian flu and other diseases.[470]

Quick and Decisive Response

Quick and decisive action is facilitated when health organizations have up-to-date contingency plans. Simple matters such as being able to contact one's manager and supervisors are essential and can be organized in advance through websites and phone hotlines or email. All teams should be encouraged to set up "calling trees" to check in with other members in a crisis. Responsibility should be assigned to specific people. Ad hoc measures taken by *Wall Street Journal*'s office in Hong Kong included wiring up employees so they could work from home, providing the right masks to protect people, and quarantining offices.

Conclusions

Biological crises are another kind of threat from the physical environment. The influenza outbreak in 1918–19 is a reminder of our vulnerability to diseases whose exact nature if not known. The global reach of such outbreaks, especially since the intensification of globalization, was demonstrated by the SARS epidemic. It showed that nations could not keep such infections a secret, that international cooperation is an imperative.

A danger in the response to biological crises is that economic and political considerations can contaminate a rational, scientific analysis of an outbreak. This was most dramatically evidenced in the response by agricultural interests and the British government to the mad cow disease, which severely crippled the British cattle and beef industry. China's initial response to SARS was also impeded by concern for its global trade and for its national image.

The response to biological crises borrows some of the hazard management strategies used with natural disasters. The emphasis, however, is more on preparedness, early detection and prevention. As with natural disasters, when a crisis erupts, a quick response is needed. Local actions are no longer sufficient, for this is increasingly a global task. A beneficial side effect may be that other forms of international cooperation will be stimulated.

Chapter 7

Technological Crises

Since the modern industrial age, crises caused by human application of science and technology are far greater in number and consequence than natural disasters. When humans attempt to harness or convert the physical environment, they encounter varying degrees of risk and uncertainty which, when pushed to extremes, create technological crises. Space exploration by NASA, construction of nuclear power facilities, extraction of oil from deep waters, and invention of genetically modified (GM) crops and new drugs represent advanced technological enterprises. More recently, nanotechnology became the new technology with many unknowns and uncertainties.

Industrial and other technological accidents raise a difficult question of classification: Are they technological crises or crises of management failure caused by negligence, faulty decisions, or skewed priorities? The explosion of BP's Deepwater Horizon rig in the Gulf of Mexico appears on the surface as a crisis of mismanagement, and is so-called by most observers, because so many wrong decisions were made. But it should also be viewed as a technological crisis because a deeper explanation is that the intricacies of deepwater drilling are still at the technological frontier. As stated in a *New York Times* summary article reporting on the rig's final hours, "Investigators have dissected BP's well design and Halliburton's cementing work, uncovering problem after problem."[471] Had well-known and ordinary technologies been involved, the explosion and sinking of the rig would simply qualify as an industrial accident, a designation that applies to "normal accidents" in airline crashes, industrial plants, and in building, road and bridge construction.

To qualify as a technological crisis, accidents must arise from relatively unknown, untested, or unsuspected aspects of technology. The collapse of Minneapolis's I-35W bridge qualifies as a technological crisis because it was later discovered that it was caused by a faulty engineering design.[472] Similarly, when the three "floating walkways" in the Kansas City Hyatt Regency crashed to the floor on July 17, 1981, killing 114 patrons, it was considered a technological disaster because a metal fabricator took a fatal shortcut.[473] Although the engineers designed two of the three walkways to hang on common, vertical metal rods, the fabricator substituted shorter rods hanging from one level to the next.

The engineers, however, were implicated because they had signed off on the final drawing showing the shorter rods.

An event may also be classified as a technological crisis when technology is complex and coupled, i.e., one sub-system of a larger system can trigger events in another sub-system, and something goes wrong in the system as a whole. It is the disruption of an entire system, such as Three Mile Island or Chernobyl, that distinguishes a crisis from an incident or accident, says Charles Perrow in his book, *Normal Accidents: Living with High-Risk Technologies*.[474] The explosion of BP's Deepwater Horizon fits Perrow's characterization of a complex and coupled system where one event led to a chain of catastrophic events.

As the Chernoybl explosion of 1986 demonstrated, nuclear power is the quintessential example of a technological crisis. Chernobyl's death rate continues to climb because of the long-term effects of radiation on the surrounding land and the workers who built an enormous shelter facility (the sarcophagus) to contain further radiation. The shelter required 400,000 tons of concrete and 7,000 tons of steel, and was later further fortified with new metal supports.[475] A 30-kilometer exclusion zone surrounds the infamous plant. Some ecologists say that the consequences of the disaster will be felt for another 150 years. Even now, bans on consumption of meat extend beyond Belarus, Russia, and the Ukraine to markets in Sweden and Britain.[476] Because of the fallout, nearly 370 farms in Britain are still restricted in the way they rear sheep and use land. This number has dropped over 95 percent since 1986, when approximately 9,700 farms and 4,225,000 sheep were restricted in the U.K.[477]

Technological crises share many similarities in hazard management with natural disasters. A big difference, however, is that while people do not hold anyone responsible for causing a natural catastrophe, they do assign blame for a technological disaster because they believe technology is subject to human manipulation. Something could presumably be done to prevent technological disasters, and various kinds of "technological fixes" could be applied. This same attitude is increasingly transferred to natural disasters as people tend to blame authorities if they fail to plan for disasters or respond to them poorly.

The public expects the users of technology to control the occurrence of accidents and to reduce harm to a tolerable level. Just what level is tolerable is itself one of the thorniest questions facing policymakers. What is known is that tolerance tends to be greater when people believe the product of the technology is essential to human well-being. Tolerance is less when proponents of a new technology make over-optimistic claims about its safety. The combination of cost/benefit factors explains the hopes and fears associated with such emerging technologies as nanotechnology discussed in the appendix of this chapter.

The Rapid Pace of Growth of Technology

Technology has been a prime mover of change throughout human history. Through the invention of tools and use of reason, humans learned to control the physical environment for their own benefit. In later history, the development of steam engines, the building of railroads, the invention of electric light, the widespread reach of the automobile, and, in the field of communication technology, the rise in the use of telephones, radio, television, cell phones, computers, and the Internet have demonstrated the impact of technology.

Ray Kurzweil, an inventor and futurist, shows how the adoption rates of communication technologies over the past century have accelerated. He states: "the time to adopt new paradigms is going down by half each decade. At this rate, technological progress in the twenty-first century will be equivalent (in the linear view) to two hundred centuries of progress at the rate of progress in 2000."[478] He predicts that by 2020 artificial intelligence will match the capability of the brain. Expressed another way, he says, "we won't experience one hundred years of technological advance in the 21st century; we will witness on the order of 20,000 years of progress . . . or about 1,000 times greater than what was achieved in the 20th century."[479] Because technology grows rapidly at an exponential rate, we must expect that society's absorption of change will not be smooth and crises are likely to occur with increasing frequency.

Relevance of Risk Analysis

The uncertainties associated with technological advances create a need for risk assessment so that the probability of undesirable consequences—death, injuries, damage, and disasters—can be averted or at least minimized. Risk assessment attempts to estimate the nature, severity and likelihood of harm to human health or the environment. Technical specialists in industrial research, design, development, testing, and engineering usually begin this process.

Others than technical specialists also participate in risk assessment because managers must factor social, economic and political values into a decision. These specialists remain free from the "risk management" biases of technical experts. In the field of biotechnology, for example, the importance of considering people's perception of the risk of using GM products is demonstrated in that to this day some consumers resist these products. Political repercussions also remain as countries such as Britain require GM products to be labeled as such.

Opposing the decisions of technical experts can, however, create dangers and cause technological crises. The *Challenger* explosion, for example, was partly blamed on National Aeronautical Space Administration (NASA) officials who neglected safety concerns out of competitive and political considerations. An excessive concern for bottom-line results is suspected of having led to shortcuts that contributed to the Deepwater Horizon explosion in the Gulf of Mexico.

Problems can also arise when experts and the public see risks differently. The U.S. Environmental Protection Agency has found that while experts consider radon, indoor air pollution, and pesticide residues to pose greater health risks than toxic waste dumps and underground storage tanks, the public fears the latter more.[480] They are more willing to take risks when they feel they are in control.

From a social, political and psychological viewpoint, therefore, managing technological crises is much more complex than managing natural crises. People increasingly want to know how management makes risk assessment decisions and, in situations involving them personally, they want a voice. If they perceive a facility to be intolerably dangerous or noxious, as, for example, in a community hazardous-waste siting situation, they will protest. Furthermore, if people perceive that escalating risks and costs of technology exceed its benefits, they may opt to sacrifice product innovation and economic growth. For these reasons, the subjects of risk perception and public attitudes toward science and technology play an important role in public reactions to technological crises.[481]

Three Recent Technological Crises

BP's Oil Rig in the Gulf of Mexico Explodes

BP's Deepwater Horizon rig, located about 50 miles from the Louisiana coast, was buffeted by a series of explosions on April 20, 2010, and sank two days later.[482] Although the crisis exemplifies mismanagement (see Chapter 10), its fuller understanding requires it also to be seen as a technological crisis. Drilling contractor Transocean Ltd., the world's largest offshore drilling contractor with more than 21,000 workers and 140 rigs, operated the drilling operation for BP,[483] and Halliburton handled a critical cementing process. The explosion killed 11 of its 126 crew members and twisted the pipe that connects the rig to the well.

Oil spewed out of the wellhead almost a mile under sea level and wasn't stopped until July 15, 87 days after the accident, when BP installed a new, tight-fitting cap on the well.[484] The well wasn't declared dead, however, until a "bottom kill" cementing process sealed it from below, which was completed on September 18.[485] BP initially estimated the gushing oil at 5,000 barrels a day, but was later found to be closer to 60,000 barrels, an error that contributed to serious miscalculations in the cementing process.[486] The final estimate was that almost 5 million barrels were spilled into the Gulf, far exceeding the 240,000 barrels in Prince William Sound when the *Exxon Valdez* hit a submerged reef in 1989.

The resulting spill became the United States' worst environmental disaster as oil slicks and submerged tar balls spread to parts of Louisiana, Mississippi, Texas, Alabama and the Florida Panhandle.[487] As the spill continued, the economies of shore communities suffered. These communities are highly dependent on shrimping, clamming, commercial and sports fishing, and tourist business. The five Gulf Coast states had $10.54 billion in combined seafood sales and employed more than 200,000 people in 2008.[488] Louisiana alone provides about 45 percent of oysters consumed in the United States. Recreational fishing alone amounts to about $41 billion a year.

Hearings by the National Commission on Deepwater Horizon Spill, established by President Obama, put a human face on the economic disaster.[489] Mayors and business groups vividly described the hardships wrought on owners of recreational and other fishing vessels, small hotels, and rod and tackle shops. Many complained that even though many areas were still open to fishing and beach recreation, national media coverage of the spill created a perception of widespread spoilage that discouraged tourists from visiting. Faced with mortgage payments, electric bills and other costs, many businesses feared they would lose their livelihoods. The damage to oyster beds, shrimp and other marine life was feared to last a long time. A mid-August report from the Woods Hole Oceanographic Institution and a Georgia Sea Grant program and the University of Georgia estimated that up to 79 percent of the oil spilled might still be in the Gulf, some in an underwater oil plume 3,000 feet below the surface, which was estimated to be 22 miles long and more than a mile wide.[490] Hopelessness was pervading citizens in coastal towns as they realized their way of life might permanently be changed.

Ironically, just weeks before the accident, President Obama announced that his administration would approve more deep sea drilling as part of his proposed energy bill to augment the country's energy needs. This need was recognized as easy "hanging fruit" oil as exploration on land and shallow waters shrank. Norwegian and British companies had found oil in the North Sea and profitably drilled for several decades.[491] The industry had convinced the administration, state governments, and even environmentalists, that the technology of ocean drilling was far enough advanced to be safe. That optimistic assumption was now questioned and the Obama administration announced that no applications for offshore drilling permits would go forward until the Department of the Interior completed a review of safety policies governing offshore drilling.[492] A six-month drilling moratorium was imposed soon after the Deepwater Horizon explosion.[493]

Especially in recent years, the optimistic view grew that the technology of deep sea drilling had progressed remarkably. In his 2008 article, "Deep Water, Deep Drilling Stimulate Gulf of Mexico," Sam Fletcher stated that over the last 10 years, oil-drilling technology advanced as much as it did in the previous 30 years.[494] From 1997 to 2005, the number of deepwater projects in the Gulf of Mexico grew from 17 to 86, and ultra-deepwater projects—those at a depth of more than 5,000 feet—more than doubled in the last two years before 2008. BP's well, called Macondo, was 5,000 feet (almost one mile) below sea level. "Cracking the Gulf" had become the cutting edge of the industry's technical expertise.

Deficiency of Deep Sea Drilling Technology

Despite enormous progress, especially in exploration, the technology of deep sea drilling is still at the frontier of knowledge and engineering know-how, which is why the BP disaster preeminently qualifies as a technological crisis. Although the oil industry contends that the Deepwater Horizon rig catastrophe was a unique event, recent history of offshore drilling suggests otherwise. The *Wall Street Journal* reviews several incidents: a blowout off the coast of Australia left oil flowing into the Timor Sea for weeks and a gas leak off the Coast of Norway in the North Sea aboard a production platform almost replicated what happened in the Gulf of Mexico. Norwegian oil companies had 37 oil and gas releases and "well incidents" in 2009, up 48 percent from 2008 and the highest level since 2003.[495]

As the confused decision-making and wrong judgments by managers, engineers and workers on the rig and at Houston headquarters indicate, the BP catastrophe is best known as a crisis of mismanagement. "The rapid push into deeper water means that some projects rely on technology that hasn't been used before," said Ben Casselman and Guy Chazan.[496] Some characterized this challenge as the counterpart of inner space to the outer space faced by astronauts and robotics operators.[497] Tony Hayward, BP's beleaguered chief executive, likened the effort to plug the company's Macondo well to the Apollo 13 spaceship rescue.[498] He acknowledged, "What is undoubtedly true is that we did not have the tools you would want in your tool kit."[499]

Extracting the natural resource of oil from difficult locations in nature requires careful and continuous analysis of the specific geological characteristics of each site. This reality was recognized by Darrell Hollek, vice president of Gulf of Mexico operations and development at Anadarko Petroleum Corp, a partner of BP, who stated, "Technology is absolutely critical in getting into deeper water—seismic imaging, drilling deeper wells of 30,000 plus feet." After details emerged from initial investigations into events leading to the explosion, Anadarko's CEO Jim Hacket commented that he was "shocked" by how "BP operated unsafely and failed to monitor and react to several critical warning signs during the drilling of the well."[500] BP's CEO, Tony Hayward acknowledged, "We underestimated the complications involved in drilling for oil at a depth of 1,500 metres."[501] BP should have known that when technology contains danger, a scientific engineering approach must be used and strict procedures followed.

BP's internal and government investigations into the explosion show that BP violated its own industry guidelines and chose risky procedures in the hope of cutting costs and saving time, as the following list by the *Guardian* illustrates:

- Adopted a cheap design for the well, choosing a single casing rather than a more sophisticated design.
- Chose the cheapest option of using just six "centralisers," which hold the casing in the center of the borehole, instead of the 21 advised by Halliburton, which was responsible for the cementing process. (Halliburton later said that BP ignored its warnings that the cement job would likely fail if BP didn't use more centralizers.)[502]

- Failed to conduct acoustic tests to measure the efficacy of the cementing of the well to block off gas flows. (The cementing process, which seals the drilling pipes to the seabed was not completed and pressure tests were skipped.[503] It was forgotten that in a 2007 study by Mineral Management Service (MMS), flaws in cementing were found to be a factor in 18 of 39 well blowouts in the Gulf of Mexico over a 14-year period.)[504]
- Failed to conduct full tests of the proper workings of the new well system by circulating drilling mud from its bottom to the surface.
- Failed to install a "lockdown sleeve" that locks the wellhead and the casing at the level of the sea floor.[505]

Pattern of Cost-Cutting

These cost-cutting measures were motivated by an excessively strong bottom-line culture, which is a symptom of skewed values.[506] Hayward's cost-cutting drive succeeded in reduced costs in 2009 by $4 billion, but at a high risk, as events proved.[507] Peter N. Spotts, a writer for *The Christian Science Monitor* notes, the spill "could be the offshore oil industry's version of the *Challenger* or *Columbia* space shuttle disasters—tragedies whose causes had as much to do with attitudes and organizational culture as with hardware or operating conditions."[508]

This culture was evidenced after BP acquired Amoco's Texas City refinery in 1998. BP's excesses of cost-cutting was blamed by the U.S. Chemical Safety Board, an independent federal agency, for an explosion that killed 15 people and injured 170. After hundreds of engineers left Amoco, they were not replaced and BP instead relied on sub-contractors. Belatedly, BP subsequently announced it would invest more than $1 billion in a multi-year improvement program to upgrade the refinery, emphasizing safety.[509] But the promise was not fulfilled, as confirmed by a fine of $50.6 million levied against BP in August 2010 for failing to fix safety hazards at its refinery.[510]

Another example of skewed values was BP's neglect of its 34-inch Arctic pipeline, linked to the TransAlaska Pipeline System, which resulting in a leakage in March 2006 of 267,000 gallons of crude oil—the worst in the history of the North Slope. Later the same year, BP's cost-cutting and poor maintenance of Alaskan pipelines caused "severe corrosion" that led to a catastrophic pipeline split that temporarily closed Alaska's entire oil production. A former BP engineer in Alaska complained, "There is no doubt that cost-cutting and profits have taken precedence over safety and the environment."[511] The corrosion of BP's safety culture was spreading.

Insufficient Pre-existing Technology to Cap the Well

Revealing the lack of research in downstream hazard management measures was the inability of BP to stop the gushing oil from the wellhead for weeks after the accident. Its initial reliance on the existing technology of unmanned remotely operated submersibles to manipulate the valves and pipes in the defunct blowout preventer (BOP) failed. So did its next attempt to position a 78-ton dome, called a coffer dam, over the mouth of the oil well. It took two weeks to build and deploy the dome, and some in the industry questioned why the idea of using a containment dome took so long and why, as part of its contingency planning, BP didn't have one ready to use, and why it was untested at this depth.[512]

As Laurent Belsie, a staff writer for *The Christian Science Monitor*, commented, "BP has in essence been trying to invent ways to stop the blowout in the Gulf on the fly."[513] A former Transocean executive said, "There should be technology that's pre-existing and ready to deploy at the drop of a hat . . . . It shouldn't have to be designed and fabricated now, from scratch." Even Hayward admitted, "probably BP didn't do enough planning in advance of the disaster." He also said there are some capabilities "that we could have available to deploy instantly, rather than creating as we go."[514] The dome failed to cap the leaking BOP because the magnitude of the spill was underestimated and the dome got clogged with crystallized gas, called hydrates. Again scientific facts and knowledge lagged.[515]

Further steps to cap the wellhead were undertaken. After assembling a team of experts from other oil companies and universities, BP successfully placed a newly designed cap made by Cameron, the manufacturer of BOPs, over the existing BOP, and on August 4 started pumping heavy drilling mud into the well to stop leaks.[516] Called "static kill," the wellhead was sealed with cement on July 15, which successfully stopped the flow of oil and gas.

Why this static kill procedure was not used earlier by BP "dumbfounded" the whole industry, said experts from Wild Well Control Inc., a Houston firm. Supporting this view was Gene Beck, professor of petroleum engineering at Texas A&M University, who commented, "it's fairly obvious they should have intervened directly on the well and not resorted to stopgap measures.[517] These criticisms further indicate that the technology of deep sea drilling was far from having established standards.

Poor Maintenance and Weak Oversight

There is widespread agreement that upstream hazard management procedures were bungled. An alarm system that should have alerted workers of danger aboard the rig, according to testimony by the vessel's chief electrician, had been switched off because Transocean rig managers "did not want people woke up at 3 o'clock in the morning due to false alarms."[518] Another critical emergency system, the emergency power system which is meant to kick on within seconds of a blackout, failed to function at the time of the explosion. It had previously failed in one of the routine inspections. It was just another part of an overall condition of overdue maintenance on equipment, which included the vital BOP.

Summary

There were serious errors of judgment on the rig, which signify mismanagement. But the fundamental fault of BP's operations decisions is that it treated deep sea drilling as routine technology, rather than recognizing its innovative and experimental aspects. Despite the enormous strides made in deep water drilling, BP insufficiently understood the magnitude of its technological hazards. More research and testing of procedures and equipment to control the flow of oil and gas from the wellhead were needed. *The Economist* believes "there is every chance that technology that is up to the job will be developed fairly quickly: it is a very innovative industry."[519]

Nuclear Accidents at Kepco and JCO in Japan

On August 9, 2004, a radioactive steam leak at the Kansai Electric Power Company (Kepco) plant in Mihama, 198 miles west of Tokyo, killed four people and seriously injured seven others. The pipe that burst apparently had not been inspected since the plant was built in 1976.[520] Earlier in the year, on February 25, eight workers were exposed to low-level radiation after being sprayed with contaminated coolant water at Japan Atomic Power's plant in northwestern Japan. Public confidence in nuclear power in Japan was further undermined by a July 2004 scandal that the Ministry of Economy, Trade and industry (METI), which regulates the energy sector, had covered up a 1994 report on the costs of using recycled fuel to power some reactors.[521]

The worst reported case of a nuclear accident was at JCO Co.'s fuel-reprocessing plant in Tokaimura, 69 miles northeast of Tokyo, at around 10:30 a.m. on September 30, 1999. It killed two workers and exposed hundreds to radiation.[522] The event demonstrated the almost complete absence of contingency planning, management failure in operating the plant, and wholly inadequate emergency response. Virtually all of the technological hazard management principles, as discussed later, were violated.

Although the accident occurred around 10:30 a.m., it was not until 3 p.m. that the necessity of measuring neutrons was recognized, and not until 5 p.m. that a measurement was taken. It showed that almost five times the level of neutron rays were emitted in an hour than the limit for safe exposure for an entire year. The 310,00 people living within about six miles of the plant who were in danger were told to stay at home, and the evacuation of neighborhood citizens was initiated on the national level. The crisis rule is that decisions regarding emergency responses should be decentralized to the locality where the crisis occurs. To reassure citizens, the government distributed a photo to the media showing the Japanese prime minister eating a slice of melon cultivated near the site of the accident. The company promised to pay damages for the nuclear accident.

Worldwide, the industry has done a poor job of reporting accidents that are variously labeled "serious" or "significant." In Japan, the Tokyo Electric Power

Co. was charged with falsification of safety records and delays in reporting accidents.[523] In a mishap in Hungary on April 10, 2003, when radioactive fuel-rod assemblies were placed in a cleaning tank a warning signal on a radiation detector went off even though no radiation was released. On March 1, 2006, a Bulgarian plant near the town of Kozloduy experienced a control-rod failure, a problem that the Bulgarian nuclear regulator didn't acknowledge for 13 days and initially said had no safety significance. But emissions of radioactive gases such as xenon and krypton occurred and the plant operator wasn't able to remove the radioactive fuel until nearly four years later. The record of the nuclear industry worldwide is not reassuring.

The Great Northeast Blackout of 2003

The Thursday, August 14, 2003, power blackout in two countries, the United States and Canada, and eight states was the worst power failure in North American history, affecting about 50 million people in the Midwest, Northeast and Canada. The blackout resembled a natural disaster in that it affected a large region and crossed political boundaries. For most residents it was only a matter of inconvenience, but for utility companies, the blackout was a true crisis because their revenue-producing ability, growth, and reputations were at stake.

The blackout knocked out twice or more power than the previous U.S. blackout in 1996 and lasted far longer.[524] Because the system failed at 4:20 p.m. when people left their work, disruptions were numerous. In New York City office buildings, elevators stopped running, lights went off, computers went down, and cellphone service was disrupted. The city's massive train system, which transports 4.5 million people on an average weekday, stopped running. In Toronto, subway trains were out of operation for the whole weekend after the Thursday blackout.[525] Airlines canceled over 1,000 flights.

In hotels, air conditioners, elevators and some keyless entry systems were disabled. Even hotels with backup generators didn't have enough power to keep the water running in guest rooms. Some hotel guests slept in lobbies and conference rooms, and in Times Square some had to bed down on the sidewalks.[526] Hospitals were able to function because they had emergency power backup. Fortunately, no deaths or injuries were attributed to the blackout and no rioting and looting occurred.[527]

Human and Regulatory Aspects

The blackout was caused by a combination of technological vulnerabilities, human error and fragmented regulation. In the United States the power system is divided into generation of electricity and transmission. Most reports of the outage agree that the blackout was caused by the sudden failure of several transmission lines in Ohio controlled by First Energy Corp., one of 23 utilities that are part of the Midwest region and one of three in the national grid. A quasi-independent organization, the Midwest ISO, is in nominal control, but lacks the authority to make crisis decisions in this highly fractured transmission grid. Thus Midwest ISO operators are left without their hands on the switch in moments of crisis and a problem can spread uncontrollably to cities as widely separated as Detroit and New York.[528]

As happens in a complex, interconnected system, a minor problem in a larger technological scheme can trigger a crisis. The minor problem was a short circuit set off when a tree rubbed a 345,000-volt line in First Energy's territory. The company was unable to contain the damage and warn neighboring grid operators in time for them to take precautionary action.[529] The grid contains switches so that overloads, which might damage equipment and power lines, automatically turn off generating facilities, such as nuclear power plants, and input of power in transmission lines.

A faulty computer alarm system at First Energy Corp was part of the "human error" problem because, as one operator said, he had no clue about what was happening. Lack of planning was another problem. The company was faulted in the final report of a U.S–Canadian task force, because it "failed to conduct rigorous long-term planning studies" of its transmission system; nor did it "conduct sufficient voltage analyses" to know what it needed to do to keep its system operating safely. Technological crises are caused not only by faulty technology, e.g., the fragmented grid, but also human error and management negligence.[530]

Hazard Management Strategies for Managing Technological Crises

The handling of uncertain and dangerous technology in deep sea drilling, the space program, and nuclear energy industry requires a deliberative and systematic management approach that applies the precautionary principle. As explained by Jason Pontin, editor of *Technology Review*, this principle states that "when something is suspected of being harmful, the burden of proof that the thing is *not* harmful rests with its proponents."[531] Management must make every effort to recognize inherent risks and to use failsafe techniques to minimize accidents. Standard operating procedures must rigorously be applied. Engineers must not blithely be overridden by managers. Group decision-making practices should be favored so that all factors and viewpoints are considered. When imminent danger exists, the voice of science should dominate. When a technology fails, management must have confidence that a fix or alternative exists or will exist because ingenious humans can devise other technologies.

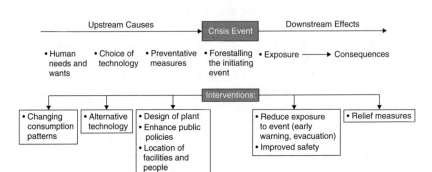

Figure 7.1 Technological hazard management.

Three Phases of Hazard Management

Hazard management strategies developed for natural disasters also apply to technological crises. These strategies fall into three phases: (1) "upstream" measures, i.e., what can be done to lessen the chances of a crisis event and to reduce its impact; (2) forestalling the "crisis-initiating event"; and (3) "downstream" measures, i.e., the kinds of mitigation efforts that can be undertaken after the crisis event, such as evacuating endangered residents and providing relief.

1. Upstream Hazard Control Methods

These consist of attempts to modify human needs and wants, consideration of alternative technologies, and adoption of preventive measures. The first two of these intervention strategies are not available for natural disasters or biological crises. Technological risks have the further advantage that they can entirely be avoided simply by not venturing into dangerous areas, such as nuclear power. Another advantage is that the choice of technology and installation of preventative and safety measures that can sharply decrease the chances that a crisis-initiating event will be initiated, whereas nothing can be done to prevent such natural phenomena as hurricanes, tornadoes, and earthquakes.

- **Modifying Human Needs and Wants—And Prohibiting Some Products and Services.** Technology exists to produce goods and services to satisfy human needs and desires. Not all things that people want, however, should be produced if doing so is dangerous or, as in the case of addictive, non-prescriptive drugs, causes undesirable social consequences.

There will always be controversy over the legitimacy of certain products and services. Increasingly, environmentally aware societies are pondering the question of what products should be banned or curtailed because of the long-lasting or irreparable harm done to the environment either by the process of production or consumption of the product. Thus the pesticide chlorofluorcarbon aerosols have been banned. Citizen action groups have placed referenda on ballots asking people to vote for a ban on nuclear power plants or to prohibit laboratory research using nuclear materials.[532]

In industries other than pesticides, attempts are made to avert some of the basic causes of crises. For example, some electric and gas utility companies encourage customers to make energy audits of their homes to find ways of conserving energy. Utilities are also experimenting with new pricing policies that discourage the use of energy during peak consumption hours. The need for building greater energy-producing capacity is thereby reduced and, along with it, the attendant risks of nuclear power accidents and pollution from oil and coal-generating plants.

- **Using Alternative Technologies.** If a particular technology is deemed unsafe or harmful to the environment, a switch may be made to less harmful alternative technologies. The whole field of alternative energy sources— windmills, water power, geothermal—is based on this principle. Interest in these technologies, as well as nuclear energy, has been heightened to reduce global warming and the dangers of deep sea drilling.

  Alternative technologies can also be sought through improvements in current technologies. With nuclear power, China and South Africa are experimenting with an inherently safer reactor design, called the Pebble Bed Modular Reactor. Instead of using fuel rods as a power source, this design uses balls of uranium-filled graphite. Should the cooling system fail, the reactor temperature would stay well below the balls' melting point and then automatically cool down.[533]

- **Adopting Preventive Measures.** Preventive measures consist of activities and decisions that reduce the probability of occurrence of a technological failure. These consist of: (1) design of plants; (2) public policies; (3) zoning and location of industry; (4) upgrading safety measures; and (5) emergency planning. Some of these measures applying to industrial facilities are similar to the preparedness measures of emergency planning for natural disasters, e.g., the need for appropriate public policies and zoning regulations.

2. Forestalling the Initiating Event

After all upstream hazard factors have been addressed, attention must be focused on the possible elimination of an initiating event, which is an opportunity not available for natural disasters. At Chernobyl, the triggering event was the conducting of unauthorized experiments by technicians; at Cape

Canaveral, it was the decision to launch *Challenger* despite warnings of freezing conditions; at Bhopal, it was inept and irresponsible behavior by workers; and at BP it was wrong decisions about cementing, testing and other procedures on the Deepwater Horizon rig. As Steven Newman, Transocean's CEO, told the Senate Environmental and Public Works Committee, there was no dictated standard regarding the order in which cementing is performed.[534]

When multinationals transfer industrial technology to third-world countries, as Union Carbide did in Bhopal, they must be prepared to compensate for the lack of industrial training and experience by workers, many of whom have agrarian backgrounds. Training programs are especially urgent when there is high turnover of personnel, as is sometimes the case when workers take industrial jobs for short periods before returning home. Differences in the infrastructure and culture of developing nations lead some experts to say that extremely rural areas of the developing world should not be used for processes requiring complex and dangerous technology.

3. Downstream Efforts to Minimize the Effects of Accidents

The manner in which a manager responds to an occurring accident, or signs of an impending one, requires careful study. Robert Bea, a safety engineering expert at the University of California, Berkeley, said, the need is to focus on how people react and interact with complex safety systems when the siren goes off. "We've neglected the human things," he says, "the designers, the people that operate [BOPs], the people that maintain them, the people who have to handle rapidly developing crises."[535] Downstream strategies must also consider the following:

- **Reducing Exposure.** Warning alerts enable people to escape danger. Compared to natural disasters, technological crises are at a disadvantage. Whereas warnings about such impending natural disasters as floods or tornadoes are unambiguous and considered authentic, managers may be uncertain about signs of a technological crisis for various reasons: (1) Events are not seen clearly, especially those that develop gradually rather than precipitately. (2) Many toxic gases are invisible and odorless. For this reason, gas utilities add a strong odor to odorless gas so that employees and customers can become aware of a leak. (3) Technological failures can occur quickly and without forewarning, with the consequence that everything happens at once. (4) Whereas communities have developed some wisdom in dealing with periodic natural catastrophes, technological hazards are not always understood and, when they occur, communities lack experience in dealing with them. The one benefit that accrues from this mystery factor is that people exhibit greater readiness to respond to such warnings by, for example, being willing to evacuate their homes.

An attendant problem is that a crisis threshold is often not defined in the contingency plan. Managers consequently tend to procrastinate.[536] In Bhopal there was a critical delay that cost many lives. When a crisis event occurred at the sister plan in Institute, West Virginia, the plan manager admitted, "We didn't believe that the emergency would affect the community because the cloud was hovering over the plant 'and would not escape the plant's boundaries.'"[537] At Three Mile Island, the owners, Metropolitan Edison, failed to sound a warning. It was a traffic reporter for a local radio station who noticed preparations for an emergency response.[538]

- **Implementing Use of Safety Gear.** This safety control method blocks the undesirable consequences of exposure to harm. Removing people from danger might be viewed as a macro-approach and implementing safety measures as a micro-approach.

  Ships carry lifeboats and life-preservers and conduct abandon-ship exercises. Every airplane trip starts with a "buckle-your-seatbelt" and emergency exit lecture by flight attendants. Public schools conduct fire drills. The principle is that if there is a chance for something to happen, prepare for it. Make appropriate safety gear and clothing available, train people how to use it, and rehearse safety procedures.

- **Relief Efforts.** Similar to dealing with natural disasters, relief efforts help people who are injured. In the aftermath of the JCO accident, this included a company promise to pay damages for the accident.

BP Scores Poorly in Applying Hazard Management Measures

BP did not adequately observe the principles of hazard management in all three phases. It neglected upstream preventive measures, its confused structure of authority on the rig contributed to human error that caused the disaster, and it inadequately prepared for a massive accident.

Reinforce Upstream Preventive Measures

The first of three upstream hazard management measures, modification of human wants, was not an issue. Neither the government nor the public questioned the need for oil, for as President George Bush noted, Americans are addicted to driving. Moreover, the whole U.S. economy is dependent on energy, with oil being a major fuel. The benefits of oil make Americans receptive to the risks involved in deep sea drilling. Nonetheless, consumer anger at BP has caused problems for BP gas stations, which are owner operated. Because sales are down and some vandalism has occurred, some want to revert to their former name, Amoco.

With the second upstream measure, choice of technology, BP should recognize that its research on deep sea technology was limited and lacking. Experts say that others in the oil industry are developing technologies that could make drilling safer and perhaps less expensive. Much could be learned from

Norway, the United Kingdom, and Australia, which have some of the world's best safety practices and regulations. For example, ExxonMobil, Shell, and Norway's Statoil have been investing in the new technology of high-tech burrowing machines that require only a small exploration ship to guide it and eliminate the need for a drill rig.[539]

The third upstream measure, taking preventive measures, was seriously flawed. Most fundamentally, BP did not conduct its contingency planning diligently. In the 1990s, it turned down Columbia University and Boeing Corporation's recommendation to plan for disasters because it would add to costs.[540] Its contingency document was slipshod, unrealistic, and perhaps faked. First, it planned for a small spill as its worst-case scenario, saying there would be only a 3 percent chance that oil would come ashore after a month in any part of the Gulf other than Plaquemines, Louisiana (which juts into the Gulf south of New Orleans).[541] Second, it mistakenly lists a wildlife expert who died in 2005 as a resource. Third, it details how walruses in the Gulf could be saved, even though they don't exist in the Gulf. The suspicion is that parts of other contingency plans, perhaps for the Arctic region, were simply photocopied.[542] As already stated, BP's worst-case scenarios were woefully unrealistic.

The most critical upstream preventive measure that was botched was the well's shut-off safety device. According to testimony of an oil worker who survived the accident, it was switched off in the weeks before the blast because it needed repair.[543] Furthermore, engineers who pulled some of the Deepwater Horizon's equipment from the seabed two weeks after the rig exploded found that a safety switch, known as a "deadman switch" wasn't functional. It would have activated the BOP when the rig erupted into flames and lost communication with the BOP.[544]

The rig also lacked a further backup system, called an acoustic switch, which can shut off a well via remote control in a disaster. It is routinely used on rigs in Norway and Brazil, but BP chose not to install it. Robert Wine, a BP spokesman in London, explained its installation was Transocean's responsibility because the drilling on the Deepwater Horizon was entirely their responsibility and "it was not appropriate to second-guess" them.[545]

Doubts were further reinforced by a 2004 study commissioned by MMS, which questioned whether the shear rams of the BOP were strong enough to cut through the thick pipes used in deep-water drilling.[546] Moreover, according to a 2008 lawsuit, both Cameron and another company, Hybrid, used defective BOP equipment, which resulted in leakage in 2007 from an offshore Louisiana well.[547] These indications should have alerted BP to the shortcomings of the BOP and the need for further testing. The importance of this technology to the safety of the rig was given insufficient attention by BP. The precautionary principle so vital in the use of uncertain technology was egregiously violated.

Establish Unified Authority Structure

To forestall human errors that trigger a crisis, a unified authority structure must be established that spells out the responsibility of each partner and designates the final decision maker. That was not the case on the Deepwater Horizon rig, where managers from the three entities that made decisions on the Deepwater Horizon rig did not always agree on who had responsibility for a decision and, as post-mortem reviews showed, blamed one another for mistakes. A unified authority structure is a crucial requirement to prevent mismanagement when technological uncertainty exists.

In relatively uncertain areas of technology with the potential of dangerous impacts, the culture of science and engineering must be paramount. As stated in an oil industry ad mentioned below, "By starting with properly designed wells, by following established procedures and best practices, by conducting relentless inspections, tests and drills, and with frequent, thorough training of personnel, accidents like this [the incident in the Gulf of Mexico] should never happen."[548] The person who has final authority over critical operations must be a science expert rather than *those* concerned with cost-cutting and other financial considerations.

Carefully Plan Downstream Measures to Protect People and the Environment

BP's downstream planning was woefully optimistic and inadequate. "They're clearly making it up as they go along," said David Pettit, an attorney with the Natural Resources Defense Council.[549] From the start, BP deployed the basic tools of well-known, existing technologies of floating booms, spraying dispersants on oil slicks, burning off the slicks, and using skimmer vessels to suck up as much oil as possible. BP innovated injecting dispersants directly underwater where oil was shooting out of the leaking well.[550]

The efficacy of the booms—whether they could withstand winds and storms—was sometimes debated, and some thought that too large a quantity of dispersants was used. Under federal direction, about 1.8 million gallons overall were sprayed, which was considered a cost-effective way of keeping spilled oil off shorelines. But a later report said dispersants may have helped some spilled oil sink to the sediment, fueling concern about how the oil below the surface might affect the range of ocean life long term.[551] A welcome addition experiment was the arrival of the Taiwanese skimmer *A Whale*, a retrofitted supertanker 1,000-feet long, with a capacity of digesting more than 21 million gallons of oily water day. In comparison, only around 28 million gallons had been collected from the time of the accident on April 20 to July 1.[552]

A consortium of oil companies—ConocoPhillips, Chevron, Shell, and ExxonMobil—is taking the right step for better downstream hazard management, driven by the disaster experience and fear of a continuing moratorium on deep sea drilling in the Gulf. In a full-page joint ad, they announce a plan "to build a $1 billion high-capacity rapid response system designed to capture and contain oil in the event of a future potential deepwater blowout in the Gulf of Mexico." The ad's headline is apt: "Engineer it. Build it. And make sure it's never needed." The nonprofit venture, called the Marine Well Containment Co., is designed to capture and contain up to 100,000 barrels of oil a day flowing 10,000 feet below the surface of the sea. It consists of several oil-collection ships and an array of subsurface containment equipment, which could be mobilized within 24 hours of a spill and be fully in place within weeks.[553]

For better results, experts say that local knowledge should be used in oil containment operations. Fire chief Jamie Hinton of Magnolia Springs, Alabama, explained he has the advantage of a deep understanding of what he calls "my river." He scoffed, therefore, when BP workers affixed a boom to barnacle-laden pylons with ropes only to see waves, sometimes more than two-feet high, sever the stays. John Wathen, a member of Waterkeeper Alliance, says BP should tap into its network, which spans six continents. Members are trained, so their presence does not create the kind of chaos that volunteers sometimes create when they try to clean up beaches.[554]

Having learned from the red tape and poor coordination in the federal response after the *Exxon Valdez* disaster, the federal government now has a unified command structure in place, which delineates the duties of the Coast Guard, state and local officials, and the oil company responsible for the spill. When the BP accident occurred, an "incident commander" was immediately designated. He was the highly qualified Coast Guard Admiral Thad Allen, who has displayed all the decisiveness and sensitivities that Hayward lacked. Overall, conformity with stricter regulations would be provided by the reorganized Bureau of Ocean Energy, Regulation and Enforcement.

Other Applications of Hazard Management

JCO Lacked Most Hazard Management Measures

The JCO case especially illustrates the inattention to several preventative measures, especially the design and location of the facility:

*   location in a residential neighborhood;
*   the plant was not clearly marked as a dangerous site;
*   the room where JCO Co.'s accident occurred had only two thin concrete walls, each only 1.6 inches thick;
*   the facility had no alarm system—"Why was no alarm sounded at the fuel enrichment plant after an accident that produced 10,000 to 20,000 times normal radiation levels in the immediate area?";[555]
*   employees were not educated about hazards and emergency treatment;
*   its staff was never equipped with a safety manual, although company

officials said one had been written for critical events but that no one had ever expected to use it!;

- no training was given and drills were not conducted. JCO had reportedly ordered workers to skip crucial procedures to save time and it had been flouting operating guidelines for years.[556]

Downstream hazard management measures were also neglected. The emergency response was grossly inadequate and mishandled, showing that plant managers were unprepared and negligent. Emergency treatment for injured employees was delayed for an hour as rescue officials searched for a hospital that could handle victims of severe radiation exposure, even though Tokaimura has 15 nuclear facilities.[557] The fire department was notified by the parent company Sumitomo Mining Co., which was located elsewhere. Three paramedicals who rushed to the scene didn't take along protective suits against radiation, even though such suits are stored at the fire station. After several telephone calls to identify an appropriate hospital, the three victims were taken to the nearby Mito Hospital, from which they could later be relocated by helicopter. In short, JCO ignored basic upstream measures of sound design and location, and downstream measures were absent or treated carelessly.

Electricity Industry Needs Technological Overhaul

A redesigned infrastructure for electrical transmission and better regulatory oversight is needed to prevent future blackouts. As *The Economist* observed, the underlying culprit in the blackout is "America's half-baked, half-hearted approach to electricity deregulation."[558] One solution favored by the magazine is to liberalize the market: "removing unfair obstacles to hooking up micro-generators to the grid, and giving consumers better price signals." Another solution would require more government involvement. For example, FERC has a plan that would create seven or eight regional transmission organizations with undisputed authority to decide who and when the grid in their regions can be used. Control over utilities' high-voltage wires would be turned over to Regional Transmission Organizations (RTOs). These RTOs could reduce power to portions of the grid when shortages occur and order companies to build new power lines.[559]

The long-term solution to the prevention of future blackouts lies with a redesigned national power system. Instead of exclusive dependency on centralized power plants and an aging web of transmission lines, a "distributed generation" system is proposed. A significant number of customers would be encouraged, partially through subsidies, to generate more of their own power locally through microturbines, combustion turbines, reciprocating engines, fuels cells, photovoltaic sources, and the wind.[560] Many companies in the alternative energy business are eager to participate.

Within the system, the Electric Power Research Institute proposes to upgrade the grid system with a "network of digitally run controls on power flows and computerized, second-to-second monitoring that would result in a 'self healing' grid." Engineers call this an "adaptive island" that enables trouble areas to be isolated quickly to prevent power failures from cascading through the rest of the nation's transmission system.[561]

The role of government and the regulatory system needs to be reexamined, for deregulation didn't work. Nor was the self-regulating industry body, the North American Electric Reliability Council, which was created after the 1965 blackout, able to ensure cooperation among the utilities, independent power companies, and transmission-system operators.[562] This is a self-regulating industry body that lacks enforcement authority. A plan that gives government greater control is proposed by the Federal Energy Regulatory Commission (FERC)[563]

The Future for Dangerous Technologies

Global Warming Leads to an Atomic Renaissance

Despite the dangers of nuclear energy as demonstrated by TMI, Chernobyl, and the Japanese accidents, a renaissance is expected because the dangers now being weighed against the growing concern about global warming. The higher this concern the lower the resistance to building more nuclear reactors. Global warming has made nuclear power an attractive alternative to coal-fired power plants. Even one of the founders of Greenpeace, Patrick Moore, changed his mind and now believes in nuclear power.[564]

In Europe, a factor favoring more construction of nuclear plants is the unreliability of natural gas from Russia, which has become a major supplier. More European nations are consequently overturning their bans on nuclear power. The Swedes are now reversing their 1980 policy of phasing out nuclear power. They had already shut down two of their ten reactors. Italy and Poland have also announced plans to build nuclear-power plants. Some nations, among them Slovakia and Bulgaria, are seeking to reopen obsolete reactors even though they are of original Soviet design.[565]

Safety concerns, in addition to cost, are a major deterrent to the future of nuclear power. This was illustrated by the Three Mile Island accident and the Chernobyl explosion. The dangers of nuclear power were further exposed by the March 11, 2011 nuclear disaster at Japan's Fukushima Daiichi nuclear facility, 150 miles north of Tokyo. A 9.0 magnitude earthquake some 100 miles off Japan's north-eastern coast, followed by a tsunami with 30-foot waves, damaged the nuclear structure and flooded the plant's cooling system and backup diesel generators. One of its four reactors came close to a meltdown and the resulting radiation eventually caused the evacuation of about a quarter of a million people within a 20-mile[566] radius of the plant. The crisis was ranked at the level of Chernobyl, which struck almost 25 years before.[567]

An upstream factor of the disaster was that the designers for the Tokyo

Electric Power Co. (Tepco) concentrated so narrowly on the danger of earthquakes that they underestimated the possibility of a powerful tsnami. They had even chopped 25 meters of a 35-meter natural seawall so that the reactors could be built on bedrock and equipment moved in easily. They thereby exposed the cooling systems and their backup pumps to the 30-foot waves of the tsunami. In the immediate response to the crisis, Tepco waited a few hours too long to pour water on Reactor 1, the most damaged. In the downstream phase, the company was indecisive in deciding on the evacuation zone necessitated by radiation.

The disaster confirmed the belief of many nuclear power opponents that you can't trust the stuff. Somewhere, eventually, reactor will get out of control.[568] The nuclear renaissance prompted by concern over global warming appeared to be over.

Conclusions

In the aftermath of technological crises, especially BP's, and concerns about such new technologies as nanotechnology, managers cannot remain complacent about technological risks. Advances in hazard management must be applied to reduce the incidence of accidents and, if they occur, to mitigate their effects. The time of voluntary and unilateral industry action, however, is rapidly disappearing, for public awareness of the dark side of technology has reached a critical level. A small incident can easily arouse latent anxieties and create resistance to technological advances.

A communication objective is to convince the public that avoidance of all risks is impossible in the modern technological world. As a champion of technological change, Kurzweil advocates replacing the precautionary principle — avoidance of risk — with a proactionary principle, which involves balancing the risks of action and inaction. He sees a need for a change in public attitude in greater tolerance for necessary risk.

Technology received a huge boost on October 12, 2010, when rescue operations began for 33 Chilean miners from the San Jose Mine after being holed up for 70 days a half-mile underground. The engineers and organizations that collaborated in applying their knowledge, skills and technology were celebrated the world over. Ms. Macarena Valdes, the topographer, is credited with successfully directing the probes. A small Pennsylvania company's powerful Schramm T-130 drill dug the escape hole and Chilean naval engineers designed the capsule, called the Phoenix, that brought them up, one by one.[569] As Peggy Noonan wrote in "Viva Chile! They Left No Man Behind," the world saw something we don't see enough: "a brilliant example of human excellence—of cohesion, of united and committed action, of planning and execution, of caring." She credited technology for being used "capably, creatively, and as a force for good."[570]

Appendix to Chapter 7: Nanotechology

Nanotechnology is one of the newer sciences that some herald as the next major development comparable to the discovery of electricity and the internal combustion engine. *Biotech Business Week* says, "Nanotechnology promises to change just about everything—our medical care, energy sources, communications and food. It is leading us to what many in government and industry care calling 'The Next Industrial Revolution.'"

Enormous promises are held out for nanotechnology. Dramatic new materials and medicines are expected that will improve existing products, ranging from sunscreens to stain-proof ties, stink-free refrigerators, and contact lenses that change color according to blood-sugar levels. Nanotechnology can be used to produce faster computer chips, more efficient batteries, "carriers" for medicines and ultra-thin coating. Rachael Rettner, a graduate student in New York University's Science, Health, and Environmental Reporting Program, learned about other benefits when she visited Brookhaven National Laboratory's Center for Functional Nanomaterials. These included the design of nanomaterial catalysts to create energy sources more efficiently, the splitting of water molecules into its components of oxygen and hydrogen, and improving solar power technology by manipulating materials at the atomic level to enhance the process of converting sunlight into electricity.[571] Another application is on farms in rural Africa where a plastic storage bag lined with nanoparticles can prolong the life of the tropical root vegetable cassava beyond one to three days after which it spoils. Cassava is a staple crop for millions of people in sub-Saharan Africa. By prolonging the life of cassava, farmers can avoid waste and sell their crop beyond their local region.[572]

Nanotechnology represents miniaturisation, industry's tiniest stage. The standard unit of measurement is a nanometer, which is a billionth of a meter. *Consumer Reports* says, "nanotechnology involves reducing the particles in standard materials to sizes as small as a nanometre, or about one-hundred-thousandth the width of a human hair.[573] Matter at this tiny scale behaves very differently from familiar materials. They "can do things they couldn't do before."[574] Carbon becomes 100 times stronger than steel, and gold melts at room termperature.[575]

A major feature of nanotechnology is the uncertainty and risks surrounding the new science. The *Financial Times* referred to nanotechnology as the science of "Franken-molecules." *Chemical Week* acknowledges that health and environmental concerns overshadow the commercialization of nanomaterials. It reports that although respected authorities such as the European Union's Scientific Committee finds that nanomaterials are not dangerous in themselves, scientific uncertainty remains about many aspects of its safety.[576]

In the United States the debate about nanomaterials is building up, driven by advocacy groups such as Greenpeace and the Natural Resources Defense Council. James Brewer states in *Lloyd's List*, "Nanotechnology could pose dangers to personal health quality in a range of products from disk drives to fuels, and some fear that it could present another asbestos-style crisis for insurance companies."[577] It is an insurance nightmare because at present there are "no official standards and no regulations in labeling or methodology, and no disclosure obligations. Neither is there sufficient experience of damage, toxicology, and classification is lacking."[578] In other words, nobody knows whether any of the nano-products already on the market are safe. "The strategy seems to be: sell first, safety later."[579]

Technology Review gives the example of a face cream sold by New York City-based Bionova, whose marketing uses such incomprehensible phrases as the "restoration of the malfunctioning biological information."[580] The writer, Apoorva Mandavilli, who bought the product at a price of $163 for half an ounce, feared that the tiny particles might creep under her skin and wreak havoc with her body. But a saleswoman reassured her with the explanation that the cream uses chemicals of regular size, just in nano amounts!

Consumers know little or nothing about nanoparticles, according to a survey by the Project on Emerging Nanotechnologies of the Woodrow Wilson International Centre for Scholars. "We should have a conversation about it," says David Rejeski, director of the project. He warns not to repeat the public backlash that poisoned the future of genetically modified foods because business and the government mishandled consumer fears. "How the public learns about nano, from whom and with what message will be crucial," says Rejeski, adding, "The government has a huge role in increasing public confidence around these emerging technologies."[581]

Part III

Crises of the Human Climate

The human climate refers to the attitudes and behavior of human beings and entities in the external environment that create conflicts with target organizations. Like crises of the physical environment, those of the human climate originate in the external environment. If the eruptions of the physical environment appear uncertain and uncontrollable, human behavior can be even more volatile and unpredictable. The limits are not set by the physical and biological sciences but by the motivations and aberrations of humankind.

Conflicts in human societies are normal because there will always be those who are dissatisfied with the status quo in their relationship with certain organizations, while others want to maintain the status quo because they benefit from it. Owners and investors are interested in maximizing shareholder value and therefore want to contain demands from other stakeholders, such as employees who seek higher pay and benefits, and communities who want to reduce possible pollution and other social costs.

Most of the demands and expectations of an organization's stakeholders are a normal part of the give-and-take between them and an organization. They may be based on the insistence that organizations live up to their social responsibilities. But occasionally, when an organization's management engages in harmful behavior or insists on maintaining the status quo while its stakeholders seek change, conflict occurs. Employees voice grievances over their benefits or treatment and seek remediation through a grievance procedure or negotiations. If an impasse is reached, a labor dispute may arise and tactics such as a strike and picketing may be employed. Such events illustrate a confrontation crisis because daily operations are interrupted and the organization may be harmed. Similar confrontations may occur when consumer groups or environmental groups boycott a company's products. Moreover, environmental groups and others that seek a change in government public policy typically choose corporations rather than government as targets because they are more vulnerable, accessible and responsive.

Another source of conflict is that society is organized on the basis of power structures. Internally, organizations operate on an hierarchical basis, which allows managers to control subordinates. Within a community and larger society, economic and government structures control a variety of functions and the behavior of its members or citizens. A feature of democratic societies is that existing power structures may be challenged by those who seek to change their policies and behavior—or even their legitimacy. When these efforts fail and the challengers become frustrated, they may resort to violence and, as a further step, to discredit or destroy existing power structures. In this book, these efforts are called crises of malevolence.

In confrontations, people and groups may escalate their tactics and engage in violence, especially when they perceive their cause as a moral one. For example, fervent for-life advocates have occasionally killed doctors in abortion clinics. In crises of malevolence, certain personality types that are angry and hateful may display their hostility through aggressive acts. Their motive may be criminal— as in cybercrime, extortion, or kidnapping—or inspired by some larger cause, such as religious or nationalistic sentiment.

Response strategies for crises of confrontation and malevolence are only slightly modeled after those in the physical environment. Surveillance of the physical environment associated with natural and biological disasters is called scanning and monitoring in the socio-political environment.

Communications, supported by social science insights, play a large role in conflict resolution. In cases of malevolence, such soft approaches are strengthened or replaced by "hard engineering" application of security forces.

Application of Issues Management

Confrontations reflect issues that are important and contentious in society. These include globalization issues such as the loss of jobs, perceived unfair distribution of benefits, poor working conditions, low wages, and abuse of human rights. Another issue of rising importance is climate change. Issues management is therefore an integral part of crisis management. Careful attention to the issues management process—issue identification, prioritization, analysis, and strategy formulation—will help to anticipate and avert crises, and, if they do occur, to control the damage caused and provide insight for the rebuilding process.

Many crises are the result of not paying enough attention to existing or emerging issues and neglecting stakeholders who espouse them. Issues are defined as those controversial matters that people argue over and that often lead to confrontations and political battles. Much of what constitutes an organization's socio-political environment is described by listing the issues of greatest importance to it. By scanning and monitoring the environment for such issues, an organization embarks on the activity known as issues management.

Stakeholder Management

Issues management automatically involves stakeholder relationships because stakeholders are the participants in the social and political arena who take sides on a particular issue. Stakeholders, however, encompass a larger group of people than those actively involved in a public policy process; they potentially include anybody who can affect the outcome of an organization's policies and actions. Thus, a listing and analysis of an organization's stakeholders and the relationship with them is an important activity, one closely associated with the field of public relations and their use of the alternative term "publics" to designate groups of people who have common interests.

One of the major political and societal developments is the greater involvement of stakeholders in decisions that affect their welfare. Within organizations, feedback systems have enlarged into stakeholder participation and forms of joint decision-making. Within society, public participation schemes include public interest groups in drafting public policies, such as environmental laws that require companies manufacturing or storing dangerous substances to disclose such information to neighboring communities and to include them in emergency planning. Whenever citizens become aware of risks affecting them, they demand a voice. This has occurred in decisions involving the location and approval of waste sites, incineration plants, nuclear power plants, and other NIMBY (Not In My Back Yard) issues.

When organizations are not responsive to stakeholders and public interest groups, these groups seek power in other ways. Employees may join labor unions and exert pressure on employers through strikes, picketing, boycotts and other forms of pressure. Consumers may join consumer organizations and boycott products. Community organizations may hold demonstrations. These are the activities of confrontation and, occasionally, malevolence, discussed in the next two chapters.

Chapter 8

Confrontation Crises

The popular meaning of confrontation is a face-to-face encounter when one person opposes another with hostility. In confrontation crises faced by an organization, the stakes are higher as one group challenges another group or organization. We have all seen activists picket in front of a store urging consumers to boycott controversial products, such as California grapes produced by farmers accused of unfair labor conditions.[582] This kind of direct confrontation also occurs when a labor union goes on strike against an employer, usually with picketers at the entrance to an office or plant who carry placards displaying their grievances. More frequently, environmental groups protest the expansion of drilling and mining sites.

Activist groups are often the organizers behind confrontations with companies whose social policies are opposed. One of the best-known cases is the organized protest by student activists and other concerned citizens against Nike for paying low wages and ignoring human rights violations in Asian plants where its athletic shoes were produced. The publicity accompanying its organized events severely hurt Nike's image and sales. Gradually it changed its practices and become a leader in reforms of overseas manufacturing operations.

Some organizations are confronted because they are associated with someone else's objectionable action or policy. The Danish dairy company Arla Foods was boycotted in the Middle East after a Danish newspaper published cartoons deemed insulting to Muhammad. Even Kuwaiti-Danish Dairy Co., which is Muslim-owned and had no formal connection with any Danish partners for more than 20 years, was boycotted.[583] Arla was not responsible for the publication of the cartoons, nor was the non-Danish company, but it was guilty by association. Some companies, such as Procter & Gamble Company and Unilever Plc/Unilever NV, skirted blame by repositioning their brands to appear as local products on store shelves.

Confrontations based on a societal issue are becoming more common as broader geopolitical, religious, or other issues play a larger role. A feature of these confrontations is that they have the potential for causing long-term harm. Animosities may persist because they often are rooted in deeply held beliefs and because there are fewer options for addressing the confrontation.[584] For example, anti-American attitudes in the Middle East and elsewhere have hurt the sales of McDonald's and other American icons, but the remedy lies chiefly in a change of U.S. policies.

What these types of confrontations have in common is that they are deliberately provoked by discontented individuals and groups who fight businesses, government, and various interest groups to win acceptance of their demands and expectations and, in extreme cases, to seek radical changes in the "system" itself.

Organizations face a crisis when confrontations affect their sales or operations or when their reputation is debased. Such crises are likely to persist and grow because an organization's stakeholders, such as customers and investors, make demands, and because more societal groups are associating themselves with social movements and championing an ever-widening variety of causes. Confrontation crises proliferated in the 1960s and 1970s in the heyday of the civil rights, consumerism, and environmental movements. During the Reagan years of the 1980s, confrontations slowed down because both government and business seemed less responsive.

By the end of the 1990s, said James H. Dowling, former president and CEO of Burson-Marsteller, there would be a "revival of activism and increased demands on business to solve a much broader array of social problems."[585] These include such major global issues as climate change, sustainable development, and world poverty. In the future, more ideologically motivated activism can be expected as the activities of corporations have become matters of public debate.[586]

The rapid growth of civil society in developed nations, along with nongovernmental organizations (NGOs) that espouse the concerns of developing nations, means that more organizations can expect to be targeted. Modern societies are replete with constituent groups, nonprofit groups, and NGOs that espouse a wide variety of issue and causes. The social and political climate is conducive to confrontations because people are more ready to participate—they have become politicized. Widespread use of the Internet makes it easier for activist groups to attract attention to issues and to mobilize support from constituents and the general public.

The Dynamics of Confrontations

A confrontation crisis develops along a fairly well-defined pattern. An activist group: (1) collects information about some issue about which they are concerned and formulates desired outcomes; (2) chooses a vulnerable target organization; (3) decides on crisis-provoking tactics; and (4) seeks media and public attention and support.[587] Organizations whose contingency planning includes likely confrontations with stakeholders and social action groups should understand how they develop.

1. Identify an Issue

As pointed out in the introduction to Part III, confrontation crises are related to controversial economic, political, and social issues and grievances. Many such disputes arise from an organization's stakeholders. Any person, group or organization that can affect an organization's performance is a potential stakeholder. Some stakeholders represent a firm's "factors of production," a term used by economists to refer to employees who provide labor, stockholders and investors who provide capital, and the local communities that provide "land," i.e., the physical setting of buildings and the infrastructure that supports them. Other stakeholders include customers who buy the output of an organization, suppliers who provide a variety of materials and services, government entities that regulate businesses (and may also be customers), nonprofit organizations that provide social services, educational and cultural resources, and the many social action groups, otherwise unrelated to an organization, that make demands on an organization.

Activist groups are largely organized around stakeholder interests. Consumer activists demand better protection against product defects or technological hazards; environmentalists want to control land use and curtail harm to the physical environment; and minority and women's groups like NOW and Operation Corporate Responsibility seek greater employment opportunities, equal pay and benefits, minority purchasing, and access to ownership. Ethnic and elderly groups seek affordable credit and utility rates; employee groups and labor unions seek higher wages and benefits, safer working conditions, curbs on plant closings, and employment guarantees; and stockholder groups demand more stockholder rights or better corporate policies on such issues as management salaries, bonuses, and "golden parachutes."

The early consumer and environmental movements increased the range of expectations by addressing the issue of the social costs of economic growth. Rachel Carson's *The Silent Spring* alerted the public to the effects of pesticides and pollutants in the environment, and Ralph Nader's *Unsafe at Any Speed* punctured the American love affair with the automobile. The two movements in concert solidified the belief that American business could be expected to produce better products and to protect the environment at the same time. Climate change has become the new overriding environmental issue. Business has failed to meet public expectations and, as a result, public confidence in business institutions has steadily eroded.

Activists, however, cannot take for granted that a politicized public will automatically favor their causes. This was evidenced in the 2001 protests against the International Monetary Fund (IMF) and World Bank meetings in Washington, D.C. The capitol had been preparing for as many as 100,000 protesters, but the September 11 attack on the World Trade Center changed the dynamics. This tragic event turned public opinion against protesters, who were then identified as pacifists. The protesters were clearly out of line with American public opinion. A *New York Times*/CBS poll found that 92 percent of Americans favored military action against "whoever is responsible for the attacks." And Americans said they were willing to make sacrifices: 84 percent said they would support tax increases and spend less money on programs such as education and social security.

These poll results were expressed by construction workers along the route of the protest in D.C. As voiced by one worker, "This is ridiculous. How can they call themselves Americans? . . . I can't believe these people don't want us to defend ourselves." His fellow workers cursed the marchers as they passed by. Some protest groups canceled their participation in the march when they saw that the event had become an anti-war rally. Other groups remained inflexible This stubborn stance was reflected by Maria Ramos, coordinator of the Washington Peace Center, who mused, "We're mourning victims, and at the same time we don't want any more victims as well."[588]

2. Choose a Vulnerable Target Organization

After championing an issue and deciding on what behaviors should be changed, activist groups choose a target organization that will best advance its cause. It may be an organization that is the worst offender, but more frequently large, visible firms are attractive targets because they attract publicity and are the pattern setters in an industry.[589] A firm must consider whether these factors increase the likelihood that it will be targeted by a campaign.

An activist group will decide on the level of harm/punishment to threaten the target organization and how it will calculate that harm. The activist group must consider what factors drive the probability that a firm will comply with an activist's demands. It is expected that a firm charged with pollution will consider the operational loss from complying with the activist demands. The strategy of the activist group is to overcome that resistance with threats of even greater harm by not complying.[590]

3. Decide on Crisis-Provoking Tactics

Activists carefully choose tactics to provoke their target opponents and to attract media attention. These tactics have been adopted from the labor, civil rights, and other social movements. One of the most quoted sources is Saul Alinsky's *Rules for Radicals*, in which he urges followers to use tactics full of surprises, irreverence, drama, and rapid change. As summarized by Harry C. Boyte: "Using military imagery, he preached the need to keep the enemy off balance, use the establishment's rules against itself, split the opposition and appeal to its self-interest, threaten embarrassment and humiliation—in short, to do whatever was necessary to win. Demonstrate, yell, picket, sue."[591]

The range of tactics used by activist groups can be viewed as falling into three categories: (1) actions within accepted social norms; (2) actions outside accepted social norms; and (3) actions that may involve civil disobedience. Examples of the first are letter writing, testifying at a public hearing, obtaining signatures on petitions, holding a media briefing, lobbying a public official, purchasing shares of stock in a targeted company, holding a vigil in a public place, organizing a march, holding a seminar or organizing a workshop, and making a survey and publicizing its findings. Examples of the second are holding a sit-in or sleep-in, boycotting an activity, holding a demonstration, holding a call-in and tying up telephone lines. Examples of the third are bringing an animal to a public hearing, heaving manure at public officials, taking over a public building, and holding a truck blockade.

Some activists prefer to use only limited tactics, such as forms of persuasion followed by threats of political/legal action. Others are skilled in lobbying and litigation. For example, the Natural Resources Defense Fund uses the techniques of coalition formation, Congressional testimony, litigation, lobbying, and participation in regulatory proceedings. On the far extreme are those social actions groups that are prepared, at least on occasion, to resort to illegal forms of violence.

4. Seek Media and Public Attention and Support

Social activists need the news media to accomplish two major purposes: to legitimize their movement and its demands; and to accelerate the process of involving the public. The literature of public interest groups fully recognizes this reality. For example, in describing publicity and other forms of public relations, Jeffrey Berry advocates the use of press releases, which can be produced with minimal resources; press conferences, which are most effective when a group can command the presence of notables like John Gardner or Ralph Nader; cultivation of sympathetic reporters like Jack Anderson or *Washington Post*'s Morton Mintz, and occasionally, all-out media campaigns involving advertising, personal appearances, films or TV and radio programs.[592]

The choice of particular confrontation tactics is guided by their capacity for attracting media attention. One of the advantages of picketing is its visibility as a media event. The Internet has also provided a powerful medium to spread awareness and mobilize support. As an article in *Public Relations Review* concludes, the Internet helps activist groups to build relationships with their constituents and to organize protests and other events.[593] The Internet has been helping activist groups to build relationships with their constituents and to organize protests and other events.[594]

Activists have an advantage over their "establishment" targets: they can afford to be more creative in obtaining publicity than corporate publicists who are restrained by notions of propriety. They are also rich in peoplepower for use in the pickets, demonstrations, rallies and marches that attract the news media. Activists and the media are linked by mutual needs, but activists are obliged to compete with one another to attract the limited amount of media attention available to them.

Greenpeace has a high success rate in competing for media attention. As described in Greenpeace's battle against Shell UK, some members were literally willing to put their lives in peril, a courageous attitude admired by the media. In other situations, however, Greenpeace engages in very rational information campaigns and media relations. As stated by David McTaggart, past chairman of Greenpeace International, Greenpeace has "always, on purpose, looked rough and haphazard, but most of it's been carefully thought out and planned, sometimes years before."[595]

Case Studies

Danish Cartoon Episode

On September 30, 2005, Flemming Rose, the cultural editor of the Danish newspaper *Jyllands-Posten*, published a series of 12 cartoons satirizing the Prophet Muhammad as a way of demonstrating Denmark's devotion to freedom of the press. One depicted Muhammad in a turban shaped like a bomb. Another showed a turbaned figure in heaven telling ascending suicide bombers to stop because "we've run out of virgins" (the reward for Islamic martyrs). The immediate response was local. A prominent cleric in Denmark, Ahmed Abu Laban, felt insulted and wrote a protesting letter to the newspaper and to the Danish culture minister, to which there was no reply. He and others formed the " European Committee for Honoring the Prophet," which claimed to represent 27 organizations across a wide spectrum of the Islamic community.[596] They also sent a petition with 17,000 signatures to Prime Minister Anders Fogh Rasmussen, who did not show the courtesy of responding. When ambassadors from 11 Muslim countries asked for a meeting with Rasmussen, he declined.

Abu Laban and his colleagues then decided to take their case outside Denmark. They prepared a 30-plus-page dossier to distribute during their travels. This document included a group of highly offensive pictures never published by the newspaper, including a photograph of a man dressed as a pig, with the caption: "this is the real picture of Muhammad."[597] By the end of January 2006, word spread so wide that protesters in the Middle East burned Danish flags and declared boycotts of Danish and other European goods. With the help of cellphone text messages and massive emails, messages reached virtually everyone in the Middle East. The response was that Denmark's diplomatic missions in Syria and Lebanon were ransacked, protesters demanded that the Danish ambassadors leave their countries, and in Lebanon, the Danish and Norwegian embassies were torched.

One of the most affected companies was Arla Foods, a Danish dairy company (the second largest dairy company in Europe) that has plants in Saudi Arabia and sells butter and cheese to Middle Eastern countries. Louis Honore, a spokesman for Aria, declared, "This is a public uprising. . . . This has spread through the region like wildfire. And the boycott has been practically

100 percent."[598] Other Danish companies, some as large and prominent as LEGO, were also affected. Peter Thagesen, a senior advisor from the Confederation of Danish Industries, said, "Danish companies are being taken as hostages in a conflict in which we have not been a part. In this conflict, as is often the case in a conflict, there have been many misunderstandings on both sides."[599]

Prime Minister Rasmussen and the editor at *Jyllands-Posten* finally became aware of the need for diplomacy. On January 2, 2006, Rasmussen apologized on Danish television, saying, "I personally have such respect for people's religious feelings that I personally would not have depicted Muhammad, Jesus or other religious figures in such a manner that would offend other people."[600] He also appeared on al-Arabiya, an Arab TV channel, and said he was "deeply distressed that the cartoons were offensive to Muslims," a response the Egyptian ambassador called unsatisfactory.[601] On January 30, Carsten Justen, editor in chief of *Jyllands-Posten*, issued a similar statement: "In our opinion, the 12 drawings were not intended to be offensive, nor were they at variance with Danish law, but they have indisputably offended many Muslims, for which we apologize."[602]

The apologies by Rasmussen and Justen are inadequate. They do not express responsibility for their offense and seem to be "blaming the victim." The wrongdoer is actually saying, "If you have a problem with being so thin-skinned, I apologize to you because of your need, or your weakness, I hope that makes you happy."[603] They seem to apologize for the perception by Muslims that the cartoons were deemed offensive, but not for their publication. European newspapers sided with the Danish publishers and added fuel to the fire by republishing the cartoons.

Company responses varied. Nestlé, Carrefour and Kuwaiti Danish Dairy took out advertisements stating they were not Danish companies or they let people know their stance on the cartoon situation. Arla, hit the hardest, reprinted the text of a news release from the Danish Embassy, which said that Denmark respects all religions.[604] Arla also advertised in two big Saudi newspapers in which the text of conciliatory remarks by the Danish prime minister were shown. The ads made no difference, however, according to Finn Hansen, head of Arla's international operations.

The company then embarked on diplomatic meetings.[605] In February, representatives attended an industry trade show in Dubai where it displayed posters stating that it was against the publication of the cartoons and anything thing else that causes religious offense. The representatives sat down with Arab businessmen and discussed ways they as a company could become more attuned to the needs of the Arab world. These discussions were effective. This was two-way symmetrical communication that showed that Arla really cared about people and improving relationships.

Having achieved some acceptance, Arla Foods placed advertisements in 25 Arab newspapers in late March, which won praise from influential Islamic scholars who were meeting in Bahrain.[606] The advertisements outlined the company's 40-year history in the Middle East and reiterated Arla's dissocia-tion from the cartoons, saying that Arla's business in the Middle East had been affected not by its own actions, but by the actions of others. Consumers were therefore asked to reconsider their attitudes toward Arla. Executive director Finn Hansen of Arla Foods commented, "We hope that the advertisement will get Arab consumers to consider whether it is fair to boycott a dairy company that has had nothing to do with these caricatures."[607]

By the end of March, after a two-month boycott, shops and supermarkets in the Middle East were starting to put butter and cheese from Arla back on their shelves. By April, Arla announced a "Breakthrough for Arla in the Middle East," saying that its products were back in 3,000 shops and supermarkets, and that 31 of its largest retail customers in Saudi Arabia confirmed that they would within the week return Arla products to their shelves.[608]

The Danish cartoon crisis exposes the blindness and insensitivity of Danish editors and government officials to the conflict between European nations and the world of Islam. Surely the Western world's value of the freedom of expres-sion deserves to be supported, but to ignore the sensitivities of Muslims to des-ecrations of Prophet Muhammed displays arrogance and social irresponsibility. There seemed to be almost universal agreement that the cartoons were offen-sive. As *The Nation* stated, "When it comes to freedom of speech, the liberal/left should not sacrifice its values one inch to those who seek censorship on religious grounds. But the right to freedom of speech equates to neither an obligation to offend nor a duty to be insensitive. If our commitment to free speech is impor-tant, our belief in antiracism should be no less so."[609]

Pepsi's Water Problems

Pepsi Cola and Coca-Cola were involved in negotiations with both NGOs and Indian states over groundwater usage. A well-known activist in India, Sunita Narain, organized a protest against Pepsi charging the company with consum-ing excessive groundwater in often parched communities and allowing pesticide reside from groundwater to get into locally made soda.[610] Coca-Cola asked for a meeting to discuss the findings of the Centre for Science and Environment, Narain's research and lobbying group, that soft drinks made by Coca -Cola and PepsiCo contained pesticide residues far above limit.

The prestigious publication *Foreign Affairs* listed Narain among the world's 100 global leaders.[611] Narain had credibility based on lifelong involvement in environmental causes, e.g., campaigning to stop developers from cutting down New Delhi trees, and by virtue of her position as director of the Centre for Sci-ence & Environment (CSE). When in 2005 she received the Stockholm Water Prize, she declared Indians were "getting poisoned by pesticides" and that CSE tests showed Pepsi contributed to this toxic assault. She announced that new research findings released in August 2006 found that Pepsi's pesticide level was 30 times that of the unadopted Indian government standards.

She appeared at news conferences and used blogs, email and other tools to get her message out. As a result, the state of Kerla banned the manufacture and sale of all Coke and Pepsi products and other states cut soft-drink sales in schools, colleges, and hospitals. Protestors smashed bottles on the streets and in Mumbai and Kolkata defaced Pepsi and Coke ads and burned placards depicting soda bottles.

Helping Narain's cause is that water is a sensitive issue in India. People attribute sacrificial aspects to water, e.g., bathing can be a sacred act. More important, India faces a shortage of water, exasperated by overpumping and poor management. The quality of water is one of the worst in the world because of poor sewage treatment, heavy pesticide use, and industrial pollution.

Soda sales fell by double digits when the scandal first broke. The media reported that Pepsi underestimated how quickly events would spread into a nationwide scandal. One factor is that the news media are plentiful in India, so news travels fast. Pepsi decided to respond through the media. It held a joint press conference with Coke (which was also implicated) and presented its version of the facts, namely that the level of pesticides in soda was far lower than what Indians put up with in most other foods.

Pepsi met with editorial boards, presented its own data in press conferences, and ran TV commercials featuring its then-president in India walking through a gleaming laboratory. It also ran splashy ads bursting with Indian celebrities: "It painted titanic versions of its red, white, and blue logo on ancient Himalayan rocks and buildings around the country, which seemed unrelated to alleviating India's water woes."[612] A final symbolic gesture was that Andra K. Nooyi, who became Pepsi CEO in October 2000, visited India. She commented that she should have taken the trip three years previously.

Pepsi engaged in another traditional response by engaging in government relations to clarify standards. It took the Bureau of Indian Standards (BIS) two years to arrive at guidelines for pesticides, caffeine, and even PH levels in soda. But it flip-flopped on the issue and, at the last minute, a letter from the Health & Family Welfare stated that the new standards should be deferred because further research was under way.

These initial defensive measures finally gave way to concrete steps to address the water shortage and contamination issues. Pepsi reduced water usage in its plants, lowering its intake to 8.6 liters for every case of two dozen 8-oz. bottles, down from the former 35 liters. (One gallon is 3.7 liters.) During her visit to India, Nooyi said, "We have to invest, too, in educating communities in how to farm better, collect water, and then work with industry to retrofit plants and recycle."[613]

Anti-Globalization Protests

With the spread of globalization, this issue became a rallying point for a coalition of activists. The so-called Battle of Seattle in 1999 is recognized as the start of the anti-globalization movement. An ad hoc coalition of environmental, labor, human rights, consumer, and other activist groups demonstrated against the World Trade Organization (WTO) meeting. They were united by one theme which contained a catalogue of related issues: "their opposition to the expansion of a system that promoted corporate-led globalization at the expense of social goals like justice, community rights, national sovereignty, cultural diversity, and ecological sustainability."[614]

The media reported that some 60,000 demonstrators participated, but the 200 radicals who were among them got all the media attention as they broke windows and engaged in other destruction. Lori Wallach, a Harvard-training lawyer, and head of the public Citizen's Global Trade Watch, was the leading planner of the demonstration. *The Economist* called the Seattle meeting "a debacle that was a setback for freer trade and a boost for critics of globalisation."[615]

The Seattle protests demonstrated the growing political power of the anti-globalists, which was confirmed in subsequent protests in Washington, D.C. in April 2000, Prague in September 2000, Davos, Switzerland in January 2001, Quebec City in April 2001, and Cancun in 2003. These confrontations yielded several lessons for negotiators and diplomats, which are discussed later.

Anti-globalization protests have mainly targeted supranational organizations, such as the WTO, IMF and World Bank. However, the overarching umbrella uniting the backlash to globalization is opposition to corporate control of the global economy. Most protesters don't agree with Tom Friedman that economic globalization is inevitable; they believe that some aspects should and can be stopped or rolled back.

Boston University's National Biocontainment Laboratory

On September 30, 2003, Boston University, in partnership with Boston Medical Center, was selected to receive $127 million to build a National Biocontainment Laboratory and to manage and direct research into emerging infectious diseases and agents of bioterrorism, such as anthrax, Ebola virus, plague, and smallpox.[616] The facility was part of the fight against terrorism in the aftermath of the 9/11 attacks because there was a shortage of Biosafety Level 3 and 4 labs.[617]

This case has both a technological and confrontation aspect. It is technological because the potential hazard arises from the uncertainties in science, but confrontational because the crisis for Boston University arose from community opposition to the building of a research laboratory dealing with emerging infectious diseases and agents of bioterrorism. It is the latter that has created a crisis for the lab. The contentious issue was the safety of the lab in Roxbury, a poor and densely populated area. According to a community newsletter, this would be the first time that a Level 4 Bio Lab would be situated in a densely populated urban area.[618]

Community Opposition

Although Mark Klemper, associate provost for research at BU, provided the assurance that the lab would be built with "extensive redundancies and safety features," community leaders were not convinced. The issue was taken up by several community groups, with Safety Net, a Roxbury community group, spearheading opposition to the BU Lab.[619] Its coordinator, Klare Allen, provided ammunition for their safety cause. At a public forum at the Harriet Tubman House on February 16, 2005, organized by the Coalition to Stop the Bioterrorism Lab, Allen broke the news that three researchers at another BU lab on the medical campus accidentally exposed themselves to an infectious agent, tularemia, a potentially lethal bacterium. Although this happened in a lower-security lab, it was on the same BU medical campus where the new lab was planned. The event led Daniel Goodenough a Harvard Medical School biologist (who is certainly a high-credibility source) to say, "the risk is real now. No laboratory is fail-safe. . . . This facility is going to be there for 30 years or longer, so we are talking about our children, not just us. Ten years from now, will the real, careful monitoring be going on?"

Further arguments against the lab were made. An outside group, The Council for Responsible Genetics (CRG), expressed skepticism about the lab's safety and pointed out several breaches associated with high-security labs which were conveyed to the public: "Reports of transit accidents, missing vials of dangerous organism, failed power and sealing of facilities with cut tape, and explosion of a West Nile package at a Federal Express facility."[620] A further argument was made by the neighborhood group, Alternative for Community & Environment (ACE), on its web page, saying, "BU will not control the research to be done in the lab and thus cannot promise what research will be done." Another safety danger was that the lab planned to use Federal Express and other such couriers to deliver dangerous materials to the lab.[621]

A report in 2006 by the inspector general of the Massachusetts Department of Health and Human Services further undermined trust in scientific assurances. It found that 11 out of 15 universities did not fulfill all the federal requirements. Several universities kept sloppy inventory records, and inspectors could not identify who was gaining access to the pathogens, according to the report. Institutions working on animal and plant pathogens did worse. None of the 10 institutions described in a 2006 report by the USDA inspector general met all standards. Many had not updated their lists of people with access to the pathogens and had failed to fully train their staffs.[622]

Opposition forces spread the fear to outlying communities. *Green News*, a newsletter of the Green Decade Coalition, in Newton, Massachusetts, warned that a Level 4 lab in Boston posed serious safety risks "for us in Newton," pointing out that "our city will be barely five miles from the facility, easily in range for pathogens that may be accidentally released into the air. We are also at risk from researchers in the lab who may contract rare infections and then carry them to our neighborhoods. This is how SARS broke out again in China recently."[623]

Some scientists, however, "dismiss" these safety concerns, citing that there had never been a documented case of illness in a community caused by an escaped pathogen from a high-security laboratory. Level 4 labs were a "safe within a safe."[624] Nevertheless, events were turning against BU and became worse when another neighborhood association, ACE, planned to sue Boston University and the Boston Redevelopment Authority to block the project on environmental grounds.[625]

The Legal Fight and Broader Criticism

The tactic of the lawsuit against BU and BU's response led to further damaging events. Ten Roxbury and South End residents sued in state court to block the project, prompting a ruling by Suffolk Superior Court Judge Ralph D. Gants in July 2006 that called for an expanded environmental review. It was the second time in two weeks that environmental reviews of the BU project were lambasted. An independent panel of scientists declared two weeks previously that a federal review of the lab was "not sound and credible" and failed to adequately address the consequences of lethal germs escaping. BU appealed that decision to the Supreme Judicial Court in Massachusetts (SJC).

BU's appeal was unsuccessful as the state's highest court delivered a victory in December 2007 to opponents of a controversial research laboratory. In a unanimous decision, the SJC upheld a lower-court decision and agreed that the state's environmental approval of the South End lab, granted by the Romney administration, was "arbitrary and capricious." The SJC also concurred that BU must complete another environmental review of the project and submit it to the state for approval.[626] One of its criticisms was that in its original environmental approval process, the state failed to adequately consider alternative sites or weigh worst-case scenarios for release of viruses or bacteria.

The legal battle stimulated criticism from groups beyond Boston. The National Research Council concluded that the federal analysis was so woefully incomplete that it did not meet basic standards applied to scientific research. Gary Smith, a report author and University of Pennsylvania epidemiologist, said that if the federal review had been submitted for publication in a medical journal, "it would have failed."[627] In its blistering report, the independent panel of scientists said BU's defense was found to be "not sound and credible" and, among other deficiencies, failed to adequately address the consequences of highly lethal germs escaping from the project.

The BU lab case highlights the role of community groups in confrontations and, specifically, the use of legal tactics. The tactic of issuing news releases and holding events, such as the forum, that attracted media and public attention, was also used.

Animal Rights

The animal rights issue covers a wide range of industry behaviors, from keeping animals in zoos and circuses to replacing the bearskin hats worn by ceremonial guards at Buckingham Palace. One of the major animal rights groups, People for the Ethical Treatment of Animals (PETA), called for a global boycott of KFC to force it to improve the conditions that 700 million chickens supplied to the chain are raised in.[628] Other groups want to banish the wearing of fur coats, halt the sale of tiger bones, rhinoceros horns, and elephant tusks. Even foie gras is targeted because goose liver is fattened by traditional force-feeding. Animal rights has become a moral issue, raising the question of whether animals should be accorded more human rights.

The biggest confrontations, however, concern the use of animals to test the safety of consumer products. In Britain, the biomedical research industry, which totaled $8 billion in 2004, is under siege. Attacks and harassment of drug companies and university labs, including their staff, suppliers, and shareholders, are on the rise. There were 235 incidents of criminal damage in the 12 months through June 2004. Animal rights groups were costing Britain $2 billion a year in investment. "We are being terrorized," said GlaxoSmithKline PLC CEO Jean-Pierre Gernier.[629]

Huntingdon Life Sciences

A group calling themselves "Stop Huntingdon Animal Cruelty" (SHAC) has confronted Huntingdon Life Sciences (HLS) to stop what they label cruelty and abuse of animals in research labs. Such abuse in research labs was authenticated by a 1997 undercover television report by Britain's Channel 4, which included footage of a lab worker punching a beagle in the face and shaking it. (The British love their dogs!) In the United States, PETA videotaped alleged abuses and violations that included cutting monkeys while they were still alive and slamming them into cages.[630]

Huntingdon is one of the world's leading research labs, which provide development services to the pharmaceutical, agrochemical, and biotechnology industries. They operate research facilities in the United Kingdom and the United States. Although some testing is done in petri dishes, most of it is done on beagles, cats, rats, rabbits, monkeys, and other animals.

SHAC's tactics include not only the usual protests, demonstrations and pickets outside the labs, but also more militant ones, such as intrusion into the lives of executives and workers and outright violence. Having obtained personal information about the directors and employees of HLS, SHAC began to protest outside the staff members' homes and made threatening phone calls to them. In one incident Brian Cass, the managing director of HLS, was attacked outside his home with a baseball bat and seriously injured. Ronnie Lee, founder of the Animal Liberation Front (ALF), which may have participated in this violence, said, "In fact, I would say that I condone this. What surprises me is that this doesn't happen more often."[631] Other violent acts included letter bombs to employees' homes and firebomb attacks on cars belonging to staff. Belatedly, Scotland Yard created a special intelligence unit to work on animal-rights protests against HLS and other targeted firms.

Showing innovations in choice of tactics, SHAC has been equally aggressive toward the financial backers and the pharmaceutical companies who have patronized HLS. These included The Royal Bank of Scotland (RBS), Barclays Bank, HSBC Bank, Credit Suisse First Boston, and Merrill Lynch. One by one these banks deserted HLS. Brokerage firms joined the rout, notably Winterflood Securities and Dresdner Kleinwort Wasserstein. Greg Avery, spokesperson for SHAC, said, "We want to remove the financial pillars from underneath it."[632]

In the United States, the president of the Biotechnology Industry Organization, Carl Feldbaum, wrote a letter to President Bush highlighting his concerns. He stated, "Their campaign against biotechnology companies is strategic, specific, unrelenting and directed toward delivering economic, and sometimes physical, damage to companies engaged in innovation for life threatening diseases such as cancer and cystic fibrosis."[633]

McDonald's has been the target of occasional attacks by animal rights groups. Demonstrations occurred outside one of their downtown Montreal restaurants where placards accused the company of "buying products from breeders who raise and kill animals cruelly."[634] PETA placed advertisements in local papers, one which showed a flayed cow's head, dripping blood, hanging from an abattoir wall, with a caption reading "Do you want fries with that?" and closes with, "McDonald's Cruelty to Go." A website, McSpotlight, accuses McDonald's as being "a symbol of multinational corporations and big business that relentlessly pursued their profits at the expense of anything that stands in their way."[635]

The most influential group in the animal rights movement, PETA, states that it seeks to achieve its objectives through public education and casework and through promotion of a cruelty-free lifestyle."[636] Its varied and sophisticated tactics go far beyond persuasion, however. While it has engaged in such activities as releasing damning video footage of animal cruelty, it has also blocked animal laboratory entrances, picketed diving-mule shows, disrupted shareholder meetings, and had its members arrested, sued and countersued. To enable it to introduce animal-rights resolutions at shareholder meetings, PETA owns more than $40,000 worth of stock in a dozen major corporations that perform animal testing or sell animal products, including IBM, Procter & Gamble, and Gillette.[637]

The most extreme animal rights group, one that literally wages war against bio-medical research, is the ALF. One of its tactics is to break into animal laboratories, which it did at the University of California's Riverside laboratories where pigeons, monkeys, cats, and other animals were kept. They emptied cages of animals, wrote graffiti on the walls, smashed computers, and painted slogans on equipment.

In Britain, the ALF raided Interfauna, one of Britain's largest animal breeders and suppliers of dogs, rabbits, guinea pigs, and mice to biomedical research laboratories. Stolen were 82 beagles and 26 rabbits, as well as documents. The ALF spray-painted "Beagles Bred for Torture" on a side entrance to the building.[638] An extreme was reached with the Hall family, which diversified from dairy and sheep farming into breeding guinea pigs for use in research laboratories. Activists stole the body of the mother-in-law of one of the Hall brothers from its grave in a churchyard. This act persuaded the family to stop breeding guinea pigs.[639] In Europe, when the Swiss drug giant Novartis AG was targeted, someone stole the ashes of its CEO's mother and set his Austrian vacation home on fire.[640]

Labor Disputes

Labor disputes, although declining in frequency, have continued to plague some industries. In September 2007, 73,000 United Auto Workers (UAW) struck General Motors plants in the first nationwide strike since 1976.[641] Labor unions in the United States have been in decline, as reflected in low membership, which is only about 12 percent of total employed population and 9 percent of the civilian work force. Facing global competition, the bargaining power of unions has been reduced. Many labor leaders now often work hand-in-hand with management to improve corporate competitiveness to protect jobs. As Jerry Tucker, a longtime U.A.W. militant said, "The message from the union leadership nowadays often is, 'We don't have any choice, we have to go down this concessionary road to see if we can do damage control.'"[642]

Only occasionally do American workers vent their anger in protests and strikes. Demonstrations were held against American International Group bonuses but, generally, American workers largely stayed off the streets, even as the unemployment rate rises and companies cut wages and benefits. American unions engaged in only 159 work stoppages in 2008, down from 1,352 in 1981, according to the Bureau of National Affairs, a publisher of legal and regulatory news.[643] Workers may have been cowed by the watershed event in 1981 when President Ronald Reagan quickly fired the 11,500 striking traffic controllers when they engaged in an illegal strike. Since November 2008, the only large strike, lasting six weeks, was by 2,500 union members at Bell Helicopter.[644]

Compared with U.S. workers, European workers are more prone to strike and demonstrate. When Danone sought to rationalize its biscuit division, strikes immediately broke out at the firm's biscuit plants. A front-page headline in France's *Le Monde* (January 10, 2001) read, "Danone Prepares to Suppress 3,000 Jobs in Europe, Including 1,700 in France." The Internet began to hurt Danone. One site featured a Danone logo modified to include the slogan "human beings are not yogurt." It also provided a list of all Danone brands to help consumers boycott the wide range of Danone products. Besides striking, the union used the tactic of allowing unbaked dough to harden like concrete in its receptacles.

Over the next two weeks, sympathetic protests widened to the public sector. A survey showed that unions were winning in the arena of public opinion as 85 percent of the French supported them, even though, on March 29, Danone presented a plan of social measures for displaced workers that went well beyond what was required by French law.[645] Support for the unions further grew when they launched a boycott. Communist and socialist mayors of big town ordered their hospitals, schools and cafeterias to stop buying Danone products. A copy-cat boycott also began in Hungary. In mid-May the press reported on rumors that Danone had lost 10–20 percent of its sales. Danone's public image continued to suffer.

During the recession, which started in 2008, 15,000 workers demonstrated at General Motors' German headquarters when the company announced huge job cuts worldwide in 2009. Early that year, more than a million workers in France demonstrated against layoffs and the government's handling of the economic crisis. They used more direct tactics too. French workers took their bosses hostage in four different labor disputes.[646] One of them was at Caterpillar in the French city of Grenoble after the company announced 700 job cuts. The CEO and other executives were subjected to a night of pounding revolutionary rock music and threats shouted by workers. They were released after French President Nicolas Sarkozy promised to meet with union leaders and save the site.[647]

Managing Confrontation Crises

The signs that an organization is facing a confrontation are clear: a group of protesters are at the factory gates or in the office lobby; they picket, demonstrate or sit-in; workers don't report to work; critics become stockholders so they can file a proxy resolution; demands are made of the CEO or plant or office manager; a boycott or other unwanted actions are threatened. A manager must know how to respond, not only immediately but on a continuing basis.

Coping with a confrontation crisis requires a deep knowledge of human behavior and political and social processes, as well as skill in listening, group dynamics, conflict resolution, and negotiations. And when the news media are involved, as they usually are, adroitness in media relations is a necessity.

Assess Power of Opposition

A good start is to assess the political power of activists who challenge an organization. The primary sources of information are newspaper and magazine reports, which can be accessed rapidly by such bibliographical computer services as Nexis, the group's own handouts and literature from other companies who have been confronted by the group, and in other published material such as files the Foundation for Public Affairs' Public Interest Profiles.[648]

It is also critical to profile an opposition group—to identify its particular strengths, the kinds of tactics it uses, and its record of success in other confrontations.

When the Baptist Church urged its members to boycott all Disney Operations, including its popular theme parks, because Disney hired homosexuals and engaged in other family-unfriendly acts, Disney could engage in a power assessment: how many members does the group have; how well organized are they; what is its geographical reach; do the members support the positions of their leaders? The attempt failed because the attractiveness of Disney offerings was greater than the urging by the Church's leader. As the Baptist Church learned, a boycott requires the voluntary participation of people. It is easy for leaders to call for a boycott but very difficult to enforce it.

A significant source of strength of an opposition group is its ability and skill in communicating with its supporters and the public. Labor unions find strength in effective internal communications. For example, the *IUE News*, the official publication of the International Union of Electrical, Radio & Machine Workers, goes to every member and regularly carries house ads identifying the products being boycotted by IUE itself and by other unions. Communications by labor unions and social action groups are protected by the First Amendment and by labor laws, specifically the National Labor Relations Act.

Don't Get Caught By Surprise

If managers have applied the principles of contingency planning, confrontations should not be complete surprises. Careful monitoring of issues and trends, as well as activist group interest in them, will forewarn them. Many firms have installed issue management and public affairs departments to "try to proactively keep track of upcoming issues or to respond as adequately as possible to any incidents."[649] In some situations, a target organization may use the accommodative strategy with activists rather than taking a defensive stance as Pepsi initially did in response to Narain's accusations. "Intelligence is the essential weapon," said Italy's deputy interior minister, Alfredo Mantavano, with regard to demonstrations.[650] Police around the world realize that the best information about protesters comes from the Internet. Additional information is obtained by infiltrating groups. It is unwise, however, to use such surveillance techniques unless a situation becomes one of malevolence.

There was no reason why the WTO should have been surprised by the huge protest in Seattle. U.S. Trade Representative Charlene Barshefsky amazingly conceded that the growing political power of the anti-globalists had taken the free-trade establishment by surprise.[651] Even the most rudimentary scanning of major newspapers and magazines would have indicated growing anti-globalism, let alone more formal monitoring activities associated with issues management. Similarly, police officials were apparently unaware of the email activity preceding the meeting and that 2,500 campaigners attended a teach-in on the evils of globalization. Too often, people in organizations are insular and don't look beyond their walls. The power of the social media is not fully recognized.

It remains uncertain how aware the editors and publisher of the Danish newspaper *Jyllands-Posten* that printed the inflammatory cartoons of Moham-mad were of Muslim anger. They wanted to express the basic Western value of editorial freedom. But whoever was responsible for Arla Foods' corporate affairs should not have been surprised at the violent reaction in the Middle East after the local Muslim leadership was shunned by the Danish prime min-ister. His office did not realize that the art of diplomacy also applied to Muslim groups in Denmark. It took the prime minister over three months to issue an apology, weak as it was, and too late to prevent the protests a few weeks later.

Assess Your Vulnerability

An organization must realistically assess its vulnerability and seek to reduce it. Vulnerability is based on: (a) visibility and size; (b) type of market in which a company's products are sold; (c) its social performance; and (d) its exposure.

Visibility and Size

Coke and McDonald's are global icons and cannot conceal their identity. They are under special pressure to be socially responsible, which is a reason they are attractive to activists. Similarly, a global icon like Nike could not escape notice. Global companies that use local names or a variety of brand names could de-emphasize their corporate brand or confuse consumers. When INFACT organized a boycott against Nestlé for selling infant formula in poor nations, consumers who wished to boycott the company had to refer to a long list of brand names. American companies have long learned to keep a low profile—not to fly the American flag in sensitive overseas locations.

Large, visible firms are attractive targets because campaigns against them are more likely to garner attention from the media and the general pub-lic. Even if a targeted firm does not comply, the publicity helps the activist group.[652] These factors were identified in a study of 90 boycotts by Monroe Friedman, a psychology professor. In developing a taxonomy of the most effective actions boycott sponsors can take, he discovered these patterns: (1) use the names of well-known organizations and/or individuals; (2) identify one or more target firms that are well-known; (3) make the complaints against targeted firms legitimate and relatively uncomplicated; and (4) use drama in the announcement whenever possible, e.g., state a hunger strike is under-way.[653] A company's vulnerability increases when a social action group can apply these actions.

Boycott organizers know that "image management" is increasingly a concern of firms serving customers in retail markets. Fear of losing consumer confidence makes American businesses responsive to boycotts. As a nationwide survey of business leaders showed, boycotts topped business leaders' list of "the most effective techniques for the consumer movement to use."[654] Organizers use this apprehension of boycotts to their advantage and find that sometimes a mere announcement that a boycott is being considered is enough pressure to achieve their goals.

Type of Market

When a company sells to other companies, or to a few large organizations such as government, public opinion is not as critical a concern, since it will not impinge directly on the company's operations. A company is particularly vulnerable when its product is clearly identified with the company, such as Coca Cola and Campbell's Soup. This factor is less likely to affect a company like Nestlé whose products are sold under many different trade labels. Similarly, in the classic case of the J.P. Stevens boycott, labor organizers were faced with the intricate communications problem of informing consumers that the company's sheets and pillowcases, to mention only one product line, were sold under the labels of Beauty-Blend, Beauticale, Fine Arts, Peanuts, Tastemaker, Utica, Utica & Mohawk, Yves St. Laurent, and Angelo Donghia.

Multiproduct and multidivision companies become increasingly vulnerable, however, when a major crisis or event receives protracted media attention. This happened to Procter & Gamble when its Rely tampons became associated with toxic shock syndrome. The company had to consider the possible negative impact on its other product lines, and was consequently in a weakened position.

Companies selling convenience goods that are purchased daily, or several times a week or month by consumers are more vulnerable than those selling durable goods. Consumers are more likely to remember unfavorable news about a company in the short time-span between hearing the news and purchasing a product sold by that company. Soft drinks, beer, milk, bread, and other groceries lead the list. Companies operating in a market in which competing products are readily available and brand loyalty is weak are likely to be highly vulnerable.

Social Performance

Companies that have become controversial or socially stigmatized are vulnerable to selective boycotting. A company may be judged to be the worst perpetrator of some injustice or its actions perceived as harmful. In the classical J.P. Stevens case, the company was singled out by the Amalgamated Clothing and Textile Workers Union because of the company's open and recalcitrant refusal to bargain with the union, even after being ordered to do so by the court, and because of its aggressive campaign against further union organizing.

A company's social policies may be offensive to some groups. A classical example is Coors beer, which was unlikely to be sold in gay bars because of the corporation's support of Anita Bryant's anti-homosexual campaign. Similarly, the grape boycott called by Cesar Chavez was particularly successful in Boston's suburbs, where the issue received a great deal of attention and peer pressure was high.

Exposure

In planning events, organizations can reduce their exposure through careful selection of locations and sites. Unlike protests against organizations in fixed locations, world organizations have flexibility in choosing their meeting sites. Referring to the Seattle demonstrations, John Sellers, the coordinator of the Berkeley-based Ruckus Society, which teaches nonviolent protest techniques to activist groups, said, "I think it's incredible for [the WTO] to have chosen this place." The reason: although one in four local jobs in the Puget Sound region is tied to either importing or exporting, "it's also knee-deep in well-networked activists, many of whom are veterans of lengthy disputes with the timber industry, among other things."[655]

The World Economic Forum, which meets in its usual location in Davos, Switzerland, decided in 2002 to move its meeting to New York City because after 9/11 Davos residents feared terrorist assaults.[656] Moreover, the 2001 session at Davos was marred by fights outside the conference between police and protesters. Citizens did not want the restful place immortalized by Thomas Mann's *The Magic Mountain* to be turned into a fortress.[657] If violence is expected, sites that are relatively inaccessible to protesters should be chosen. Doha was one of those sites; so was the convention center in Cancun situated on a strip of sand jutting into the Caribbean and accessible by land on only two highway points.[658]

Take Initiative in Dealing with Media

Confrontations are media events, and the opposition must not be allowed to monopolize the media by default. Public perceptions are based on media reports, and accusations may be given credit if they are not challenged. A general assumption in crisis communication is that "those who are able to define what the crisis is all about also hold the key to defining the appropriate strategies for resolution." Protagonists generally assume "that the truth will out in the news media, and that the effects of mistruths will be devastating on public opinion and authorities."[659] One global consulting firm advises: "Stay open, frank and honest, and you will control who speaks the truth, in which circumstances, and when to reveal."[660] In other words, transparency serves to frame the limits of acceptable debate by providing continuous information that dominates the facts available to public opinion.

Many activist groups have become more media-savvy. Some protest groups in Seattle had valuable previous media experience, e.g., the Independent Media Exchange, Action Resource Center, Direct Action Media Network, Global Exchange, Citizens Trade Campaign, United Students Against Sweatshops, and Global Trade Watch.[661] Some had received support from foundations, such as the Charles Stewart Mott Foundation and the Rockefeller Brothers Fund, whose motivation was their commitment to working internationally to protect the environment.[662] It has become typical for these groups to hold media training seminars and teach protesters how to get their messages out. They have learned to look for independent channels not mediated by conventional media like the *New York Times*.

Videotaping of protests has itself become a brand of protest for the antiglobalization movement. Video activists, as they are known, show up in growing numbers at anticorporate protests around the world, filming police brutality. This new culture of "guerrilla media activism" eschews objectivity, says Thomas Harding, author of *The Video Activist Handbook*, a how-too guide. He says many guerrilla cameramen see the mass media as pawns of large corporations, so they need to cover events themselves.[663] The ubiquity of cell phones with cameras are today increasing the chances that acts of violence will be captured and broadcast widely.

In Danone's confrontation with labor unions, the media war was won by the unions. Danone failed to get media support and messages on the Internet further hurt it. The particulars of French law also injured it because it limits the right of companies to publicly discuss alternatives. The researchers of the case warn that "crisis communication strategies that give priority to influencing public opinion may increase the risk of conflict with key stakeholders. . . ." The aim should not have been to involve the general public but to deepen dialog with key stakeholders.

Enforce the Law But Use Police Force Sparingly

Legal action tends to shift a situation further into the confrontation mode. Its use is appropriate if an opposing group plans to use illegal tactics. An example is the stance taken by Kohler in its long labor dispute. It said, "Let them know they're in for a lawsuit if they step over the line."[664] If, on the other hand, the opposition group is genuinely eager to resolve a dispute, the resort to legal action will be damaging.

The tactic of legal action can be used by both sides of a confrontation. After community groups sued Boston University, it in turn decided to appeal the decision to the Massachusetts Supreme Court, where it lost the case. It may have been more productive for both sides to rethink the legal strategy and consider whether more could be gained through accommodation and negotiation.

Organizations faced with demonstrations often ask for protection from the legal authorities and the police. In the meeting of the World Economic Forum in Davos, Switzerland, in January 2001, protesters applied to hold a Saturday demonstration. City authorities, however, rejected the request, partly because businesspeople were opposed. The forum brings in about $10 million in business during the week and gets priceless publicity. The regional police manned roadblocks at all road and rail entrances to the town. Hotels installed airport-style X-ray machines at their front doors. As a precaution, McDonald's had bars and metal shutters ready to be deployed, as well as private security guards standing watch at the counter. Some shops were planning to be shuttered Saturday afternoon.[665]

The use of police force requires careful judgment. It is not unusual for the police to fire tear gas on protesters as they did at those who attempted to pull down a stretch of a perimeter fence to keep activists out of the Summit of the Americas trade meeting in Quebec City in 2001.[666] It is generally agreed, however, that the police often overreact.

The G8 meeting in Genoa, attended by more than 100,000 people in July 2001, will be remembered for a brutal police attack.[667] In an early morning raid on July 22, at the Armando Diaz school complex, where protest organizers had made a headquarters, some 70 Italian SWAT team police smashed through the doors and beat the demonstrators. Some 61 subsequently required hospitalization. One of them was Miriam Heigl, a political science student from Munich, who was among about 30 others who were arrested and taken to a police barracks. There, she said, she was humiliated and deprived of basic civil liberties by being made to strip. Another victim was Melanie Jonasch, an archeology student from Berlin, who was hit on the head with a truncheon and woke up in a Genoese hospital, where she has had surgery for a broken mastoid bone behind her left ear.[668] Police records show that 430 violent protestors were arrested and 150 were injured. At the G20 meeting in April 2009 in London, police brutality again became an issue as Twitter evidence was presented to the British newspaper the *Guardian*.[669]

Engage Opposition Groups

Meet with Reasonable Groups

Protesters sometimes complain, "We're called terrorists and militants by the corporate media," and claim that a prejudgment is made when they are characterized as "protesters."[670] Instead, distinctions should be made among different types of activist groups. A useful typology developed by Alan Marsh, a London social survey analyst, lists five types of activist groups: inactives, conformists, reformists, activists, and protesters.[671] The latter are considered the most radical.

In another typology used by veteran public relations counselor Philip Lesly, extremists are called zealots. Lesly described them as being "distinguished by overriding single-mindedness, absorbed with one issue such as stopping a power plant or liberating a geographic area of social groups. Egocentric, must run the show, consider moderates to be enemies."[672] Both zealots and protestors are known to use the most aggressive tactics.

In the anti-globalization demonstrations, "protestors" included many advocates, dissidents, and activists who simply wanted to change things through reason and nonviolent means. Of the some 60,000 demonstrators in Seattle, only 200 radicals were identified as breaking windows and engaging in other destruction, but they got most media attention.[673] Being willing to meet with the leaders of reasonable activist groups and listening to their concerns can help defuse a confrontation. It can also avoid being characterized as arrogant, unapproachable and undemocratic. If, however, there is reason to believe that a confrontation group's purpose is solely to embarrass an organization, a meeting should be avoided or a condition set that the media be excluded. Groups classified as terrorists, or even extremists, should almost always be shunned.

Despite the risk involved, managements are becoming more willing to meet with the leaders of an activist group and listen to their grievances and demands. The advice is: Don't wall yourself off; don't turn a deaf ear, even to your harshest critics. An organization does not want to be portrayed as arrogant, unapproachable, and undemocratic. It does not want to enable critics to raise the moral issue: "management won't even sit down and talk with us."

Be Ready to Accommodate and Negotiate

Some confrontations can be reduced or eliminated by voluntarily changing the policies and behavior that caused them. This is slowly being done with the animal rights controversy. The Organisation for Economic Cooperation and Development (OECD), the private club of the world's richest nations, agreed in May 2002 to approve four tests for chemical safety that don't rely on live rabbits and rodents. For example, instead of dabbing chemical onto a live rabbit's skin to identify corrosive chemicals, the same check is done by putting chemicals onto discs of skin cultured from humans or rodents. The underlying principle is to work towards the "three Rs": reduction, refinement and replacement.[674]

Procter & Gamble announced that it will stop testing current products on animals. But it will continue to test new products and ingredients on animals. "So keep boycotting!" advise P&G's critics. Neiman Marcus's response to a group was to send a "form letter" rather than recognize it. The activist group consequently gave up negotiation attempts and instead used the tactics of distributing anti-Neiman Marcus literature in front of the store (and even in the store, risking arrest), engaging in a sit-in and brandishing a banner "Neiman Kills Animals," and to demonstrate outside the annual meeting site.

Instead of taking unilateral action, an organization may find advantages in negotiating with an opposition group. Resolving problems by negotiation removes the need for confrontation and avoids bad publicity, damage to the corporate image, loss of sales, and lower profits. The willingness to bargain, along with a general interactive approach, should be used if mutually beneficial. It can reduce or eliminate disturbances and enable an organization to achieve a more stable equilibrium with others. Nevertheless, some managers resist bargaining because they see it as a surrender of management prerogatives and a loss of power. Some also rationalize that a willingness to bargain may escalate an activist group's demands.

The rationale for bargaining rather than fighting with critics is explained in Lawrence Susskind and Patrick Field's book, *Dealing with an Angry Public: The Mutual Gains Approach to Resolving Disputes*.[675] The techniques for doing so are discussed in another well-known book, Roger Fisher and William Ury's *Getting to Yes: Negotiating Agreement Without Giving In*.[676]

Danone might have been helped by negotiating with the union. It could have acknowledged the specific impacts of the boycott and, in consultation with its stakeholders, sought alternatives to restructuring and closing operations. As was pointed out, "Danone and its biscuit operations were profitable, and structuring, though desirable for investors, was not urgent. Maintaining management credibility was urgent." We want to stay French," said Yves Savoyat, head of the works council at Lu.[677]

As Danone learned,

> Managing a crisis does not, and cannot, only mean winning over the firm's adversaries in the domain of public opinion; management's urgent tasks include averting, or failing that, healing conflict with direct stakeholders. The nature of crises has changed. They are more than ever rooted in clashes of values, and all who participate in them now own a public voice. Organizational leaders who seek to manage social crises by control of information, and through it, control of opinion, are fighting a battle that they will lose.[678]

Consider Involving Public Interest Groups in Decision-Making

Besides meeting with environmentalists and its other critics, the World Bank went one step further by incorporating their views of into its decision-making.[679] It had to overcome its past reaction that interpreted all criticisms only as a matter of perceptions that had to be corrected. "This is the classical response of a big bureaucracy," says Bruce Rich, senior attorney for the Environmental Defense Fund. It follows that "a problem is conveniently explained as one of misperceptions and misunderstandings which, of course, can be corrected by properly educating the critics."[680]

The bank's approach, after James Wolfensohn took over in 1995, was to create an atmosphere of being more open to civil society. John Clark, principal "social-development specialist" at the bank, explained the six strands employed in this strategy:

- Expanded collaboration in operations, emphasizing early involvement by civil society in project design;
- Engaged civil society in discussing strategies within each country;
- Begun a new disclosure policy, making public a wider array of information;
- Established a regular dialogue on big policy issues such as environment and debt relief, replacing more informal consultations;
- Used its influence over borrowing governments to encourage greater tolerance of civil groups.
- Broadened the range of groups it consults: trade unions, religious organizations, civic associations and other groups that shape local societies.[681]

The World Bank's openness to greater participation by NGOs has helped it overcome some public criticisms.

Conclusions

Confrontations are a normal aspect of a democratic society. But the frequency and intensity mostly depends on the soundness of an organization's policies and actions that affect its stakeholders and the public and the adequacy of it communications. Some confrontations may occur to organizations that are blameless. A corporation may be implicated because it is a convenient and strategic target for promoting a social issue, or because people are angry at some action taken by its home country.

An organization must continually monitor issues and groups that might give rise to a conflict. When a confrontation appears imminent, it should use the tools of political science to study the nature and power of its challenger. By understanding the dynamics of confrontations, a targeted organization can decide how best to respond—again choosing between the strategies of defense and accommodation. The lessons learned from various confrontations, summarized under the heading of managing confrontation crises, should be applied.

Coping with a confrontation crisis requires a deep knowledge of human behavior and political and social processes, as well as skill in listening, group dynamics, conflict resolution, and negotiations. And when the news media are involved, as they usually are, adroitness in media relations is essential.

Chapter 9

Crises of Malevolence

An organization faces a crisis of malevolence when opponents or miscreant individuals use extreme and often criminal tactics for the purpose of expressing hostility toward, or seeking gain from, a company, country or economic system, perhaps with the aim of destabilizing or destroying it. Terrorist acts committed against governments are the clearest expression of malevolence, with the September 11, 2001, attack on the twin World Trade Center towers as the prime example.

Terrorism

Terrorism is the use of extreme tactics by one or more antagonists in a conflict.[682] In particular, it is the psychological element of malice that makes each terrorist act, no matter how small, deeply repugnant. Not surprisingly, one definition of terrorism is "the deliberate maiming and menacing of the innocent to inspire fear for political ends."[683] Another definition sees terrorism as a "special form of clandestine, undeclared and unconventional warfare without any humanitarian restraints or rules."[684] The FBI's definition is: "The unlawful use of force or violence against persons or property to intimidate or coerce a government, the civilian population, or any segment thereof, in furtherance of political or social objectives."[685]

The 9/11 attack revealed the need for better crisis recognition and preparation. As now known, federal agencies and the military were poorly prepared for the 9/11 emergency. There was chain-of-command confusion among the White House, the military and other federal agencies as the nation was under attack. There was no coordination between the Pentagon and Federal Aviation Authority (FAA) headquarters. Traffic control centers initially failed to notice that hijackers had altered the transponder signal from the second plane bound for the World Trade Center. They also missed the turn by American Airlines, which was supposed to go to California but instead flew undetected for 36 minutes back toward Washington. When military fighters were scrambled, they first flew in the wrong direction.[686]

The persistent fear is that the ultimate expression of terrorism—an atom bomb or bacterial attack—may yet come. We're living in a nasty world. Road bombs in Afghanistan are the symbol of omnipresent danger. We have to expect more malevolence and prepare for it.

Business as a Vulnerable Terrorist Target

Although terrorist acts are usually aimed at governmental or military/police hierarchies, business establishments and executives have been more frequent targets. The reason is that corporations serve as highly visible symbols of what terrorists call the "exploitative imperialist elements or part of the repressive organizations of state."[687] The boundaries between public and private targets were blurred when ten terrorists wielding AK-47s launched an onslaught in Mumbai, India, on November 27, 2008. Their targets were a railroad station, two luxury hotels—the Taj Mahal and the Trident Oberoi,—Cafe Leopold, a hospital, and a Jewish center.[688] The attack killed 166 people and wounded many others. Most were businesspeople and tourists. The traumatized citizens of Mumbai no longer felt secure and were angry with local authorities for failing to stop the attack. Many turned to private sector security and emergency services.[689] The terrorists succeeded in undermining citizen faith in their government.

The private sector must be prepared for terrorist acts on a smaller scale. All organizations must consider the possibility of the kidnapping of executives, workplace violence, mailing of bomb or anthrax-laden letters, extortion attempts, corporate espionage, cybercrime, placement of malicious rumors, and defamation through the Internet. The cost of protecting a top executive can be high. It cost $1.2 million in 2007 in security and protection for Jeff Bezos, Amazon.com's CEO. The costs of other top executives were $727,199 for Patrick Soon-Shiong, Abraxis BioScience chairman and CEO; $571,447 for Frank Fertitta III, Station Casinos chairman and CEO; $158,478 for Maurice Marciano, chairman of Guess?; and $134,000 for Fred Hassan, Schering-Plough chairman and CEO.[690]

Vulnerable industries, such as chemical, transportation and public utilities, should engage in appropriate mitigation and preparedness activities, but they are worried about the costs. In 2003, Senator Jon Corzine (N.J.-Dem), introduced the Chemical Security Act as a measure to combat terrorism. One of its goals was to reduce the usage and storage of chemicals by changing production methods and processes. The bill was opposed by the industry's two big lobbying groups—the American Chemistry Council (ACC) and the American Petroleum Institute (IPI). They were especially concerned about the prospects of regulators demanding "inherently safer technologies."[691] Senator Corzine's attempt to frame the issue around homeland security was insufficient to change the stand of the ACC and IPI.

Varieties of Malevolent Acts

Some of the most publicized malevolent acts against corporations in the past were the product tampering of Johnson & Johnson's Tylenol, the placement of syringes and needles in Pepsi soda cans, rumors that Procter & Gamble was consorting with the devil, and that the Tropical Fantasy drink was sterilizing African-American men. The new cases included below are more insidious and violent. They include bioterrorism, cybercrime, violence in the workplace and universities, and rumors spread through the Internet.

Bioterrorism

Anthrax

Americans became familiar with bioterrorism in September 2001, when a series of anthrax-laced letters were mailed by an unknown individual. At least seven such letters were sent to lawmakers and the media from a mailbox near Princeton University, New Jersey. The letters killed five people and injured 17.[692] The letters also caused significant disruptions, e.g., Congress was shut down for several months to allow a thorough examination of buildings used by the House and Senate after Senator Patrick Leahy of Vermont received one of the letters.[693]

The psychological impact of these anthrax-laced letters was heightened because they appeared shortly after the attacks on the World Trade Center and the Pentagon. Further heightening the severity of this form of terrorism was its ubiquity—it could happen at any location served by the U.S. Postal Service, and to postal employees as well as recipients. Moreover, the symptoms of anthrax are difficult to diagnose because they are confused with common illnesses such as the common cold or the more dangerous flu. A runny or stuffy nose is not the flu, whose symptoms are systemic, i.e., victims feel sick all over their bodies, and profoundly tired. The similarity of anthrax to the flu is that its victims complain of chills, vague chest tightness, nausea, high temperature, and body ache.[694]

Exacerbating correct diagnosis is the nation's deficit in public-health agencies equipped to handle such crises. They are the first line of defense, but because of the nation's relative health, their number and staffing has been reduced and 1,140 U.S. counties don't even have a health department.[695] The Centers for Disease Control & Prevention (CDC) can play a vital role in monitoring health outbreaks and seeing patterns, but its role is to support the public health mission of states—if asked.

Future Scenarios

"Bioterrorism will be the next event," predicts Dr. Bertram S. Brown, co-founder of the Potomac Institute for Policy Studies.[696] The cult that released sarin in Tokyo subways in 1995 had plans to use anthrax.[697] Some "worst scenarios" of other forms of bioterrorism include the unleashing of smallpox and other deadly bugs such as anthrax, bubonic plague, hemorrhagic fevers, Ebola, and gene-spliced bacteria. Smallpox would represent the gravest danger because of its high contagiousness and because the general U.S. public hasn't been vaccinated since 1972. It could leave thousands, or millions, of Americans dead, as the influenza did in 1918. The biggest fear is that bioterrorism might be a new weapon in war. A book by Judith Miller, Stephen Engelberg and William Broad, *Biological Weapons and America's Secret War*, recounts the many efforts by nations around the globe to develop bio-weapons, including the U.S.[698] There is evidence that Iraq, Iran, Libya, China, North Korea, Russia, Israel, Pakistan, and Taiwan have biological arsenals.

Bioterrorism has also been used in local conflicts. In 2001, The Dalles, an Oregon town of 10,000, was struck with salmonella poisoning which, while killing only one person, filled all 125 beds in the town's only hospital. The salmonella outbreak, it was learned, was caused by followers of Shree Rajneesh, the founder of a huge cult with a settlement in town. Angered by town efforts to prevent expansion of their 4,000-member community, they had sprayed salad bars around town with salmonella.[699]

Cybercrime

Cybercrime is the application of computer technology to various kinds of undesirable activity. It usually refers to "new" crimes such as the unauthorized "hacking" into computer systems and data banks to steal valuable intellectual property or other information for purposes of spying or self-gain. Cybercrime also refers to the use of computers to facilitate the commission of such conventional crimes as theft, fraud, extortion, and stalking. A feature of cybercrime is its ability to transcend national boundaries, thus eluding local law enforcement.[700] In response, a Convention on Cybercrime was organized in 2001 to consider establishment of a sort of super-Interpol to coordinate investigations among national law enforcement officers.[701]

Headlines announce the severity of cybercrime. A page one article, "Arrest in Epic Cyber Swindle" appeared in the August 18, 2009 issue of the *Wall Street Journal*.[702] It described how a 28-year-old, Albert Gonzalez, and two Russian accomplices, carried out the largest hacking and identify-theft caper in U.S. history by allegedly stealing 130 million card numbers.

A 2006 Computer Crime and Security Survey of some 616 IT security practitioners from U.S. businesses and other organizations listed the top new types of cybercrimes as virus attacks, unauthorized access to networks, lost and stolen laptops or mobile hardware, and theft of proprietary information or intellectual property.[703] Spies in China and other countries were targeting traveling U.S. corporate and government officials. Their electronic devices are often targeted by foreign governments, using such tactics as copying information contained in laptop computers at airport checkpoints or hotel rooms, wirelessly inserting spyware on BlackBerry devices, and a new technique dubbed "slurping" that uses Bluetooth technology to steal data from electronic devices.[704]

Data Theft at TJX Cos

The biggest theft of credit-card numbers in history occurred in 2005 when hackers pointed a telescope-shaped antenna toward a Marshalls discount clothing store near St. Paul, Minnesota, and used a laptop computer to decode data streaming through the air between hand-held price-checking devices, cash registers, and the store's computers.[705] Hackers were then able to penetrate the central database of Marshalls' parent, TJX Cos, in Framingham, Massachusetts, to obtain more customer information. The hackers downloaded at least 45.7 million credit- and debit-card numbers from about a year's worth of records, and may have obtained as many as 200 million card numbers from four years' records. They also got personal information—such as driver's license numbers, military identification and Social Security numbers—of 451,000 customers, which could be used for identity theft.

Hackers used the method of working through middlemen to sell the data to other thieves on password-protected Internet bartering sites. The hackers are suspected of being members of "Romanian hackers" and Russian-organized crime groups. Criminals pay as much s $200 a card, depending on the card's limit and other factors.[706] Fraudulent cards are then produced that start showing up in credit-card statements. In Florida alone, one gang that bought some of the hacked TJX card data used it to steal $8 million in small transactions at Wal-Mart Stores Inc., Sam's Club and other stores across the state. One California customer found a whole page of $450 charges for gift cards from a Wal-Mart in Florida. Fidelity Homestead Bank in Louisiana and Middlesex Savings Bank in Natick, Massachusetts, suffered losses.

Losses stemming from data theft are enormous. TJX's breach-related bill could surpass $1 billion over five years in costs for consultants, security upgrades, attorney fees, and added marketing to reassure customers, but not lawsuit liabilities. In June 2009 TJX agreed to pay $9.75 million to 41 states, including California, to settle the massive data breech. For U.S. individuals, the risk is limited: consumer debit-card holders can only be held liable for unauthorized transactions if they don't report the fraud within 60 days. Credit-card customers can only be liable for the first $50 in fraudulent charges. Credit- card companies bear the brunt of costs. But new legislation is considered, for example, requiring a company responsible for allowing a breach to bear the costs of notifying customers and reissuing cards, or imposing full financial responsibility for any fraud-related losses on companies whose security systems are breached.[707]

TJX did not give high enough priority to its data security system. It ignored flaws in its credit-card database until hackers broke into it. It wasn't detected for more than a year. It wasn't until January 2007 that the company acknowledged that hackers had breached the system.[708]

Competitive Intelligence

Such cyberspying should be differentiated, however, from the legal practice of competitive intelligence (CI). This activity has been revolutionized by electronic exchanges and the Internet, especially in the age of globalization. The Internet has made it simple to gather information from both primary sources, such as corporate annual reports, and secondary sources, such as newspapers, magazines, books, and other edited media. Information that has been gathered and analyzed can also easily and quickly be disseminated.

International Cyberspying

On the international level, cyber warriors are seeking to harm the United States, as foreign governments and terrorist groups focus on cyber offensives.[709] The Center for Strategic and International Studies reported in 2008 that the departments of Defense, State, Homeland Security, and Commerce all had intrusions by unknown foreign entities. Russia and China are the main suspects. U.S. government agencies are vulnerable because they are organized along hierarchical, relatively independent "stovepipes," whereby the weakest link compromises all.

In an article titled "The Taking of NASA's Secrets," *BusinessWeek* describes how hackers and foreign operatives have been penetrating NASA's computers for years. NASA documents reveal a pattern of significant electronic invasions dating at least to the late 1990s.[710] Sometimes, hackers find invasions easy, such as using obvious passwords like "administrator." "America's military and scientific institutions, along with the defense industry that serves them, are being rolled of secret information on satellites, rocket engines, launch systems, and even the Space Shuttle."[711] The breaches at the Marshall Space Flight Center in Huntsville, Alabama, were especially penetrating. As a precaution, NASA has stopped using email before shuttle launches. Lost technology cost U.S. taxpayers an estimated $1.9 billion—for the value of intellectual property lost, e.g., the cost of 50 years of rocket engine development in the United States.

In Europe, an attack in Estonia in 2007 became a "loud wake-up call." "For the first time, a state faced a frontal, anonymous attack that swamped the websites of banks, ministries, newspapers and broadcasters.[712] It was a level of sophistication not seen before. Telephone exchanges were targeted; packet "bombs" of hundreds of megabytes in size would be sent first to one address, then another," showing the involvement of a state and large telecom firms. "Botnets"—swarms of computers hijacked by surreptitiously placed codes— swamped sites by deluging them with bogus requests for information. This so-called "distributed denial of service" (DDOS) attack involved more than one million computers. Hackers penetrate and seize control of thousands of private computers and use them to flood messages to a targeted organization.

Defaming Someone by Blogging

Malevolence can be expressed by criticizing or bullying someone on a blog. As stated by Reid Goldsborough, "Venting harsh criticism anonymously is—unfortunately—part of online culture."[713] Liskula Cohen, a former professional model who has appeared on the cover of *Vogue*, was called offensive names on a now-defunct site called "Skanks in NYC." A photo of her was posted on the blog. Unexpectedly, the blogger's identity was exposed after the New York Supreme Court ruled that Google must reveal any identifying information it had about the blogger. Although matters were politely resolved, the case demonstrated that the expression of malevolence through the Internet has bounds.

Workplace Violence

Workplace violence—physical assault, threatening behavior, or verbal abuse—is a form of malevolence aimed at employers and fellow employees. It occurs more frequently than the occasional news story in local papers would suggest.[714] A study by Northwestern National Life insurance Company (Minneapolis) called "Fear and Violence in the Workplace," reported that from July 1992 to July 1993, more than two million Americans were victims of physical attack on the job. An additional six million workers were threatened and 16 million were harassed, the report said.[715]

In the 1990s, on average, 19 people were murdered at work each week or close to 1,000 people on an annual basis. In this century, workplace homicides have averaged 603 annually. A 13 percent increase in incidents occurred from 2006 to 2007, according to the Bureau of Labor Statistics. In a 2006 survey, National Institute for Occupational Safety and Health (NIOSH) said nearly 5 percent of U.S. businesses had an incident of workplace violence in the previous 12 months.[716] The estimated cost for a workplace homicide is $850,000 per incident.[717]

Besides economic and legal liabilities, workplace violence becomes a crisis when it throws an entire organization into the spotlight, which is likely because of its newsworthiness and often front-page coverage by national newspapers and evening television. One study showed shareholder value declining almost 8 percent in the short term (but it recovers fully in an average of just over 50 trading days). The final outcome is not always positive: Some companies lost millions or went out of business entirely."[718]

Human resources managers are encouraged to engage in contingency planning for workplace violence as part of an overall contingency plan. This includes a crisis planning team and concrete plans for managing specific situations. Attention must be given to employee communications during a crisis.

After a crisis, assistance must be made available to all affected persons. Employees should recognize the effects of "critical incident stress" and the value of acknowledging their emotions. They should be informed of the resources available to them.[719]

U.S. Postal Service

As the largest employer in the United States, the U.S. Postal Service with 730,000 employees, workplace violence has been a major concern. As a Center for Disease Control and Prevention study indicated, co-workers appear to be disproportionately responsible for homicides that occur in the Postal Service. Between 1983 and 1993, ten incidents of violence at U.S. Postal Service locations occurred, with 34 employees and two family members dead. The deadliest incident occurred in 1984 when Patrick Sherrill, a part-time letter carrier about to be terminated from the Edmond, Oklahoma, post office, shot 14 people and killed himself.[720]

Vulnerability to workplace violence can be reduced by careful recruitment that hires the right person for the right job and through sound employee relations practices that encourage open communications with supervisors and management practices that reduce stress on the job. The U.S. Postal Service reviews these practices by conducting an annual employee opinion survey.[721] To help reduce workplace violence, the U.S. Postal Service conducted a leadership awareness program on workplace violence that covered such techniques as conflict resolution, the value of positive reinforcement, and employee empowerment. Employee communications was widely used, e.g., postings on bulletin boards, articles in newsletters, and mention at occasional Town Hall meetings.[722]

University Rape Case

A Boston University student was raped on Sunday, September 12, 1999, in an Emmanuel College dormitory, which the university had rented. When the student went to the shower stall, a man seized her, placed a knife at her throat, began to rape her, and moved to her room, where he raped her. He asked the victim how to exit the building and they went out into the corridor, as the victim cried.

The police caught a suspect after a security guard was alerted. He informed a police cruiser in the area and, using surveillance cameras, was able to tell police where the suspect was. Within two minutes the suspect was caught as he tried to scale a fence. He was arrested, and taken to Brighton Police Station where he was detained by the BU Police. The victim was taken to the nearby Beth Israel hospital for treatment.

When the suspect was arraigned, a judge, known to be liberal, released him on $75,000 bail (the usual amount for such an offense is $500,000), which was provided by the suspect's employer, Gentle Giant Moving Co. of Somerville, Massachusetts. The firm was started by an Irish immigrant who was known as "a nice and generous guy" who liked to hire other immigrants. The suspect, who was a Moroccan citizen, was ordered to surrender his passport.

Communications

Kevin Carlton, BU's director of public relations, was notified at 9:30 a.m., four hours after the incident. He decided not to hold a news conference, but instead dealt with reporters on a one-on-one basis, which was his preference because of his advantage of knowing many of them over the numerous years he was public relations director. Only he and two staff members who were familiar with the situation were authorized to talk to reporters.

At 10 a.m. Carlton activated the crisis management committee, which included the dean of students, legal counsel, representative of the counseling center, and a representative from the president's office. That evening, the dean of students and residence life held a meeting with students in the dormitory where the raped student lived. The "gripe session" part lasted one hour; another one-and-a-half hours was spent getting suggestions. One was that peep-holes be placed on doors, which was immediately implemented. The university also added an extra security guard (making a total of two) for night duty, and a police cruiser would patrol the dormitory area.

The Boston media were interested in the story, which went public on Monday morning when the suspect was arraigned in court. The suspect's face was shown on every channel, which led to comments by some Emmanuel College students that when they returned from a party, this man "groped" one of them. Consequently two new charges were filed against the suspect, who was arrested at his attorney's office, and a new bail set at $125,000.

The student newspaper, *Boston University Free Press*, ran the story for three days, but had waited until Tuesday, the day after the arraignment, even though it had full access to the university's police log, which could have been examined on Monday. Carlton did not notify the Free Press. He also doubted that the story was newsworthy to the regional or national media. At the time, the university was "almost there" with a planned website, but it was not yet functioning.

Massacre at Virginia Techap[723]

Universities and other schools must face the serious contingency that violence may occur on their campuses, making large populations of students vulnerable. Universities are known for their open grounds and buildings and a minimum presence of security personnel.

Some highly publicized shootings have occurred. In 1966, Charles Whitman, climbed to the top of the University of Texas Tower in Austin and murdered 16 people and wounded 31 others with a hunting rifle. The most notorious incident is the Columbine High School shooting spree on April 20, 1999, when two videogame-addled teenage students, Eric Harris and Dylan Diebold, killed 13 students.[724]

Those incidents pale against what has been called "the worst peacetime shooting in American history."[725] On April 16, 2007, a despondent student killed 32 people and wounded an equal number at Virginia Tech University in Blacksburg, Virginia. The student was Seung-Hui Cho, who was studying English. He was a native South Korean, but had lived in the United States since he was eight years old and was a legal, permanent resident. His murderous venture started around 7:15 a.m. when he shot and killed Emily Hilscher, a 19-year-old would-be vet in the West Ambler-Johnston Hall dormitory. He also shot a nearby student, Ryan Clark, a popular member of the university marching band.

In what turned out to be a fatal error, the campus police who were called did not sound a campus alert. They had erroneously assumed Hilscher's death was the result of a domestic dispute with her boyfriend who had dropped her off in his pick-up truck that morning. The boyfriend was immediately tracked and found to be innocent. A report by an eight-member state investigative panel noted that the premature and mistaken assumption contributed to the two-hour gap between the first shooting and the university's notification of students and faculty—a warning that "might have made a difference."[726]

Before he continued his escapade, Cho went to the post office to mail a manifesto to NBC News in New York, including "pictures of him posing with guns, video clips and a rambling and obscene diatribe against wealthy people." At 9:05 a.m., Cho entered Norris Hall, about a mile from the dormitory, and locked the doors with chains to prevent anyone from escaping. He then walked into classrooms, one by one, and tried to kill everyone inside. When he was finished, he shot himself. His weapons were a Glock 9 mm and a Walther P22, both semi-automatics.[727] He had plenty of ammunition. In February and March, he had legally purchased guns at a pawn shop and at a gun shop in a nearby town. He had all the necessary documents and had no criminal record.

Media coverage, as might be expected, was huge. CNN's traffic spike was 19 million from the usual 7 million and ABC abcnews.com received 2.3 million unique visitors in one day, a 210 percent jump from the previous week.[728] Virginia Tech faced a major image problem of lax security.

Other campus shootings followed Virginia Tech's. At Louisiana Technical College in Baton Rouge, two students were shot by a female student in a class and one of two students died after being shot in a Delaware State University dining hall.[729] At Northern Illinois University, a former student stepped out from behind the curtain on the stage of an auditorium where an undergraduate course was coming to a close and killed five students and wounded 16 others, two of them critically.[730] Magara, the university's assistant vice president for public affairs, held the first news conference about two hours after the shooting. Time was saved by not being required to have a meeting before holding a new conference. She believed that addressing all of the media together as quickly as possible and letting reporters ask questions would put the brakes on a lot of speculation. Students and staff were neither encouraged nor discouraged from speaking with the media, but they were told to stick with what they knew.

Guns

The usual admonitions for tighter gun controls were heard after the shootings. At the National Rifle Association's (NRA) Virginia headquarters, flags were flying at half-mast, but its main reaction was to defend the right of people to bear arms. The NRA argues that without their 240 million guns, Americans would be defenseless not only against criminals but also against tyranny. Some students and other advocates of the Second Amendment argued that if his victims had been armed, they could have shot him.

Most attempts to restrict the use of guns fail. After President Bill Clinton signed a modest gun control law in 1994, which banned assault weapons, the military type rapid-fire rifles with no conceivable civilian use, President Bush allowed this ban to lapse in 2004. Many cities have stiff anti-gun laws, but when the District of Columbia tried to outlaw the possession of guns, the Supreme Court sided with the NRA. The NRA is so powerful that few politicians propose stricter gun control laws.

The Virginia Tech shootings had the effect of increasing the popularity of guns in Virginia. In 2007 there was a rise of more than 44,000 applications over the previous year in concealed-handgun permit applications. Also, the state legislature refused the governor's request to close a loophole in the firearms laws that allows purchases from unlicensed dealers at gun shows without an on-the-spot background investigation.[731]

One policy that some campuses are reviewing is whether their police should carry guns. At Brandeis University an eight-member panel deliberated the question and unequivocally recommended that their previously unarmed police be armed. Roughly 20 police officers on the 4,100-student campus in Waltham, Massachusetts, would be armed by summer 2008.[732]

Safety vs. Privacy

As at Columbine High School, questions were asked about why students with behavioral problems are not early identified and counseled. At Virginia Tech, an essay found in Cho's room said, "You caused me to do this."[733] He was known to have raged against religion, women, "rich kids," "debauchery" and "deceitful charlatans."[734]

In his creative writing class, he wrote two "twisted, blood-drenched" short plays, with plots "suffused with anxious fury: about money, sex, religion and overbearing adults." Viewing his writing, the English department's chairwoman, Professor Carolyn Rude, found his writing so disturbing that she referred Cho to the school's counseling service.[735] His classmates said he had always been quiet in class and hid behind sunglasses, a hat and a blank expression. Critics asked why more could not have been done about Cho's obviously troubled mental state.

The panel that investigated the event said that the university did not intervene effectively even though people at the school knew of "numerous incidents" during Cho's junior year that were "warnings of mental instability." The panel found that when Cho arrived at Virginia Tech, he had not received the mental health service he needed in late 2005 and 2006. Records of Cho's treatment at Virginia Tech's Cook Counseling Center were missing.[736]

In 2005, two female students complained to the police that Cho was stalking them, but didn't press charges and the police didn't arrest him. Yet a district court considered him "mentally ill" and "an imminent danger to self or others" and ordered him to undergo a psychiatric test. But he was discharged after the health authorities said that "his insight and judgment are normal."[737]

Making remedial measures difficult is that most universities zealously guard the confidentiality of their students, citing privacy laws and support of students' independence.[738] Because students are legally considered adults at age 18, federal and state laws generally prohibit colleges from sharing details about a student's health or academic record with parents or outside authorities.[739] But security may be sacrificed in favor of too much privacy. Administrators essentially have to choose between possibly violating privacy rights and trying to head off wrongful death or injury. Karen-Ann Broe, senior risk analyst at United Educators, which insures 1,200 educational institutions in the United States, says, "I think there's been a hesitancy to share information in deference to student privacy probably more than the law requires."[740] This hesitancy extends to high schools in that valuable student profiles are not carried forward.

Rumors

The planting of rumors — propositions that are unverified and in general circulation — may be motivated by malevolence to harm some individual or organization. In other cases, the instigator may not have a criminal intent but the damage to targeted companies is nonetheless real and may justify civil suits. Firms are being forced to defend themselves, knowing that their reputations can be destroyed and stock values punctured.

Procter & Gamble (P&G), which for years was accused in a rumor of consorting with the devil,[741] faced an additional rumor that its tampons contained asbestos and that Febreze, its odor-eliminating spray, kills pets. A March 1999 warning appeared on the Internet saying, "Febreze Is Dangerous to Pets. There have been multiple instances of dogs and birds who have died or became very ill after being exposed to Febreze, a deodorizer/air freshener. Febreze contains zinc chloride, which is very dangerous for animals." These cybersmears force firms to defend their reputations. P&G used its website to write a question-and-answer response and say "These rumors are not true."[742]

A vacuum of information can start a rumor. The health of Steve Jobs, the visionary head of Apple, became the subject of rumor when in a summer 2007 product announcement meeting he appeared gaunt. The ground for such speculation was prepared when he went for cancer surgery in 2004. Anxiety fueled the rumor because without Jobs, Apple would be a much-diminished company and its stock value would drop. After months of denying that anything was seriously wrong with Jobs' health, rumors abounded. In early January, the company reversed itself and provided information. Jobs would be stepping aside from his day-to-day responsibilities until June to focus on recovery.[743] Other instances when incomplete information about a matter of concern to people generates rumors are with company investment plans, mergers, employee layoffs, and so forth. When the Samsung Group, for example, was exploring various investment opportunities in Southeast Asian countries, the rumor originated that Penang was favored because of the quality of its labor force and the availability of land.[744]

The power of rumors stems from their emotional nature. In their purest form, they deal with uncertainty about matters of concern. The formula for determining the origin of a rumor is sometimes seen as the product of likelihood and consequence. People are pretty impervious to facts once they get into the gossip mode. Hearing a rumor repeated by several different sources, or even by the same person, makes people more likely to believe it, especially if they tap into existing biases, prejudices, and anxieties. As David Bartlett, a crisis communication strategist and blogger, states, "Even the smartest people are easy prey. Verifiable facts, and even simple common sense, have little or nothing to do with the way a rumour spreads. Utterly improbable urban legends persist even though they can be easily disproven. And, of course, once a rumour finds its way to the web, it lives forever."[745]

Rumors on the Internet

Businesses are becoming increasingly vulnerable to rumors spread over the Internet by angry and bitter customers, employees, and anti-business activists. Rumors are likely to grow in number and accelerate in spread because of the new social media: the Internet; blogs; cell phones; MySpace; Facebook; Twitter; and other social networks. Richard Weiner says that blogs were invented for gossiping, which is a broader concept than rumors and typically deals with the private lives of others, especially celebrities.[746] Both gossip and rumors flourish within existing social networks—in the workplace, at Starbucks, among friends and relatives, conferences, and community and neighborhood gatherings. For those who become the subject of gossip or rumors, the management of reputation becomes paramount.

When the dot-com era collapsed at the end of the 1990s several sites became magnets for disgruntled employees. One of the most popular was Fucked-Company.com. Other types of anger are expressed in hundreds of other sites that contain the word "suck," e.g., PayPalsucks.com, WalMartsucks.com, and HomeDepotsucks.com. Leonard M. Fuld, author of *The Secret Language of Competitive Intelligence*, reads these postings to obtain valuable information about competitors.[747]

Financial Rumors

Rumors are commonplace in the financial world. Before securities and exchange regulations, so-called "bear" rumors were routinely placed by large investors who sold "short"—they sold stocks that they did not yet own—and waited for negative rumors (often prompted by them) about the companies whose stock they bought to lose value so they could then buy shares cheaply to cover the ones they sold short. They would profit from the difference between the low price at which they bought stocks and the higher price at which they sold them. That practice is still alive, particularly abroad. London's Stock Exchange investigated "suspicious dealings" in more than a dozen British stocks that might have been targets of illegal bear raids.[748]

Emulex

A notable financial rumor targeted Emulex, a California-based maker of fiber optic communication equipment.[749] On August 25, 2000, Internet Wire, the smallest of the three major press release wires, issued a news release stating that Emulex was revising its earnings for its quarter ending on July 2 from a profit of 25 cents a share to a loss of 15 cents a share due to some accounting revisions. The release also stated that the company's CEO, Paul Folino, had resigned and that the SEC had begun an investigation into the accounting procedures. Once the news hit the wire at 9:30 a.m. EST, it was automatically posted on most financial websites, including CBS Marketwatch, Bloomberg News, TheStreet.com, CNBC and Dow Jones Service. One message read, "EMLX SEC investigation SELLLLL."

The release, which supposedly came from Emulex, was false and was actually written by a perpetrator who had worked for Internet Wire. He convinced the night shift by using specific billing terms used by the wire service. His apparent motive for the fraud was to cause Emulex's stock to plunge so he could profit from selling the stock short. Indeed, when the news got out, investors rushed to sell their Emulex shares and the stock plunged from $113 to $43, reducing the company's market value by $2.4 billion before the Nasdaq stock exchange halted trading at about 10:30 a.m.[750]

At Emulex headquarters, crisis management went into high gear. When CEO Paul Folino arrived in the office at 10 a.m., he heard about the stock's free fall, as did his senior vice president, Kirk Roller. Before they ended their brainstorming over the news releases, it was too late—Bloomberg News had already run its story at 10:13. At 10:25 the senior vice president's administrative assistant called, saying an Emulex salesman in Washington had found the Emulex "press release" and would fax it over. Then, when Nasdaq's general counsel's office called, Folino denied news about his resignation and Nasdaq said it would halt trading. At 10:57 Dow Jones Newswires called the earlier release a hoax and Bloomberg followed with a similar headline. The Federal Bureau of Investigation (FBI) arrested the suspect, Mark Jakob, six days later.

A few hours later (in the financial world, every minute and every hour counts), Dow Jones Newswire quoted an Emulex spokesperson who called the release a hoax. Business Wire carried a news release from Emulex that rebutted the earlier "news." Bloomberg's editor-in-chief acknowledged that his organization broke one of journalism's basic principles of always checking sources and to have at least two credible ones. Its release should have clearly explained that it had been unable to confirm the release or get comment from the company.

Banking Crisis

Rumors sprouted during the turmoil of the 2008–09 banking crisis. For example, after traders reported rumors that Countrywide Financial Corp., the United States' largest mortgage originator, might seek bankruptcy protection, its shares suffered their biggest decline since the 1987 stock market crash. The rumors were triggered by a *New York Times* article citing court records it said showed the lender had fabricated documents relating to the bankruptcy of a Pennsylvania borrower. The company denied the speculation by issuing a statement saying, "there is no substance to the rumor that Countrywide is planning to file for bankruptcy, and we are not aware of any basis for the rumor that any of the major rating agencies are contemplating negative action relative to the company."[751] This statement, however, did not end speculation and Countrywide did later default and was taken over by the Bank of America.

Merger rumors are also common when acquisition and merger (A&M) activity is high. For example, after the ailing Chrysler agreed to give Fiat a 35 percent stake in the company in return for access to the Italian automaker's line of small cars and international sales network, rumors appeared about other potential partners for Chrysler, including GM and Niss.[752]

Rumors in the Marketplace

Many other rumors have circulated in the marketplace. Some past ones are when Wendy's and McDonald's had to combat rumors that they ground red worms into their hamburger meat; Hygrade Food Products that razor blades were found in its Ball Park Franks; Tropical Fantasy that it produced a drink that sterilized black men; Snapple that it was racist; Procter & Gamble that it consorted with the devil; and Entenmann's that it was owned by the Moonies. Rumors found in the marketplace are often premeditated, motivated by self-gain and intent to hurt. The targets may be individual competitors or the entire American business system, vulnerable because the American public has a latent distrust of powerful corporations. Rumors have hurt companies by cutting into sales, undermining product lines, reducing employee morale and productivity, and sullying company reputations.

Strategies for Countering Acts of Malevolence

Five strategies apply to the different types of crises of malevolence discussed in this chapter: (1) reduce vulnerability to the threat; (2) engage in intelligence activities; (3) improve preparedness; (4) seek law enforcement; and (5) take defensive action, such as recalling products.

Mitigation: Reduce Vulnerability to Threats

Preparation for crises of malevolence begins by becoming aware of an organization's vulnerabilities and seeking ways of reducing them. Vulnerability to acts of malevolence can be reduced by lowering the organization's visibility and exposure, by strengthening security measures, and reducing the frustrations that lead to aggressive acts. In all situations, the degree of vulnerability must be appraised. For example, in addressing workplace violence, W. Barry Nixon, director of the National Institute for Prevention of Workplace Violence, recommends that the first step in addressing workplace violence is to assess its potential threat based on the nature of the organization, its types of facilities, and their locations. Such vulnerability assessments can then be rated as devastating, severe, noticeable, or minor, and attention given to the most serious ones.[753] Hiring the right employees and paying attention to their concerns is always a way to minimize problems. Providing them with an opportunity to speak to their supervisors and to make their grievances known reduces confrontations and workplace violence.

TJX made itself vulnerable by not giving high enough priority to its data security system. It ignored flaws in its credit-card database until hackers broke into it. It wasn't detected for more than a year after which, in January 2007, the company acknowledged that hackers had breached the system.[754] The lesson was now clear: mitigation efforts required a significant strengthening of its security system.

Reduce Visibility and Exposure

Businesses are vulnerable to attacks because its facilities are typically in public places and its activities are visible to the public. To reduce vulnerability, most large office buildings have installed security systems and require visitors to check in. A company's vulnerability depends on the degree of visibility, the nature of the industry to which it belongs, its image, and situational factors like the nature of the threat and the physical features of its buildings and contents.[755] During the Tylenol crisis, Johnson & Johnson's CEO, Burke, realized that the company was highly vulnerable because it is a highly visible manufacturer of widely used consumer products, which includes such sensitive items as non-prescription drugs. Furthermore, loss of product reputation for Tylenol could spread across its entire product line.

Technological innovations should be assessed in terms of whether they increase an organization's public exposure. Some computer experts, for example, believe that cybersecurity is threatened by so-called "Cloud Comput-ing"—the storing of information and services, such as email, remotely on sup-posedly secure servers. They discourage it because it provides possible access by foreign intelligence agencies and commercial snoops.[756] Mark Anderson, the writer behind the influential Strategic News Service predicted on BBC that cloud computing will face a catastrophe within a year.[757]

Special occasions also become opportunities for snooping. Foreign visitors to the Olympics in Beijing must assume that their PCs and BlackBerrys might be compromised. Employers therefore advised employees to leave laptops behind or use a stripped-down travel laptop and encrypted hard drives; disable boot-ing from CD, USB or other external drives; use disposable cell phones while in China; install only necessary applications on laptops; and place files on an encrypted flash drive and keep it in a pocket at all times.

Strengthen Security Measures

Companies vulnerable to acts of malevolence have opened or beefed up security offices, often assigning the intelligence function to them. Executives assigned to dangerous overseas posts are again preferring American enclaves, protected by security guards. More are using bodyguards and following defensive driv-ing techniques, such as never using the same route to work or leaving at the same time of day. The really vulnerable wear body shields and carry armored briefcases. In addition to providing for physical security, other measures are undertaken, including the screening of job applicants for sensitive positions, detecting dangerous objects or events, and providing employee security aware-ness and training programs.

Another activity that is given higher priority, sometimes even by the board of directors, is cybersecurity.[758] Many vulnerable companies now have a chief security officer, many of whom are increasingly morphing into chief risk miti-gation officers. The scope of their remit is expanding into functions such as e-discovery, records retention, privacy, compliance, and disaster recovery.

Companies are expected to continue to make substantial investments in secu-rity and information protection software.[759] After its serious security breach, TJX is planning to do so. A special investment is planned by companies that have been subject to a "distributed denial of service (DDOS)" type of attack. They plan to buy lots of extra computers and bandwidth to handle an unexpected spike in traffic. Cyber-attackers must then hit many more targets simultaneously before disrupting anything. At a minimum, any international cybercrime convention would likely oblige Internet service providers to cooperate in blocking DDOS attacks coming from their subscribers' computers.[760]

Defuse Frustrations

Anger and aggression can sometimes be reduced by removing the conditions that frustrate people. Being kept in the dark about important events that affect their lives lead employees to spread rumors or seek recourse by Internet attacks. The best preventer of rumors is to keep people informed about matters of concern to them—and being sensitive to what might confuse them.

Aggressive behavior can often be defused by trying to understand the motivations of the instigators of such acts. Psychologists point out that aggression is one reaction to a frustrating situation. When goal-attainment is thwarted, a person becomes angry and directs it upon the obstacle or barrier to goal-attainment. Sometimes frustrations don't stem from an identifiable barrier at all; they are the result of aggression toward a convenient target that is entirely innocent. For example, historical studies found that there is a significant correlation through the years between the price of cotton and the number of lynchings in the Deep South. As the price of cotton goes up and brings greater prosperity to more Southerners, the number of lynchings goes down, and vice versa.[761] Negroes became convenient "scapegoats." Similarly, people may target highly visible corporations during times of economic stress simply because they are visible and accessible.

Business organizations can reduce frustrations and, therefore, hostile acts, by providing employee grievance systems and customer complaint systems. Some companies go a step further by giving stakeholders an opportunity to participate in decision-making through such devices as consumer roundtables.

Engage in Intelligence Activities

A company that becomes the target for a malevolent act is at a considerable disadvantage because of lack of intelligence information. It is extremely difficult and sometimes virtually impossible to anticipate a crisis of malevolence, however, because perpetrators operate furtively and often rely on the element of surprise.

This feature particularly applies to terrorist activities. Since terrorists operate on the surprise principle, infiltration of terrorist groups by intelligence personnel may alert a target person or organization of an impending action. Furthermore, knowledge about specific terrorist groups and their members, as well as about their past and current activities, can be helpful. As with crises of confrontation, typologies of groups using terrorist tactics have been devised.[762] Several organizations, such as Control Risks Ltd. (London), Mid-Atlantic Research Associates (Washington, D.C.) and Rand Corporation (Santa Monica, Calif.) offer intelligence reports.[763] Demographic and motivational approaches have been used in attempts to look at terrorism from the inside in an effort to try to understand why terrorists do what they do.[764]

Intelligence activities, or the more gentle process of environmental scanning and monitoring, can also be applied to rumors. Organizations can do simple searches of Internet newsgroups to see what is being said about them, using search engines such as Google and looking under "groups." Larger firms can hire specialty firms, such as eWatch, to conduct broader searches, or Planet-Feedback to take complaints from consumers and relay them to business clients. Information should be sought on who is disseminating the rumor and whether the source is legitimate.

Companies respond to critical comments in both soft and hard ways. To discourage the sending of critical Internet messages, some firms set up their own online complaint system, have a chat room where people can air their grievances, and a few assign representatives to answer complaints in chat rooms. They may call up complainers in the hope of soothing their anger. They may issue a press release or website announcement, but must be aware of the danger that they may divert the attention of important groups from other messages. Organizations can also use the hard approach by fighting back aggressively by attempting to unmask anonymous posters. They also serve subpoenas on Internet service providers and operators of Web portals such as America OnLine and Yahoo, forcing them to reveal the identity of anonymous posters of false rumors.

Another way to monitor rumors is to ask all employees, distributors, and retailers to be alert to rumors and to report them to a specific individual in the organization, such as a human resources director for internal rumors, and the public relations or marketing director for external ones. Facts should be collected about what the rumor is about, its sources, and how widespread it is. If necessary, a discreet survey should be conducted. Since rumors are nourished by anxieties, the opportunity should be seized to learn more about the issues that bother people. With internal rumors, for example, reports of imminent layoffs often lead to a variety of rumors about layoffs in specific departments.

Improve Preparedness

Employee Awareness and Education Programs

Computer hacking and industrial espionage can be discouraged and prevented by employee awareness and education programs that make a company-wide counter-espionage mindset part of the corporate culture. These communication programs must be specific about what information is deemed sensitive enough to require protection. Included in such lists are trade secrets, advertising strategies, plans and samples, pay records, addresses of key personnel, legal briefs, computer software, and any programs or research materials that the company has invested time and money in developing. To supplement education efforts, and specifically to guard against loss of proprietary information, some employers request employees to sign noncompetitive agreements. One prominent survey research firm's agreement prevents executives from contacting any client firm for whom they worked.[765]

To combat terrorism, companies offer employees advice on how to minimize exposure and to blunt attacks. Corporate travelers are advised not to loiter in airports, to move through the check-in as quickly as possible, not to go to known hangouts of Americans, and to melt with the masses.[766]

These efforts must be reinforced through periodic reminders and training sessions. Reminders can appear in a column in a company publication, strategically placed posters, and information flyers. Testing can be conducted by organizing so-called "tiger teams" whose role it is, for example, to continually test computer security by trying to break in.[767] Another way is to establish SWAT units, such as the Computer Emergency Response Team (CERT), which tries to track down unauthorized entries and inform network users of security breaches and safety procedures.[768] Some companies punish and even fire those who violate secrecy restrictions. By increasing the certainty that violators will be caught and severely punished, security measures are more likely to be observed.

Improve Alert Systems

Improving emergency alert systems is part of preparedness that enables crisis responders to reach vulnerable audiences. Spurred by Virginia Tech killings, universities across the country are reexamining their policies for swiftly notifying students and faculty of an emergency. This failure of the warning system led some critics to ask for the resignation of Virginia Tech's president and the chief of campus policy. The lack of aggressive, timely communication at Virginia Tech may have cost lives. University officials reportedly spent more than two hours in internal meetings before sending out its first advisory via email, and that message asked students to report danger rather than warn them to seek safety.

Internet-based communication tools, from text messaging to "Twittering," can help get the word out quickly. Many schools have instituted email and cell phone alerts. Communicating by social media, however, assumes that the sender has each recipient's cell phone number and email address and that all recipients are online and reading their emails or listening to their cell phones.[769] Furthermore, email can't reach people on athletic fields and professors typically demand that students stow cell phones.

Traditional "low tech" channels should also be used. Virginia Tech ignored a campus-wide public address loudspeaker system that could have reached students everywhere—in their dorm rooms or classrooms as well as those walking on campus, perhaps to Morris Hall where the shooting occurred. At the University of Vermont, police chief Gary Margolis said he expects a siren-and-loudspeaker system to be up and running by summer of 2008 on the 645-acre campus.[770] A service called e2Campus claims it is used by more than 600 campuses around the United States, enabling school officials to self-administer and send time-sensitive messages to multiple communication devices, including fire/security systems, LCD/LED digital signage, alert beacons, Facebook pages, Twitter accounts, and relevant school Web pages.[771]

Exercise Security Measures and Enforce Laws

Terrorist acts require the full force of security measures. It is difficult to track down perpetrators of terrorist acts. The Federal Bureau of Investigation's (FBI) search for the possible killer in the anthrax postal attacks centered around the labs where anthrax was stored and experimented with. The makeup of the anthrax found in the victims was a combination of two strains, one from Dugway Proving Grounds, and the other from a third lab. Both strains intersected in one place: the bacteriology division of the lab at Fort Detrick. Scientists at the lab were subjected to lie-detector tests in 2001. The prime suspects became two scientists at this lab, first Steven Hatfill, and by late 2006, Dr. Bruce Ivins. His home and laboratory office were searched and members of the family interrogated. On March 19, 2008, Ivins committed suicide after learning that the FBI was planning to accuse him.[772]

Law enforcement is an essential strategy, and, if a law does not exist, one should be sought. The expected impact of such law enforcement is both to deter illegal actions and, if possible, apprehend and confine those who commit them. During and after its Tylenol crisis, Johnson & Johnson was actively involved and cooperated with law enforcement agencies, including the FBI. Furthermore, it announced a reward of $100,000 for information leading to the arrest and conviction of the tamperer. Subsequently, Johnson & Johnson's government relations personnel were directed to lobby for legislation to make product tampering a felony.

When necessary to protect companies against such attacks as product tampering and computer break-ins, new or more stringent laws may have to be sought. California now outlaws the knowing introduction of "computer contaminants" into computer systems or networks. The law's penalties include jail terms, fines, and the confiscation of computers and software owned by people who commit such crimes.[773]

Take Defensive Action—Product Recalls

As contingency plans indicate, when a crisis strikes a company must take immediate defensive action to limit crisis damage. In serious cases of product tampering where the health and safety of people are at stake, a product recall must be undertaken. Product liability is another consideration. Product tampering cases get high media coverage and a seller must demonstrate that the health and safety of its customers are its paramount consideration.

Syringes and razor blades seem to be popular in product tampering cases. In November 2006, Canada's largest food manufacturer, Maple Leaf Foods, issued a nationwide recall after three syringes were found in a pork-processing plant. The police were called in to investigate possible criminal tampering.[774] In Australia, Top Taste pulled hundreds of thousands of cakes off supermarket shelves after razor blades and needles were found in some of them.[775]

To discourage copycat acts, business and the media should not publicize unsubstantiated warnings of product tampering. If undangerous evidence of tampering is found, the affected products, or lots thereof, can quietly be removed from shelves without risk to customers. But if products have already been sold and there is reason to believe lives are at risk, companies and stores must publicize the threat. If they do not, public officials will.

Conclusions

In crises of malevolence, organizations and innocent third parties are victims of terrorism, product tampering, cybercrime, employee and student violence, and rumors. A company cannot prevent such acts, but it can discourage them and mitigate their effects through a variety of means.

The threat or actuality of terrorism is managed by conducting a vulnerability audit, engaging in intelligence operations, and intensifying security measures. A specific form of terrorism, computer vandalism, can be warded off by a variety of detection and protective measures. Product tampering typically requires product recalls and cooperation with public authorities to determine cause. Better protective packaging helps to reduce future incidents. Rumors require the antidote of truth but administered only to those who have been infected by the rumor. All kinds of malevolence can be discouraged through the existence of relevant laws and their strict enforcement.

Part IV

Crises of Management Failure

The actions and inactions of managers inside an organization are the primary cause of crises of management failure. In the previous two types of crises—confrontation and malevolence—people outside the organization precipitated the crisis. And in natural and technological crises, external factors were the main cause. Crises of management failure in Part IV focus on the attitudes and ability of management in anticipating, preparing for, and responding to crises. It consists of four sub-types: crises of mismanagement (Chapter 10); crises of skewed management values (Chapter 11); crises of deception (Chapter 12); and crises of management misconduct (Chapter 13).

Crises of mismanagement represent the most general type of management failure, which are caused by inadequacies in the quality of management. These inadequacies manifest themselves through incompetence, negligence, and callousness. The other three types of management failure may also reflect such inadequacies but focus on three primary failings: crises of skewed management values violate important societal values and the rights of stakeholders; deception is a deliberate attempt to deceive investors, customers and others; and, most egregious, misconduct consists of outright violations of the social norms and laws of society.

The first edition of this book gave examples of each crisis subtype. A case of skewed management values was the *Exxon Valdez* accident in Prince William Sound, which resulted in an oil spill that fouled the pristine waters of "little Switzerland of Alaska." The operational values of meeting scheduled deliveries of oil and doing so in the most economical and profitable manner led to assigning too low a priority to the risk of environmental harm. The second subtype, crises of deception, was exemplified by the silicone breast implant controversy that implicated Dow Corning. The company had misled doctors and consumers about the dangers of breast implants. Finally, crises of misconduct were illustrated by the corrupt handling of defense contracts and violation of the SEC's insider trading laws.

In the past decade, the incidence of serious crises of management failure has soared. These were represented by stories about salmonella in peanut butter; tainted milk products fed to babies in China; lead-laced toys imported by

Mattel from China; defective tires sold by Firestone and placed on Ford SUVs; excessive risk-taking by the "masters of the universe" in the worldwide banking industry; illegal payments by Siemens to win buyers to their products; and outright fraud in Italy's Parmalat and India's Satyam companies. These crises have arisen from faulty, unethical, or illegal actions and inactions by managers inside an organization.

Damaged Relationships

The four subtypes of crises of management failure share the common feature that they reflect an organization's damaged relationships with its stakeholders, other organizations, and society. In an article on "Repairing Relationships Within and Between Organizations," three organizational theorists draw a useful distinction among three types of damage caused by an organization's transgressions (which can be translated to crises): trust, negative affect, and negative exchange:[776]

- Trust serves as the lens through which an organization's behavior is interpreted, e.g., determining whether and how to interact with the organization. Victims will examine a transgression to determine whether it is a matter of competence or, more seriously, of the integrity and values of the transgressor.
- Negative affect is reflected in immediate emotions such as disappointment, frustration, anger, and outrage following a transgression. It also affects the long-term impact on a stable affective relationship, e.g., whether a general dislike and feelings of injustice linger.
- Negative exchange may lead to a suspension of cooperation or, worse, a desire for retribution and revenge.

Crisis managers must distinguish among these three types of damage when deciding on appropriate repair strategies. They must realize that it might not be possible to repair all three types, at least not immediately. To repair trust, an organization must convince the wronged party that the violation does not reflect the violator's true nature or that the violator has experienced redemption. As Ralph Waldo Emerson warned: "no change of circumstances can repair a defect of character."[777] The elements of trust—reliability, predictability, and fairness—must be examined. Attribution theory discussed in Chapter 4 reviews some repair remedies, such making a sincere apology.

The reduction of negative affect, which results in a disruption of what sociologists call social equilibrium, requires an examination of the conventions or norms that govern the relationship. These norms are embedded in an organization's culture. Outside of the organization they reflect the ethics codes of professional societies, such as the Association of Certified Accountants, and legal requirements, such as the SEC's "full and timely disclosure" rules. Certain social rituals may also be required, such as penance, punishment, and apologies. "These rituals help to 'settle the accounts' in the relationship as well as to reestablish the expectations in the relationship."[778]

Restoration of positive exchange requires a structural approach which examines "formal organizational, group, or interpersonal structures, systems, and incentives that may be put in place following a transgression. . . ."[779] Corporate governance is at the heart of structural changes and may involve such remedies as instituting various controls through policies, procedures, contracts, and monitoring that increase the reliability of future behavior—and also help restore trust.

Central Role of Ethics

Ethics pervades all aspects of an organization—whether its board of directors shows a concern for how an organization affects others in society and whether on-going decision-making follows ethical principles.[780] A Conference Board study shows that in most participating companies, boards play a key institutional role in establishing ethics programs. In Western Europe and elsewhere nearly all company ethics programs were established by board resolution. The general counsel has principal responsibility for reporting to the board on ethics compliance issues in nearly half of the U.S. participating companies.[781]

Ethics has several meanings. The common-sense meaning is that it pertains to judgments about what is right and wrong, good and bad, virtuous and evil. Another meaning of ethics is that it deals with the abstract ideals of fairness, justice, and due process. Some are embodied in law; others transcend the law. These ideals are reflected in several values and rules of moral common sense that people follow in their personal and professional lives:

- Avoid and prevent harm to others;
- Respect the rights of others;
- Do not lie or cheat;
- Keep promises and contracts;
- Obey the law;
- Help those in need;
- Be fair;
- Reinforce these imperatives in others.

Immoral, Amoral, and Moral Managers

The common-sense imperatives of ethics have been applied to managerial conduct by Archie B. Carroll, holder of the Georgia Power Company Chair of Corporate Public Affairs at the University of Georgia. He classifies executive moral behavior into three categories: immoral, amoral, and moral.[782] His description of the first two is enlightening.

Immoral managers are those who are motivated by greed and whose goals are profitability and organizational success at almost any price. They regard legal standards or contractual agreements as barriers to be overcome. They choose to do wrong even when they know the difference between right and wrong. The cases of management misconduct in Chapter 13, e.g., bribery by Siemens and fraud by Parmalot, best illustrate immoral managers. Deceptive practices by many mortgage lenders also illustrate that self-gain harmed borrowers.

But it is not so much immorality as amorality that is the chief ethical problem in organizations, says Carroll. On a distribution curve ranging from immoral to amoral and moral managers, most managers fall in the middle. Amorality is neutral, a hybrid of morality and immorality. Some managers are intentionally amoral by simply thinking that different rules of the game apply in business than elsewhere. This happens in politics where political candidates justify "dirty tricks," such as making deceptive statements, during a campaign but reject such behavior as an office holder. Others managers are unintentionally amoral by being too casual, careless, or inattentive to the negative or deleterious effects of their decisions and actions on others. The only constraint recognized by amoral managers is the law. Ethical conduct, however, must transcend the law. A firm may do something that is perfectly legal, yet unethical.

Carroll's distinctions among immoral, amoral, and moral managers demonstrate the complexity of corporate ethics. As Barbara Ley Toffler's book title, *Tough Choices*, affirms, managers often face difficult ethical dilemmas.[783] Situations do not usually present themselves as clearly right or wrong. Yet every decision invokes values implicit in an organization's culture and its supporting managerial performance standards.

Personal values have an important influence on business conduct, but it is also known that good people do bad things. Philip Zimbardo, a social psychologist, observes that "almost all of us are susceptible to being drawn over to the dark side, because human behavior is determined more by situational forces and group dynamics than by our inherent nature."[784] Organizational culture is a major situational factor.

Ethics apply to all types of crises of management failures. Most of all they apply to crises of misconduct because they violate both the law and the norms of society. Examples are tolerating adulteration of food, committing fraud, engaging in insider trading and bribery, and violating professional and societal norms and codes. Ethics next applies to crises of deception, which violate the growing concern with transparency and lack of "authenticity." Deception refers to providing misleading information or lying outright about products, finances, environmental compliance. Ethics also applies to crises of skewed management values because the norms of fairness and justice with stakeholders are violated when the interests of an organization's stakeholders are ignored or minimized. The legal concept of a business is that the responsibility of management is to maximize profits and stockholder wealth. In contrast, ethics requires management also to include obligations to other stakeholders, such as customers, employees, and the community. It considers broader social values and not only economics.

Economic Relationships Embody Moral Dimensions

All economic transactions embody moral relationships, as illustrated in the relationship between sellers and buyers in the marketplace. Sellers distinguish between a transaction and a relationship with customers. A transaction represents a narrow relationship, a kind of anonymous encounter, symbolized by the primitive principle of *caveat emptor*—let the buyer beware. Such a seller does not ask the basic moral question: Is anybody likely to get hurt from this transaction? In the relationship model, however, a seller asks: How can the needs of the customer be met? This model is reflected in the new marketing mantra called customer relationship management (CRM). It requires sellers to make a conscious effort to know their customers and to satisfy their rights and expectations. The same concern for others in a relationship is applied to other stakeholders: employees, investors, the local community, suppliers, dealers, and others.

Acceptance of Social Responsibility

The acceptance of social responsibility is an expression of ethical behavior. Ethics here deals with the conflict between competing claims among stakeholders.[785] The ethical proscription facing a corporate manager is to achieve a more equitable balance between corporate self-interest and the interests of others in society, including safeguarding of the environment. This view is reflected in the highly regarded statement made by the Committee for Economic Development. It specifies three levels of social responsibility: (1) providing goods and services and jobs; (2) reducing or eliminating social costs; and (3) helping to solve social problems.[786]

Although neo-classical economists like Milton Friedman still want business to restrict itself to its economic function (the first level), modern socio-political realities make that impossible. Providing goods and services raises questions about safety, disclosure of product information, complaint procedures and redress; and providing jobs implies at least some consideration for worker satisfaction and quality of life. Ethics very much applies to the second level of social responsibility concerning social costs, because such costs refer to harm to people or the environment. Helping to solve social problems, the third level, is not an ethical imperative unless the problem is caused by a company and harms others. Few would argue, for example, that caring for homeless people is an ethical obligation of business.

Understanding the various meanings of business ethics is just a start toward ethical behavior. The challenge is to incorporate an ethical perspective into everyday business decisions and actions, which is done when members of an organization internalize ethical principles and they become part of the corporate culture. As stated by Chester Barnard in his classic, *Functions of an Executive*, an executive must hold a personal moral code and be able to create a moral code for others.[787]

Integrating Ethics into Decision-making

Ethics must become part of the fabric of everyday life and organizational decision-making. Ethics can be incorporated into the corporate culture by developing a corporate conscience, says Kenneth E. Goodpaster, the Barbara and David Koch Professor of Ethics at the College of St. Thomas and a frequent writer on ethics.[788] He points out that conscience works against a kind of entropy in human nature, namely, "backsliding toward the pursuit of self-centered purposes . . . . Other persons—and the environment—are not simply resources to be used but invite and deserve consideration independently."[789] This view is supported by Harvard University's Josiah Royce, who advises that there must be the resolution to treat one's neighbor "as if he were real, that is, to treat him unselfishly."[790]

A survey by the Center for Business Ethics at Bentley College in Waltham, Massachusetts, and the Ethics Resource Center in Washington, D.C., showed that in the world's top 50 graduate business schools there has been a fivefold increase in the number of ethics courses over the past two decades. Reflecting their importance, just over half of these schools have made ethics study a graduation requirement. Bentley College offers an MBA with a concentration in business ethics and the New England College of Business and Finance offers a master's degree in business ethics and compliance. Other schools nationwide offer business doctorates that include a heavy dose of ethics studies. Spurred by moral meltdowns, such as Enron, about 70 percent of U.S. employers have implemented ethics training—up 14 percentage points from 2003.[791]

Measuring Degree of Success

In their article "Reframing Crisis Management," Christine M. Pearson and Judith A. Clair state that the ultimate test of effective crisis management is the viability of an organization—whether the outcome is successful or fails.[792] Efforts are successful and effective when operations are sustained or resumed and the needs of keys customers and stakeholders are satisfied. The authors list several criteria of successful outcomes:

- Signals of a crisis are detected early, so that appropriate responses are brought to bear.
- The crisis incident is contained within the organization and there are no injuries or deaths.
- Business is maintained as usual during and after the crisis.
- Learning occurs: policies and procedures of an organization are changed as a result of the crisis and lessons are applied to future incidents.

- Reputation is improved by the organization's effectiveness in managing the crisis.
- Resources are available from the organization or external stakeholders.
- Evidence is ample of timely, accurate decisions grounded in facts.[793]

In addition, Pearson and Clair believe that a team response is better than an individual one and that the sharing of information and coordination with stakeholders and leads to better outcomes.[794]

Chapter 10

Crises of Mismanagement

Many crises of management failure are primarily caused by negligence, incompetence, lack of ethics, and inadequate control and oversight. These are general failures that can appropriately be called crises of mismanagement in that they do not to any strong degree exhibit the specific failures discussed in the next three chapters, namely, skewed values, deception, and misconduct.

Mismanagement means that basic management principles are violated, such as not executing the procedures necessary to achieve objectives. Often, the problem is the absence of feedback systems and the setting of thresholds to signal when corrective action must be taken.

More generally, the shortcomings of mismanagement cover topics typically included in basic management courses, especially the basic "OB" (Organizational Behavior) course. They include job assignments to individuals; division of labor among departments; hierarchy of authority that coordinates and controls activities; a rewards system that provides incentives, and a feedback system that lets those in command know whether goals are met. In his seminal book, *Management: Tasks, Responsibilities, Practices*, Peter F. Drucker discusses the important function of controls in an organization that enable a manager to collect reliable information about the achievement of desired results.[795]

Because of the key role of reliable information, openness and transparency of the decision-making process is of critical importance, as discussed by James O'Toole and Warren Bennis in "A Culture of Candor." They look at "the degree to which information flows freely within an organization, among managers and employees, and outward to stakeholders."[796] They refer to such cases as when an aircraft pilot accidentally crashes a plane because of an authoritarian cockpit culture that forbids the co-pilot or other crew members who are aware of the danger from warning the pilot. Organizational openness is reflected in answers to several questions: (a) Are people who need to communicate upward able to do so honestly? (b) Are teams able to challenge their own assumptions openly? (c) Are boards of directors able to communicate important messages to the company's leadership? (d) Is there collective denial and self-deception? These questions identify the criteria of an open and transparent organization.

In discussing lack of transparency, O'Toole and Bennis use the apt image of a "mushroom farm," which they describe as "people around here are kept in the dark and fed manure."[797] The authors note that hoarding information is far too persistent in organizations of all kinds. Their advice is to adopt the default position of "when in doubt, let it out."[798] They also recommend listening to more feedback from contrarians and even rewarding them.

Managers must receive and have access to information, which, as discussed above, they are more likely to obtain in open organizations. Not constrained by bureaucratic hierarchies and "silos" of specialization, managers are more likely to become aware of early warning signals through contact with others, through group meetings, through access to organizational publications and websites, and through formal issues management systems. Transparency lubricates communications and promotes accuracy and completeness. Decisions are less likely to be wrong and insensitive to important constituencies.

Cases of Mismanagement

All companies are susceptible to mismanagement. In the cases that follow, BP in the oil industry dominates because management errors led to enormous damage to the environment and harm to people. In the pharmaceutical industry where standards should be the highest, some reputable companies seriously neglected quality control. In the food and beverage industries, a wide range of products were found faulty, including such basic products as peanuts, meat, and eggs. Where safety is paramount, the performance of airlines ranged from enormous laxity to heroism.

BP's Deepwater Horizon Explosion Blamed on Mismanagement

The explosion of the Deepwater Horizon rig in the Gulf of Mexico has become a major example of a crisis of mismanagement, a designation that is the prevailing contention of government and other reports on the disaster. The avoidable disaster was caused by management failures by BP and its contractors Transocean and Halliburton, as evidenced by questionable decision-making and wrong judgments by managers, engineers, and workers on the rig and at Houston headquarters. Because decision-making occurred in the context of the risks and uncertainties associated with technological crises, the disaster is first described in Chapter 7, which deals with technological crises. Only by understanding the technological complexities of deep sea drilling can the challenges to management that led to faulty decisions be understood.

As reported by the National Commission on the BP Deepwater Horizon Oil Spill and Offshore Drilling, of the nine decisions made that increased risk while potentially saving time, seven are attributed to BP.[799] An illustration is the confusion aboard the rig about the final safety testing just before the explosion. An email on the morning of April 20 by a young BP engineer in Houston notified his colleagues about a change in a key pressure test that would help determine the well's safety. It called for removing an unusually amount of the thick drilling fluid, called mud, from the well before running the test. This unorthodox decision perplexed BP's day-shift manager, Robert Kaluza, and Jimmy Wayne Harrell, the offshore installation manager and most senior of the Transocean workers aboard the rig. But after a consultation with Donald Vidrine, BP's top operations official on duty when the blowout occurred, Kaluza called Houston and said he was satisfied with the test. That was around 9:30 p.m. At 9:50 p.m., the assistant driller called with the ominous message, "We have a situation," and minutes afterwards the first explosion occurred.[800]

The stress caused by time compression in a crisis situation was evident when Caleb Holloway, a 28-year-old floorhand, and a co-worker who were on the main deck, glanced up and saw the dangerous symptom that drilling mud was gushing up from the well. Floorhands like Holloway serve as first responders and would have to decide whether to declare a "Blowout." Quick action would then be necessary to install a special valve on the drill pipe, as operating manuals specified. The window for effective action was limited to nine minutes, investigators later said. Unfortunately, in this real situation Holloway found no other floorhands on the deck to execute the task and the gas continued to spread. He tried to call his boss, Dewey Revette, on his radio but got no response.

At this point a decision had to be made whether to divert the blowout out to sea or contain it on the rig by funneling it through a device called a mud-gas separator. Transocean's manual offered contradictory advice. But by this time, as the gas seeped to other floors, Holloway and his partner realized they were losing control. There were no communications or coordination among several floors and sections: the bridge, the drill shack, and the engine control room. Many of the workers were asleep in their rooms because the alarm had been deactivated as, "They did not want people woke up at 3 o'clock in the morning due to false alarms."[801] Furthermore, the red button to activate the "ultimate failsafe," the blowout preventer (BOP), was never pushed, and even if it had, it was likely inoperable.

Sloppy maintenance of the BOP is another example of mismanagement. As one BP employee, Ronald Sepulvado, overseeing the rig's operations told a federal investigative panel, workers had detected a leak in the hydraulic system that controls the BOP. He said he had raised concerns about maintenance, noting that some pieces of equipment had been out of service for extended periods of time.[802] This kind of failing was supported by a 2006 Mineral Management Service (MMS) finding that debris had gotten into a BOP and reduced its effectiveness. Even Cameron International Corp., the manufacturer of the BOP, questioned its reliability with the Deepwater Horizon rig, saying, "Our preventers have never been involved in an accident like this."[803]

Disagreement among the three operatives, another sign of mismanagement, was apparent before the explosion. According to Halliburton, BP ignored its advice on the design of the well and failed to do all the necessary tests. But as federal investigators reported, months before the disaster Halliburton performed four tests on the cement mixture it planned to use and only the fourth passed the tests after engineers changed the testing procedure. The report stated that it wasn't clear what BP knew about the tests and in any case there was no indication that Halliburton highlighted to BP the significance of the results.[804] This lack of communication was a further sign of mismanagement, as well as reflecting BP's failure to recognize technological dangers and uncertainties.

BP's Communication Blunders

Further damage was caused by early communication blunders that created public skepticism and raised questions about BP's transparency and honesty."[805] A month after the accident, the Obama administration accused BP of having "fallen short" of commitments to keep public and government officials fully informed about the spill. Officials said it was "imperative" that they be provided with the results of internal corporate investigations and other data pertinent to the gulf disaster.[806]

Three communication failures were conspicuous. First, although BP promised to be transparent about the spill, for weeks it resisted putting up a live video feed showing in excruciating detail the massive oil geyser fouling the Gulf of Mexico.[807] Second, BP initially underestimated the size of the leak. BP consistently refused to apply widely used scientific techniques to measure the spill, likely motivated by knowing that the EPA's fine for the spill would be on a per barrel basis.[808]

Although it is appropriate for the CEO of an organization involved in a major crisis to make a statement, BP's CEO Tony Hayward, a brainy geologist, was the wrong person to restore confidence in BP. In his opening statement to a congressional committee on June 17, he followed the ritual of apologizing for what happened, saying, "The explosion and fire aboard the Deepwater Horizon and the resulting oil spill in the Gulf of Mexico never should have happened, and I am deeply sorry that it did."[809] But he exhibited an unfriendly and uncooperative demeanor that angered some members of Congress; nor did his so-called apology meet the criteria of a sincere apology that acknowledges the harm done.

On the occasion when he met with the families of the 11 men who died on the rig to extend his condolences, he insensitively commented, "You know, I'd like my life back," a remark he later acknowledged as "wrong."[810] As Robbie Vorhaus, a crisis expert at Vorhaus Communications, Inc., said, "A true leader needs to be able to come from the heart and make these people feel that there is a connection."[811] Hayward was not an empathic person; he lacked what Daniel Goleman called "emotional intelligence."[812]

Hayward's comment further revealed his lack of empathy when it was reported that he spent a subsequent weekend on his 52-foot yacht watching a yacht race around the Isle of Wight. As Phil Hall, the former *News of the World* editor who runs PHA, a crisis management firm, bluntly said, "Going on holiday absolutely sends the most horrific signal . . . . Lying back on a yacht feels like arrogance at best and rank stupidity at worst."[813] It ranked close to that of the boss of investment bank Bear Stearns, Jimmy Cayne, who famously took part in a bridge competition in Nashville while his firm veered toward collapse. To Ian Monk, a celebrity public relations man, Hayward's behavior was death-wish stuff and left him looking like "a dead man walking."[814]

When the *New York Times* described Hayward as "gaffe-prone," it referred to other memorable lines, such as saying that the spill wasn't going to cause big problems because the gulf "is a very big ocean," and "the environmental impact of this disaster is likely to have been very, very modest."[815] He also lacked such facts as the number of similarly designed wells in the Gulf. No wonder President Obama publicly called for him to be fired.[816]

Neglect of Quality Control by Pharmaceutical Companies

Johnson & Johnson's Recalls

Mismanagement has affected even the most reputable companies. For years, Johnson & Johnson (J&J) has been first on surveys such as the Harris Interactive/Reputation Institute, which measure the reputations of leading companies, and was cited as the most-reputable company in the United States by the Reputation Institute in April 2010.[817] Its reputation is likely to drop in the future because flaws have been found in the quality of three products that required recalls: several pediatric drugs were found to contain contaminants;[818] contact lenses sold in Asia and Europe were defective, causing complaints of pain, stinging or redness;[819] and two of its hip-repair implants were recalled because too many patients needed surgeries to replace the devices.[820]

Particularly affected was J&J's McNeil Consumer Healthcare division amid a slew of quality-control issues and product recalls. The constant recalls hurt J&J's reputation as a trusted branded supplier. Beginning in January and through 2010, NcNeil issued recalls on 40 brands, including Tylenol, Motrin, Zyrtec and 140 million bottles of children's and infants' products. Even in late December, the company had to recall 13 million packages of Rolaids because wood and metal particles were found in the drug. In addition to these manufacturing violations in 2010, McNeil was charged with an ethical violation in a "phantom recall" conducted two years earlier. It had hired contractors to buy back travel vials of adult Motrin from retailers, rather than conducting a recall. Contractor's employees were instructed to act as though they were ordinary customers.[821] The company that was lauded for its excellent crisis communications during the 1982 Tylenol poisoning scare, now had to admit that it stumbled seriously with manufacturing quality.

GlaxoSmithKline's Faulty Puerto Rico Plant

60 Minutes ran a segment called "GlaxoSmithKline's Whistleblower," which exposed serious failures in the manufacture and labeling of drugs in GSK's Cidra, Puerto Rico, plant. This was a premier manufacturing facility that produced $5.5 billion worth of drugs each year. The discoveries were made by Cheryl Eckard, the company's quality manager who led a team of quality experts in August 2002 to fix problems cited by a FDA warning letter a month earlier.[822]

What she found was startling: "All the systems were broken, the facility was broken, the equipment was broken, the processes were broken." Among her specific findings were that the water was tainted with bacteria, that employees were contaminating such products as the anti-bacterial ointment Bactioban, and that powerful medications were getting mixed up in bottles. A grandmother, worried about her grandchild's reaction to a drug, opened a bottle in the presence of a pharmacist in which they found two different colored pills, indicating different dosages. Eckhart reported her findings to the company's vice president responsible for quality control and pleaded that the plant be shut down. After five months, she found that no action was taken; when she complained she was fired.

The company finally agreed to pay $750 million to settle criminal and civil charges that the company for years knowingly sold contaminated baby ointment and an ineffective antidepressant; $96 million will go to Eckard, a whistle-blower record. Altogether, GSK had sold 20 problematic drugs manufactured at the huge Puerto Rico plant that for years was rife with contamination. Among the drugs were Avandia, Paxil, Tagmet, Coreg, and Bactroban. It was only after Eckhart reported her finding to the FDA and a multimillion-dollar settlement of criminal and civil complaints that the plant was closed. This was a case of gross mismanagement with potentially serious health consequences.

Baxter International's Tainted Heparin

Negligence can be blamed for tainted heparin sold by Baxter International Inc. It received the drug from a Shenzhen Hepalink plant in China. The plant produces heparin from pig innards from government-regulated slaughter houses, which are supposed to follow strict rules to minimize contamination. The company claims that its employees are stationed in quality-assurance labs on the premises of each supplier whose material is destined for the United States, but enforcement was often spotty. To cut costs, some intestines from pigs infected with a virus may have been used. When the FDA officials toured the factory they found flaws in record-keeping and a lack of evidence that appropriate steps were being taken to effectively rid crude heparin of possible contaminants. The report also stated that "manufacturing instructions" followed at the plant were "incomplete."[823]

Food Recalls Reveal Sloppy Practices

About 76 million people are stricken with food-borne illnesses every year in the United States, which result in 325,000 hospitalizations and 5,000 deaths, according to the Centers for Disease Control and Prevention (CDC). Major food outbreaks occurred toward the end of the first decade of the 21st century: 72 illnesses stemmed from E.coli in cookie dough in 2009; 272 illnesses in 2009 and 2010 from salmonella in red/black pepper and Italian style meat; 1,442 illnesses in 2008 from salmonella in jalapenos and tomatoes; three deaths and 199 illnesses in 2006 from E.coli in spinach; nine deaths and 714 illnesses in 2008 and 2009 from salmonella bacteria in peanut butter; and 1,600 illnesses in 2010 from salmonella in eggs.[824] Because food distribution systems are widespread, most scares cover several states and often the entire United States. Sometimes, however, scares are misplaced. Tomatoes were mistakenly recalled when, as later discovered, the problem of salmonella was actually with jalapenos.[825] Tomato growers, who saw much of their crop destroyed, endured millions in losses.

E.coli caused by unsanitary practices was the main culprit when Nestlé's Toll House refrigerated cookie dough products made in a Danville, Virginia, factory were blamed for sickening 69 people in 29 states.[826] Topps Meat Co. was another company stricken with E.coli in 2007. After recalling nearly 22-million pounds of contaminated beef in 2007, the company, which had been in business more than 60 years, was forced out of business in early 2008.[827] Sloppy management can be blamed for most of the outbreaks that are responsible for deaths and illnesses.

Peanut Corporation of America

One of the worst cases of food contamination involved two plants of the Peanut Corporation of America (PCA). It sent out batches of peanuts, peanut butter and paste that it knew to be contaminated with salmonella. These products were used in more than 2,000 processed and packaged foods by some of the largest food makers in the country, such as Kellogg, Kraft, and General Mills. While big companies have experience and staff to handle recalls, many smaller businesses have neither. One of the victims was King Nut Cos., in Solon, Ohio, which sells peanut butter under its King Nut and Parnell's Pride brands.[828] Martin Kanan, CEO of the company, issued a recall and said in a release, "We are very sorry this happened. We are taking immediate and voluntary action because the health and safety of those who use our products is always our highest priority."[829]

In all, CDC tied 637 illnesses to the salmonella outbreak and probably nine deaths. When investigators examined PCA's Blakely, Georgia, plant, they found a leaky roof, mold and roaches. In its Plainview, Texas, plant they found rodents, rodent excrement and bird feathers in crawl spaces above the production area. During a FDA inspectors' visit in late 2001, they noticed pea-nut-processing equipment had been improperly repaired with duct or cello-phane tape, a condition that was hard to sanitize and could lead to adulterated food.[830]

The company's first public statement was to disagree with some of the gov-ernment's findings—sometimes called "attacking the accuser"—and state that it had "taken extraordinary measures to identify and recall all products that have been identified as presenting a potential risk."[831] Company officials could not be located for a comment and did not speak publicly. When mismanagement is as gross as in this case, an attempt by a company to repair damage—both to retain customers and restore its reputation—is extremely difficult. Extensive recalls of its products left it no choice but to file for bankruptcy protection.

Hallmark/Westland Meat Co. Exposed by Humane Society

In the nation's largest meat recall at the time, Hallmark/Westland Meat Co.'s Chino, California, slaughter house recalled 143 million pounds of beef dat-ing back two years after an employee member of the Humane Society secretly video-taped two employees using a forklift and electric prongs to get "downer cows" to stand up and be moved to where they would be slaughtered for human consumption.[832] Downer cows are known to carry a number of bacte-rial infections and possibly mad cow disease. Before knowing about the taped incident, Steve Mendall, the company's president claimed the sick cows "were not slaughtered, ground or sold. They were euthanized and removed."[833] The incriminating tape was posted on a website and widely circulated on the Inter-net. The Humane Society used the tape when it sued the Agriculture Dept. for creating a "loophole" that it said permitted potentially sick cows to enter into the food supply.

Other slaughter houses have also been negligent. Nebraska Beef Ltd. recalled 1.2 million pounds of beef and then another 53 million after it was linked to E.coli outbreaks in ten states and Canada. The company hadn't thoroughly cleaned its equipment so there was no way to ensure the meat produced later in the day was safe.[834] In western New York, Fairbank Farms voluntarily recalled 545,699 pounds of ground beef products after two people, one from New Hampshire and another from upstate New York, died after eating ground beef and more than two dozen people became ill. [835]

Half a Million Eggs Recalled

Wright County Egg Co. of Galt, Iowa, was at the center of a salmonella out-break in eggs in August 2010 that sickened at least 1,500 Americans in at least ten states. Together with Hillandale Farms with which it is affiliated, Wright County Egg recalled more than half a billion eggs in August. Food retailers and manufacturers were rushing to reassure their customers.[836]

The egg industry is regulated by two federal agencies: the Food and Drug Administration (FDA) and the U.S. Department of Agriculture (USDA). They sharply divide their responsibilities, with the FDA having overall responsibility for egg safety and the USDA for grading eggs and daily reviewing 22 categories of cleanliness. Although the USDA found conditions generally satisfactory until around mid-May, the marks then shifted to "unsatisfactory" in several areas, including some deemed "critical." Among the sanitation problems found at Wright's henhouses were flies, frogs, pigeons, piles of chicken manure, and bird droppings. When the FDA finally inspected Wright's facilities it found many sanitation problems such as mice, maggots and manure piles as high as eight feet. Contributing to the problem was a serious lack of communications between the FDA and USDA, even when inspectors were only a few dozen feet away from each other at a facility. The FDA says it never heard from the USDA about problems such as dirt and mold.[837]

The blame game was also in full swing, with egg farmers blaming the feed companies for the contamination; there are about 750 commercial feed mills in Iowa. The FDA found that sanitary conditions in the Quality Egg feed mill showed multiple points of possible contamination, such as rodents that appeared to have access to many parts of the barn and rusted and porous bins exposed to live birds and avian feces.[838]

The egg industry also has continuing animal rights problems. California passed a law, known as Proposition 2, which will by 2015 require egg producers to get bigger cages or let the hens roam free. The law, which was sponsored by the Humane Society of the United States, requires that egg-laying hens must be able to fully extend their limbs, lie down and turn in a circle within their enclosures. "That's carrying reforms too far," said Eric Benson, president of J.S. West, a California egg producer, "hens are simple creatures and don't need much to be happy."[839]

Tainted Coke in Europe

As the world's leading brand, Coca-Cola must carefully guard against any harm to this valuable intangible asset. Yet this happened in June 1999 when newspapers reported that some people in Belgium became ill after drinking Coke. The first incident occurred at a bar near Antwerp where four adults were affected. It is assumed that Coke made normal inquiries about the circumstances and that there was no justification for further action. The second incident occurred on June 8 when school children in Bornem felt dizziness, nausea and other symptoms after drinking Coca-Cola at school. Forty-two were hospitalized over the next 24 hours. This was the tipping point when Coke should have realized that it was facing a crisis and that it should immediately engage in crisis communication. However, it remained silent. In a third incident on June 10, eight children were hospitalized in Bruges after drinking Coke and Fanta (a Coke product). This event should have confirmed that the problem was serious enough to justify a regional product recall.

Instead of initiating action, Coke officials procrastinated until they were forced to react. On June 11, they were summoned to a meeting at the Belgian Health Ministry, which had established a call center for health complaints about Coke products. Between June 12 and 14, it received 200 calls. Some European newspapers were now speculating that Coke cans were contaminated with rat poison. On June 14, the Belgian Health Minister Luc Van den Bossehe ordered all Coca-Cola products off the market and for production to be halted in bottling plants at Antwerp and Ghent. For him, the crisis threshold, which Coke had hesitated to acknowledge, had been reached. When a company fails to decide on a voluntary recall and is ordered to do so by the government, it has already lost ground in the arena of public opinion and consumer attitudes. Its brand is jeopardized.

After further reports—some now coming from Luxembourg, France, Netherlands and Germany—and orders by France to stop product at a bottling plant in Dunkirk, Coke recognized that it faced a major crisis. On June 15, Coke held a press conference (described by some as chaotic) and issued its first press release that acknowledged that products sold mainly in the Belgian market had been tainted. One source was the accidental injection of "defective" carbon dioxide gas (which gives soft drinks fizz) into some cola and the other source was contamination of the outside of soft drink cans by a fungicide used to treat wooden shipping pallets. Coke had violated its own rules by not requiring certificates of analysis from the gas's supplier (Aga Gas AB of Sweden) and by worker failure to perform the routine test of confirming that each batch of carbon dioxide smelled and tasted fine.

Confirming that the Belgian incidents constituted a major crisis, the situation now received the attention of its CEO Douglas Ivester. In an open letter to the public, he issued the company's first apology to European consumers, saying that it was "taking all necessary steps" to ensure quality. The next day he flew to Brussels, arriving on June 18—ten days after the first incident of ill school children. The lack of immediacy harmed the effectiveness of the apology and his visit. He told Coke employees that quality control in Belgium failed. It wasn't until June 23 that Belgium lifted its ban and on June 25 when other countries did so.

In summary, Coke displayed mismanagement by responding too slowly to early warnings and by procrastinating. It should have acted sooner in recalling the affected products and being open with consumers about what went wrong. Richard Tomkins of the *Financial Times* adds that its apology should also have shown contrition, which is an ingredient of a good apology.[840] Although recalls are costly (over one million bottles were recalled), the potential harm to its global brand and reputation would be even greater.

The Coke case illustrates the importance of issues management, discussed earlier in Chapter 8, as a way to spot early warning signals of crises of management failure. It would also have helped the Coke representative who met with Belgian's health minister, for he would have known about a then-current food scandal, including the discovery of cancer-causing dioxin in animal feed, which embarrassed the minister and made product safety a prominent issue.

Other Cases of Incompetence and Negligence

Airline Mishaps

The crash of Continental Flight 3407 on February 12, 2009, which encountered wintry weather in its flight from Newark to Buffalo, killing all 49 people aboard, was blamed on pilot fatigue, inexperience and misjudgment. The flight was operated for Continental Airlines by Colgan Air Inc., a unit of Memphis-based Pinnacle Airlines Corp.[841] Colgan's safety practices were less rigorous than those of major carriers. Salaries were also smaller. The average annual pay for a co-pilot on the type of plane flown was about $24,000 and about $67,000 for a pilot. The co-pilot, Rebecca Shaw, had flown overnight from her home in Seattle and arrived at the Newark International Airport at 6:30 a.m. on the day of the crash raising the question of fatigue. She made less than $17,000 a year and was holding down a second job at a coffee shop.[842]

The pilot had reportedly failed test flights before he was hired and was never adequately taught how to respond to the type of emergency he encountered. When a signal indicated falling air speed, he pulled on the stick instead of pushing it to accelerate speed, as the training manuals advised. By pulling on the stick, which makes the plane ascend, speed dropped even further and the plane crashed.[843] The co-pilot's final words were "I've never seen icing conditions. I've never deiced. . . . I don't want to have to experience that and make those kinds of calls. . . oh my gosh we're going to crash."[844]

Such misjudgment should be compared with the laudatory actions of other pilots. One of these is Captain Chesley Sullenberger I whose jetliner engines were disabled after flying into a flock of geese. He skillfully glided the aircraft into the Hudson River without losing a single passenger.[845] Another example is how a crew of five senior pilots of a Quantas Airways airliner flying from Singapore to Sydney, Australia, handled an explosive engine failure. They "relied on discipline, calm teamwork and in the end, manual flying skills to turn a harrowing situation into a safe emergency landing."[846] Competence may determine whether a situation results in a serious crisis.

The safety of regional airlines has been scrutinized since the Colgan Air crash. Another feeder carrier for Continental Airlines, Gulfstream, was criticized by pilots for alleged unsafe practices. One instance was when one of its captains refused to fly a Beech 11900 turboprop that had a malfunctioning collision-avoidance system. He was allegedly fired on the spot for insubordination. David Hackett, CEO and president of the airline's parent company, Gulfstream International Group, Inc., defended Colgan Air. In May 2009 the Federal Aviation Authority (FAA) proposed a $1.3 million penalty against Gulfstream for alleged faulty record-keeping and substandard aircraft maintenance.[847]

Mismanagement took the form of inattention when the pilots of Northwest's Flight 188 from San Diego overshot their destination in Minneapolis and were out of radio communication for over an hour. They claimed they were distracted by viewing company scheduling policies on a laptop and engaging in a heated discussion, thus challenging the suspicion that they might have been napping. Neither pilot monitored the progress of the airplane nor air-traffic control communications.[848] A Federal Aviation Administration (FAA) air-traffic facility tried to reach the pilots by radio more than a dozen times, and Northwest officials tried with eight separate text messages to the cockpit. FAA violated its own rules by taking more than 40 minutes to alert the military after losing contact with the flight.[849] When public safety is at risk, such lapses by pilots and flight-control operators are unconscionable.

Strategies for Responding to Crises of Mismanagement

The strategies for responding to crises of mismanagement basically seek to attain the criteria of crisis-avoidance management discussed in the introduction to this chapter. Overcoming management inadequacies and vulnerabilities is the basic goal. Specific strategies include quality assurance, repairing reputational damage, and improving organizational and government oversight.

Quality Assurance

Responding to negative reports about its recalls, J&J CEO William Weldon provided the reassurance that "The people who use our products are our first priority, and we've let them down."[850] He also announced that J&J would restructure its manufacturing hierarchy and create a new position to ensure quality products. The plan calls for the appointment of chief quality officers for each of the three major business segments, who will report to a corporate vice president.[851] Weldon was criticized for not taking a more active role in the recall crisis earlier in the process and not fully centralizing all crisis communications. Too much was left in the hands of its business units and Colleen Goggins, J&J's consumer products chief.[852]

Quality assurance requires more than a reassuring announcement that someone has been appointed as a vice president of quality assurance. GSK's senior vice president responsible for global quality assurance, Ian McCubbin, didn't recall questionable products nor stop production. His response to the *60 Minutes* story was, "GSK regrets the manufacturing issues at the Cidra facility, which were inconsistent with GSK's commitment to manufacturing quality." He also pointed out that the events occurred between 2001 and early 2005, and that the company had been working with the U.S. FDA to improve the plant's performance. As reassurance, he further explained that, "patients were not harmed as a result of production problems at a plant it once operated in

Puerto Rico."[853] The slowness in taking corrective action is inconsistent with GSK's responsibility to its consumers. Greater vigilance by the board of directors is needed to strengthen the company's culture of safety.

As shown in the heparin case, those responsible for quality assurance must conscientiously execute their assigned responsibilities. Whenever ingredients, parts, or entire products are received from elsewhere, they must be checked to make sure they meet required specifications and quality. This is a function of supplier relations, which is performed by purchasing managers. When large quantities of supplies are involved, a quality assurance procedure is necessary. It should not be left to the supplier. At Cardill, a grain operator, agricultural products are conscientiously inspected and assessed and each shipment graded accordingly.

Standards Vary in the Food Industry

Companies in the food industry vary in their quality assurance standards. After twice inspecting PCA plants, Nestlé chose not to accept PCA as a supplier because it didn't meet the company's food-safety standards, according to Nestlé's audit reports in 2002 and 2006. The reports said the plant needed a "better understanding of the concept of deep cleaning" and failed to adequately separate roasted raw peanuts from unroasted ones, which could allow bacteria on raw nuts to contaminate roasted ones. Nestlé's auditor Richard Hutson said he shared his concerns with PCA officials at the time, but "they didn't pursue it further" with Nestlé.[854]

Other customers of PCA, however, including Kellogg, never audited the Blakely plants themselves, relying instead on inspection by an auditing firm that was paid by PCA. Kellogg got certificates from PCA, issued by private labs paid by PCA, saying the product was salmonella-free. According to Rep. Bart Stupak (D.-Mich.), AIB International, which is the most commonly used auditor in the United States, rates almost every client "excellent" or "superior."[855] AIB's rating of PCA has since come under attack, along with the all-too common practice of foodmakers paying for their own audits. Little solace can be found in AIB's defense that between its audit in mid-2008 and the FDA's inspection in January 2009, the Blakely plant ran for months without a manager, thus allowing conditions to deteriorate. In the food industry, basic hygienic and sanitary conditions and employee practices must routinely be inspected.

Trade associations should consider providing a quality assurance service for their members. In the meat industry, this could be done by the American Meat Institute (AMI), which represents the interests of packers and processors of beef, pork, lamb, veal and turkey products and their suppliers throughout North America. It provides legislative, regulatory, public relations, technical, scientific and educational services to the meat and poultry packing and processing industry. Quality assurance should be included.[856]

Problems of Outsourcing

Recognizing that outsourcing increases a company's vulnerability, the historical vertical integration of giants like Carnegie Steel Co. and Ford Motor Co. is being reconsidered. In the past, these companies owned their own iron-ore mines and controlled everything else from manufacturing to sales. The modern trend has been for companies to concentrate in certain core operations, such as assembling cars, and to subcontract everything else. Boeing carried that model to the extreme by assembling the 787 Dreamliner jet from parts made by hundreds of suppliers. Discovering problems with some of the parts received, its delivery schedule fell behind by more than three years.[857] Boeing and others are now reversing the historical trend of "disintegration" to the new model of "integration," says Harold Sirkin, global head of Boston Consulting Group's operations practice.[858]

Outsourcing has raised concerns over the safety of foreign-produced products whose origins can be difficult to track. About 88 percent of the bulk ingredients used by U.S. drug manufacturers comes from overseas, with China and India producing about 40 percent of the world's active pharmaceutical ingredients.[859] As the recall of Baxter's China-produced blood-thinner heparin demonstrated, this dependence can cause problems unless strict quality assurance is exercised.

Hospitals have traditionally paid scant attention to outsourcing, but that's beginning to change, say Frank Fernandez, corporate director of material management for Baptist Health South Florida, a five-hospital group, in Coral Gables, Florida. "The problem is we don't know where a lot of these products are produced. We see product labels that say 'made for' but not 'made by,'" says Fernandez.[860] Although most outsourcing manufacturers say they have internal process and quality-assurance programs, they may not go far enough. Many drug companies and device makers have downsized their quality-assurance staffs, they have turned over quality-assurance responsibilities to their contracted production facilities.

Repair Reputational Damage

The explosion on April 20 and sinking of the Deepwater Horizon rig created a huge reputational and financial crisis for BP. Its image as a leader in deep sea technology was shattered, as well as its professed dedication to corporate social responsibility and the environment. It now had to restore its reputation to stem financial liability and ensure that it would continue to be allowed to operate in U.S. waters. The attitudes of public officials and the general public might influence the size of the fines and the harshness of various judgments. Investors would also consider how seriously BP's reputation was damaged, which would be reflected in the company's stock market price.

BP's effort throughout the crisis was to minimize erosion of its reputation as a forward-looking oil industry giant. BP's failed attempts to cap the leak at the sea bed, the continuing spread of oil in the Gulf, and BP's dangerous cost-cutting severely damaged the company's reputation. Under Lord John Browne, BP positioned itself as a leader in thinking about alternative energy sources, using the slogan that BP stood for "Beyond Petroleum." But the $200 million spent on the image campaign was never backed up by expenditures on necessary research. Its resources went into its merger with Amoco for $52 billion in 1998 and its acquisition of Atlantic Richfield in 2000. Its post-merger cost-cutting led to serious lapses in safety and maintenance.

BP's Advertising and Social Media Campaign

Even before the spill was stopped, BP used advertising and other communication techniques to report on its actions. To counter images of the mounting disaster, BP spent more than $5 million a week on advertising during the weeks of media coverage of the oil spill. The ads were intended to ensure transparency and to keep residents informed on issues related to the spill. Although the cost of the ads was criticized by some, the ads were effective. Favorable marks for handling the spill more than doubled from June to August, rising to 33 percent.[861]

On June 3, BP began showing a new television ad in which CEO Hayward spoke directly into a camera and pledged to spare no effort to clean up the spill.[862] The company took out full-page ads in major newspapers, starting with "Gulf of Mexico Oil Spill Response," in which it reaffirmed that "BP has taken full responsibility for dealing with the spill. We are determined to do everything we can to minimize any impact. We will honor all legitimate claims."[863]

The ads continued over the weeks with the banner "Making This Right," which reported updates on actions taken on claims, economic investment, environmental restoration, health and safety, and wildlife. Its July 30 ad reiterated, "Our commitment is that we'll be here for as long as it takes." The ads humanized the effort by showing workers, among the 33,000 people involved in the cleanup operation, on a beach, and including a photo of one of the workers who is quoted, "I am from Louisiana and I know our beaches are our home, our way of life and our livelihoods. Protecting the coast and cleaning up the beaches is very personal to me."[864] BP enlisted the help of the Brunswick Group, a public relations and crisis management firm, to help in these communication efforts.[865]

Upon the advice of Ogilvy Worldwide, BP also used the social media extensively, partly as a defensive measure. The Facebook group Boycott BP had more than 181,600 members as of Friday, May 29 and the parody Twitter feed BPGlobalPR had more than 75,800 followers.[866] BP worked with Mindshare, a WPP Group, and opened a website, "BP Oil Spill Response." *AdWeek* commented, "The Gulf of Mexico Response hub that BP set up would make most social media strategists proud. It's fed with information broadcast through Twitter, Facebook, YouTube and Flickr."[867]

On an optimistic note, one senior BP executive insisted that although the situation is grim, it is not helpless. "The actual damage inflected to BP's brand is significant, but the ultimate way to restore a brand is to do the right thing. . . . We need BP to be a healthy, viable company."[868]

BP's Board Actions

A standard practice in serious crises of management failure is to replace errant managers. Accordingly, Hayward who was seen as harming BP's efforts to restore its credibility was fired on July 27, well-timed to occur shortly after the well was brought under control. The board named Robert Dudley, BP's managing director, as the new chief executive officer. Dudley had the advantage of being American born and brought up in Louisiana, and was reputed to be a "more caring, individual than Hayward."[869]

This appeal would be valuable when Congress and the administration ultimately decide on the penalties BP would have to pay for the environmental damage. Until the total bill is added up, BP agreed to a $20 billion escrow fund as a political settlement with the U.S. administration to compensate for the liabilities stemming from the spill. Perhaps more important, he could help "BP retain its ability to continue as an operator in high-profile areas such as Alaska and the deep-water Gulf of Mexico."[870]

BP's board also decided on further restitution. When its board met in late July, it set aside $32.2 billion to pay for damages. To finance the cost of the spill, BP planned to raise $30 billion from asset sales.[871] BP's market value fell $89 billion since the well erupted, nearly 40 percent of its market value.[872] Preparing the way for negotiations with the government and claimants, Dudley tried to dismiss the argument that BP was negligent. He said: "It's a very complicated industrial accident" which resulted from "a series of individual misjudgments by very experienced people and a multiple series of failures of equipment and processes of using equipment that is going to involve multiple companies here."[873] The legal drama is expected to last many years. The damage to BP's reputation will be difficult to repair.

Mainly, BP had to salvage its reputation as a socially responsible corporation and to restore its credibility as a leader in the technology of deep sea drilling. It would have to convince government officials that it had learned valuable technological lessons from the BP disaster and could be trusted to drill safely in the Gulf in the future. Mindful of government's role, BP hired a bevy of Washington insiders to buy extra credibility with government officials and to protect itself from lawsuits. Included in this arsenal was James Lee Witt, the highly regarded former FEMA director.

Provide Better Organizational and Government Oversight

Careful supervision and systems of control are needed to assure that operations are properly performed in accordance with organizational plans and policies.

Negligence is then readily spotted and corrective action taken. On lower levels of an organization's hierarchy, office and shop supervisors perform the oversight function. On the highest level, it is the board of directors that establishes control systems and provides oversight.

PCA's Dysfunctional Board

In the PCA case, the board simply did not function. The companies that bought peanut products need to heed the advice of the Grocery Manufacturers Association, which advises small business to know their suppliers' food safety culture and practices, and whether the suppliers are capable of doing the right thing. Some buyers protect and prepare themselves in a variety of ways—by requiring a Certificate of Analysis, essentially a contract for quality; by obtaining recall insurance; and by undergoing mock recalls every six months. Interest in the subject was indicated by the attendance of 60 participants in a seminar on "The Ingredient Supply chain: Do You Know Who You're in Bed With?" given by the association's microbiologist and vice president of science policy and food protection.[874]

The PCA case demonstrated that every key link in the chain of protection failed. William Hubbard, a former FDA associate commission, said the outbreak "is a poster child for everything that went wrong" with the USA's food-safety system. . . . Down the line, you can find flaws and failures." Even after problems were brought to PCA's attention, it failed to fix the problems.[875]

Better Government Food Safety Oversight

Oversight is one of the functions of government regulation that compensates for company mismanagement and helps avoid crises. When the jalapeno pepper grown in Mexico was found to be the cause of a salmonella outbreak in 2008, flaws were discovered, such as poor record-keeping for tracking fresh produce and the common practice of mixing and processing tomatoes from many different farms together. Michael Doyle, director of the University of Georgia's Center for Food Safety, commented: "It's a mess—that's part of the problem with the food-safety system we have today."[876]

Over 12 federal agencies are responsible for food safety, and much of the tracking is heavily dependent on state health departments. Many states have decided to adopt tougher safety laws independent of federal rules. By the middle of May 2009, some 600 bills addressing food safety were introduced in state legislation since the beginning of the year. After Georgia's peanut industry was hit hard by the salmonella outbreak, the state enacted legislation that give food processors 24 hours to report internal tests that find tainted products. California lawmakers also introduced legislation to strengthen food safety after a massive recall of pistachios from Setton Pistachio of Terra Bella Inc.[877] It had shipped about one million pounds of the nuts.[878]

In September 2009, the FDA launched a system for quick reporting of potential food-borne illnesses by setting up an electronic food registry. If food facilities find any contaminant in a product that might severely sicken or kill people or animals, they must alert the FDA within 24 hours. Failure to do so would subject a company to an injunction, fines or other punishment. A poll released by the Pew Charitable Trusts found that 89 percent of likely voters support these food safety measures.[879] In December 2010, the Senate passed a measure that would give the FDA the power to order food recalls, which were still voluntary. It would also give the FDA greater authority to track fruit and vegetable shipments, as well as mandate that producers write safety plans.[880]

Replacing MMS

One reason for BP's mismanagement, including negligent maintenance of the blowout preventer, was the lack of oversight by the Department of Interior's Minerals Management Service (MMS), the official regulatory body for deep sea drilling. As stated in a *Wall Street Journal* headline, "Regulator Ceded Oversight of Rig Safety to Oil Drillers," it was a failed agency accused of being "too cozy" with the industry it regulates.[881] Following the prevailing free-market system of industry self-regulation, the MMS saw its role as setting broad performance goals for the industry and letting oil producers and drilling companies decide how to meet those goals. It ritualistically approved most plans. In one reported instance it approved permits for a change of plans within seven minutes and another four and one-half minutes after being shown them, which hardly allowed time seriously to review the changes.[882]

MMS's main function was to collect gas and oil royalties, and even then the agency was accused by the Interior Department Inspector General of modifying royalty payment contracts in ways that "appeared to inappropriately benefit the oil companies."[883] The inspector general concluded in 2008 that MMS employees created a "culture of ethical failure."[884] As a result of the crisis, the functions of MMS were split between a regulatory function and a fiscal function, just as the Nuclear Regulatory Administration separated its promotional activities for nuclear energy from its regulatory function. The agency is now called the Bureau of Ocean Energy, Regulation and Enforcement.

Overhaul Deficient Systems—Safety Reforms in China's Airlines

China has become a model of successfully reversing a terrible record of aircraft crashes to having the best safety record in the industry. Its experience shows how mismanagement can be corrected. China's air safety record was one of the worst in the world. After a string of crashes stretching from the mid-1990s to 2002, the Chinese airlines were known as arguably the world's most dangerous. They were "beset by persistent pilot errors, unreliable maintenance and erratic government oversight."[885] Pilots flouted basic rules, such as flying into violent storms and haphazardly programming autopilots. Two major accidents occurred in 2002 when an Air China Boeing 767 crashed near Busan, South Korea, killing 129 and injuring 37 others, followed by a crash off the northern port city of Dalian, killing 112.

The Chinese government was intent on transforming the Chinese airline industry, realizing that its poor safety record was tarnishing its national image. The goal was to balance safety and growth. After a slow start, it put an "hard-charging aviation official," Mr. Yang Yuanyuan, deputy director of Civil Aviation Administration of China (CAAC), in charge. This appointment was important because, as recognized by Ma Tao, China's representative to the International Civil Aviation Organization, "You must have a very strong, central agency to establish rules."[886]

Following the precepts of O'Toole and Bennis, China's communication became exceedingly open and candid by revealing its shortcomings. As the head of the Federal Aviation Authority (FAA) Marion Blakey observed, Chinese authorities recognized early on "there simply was no place for secrets when it came to aviation safety. They never let egos get in the way."[887] China was also open in being willing to learn from U.S. aircraft manufacturers who were worried that sales of its aircraft might be hurt. Boeing offered free safety-management courses for hundreds of Chinese controllers and airline flight-operations personnel. It offered free time on flight simulators to Chinese pilots. Together with rival Airbus it set up permanent pilot training programs in China and sent foreign experts to train mechanics. Their efforts were joined by over two dozen U.S. companies, ranging from engine makers to cockpit-instrument suppliers, that provided technical help.

China recognized that the airline industry is international. Not surprisingly, therefore, it pledged close cooperation with foreign crash investigators and relied on international aviation safety organizations to conduct audits and recommend improvements. China worked with Boeing and later the FAA to write new aviation regulations and to beef up air-traffic control designs and inspection procedures.

Conclusions

Management inadequacies and damaging flaws of sloppiness, negligence, and callousness can cause crises. These affect issues ranging from consumer safety to safety on oil rigs. Flaws can occur in all industries, as illustrated in the oil, pharmaceutical, airlines and food processing cases. Global supply chains have increased a firm's vulnerability and require quality assurance procedures by receivers of those products.

When mismanagement is caused by an overall organizational deficiency, it must be compensated by greater oversight by the board of governors, assuming it is functional, and by government. The whole culture of an organization needs renewal, which usually requires the assistance of outside consultants in such fields as organizational development. Drastic overhaul is sometimes necessary, applying the basic principles of organizational structure and behavior. Such corrective measures were undertaken by China's airlines where massive changes were made in personnel and retraining of pilots.

Crises of mismanagement also draw attention to the emotional capabilities of managers as well as their ability for on-the-spot creative thinking.[888] Lack of sensitivity to the concerns of stakeholders and lack of attention to warning signs of a developing crisis are characteristic of crises of mismanagement.

Chapter 11

Crises of Skewed Management Values

Crises of skewed management values are caused when managers favor short-term economic gain and neglect broader social values and standards of stakeholder fairness and justice. Sacrificing safety in favor of profits is a common theme in many of these crises. This state of lopsided values is rooted in the classical business creed that focuses on the interests of stockholders and tends to view the interests of other stakeholders—such as customers, employees, and the community—as subsidiary and relatively unimportant. A blunt advocate of this skewed view was Albert J. Dunlap, former chairman and CEO of Scott Paper Co., who said, "Stakeholders are total rubbish. . . . It's the shareholders who own the company."[889] The alternative view is embodied in the modern concept of stakeholder management, which, as stated by James O'Toole in Vanguard Management, seeks "stakeholder symmetry."[890] This view holds that managers act in a trusteeship function for all stakeholders.

Crises of skewed management values are also more likely to arise in the absence of corporate social responsibility (CSR). It holds that management must include broader values in its decision-making than profit maximization. It is a revolutionary change in management thought and practice. It affirmatively seeks to avoid harm to employees by being attentive to safety practices and violations of human rights; it is mindful of providing consumer satisfaction. It is also aware of the social costs of doing business by seeking to avoid harm to the local communities where business is conducted and harm to the physical environment.

CSR also implies ethical behavior, an endeavor to relate business to society, and an effort to achieve sustainability in all operations. Ian Mitroff and Thierry C. Pauchant, in We're So Big and Powerful Nothing Bad Can Happen to Us, vividly explain this change and the need for it. They assert that "the basic conceptions and principles by which virtually all organizations operate are inherently flawed and outmoded."[891] They argue that this condition makes a corporation crisis-prone and that when a crisis does occur an organization's fundamental belief system collapses. The value of relating to a broad array of stakeholders is appreciated as a way to improve decision-making and to lessen the incidence of crises.

Managers often ascribe their skewed values to increasing pressures from domestic and global competition, deregulation, the financial community's unrelenting earnings expectations, and challenges from corporate activists. But the difficult external environment is only part of the cause. The main part lies in the attitudes, mindsets, and beliefs of managers. Sometimes managers are slow learners and hold too rigidly to past repertoires of responses. Other times they learn too fast to accommodate to new circumstances and thereby recklessly abandon the codes of business morality and social obligations that serve as a gyroscope for socially responsible behavior.

Cases of Skewed Values

Update on Exxon Valdez

Exxon, now ExxonMobil, remains a classic case of exercising skewed values and continues to be mentioned in the crisis literature. Pearson and Clair gave Exxon's handling of the *Exxon Valdez* incident a low grade, "warning signals were ignored; plans and preparations for such an event were substandard, and public statements made by Exxon's CEO Rawl riled stakeholders."[892] The authors also criticized Exxon for being generally unwilling to learn from the crisis. The company exemplifies the classical business creed that believes in profit maximization and growth in stockholder values. With this belief, the company became the largest and most profitable corporation in the United States. During his 13-year tenure as CEO, Lee Raymond was amply rewarded, with $686 million in compensation, or about $144,000 a day.[893] In 2008, company profits reached $45.2 billion, the largest in U.S. history.[894]

Economic values predominated to such an extent that one of society's most important values, concern for the environment, was given inadequate priority. When the *Exxon Valdez* supertanker crashed into Bligh Reef on March 24, 1989, its "pipeline vision"—as it was characterized in the first edition of this book—caused 240,000 barrels of oil to gush into the waters of Prince William Sound, Alaska.[895]

ExxonMobil continues to use tankers with one hull even after 79 percent of the world supertanker fleet has been replaced by ships with two hulls, which are better than one for preventing oil spills. Double-hull tankers have an outer layer of steel, normally about 2 centimeters thick, that acts as a buffer in an accident. Single-hull ships, however, cost about 20 percent less to hire, so economies are obtained. One hundred and fifty-one countries have pledged to ban single-hull supertankers by 2015.[896]

Fortunately, the United States has reduced the amount of oil spilled since the *Exxon Valdez* incident. Between 1991 and 2004 there were no spills over 1 million gallons and the number of spills greater than 5,000 gallons decreased from 55 to 14. Better technology and communications largely account for the improved record.[897] The *Exxon Valdez* Oil Spill Trustees Council reports that

Alaska now has "the best and safest oil transportation system in the world." It includes specially trained pilots and escort tugs for tankers, larger quantities of containment booms, greater capacity skimming systems and barges, and improved contingency plans for spills in the Sound. But the Council also reports the pessimistic finding that despite the enormous cleanup effort, oil "persists in the environment and, in places, is nearly as toxic as it was the first few weeks after the spill." The oil is apparently decreasing at a very slow rate.[898] The good news for ExxonMobil was that on June 25, 2008, the Supreme Court overturned the $2.5 billion in punitive damages against ExxonMobil Corp.[899]

In May 2008, 60 American institutional investors backed the Rockefeller family's campaign for a "new, modern chairman" at ExxonMobil.[900] Included among them is Ceres, a group dedicated to addressing global warming. It advocated that Rex Tillerson, the company's joint chairman and chief executive, relinquish his chairmanship to make way for an outsider with fresh ideas. They are concerned that the company relies too heavily on traditional areas of oil exploration and not enough on renewable technology, such as wind- and solar-power. They argue that a greater focus on new technologies would be good for both business and the environment in the long term.

The shareholder proposal that was submitted received 39.5 percent of the vote in 2008.[901] One sign that Exxon Mobil Corp. is taking the issues of alternative energy and global warming more seriously was its decision in July 2009 to invest $600 million into researching how to turn algae into a biofuel. Partnering with scientist J. Craig Venter, known for his work on mapping the human genome, and his company Synthetic Genomics, they hope to create biofuel that can be fed into refineries alongside conventional crude oil. They also expect the algae to suck up greenhouse gases in fighting global warming. Because the partnership will be focused on research, it is expected to take up to a decade to produce commercial quantities of fuel from algae.[902]

BP's Gap Between Rhetoric and Performance

BP has been lauded for its stance on global warming when its CEO Lord John Browne announced that BP stood for "Beyond Petroleum"—that it was looking for alternative energy sources and espoused environmental values. But the $200 million spent on the image campaign was never backed up by expenditures on necessary research. Its resources went into its merger with Amoco for $52 billion in 1998 and its acquisition of Atlantic Richfield in 2000. Its post-merger cost-cutting led to serious lapses in safety and maintenance.

Neglect of safety in its refinery in Texas City, Texas, led to a deadly explosion in 2005, killing 15 and injuring more than 170 others.[903] Neglect in erosion prevention in BP's oil field in Alaska led to oil spills in 2006, which required a partial shutdown of the Prudhoe Bay oil field.[904] BP was also charged with manipulating and cornering the propane market in 2004, spiking prices 50 percent higher at the height of the home-heating season. Quite contrary to the image it portrayed, its values were grossly skewed toward profitability and growth and against environmental values and consumer welfare.[905]

Browne resigned in May 2007 because of a personal scandal.[906] In October 2007, the new CEO, Tony Hayward, pleaded guilty to criminal charges and agreed to pay a $50 million fine related to the deadly refinery blast. He also made sweeping moves to clean up the oil giant's operational and regulatory troubles, as well as submitting to a government-appointed compliance monitor's oversight for the next three to five years.[907]

Turner Broadcasting System's Guerrilla Marketing

Almost by definition, guerrilla marketing is skewed in favor of a marketer at the expense of the public. Michael Levine likens this form of marketing as "battling a sort of urban war and hunting down prey"—the prey being that key customer . . . that will give "your client 'free advertising.'"[908] Turner Broadcasting System engaged in a guerrilla marketing scheme to publicize Cartoon Network's "Aqua Teen Hunger Force" television show that ignored social costs. In 80 cities, including Boston, New York, Los Angeles, Chicago, Atlanta, Seattle, Portland, San Francisco and Philadelphia, billboard types of boxes illuminated by magnetic lights were placed in heavily trafficked locations.

After a motorist in Boston reported seeing one at the end of busy Longfellow Bridge connecting Cambridge and Boston over the Charles River, he alerted the police. They assumed the worst and viewed the situation as a terrorist threat (perhaps because 9/11 terrorists boarded at Boston's Logan Airport). Authorities closed part of the transportation system and a section of a highway, and the Coast Guard shut down portions of the Charles River. To pay for the response costs, Boston Mayor Menino demanded reparations from Turner. An apology was rendered, along with an agreement to pay $2 million. The cost to pedestrians and motorists was not calculated.

Mattel's Toy Recall

Mattel Inc., the United States' largest seller of toys, faced a major crisis following a series of recalls in early September 2007. It announced that it took nearly one million lead-tainted toys off the market. Most of the recalls involved accessories associated with Barbie, Mattel's most popular brand. Earlier in the summer it recalled about 1.5 million toys believed to contain lead contamination, including items featuring characters such as Elmo. A second recall late in August involved a quarter-million "Sarge" toy cars from the Walt Disney Co. movie *Cars*, and four other items involving more than 18 million toys sold in the past four years.[909] In all, Mattel recalled more than 21 million toys made in China, including some Elmo and Dora the Explorer toys.[910] The case highlights the importance of safety in consumer relations and the extension of crisis management to international relations.

Mattel At First Blames China for Toy Recalls

These events added up to a major crisis for Mattel, affecting its reputation with consumers and the possibility of more stringent U.S. safety regulations. China faced a reputational crisis because it was prominently named in news articles. It manufactures about 65 percent of Mattel's toys and nearly 80 percent of all the toys imported by the United States.[911]

In its initial posture in the recall crisis, Mattel acted as an innocent victim whose product safety standards were violated by Chinese manufacturers. This posturing was evident in its full-page ad on September 5 with the headline "we take our promises seriously." The ad continued, "As promised, in recent weeks, we have been busy testing and retesting toys before they leave factories. Our recent voluntary recalls are part of our ongoing promise to ensure the safety of your children." The ad was unsigned. But on September 11 an op-ed article appeared in *Wall Street Journal* written by Mattel's chairman and CEO Bob Eckhart. In it he laments that because of media bias, "the character of Mattel has been maligned." He then explains the company's existing and strengthened safety check system "to prevent lead in paint." He concludes with his "sincere pledge that we will face this challenge with integrity and reaffirm that we will do the right thing."[912]

At a Senate subcommittee hearing, Eckhart blamed China as well as the media for its problems. They were caused by Mattel vendors, he said, who did not check closely enough on subcontractors in China. An internal Mattel investigation showed "that certain vendors or their subcontractors violated our well-established rules." "In some cases, they appear to have been careless. In others they appear to have deliberately avoided doing what they knew they were required to do."[913] In other words, Mattel considered the recall crisis China's fault.

"Made in China" Becomes a Safety Issue

Toy recalls for which lead paint was blamed followed an earlier May 2007 report that cats and dogs were becoming ill, and some dying, from tainted pet food. All the brands came from one Canadian firm, which bought wheat glutton from a single source: China. The glutton contained an industrial chemical, melamine, which was used as an inexpensive fortifier. The chemical is used in plastics and fire retardants and is unfit for use in food. So many brands of pet food were involved that none stood out, but China as the supplier of glutton became suspect for violating safety standards.

China's nation brand was being severely damaged by stories suggesting that the fault lay with China's culture. One was by *Wall Street Journal* reporter Emily Parker who blamed defects in Chinese products on China's single-minded goal of economic development, which, she says, has skewed its actions to the detriment of consumer and worker safety and the environment. She described the managerial attitude behind the "Made in China" label as "anything-for-profit." Every man is for himself in this kind of society, she says. She suspects that since many Chinese have lost faith in communist ideology, "getting rich has, in a sense, become the national religion." She acknowledged, however, that relentless demand by such foreign purchasers as Wal-Mart and Mattel contributed to the almost complete bottom-line mentality of Chinese managers.[914] Parker also pointed to weak government regulation and lax enforcement as contributing to the crisis. She says, "the large problem is that in a country without a real rule of law, where everything is subject to Communist Party 'interpretation,' there is no codified set of ethics to guide national behavior."[915]

China Retaliates

As safety became a hot issue, China at first treated the recalls as a broader trade issue that included Chinese imports from the United States In July 2007. Chinese authorities announced a temporary suspension of imports of some products from several U.S. meat processors, saying tests had found safety problems, including salmonella in frozen chicken and residues of growth hormones in frozen pork ribs. The growth hormone is approved for use by the United States but isn't allowed in China. (The Chinese also turned back French bottled water, Australian seafood, and a U.S. drink mix that authorities said were contaminated or failed safety tests.)[916]

China's strategy seemed to be "defiance and denial," for instance, saying the U.S. authorities were exaggerating the risks and playing up dangers because of trade disputes. A team of Chinese diplomats in Washington, D.C., went to Capitol Hill to present its case and began briefing legislators and reporters. They distributed three-page fact sheets arguing that tainted products represent only a small portion of the country's sales and risks shouldn't be overblown. "The quality rate of Chinese food exports are above 99 percent," the report said. But the team's ability to communicate was reportedly "hampered by its overall inexperience at managing public perceptions in a world of instant communications."[917]

Besides toys, other products were found deficient. The U.S. Food and Drug Administration (FDA) blocked shipments of Chinese-made toothpaste and of several types of farm-raised Chinese seafood because of worries about chemical contamination. Earlier, in spring 2006, more than ten people fell ill after injections of a gallbladder medicine made by a Chinese pharmaceutical company. However, China soon acknowledged the safety problem and took two major remedial actions. First, it meted out punishment, including the extreme measure of sentencing to death the head of the State Food and Drug Administration for having received bribes of cash and gifts worth about $8,950,000 from eight pharmaceutical companies. Second, the Chinese General Administration of Quality Supervision, Inspection and Quarantine, which found 23,000 cases of infractions between December and May 2007, shut down implicated plants that were found to have used industrial chemicals and additives in food products. For example, dyes, mineral oils, paraffin wax, formaldehyde and the carcinogenic malachite green were used in producing flour, candy, pickles, biscuits, black fungus, melon seeds, bean curd and seafood. Most were small, unlicensed food plants with fewer than ten employees among the about one million food factories.[918]

Months later, China took further remedial actions. In late October 2007, Li Changjiang, the head of the government's inspection service, announced the arrest of 774 people allegedly involved in the sale and manufacture of counterfeit and low-quality food and drugs. But Li also named nearly a dozen examples of American products such as General Electric Co. turbines and Deere & Co. cotton pickers that had safety and quality problems.[919]

Mattel Shifts Concern to Relations with China

Having concentrated on its U.S. publics—consumers and government lawmakers and regulators—Mattel recognized that it was endangering its important economic relationship with China. Diplomacy became important, as reflected in a *Wall Street Journal* headline "Mattel Seeks to Placate China With Apology."[920] Mattel now sought to assuage the anger of Chinese officials who felt their country was being scapegoated. A top-level Mattel officer, Thomas A. Debrowski, Mattel's executive vice president for worldwide operations, flew to Beijing to meet with Mr. Li, the Chinese product-safety chief who heads the General Administration of Quality Supervision, Inspection and Quarantine, which employs 30,000 people. After listening to criticism of Mattel's actions, Debrowski humbly recanted:

> Mattel takes full responsibility for these recalls and apologizes personally to you, the Chinese people, and all of our customers who received the toys. It's important for everyone to understand that the vast majority of those products that we called were the result of a design flaw in Mattel's design, not through a manufacturing flaw in Chinese manufacturers.

Mattel switched from a defensive stance to an accommodative one. In related statements, Mattel admitted that the vast majority of the recalled toys didn't have a lead problem and that most involved tiny magnets that can fall off toys and become deadly if swallowed. Mattel's own flawed designs were acknowledge to be at fault.[921]

The apology was astonishing, and Mattel knew it because it almost immediately tried to downplay its significance by saying the company "apologized to the Chinese today just as it has wherever its toys are sold."[922] Lawyers are most worried by such admissions because it makes a company vulnerable to lawsuits. Mattel has consistently employed a formidable team of outside lawyers, said the *Wall Street Journal*, "to deny defects with its toys, in some cases even after millions of them had been recalled and determined to be unsafe and defective by U.S. regulators."[923] Mattel's willingness to accept litigation risks demonstrates the severity of the dual crisis: the recall crisis itself and the diplomatic crisis with Chinese authorities.

Mattel recognized the need for diplomatic overtures with the nation-state of China. Its own efforts followed those of the U.S. Department of Health and Human Services, which in early August 2007 started negotiations with a senior official in China to try to reach agreements to improve Chinese food and drug safety by the end of 2007. In May, a second U.S.-China Strategic Economic Dialogue was held, on which occasion American officials stressed the need for better cooperation and information and "to have the Chinese devise and enforce regulations that we can understand, with which we agree and in which we feel confident," said Mike Leavitt, Secretary of Health and Human Services.[924] The emphasis of these talks, however, was in line with Mattel's earlier stance of blaming China for its problems.

Merck's Delayed Decision to Withdraw Vioxx

Merck surely had a crisis on its hands when CEO Raymond V. Gilmartin announced the voluntary withdrawal of Vioxx, its acute-pain medication, on September 30, 2004. The following day the value of its stock fell 27 percent, erasing $26.8 million from its market capitalization, and a few weeks later to 40 percent.[925] Introduced in 1999, Vioxx was the first among COX-2 inhibitors, which were developed to reduce pain and inflammation without the risk of ulcers and other gastrointestinal side effects posed by aspirin and other over-the-counter medications. More than 80 million patients had taken Vioxx, with annual sales topping $2.5 billion. It was a blockbuster—defined as drugs in excess of $1 billion per year—that make or break pharmaceutical companies. It was also the largest prescription-drug withdrawal in history.[926]

Background

The week before the withdrawal announcement, CEO Gilmartin received a call from his research chief Peter Kim saying that an outside panel overseeing a clinical trial of Vioxx had urged Merck to halt the trial and immediately stop patients from taking the drug. Findings, he said, showed that patients on the drug were twice as likely to have a heart attack or stroke as those on a placebo.[927] After Merck executives consulted about two-dozen outside experts and the board of directors reviewed evidence, the directors agreed that Merck should withdraw the drug.[928] Gilmartin said the company took this drastic action because its professed belief was "patient safety first." This was the credo of George Merck, Gilmartin's predecessor, who proclaimed, "We try never to forget that medicine is for the people. It is not for the profits. The profits follow, and if we have remembered that, they have never failed to appear."[929]

Not everyone, however, believed Gilmartin. One was Eric J. Topol, an M.D., who blasted Merck in his article in the *New England Journal of Medicine* for inverting its values by placing "sales over safety." "Sadly, it is clear to me that Merck's commercial interest in rofecoxib [Vioxx] sales exceeded its concern about the drug's potential cardiovascular toxicity." He warned, "we are dealing with an enormous public health issue," estimating "there may be tens of thousands of patients who have had major adverse events attributable to rofecoxib."[930]

Another critic was Federal Drug Administration (FDA) scientist Dr. David Graham whose estimate was more specific, stating that Vioxx had been associated with nearly 27,000 heart attacks or deaths linked to cardiac problems.[931] High doses of Vioxx, he said, increased the risk of heart disease 3.7 times.[932] Graham also estimated that Vioxx might have caused as many as 140,000 excess cases of serious coronary heart disease in the United States up until the drug's withdrawal from the market.[933] His testimony before the Senate Finance Committee on November 18 was foreboding: "Today, in 2004, you, we, are faced with what may be the single greatest drug safety catastrophe in the history of this country or the history of the world. We are talking about a catastrophe that I strongly believe could have, should have been largely or completely avoided. But it wasn't and over 100,000 Americans have paid dearly for this failure."[934]

Warning Signs Ignored

This was not a sudden crisis that erupted when Gilmartin received the report of his research chief. It is an extreme example of *Predictable Surprises*—the title of a new book with the subtitle, *The Disasters You Should Have Seen Coming and How to Prevent Them*.[935] Topol asserts that had Merck heeded the many warning signs along the way, such a debacle could have been prevented.[936] He, among others, thought the drug should have been removed four years earlier. In March 2000, a research study of 8,100 rheumatoid arthritis patients known as Vigor (Vioxx gastrointestinal outcomes research) showed that five times as many patients taking Vioxx had heart attack as those taking the older pain reliever naproxen.[937] But Merck dismissed this finding, arguing that the results were accounted for by naproxen's cardioprotective qualities—not that Vioxx had cardiovascular toxicity.[938] As FDA reviewer Maria Lourdes Villalba told the Senate Finance Committee, it was "not very convincing to us" that good effects from naproxen were the whole explanation of Vigor study findings. Another FDA doctor wrote that "it would be difficult to imagine" including the Vigor results in Vioxx's label without flagging the cardiovascular issues in the warnings sections.[939]

Misleading Direct-to-Consumer Advertising (DTC)

Despite these negative evaluations, Merck denied the implications of the research findings and went on the offensive to proclaim that Vioxx was safe.

On May 22, 2001, it issued a press release titled "Merck Reconfirms Favorable Cardiovascular Safety of Vioxx." The same theme appeared in numerous papers in peer-reviewed medical company literature written by Merck employees and their consultants. It continued to debunk concern about adverse cardiovascular effects in its numerous medical education symposiums at national meetings. The company's direct-to-consumer advertising (DTC) with the positive message that Vioxx minimizes gastrointestinal side effects was not interrupted.[940] In 2003, such advertising by the pharmaceuticals contributed about $3.4 billion in media spending[941] and in 2004 rose to $4.44 billion.[942] Senator Edward M. Kennedy attacked these ads by saying that "Celebrex and Vioxx were 'peddled' indiscriminately through widespread TV ads even though only 5 percent of all the people taking painkillers actually needed the new drug's stomach-protecting benefits."[943]

Another problem is that consumer marketing campaigns help create a distorted view that drugs are essentially risk free.[944] According to *BusinessWeek*, studies show that "people typically overestimate the benefits of drugs and underestimate their risks, especially for heavily advertised medicines. That is why DTC ads contribute to the mistaken notion that there is a safe pill for every problem. The FDA's Cox-2 panel called for an end to ads for the drugs."[945]

After Pfizer's Celebrex, another Cox-2 drug, was found to face similar risks as Vioxx, its CEO Henry A. McKinnell, Jr. acknowledged a downside to the drugmakers' marketing successes: "We've managed with our advertising to create this image of a perfectly safe drug. And that is never true."[946] To correct this perception, Johnson & Johnson planned to use a new approach in its advertising by dealing head-on with safety, "putting drug risks on more-equal footing with drug benefits." In his acceptance speech upon becoming the new chairman of PhRMA, J&J's CEO William Weldon stated: "If our industry is to retain the important right to talk directly to consumers, each of our companies in its own way must work to make DTC what it very definitely can be—a way to educate and counsel consumers in improving their health."[947]

Direct-to-consumer advertising is almost purely promotional, even though its advocates claim its purpose is informational. The propensity for promotional advertising is easy to understand: to successfully recoup research expenditures on a new drug, a company must engage in a product launch that quickly achieves adoption by as many potential customers as possible. In that way a "blockbuster" is created. Television and other mass media advertising remain ideal vehicles to achieve this objective. In 2003, direct-to-consumer pharmaceuticals were the 10th largest industry category in U.S. advertising. It is estimated that the category represents about 7 percent to 8 percent of spending on national network broadcasting and syndication and about 5 percent to 6 percent of spending on national magazines.[948]

What Merck failed to do after receiving early negative information was to develop a cardiovascular risk study expressly to prove or disprove the findings of the Vigor. This option was rejected during a top policy-making group in

May 2000 to discuss ways to defend Vioxx against competing drug makers' accusations that it posed risks. Instead, Merck decided to start a clinical trial for a different purpose: to determine whether Vioxx could prevent the recurrence of colon polyps—not to check on the safety of Vioxx. The cardiovascular condition of patients in that test (known as the Approve trial) as well as subsequent studies would be intensely monitored.[949] Revealing Merck's lack of interest in checking the safety of Vioxx at this time, none of the 2,600 patients with colon polyps would be eligible for the study if they had had any cardiovascular disease. Thus it was only by happenstance, said Topol, that it was discovered that 3.5 percent of the patients assigned to rofecoxib had myocardial infarction or stroke, as compared with 1.9 percent of the patients assigned to placebo. It was this discovery that led to Merck's "premature cessation of the trial and the decision to discontinue treatment with rofecoxib."[950] Merck finally faced the reality that Vioxx posed unacceptable risks.

FDA Faulted

The Vioxx crisis has also raised the question of whether the FDA conscientiously monitors the safety of approved drugs. The agency was severely criticized by David J. Graham, its associate director for Science and Medicine in FDA's Office of Drug Safety, at the Senate Finance Committee hearing. He said, "Vioxx is a terrible tragedy and a profound regulatory failure," adding the dire warning: "I would argue that the FDA, as currently configured, is incapable of protecting America against another Vioxx. . . . Simply put, FDA and its Center for Drug Evaluation and Research are broken."[951]

The FDA's typical response to adverse research has been to issue warnings. Its strongest one came on September 17, 2001, on the heels of the critical Vigor study, when it wrote to Merck's CEO complaining that Merck engaged "in a promotional campaign for Vioxx that minimizes the potentially serious cardiovascular findings that were observed." Specifically, the campaign failed to mentioned that "patients on Vioxx were observed to have a four- to five-fold increase" in heart attacks, compared with patients on naproxen. The only other significant FDA action in response to Vigor and other studies was on April 11, 2002, when it instructed Merck to include certain precautions about cardiovascular risks in its package inserts.[952]

Pressures Grow

Merck and its CEO Gilmartin faced a gargantuan crisis. Not only had a major flow of revenue been halted, but lawsuits were also piling up. Merck's general counsel, Kenneth Frazier, reported that 475 Vioxx-related lawsuits against Merck had been filed in the United States by November 30, 2004.[953] Wall Street analysts estimated legal liability at $4 billion; Merrill Lynch's estimate was between $4 billion and $18 billion.[954] The main damage, however, was to

Merck's reputation and the erosion of its customers' trust. Investigations by the U.S. Justice Department, the Securities & Exchange Commission, and Congress would for many months result in unfavorable media coverage that further reinforced the damage.[955]

In the aftermath of the Vioxx crisis, pressures for an independent drug safety office at FDA have been growing. At the three-day Senate Health, Education, Labor & Pensions Committee hearing in February 2005 the FDA proposed creating a Drug Safety Oversight Board to review safety issues. But its powers would be limited. While it would be charged with making recommendations, e.g., say when consumers should be alerted, and making its findings public, it would lack authority to pull drugs off the market or change labeling.[956] Lawmakers were also considering the establishment of an Office of Patient Protection, which would independently review the safety of already-approved drugs; they would also examine several other issues that would affect the drug industry, such as reviewing the quick approval process for new drugs.[957]

Pressures were mounting for Gilmartin to resign, which he did on May 5, 2005, and to consider options previously rejected by him, namely, the possibility of a merger.[958] The January 10, 2005, issue of *Business Week* named Gilmartin as one of the worst CEOs of 2003. However, Gilmartin reiterated his position that the company wouldn't change its strategy of rejecting the merger option and would continue to license new medicines from smaller biotech firms and drug makers.[959] *Business Week* even raised the question of possible bankruptcy, but concluded this was unlikely.[960] In the short run, Merck was engaged in cost-cutting efforts and by the end of 2004 would have eliminated 5,100 positions.

Merck may also reconsider its total withdrawal of Vioxx as a result of the 17 to 15 vote of a panel of medical experts in February 2005 that Vioxx could be sold to at least some patients, but with strong warning labels and other restrictions.[961] Pfizer, it should be noted, continued to make Celebrex available to patients.

In summary, Merck violated major principles of crisis management: denying signs of a simmering crisis; deceiving patients and their doctors about the safety of the product; refusing to provide more information about the drug's side effects; and not allowing adequate voice to those who disagreed with management's decision not to withdraw Vioxx.

Strategies for Managing Crises of Skewed Values

In all the above cases, management failed to integrate ethical concerns and social values into their decision-making process. To overcome this skewed approach, management can use four strategies: (1) reevaluate its risk analysis premises; (2) revise its corporate culture, specifically by listening to dissenting opinions and creating company-wide environmental awareness; (3) broaden corporate governance; and (4) institute a system of social accountancy.

Reexamine Risk Analysis

Risk analysis, which is central in technological and scientific activities, is a factor in crises of skewed values. As a producer of pharmaceutical products, Merck is obligated by the FDA to follow stringent procedures to test new products. Once a drug is approved, the same diligence is seemingly not applied to patients' experience with it, as the Vioxx case illustrates. The findings of critical studies were brushed aside and the standards of full disclosure were not fully adhered to. Another pharmaceutical company, Pfizer, illustrates another deviation from sound risk analysis. It actively promoted the off-label use of its drug Celebrex, e.g., to reduce pain after surgery despite attendant risk, and it paid doctors to attend strategy meetings.

With all products people learn to accept risk because they recognize the benefits of consumption. But they want to minimize risk and are all-too-ready to sue manufacturers when they are harmed—or think they are harmed. Consumers expect businesses to do all within their power to make products as safe as possible. And because of the growing incidence of product liability cases, along with high jury awards, businesses are motivated to reduce product risks.

Inspection of Products—Dropping the "Blame Game"

As the Mattel toy case indicates, more attention must be given to inspection of facilities and sampling of products as a way to reduce risk. Mattel blamed vendors and subcontractors for failing to check for leaded paint. It had not learned the lesson of Nike that it cannot claim immunity from responsibility because the factories that produce a product are not legally owned by it—that someone else is to blame. When Campbell Soup was charged with using child labor, paying low wages, and tolerating poor health and housing conditions, and, in general, mistreating Mexican American migrants who picked its tomatoes in Ohio, and accused of paying low wages to farm workers in Ohio who supplied peas, the company denied the charges and disowned responsibility by saying that growers under contract, not Campbell, hire the farm workers.[962] It is increasingly recognized that in an interrelated economy with many global supply chains, a seller must take responsibility for all stages of the manufacture of a product.

Mattel was not released from ultimate responsibility for the lead paint on toys by saying that it expected the vendors and subcontractors who produced the toys to check on compliance with paint requirements. In the global economy, the blame game is no longer acceptable. Mattel was negligent in not testing the paint on its toys for lead. Its organizational structure was over-focused on marketing and lacked an adequate system of inspection. Its penchant for blaming the Chinese producers showed an unwillingness to accept managerial responsibility for product quality and safety.

Failure to inspect its products—a form of risk analysis—also portrays Mattel as failing to engage in contingency planning. All possible events that could cause a crisis should be considered in this process. Simply assuming rosy scenarios does not remove a threat and is another aspect of risk analysis that has caused problems. Although having an optimistic outlook is generally a healthy personal attribute of an executive, it is dysfunctional in the realm of risk assessment. As *Business Week* observed, some companies do not factor in the possibility of major disasters, or their potential costs, when making decisions.[963] Mattel apparently did not give serious consideration to the possibility of defective paint on their toys.

Reform Corporate Culture

Of the many ways in which an organization's culture is studied, the manner in which critical incidents are handled is most revealing. Such precepts as "Don't be a bearer of bad news"; "See no evil, hear no evil, and speak no evil"; and "Don't rock the boat" may determine how soon an organization becomes aware of an impending crisis and how it responds to one. When Lawrence Rawl initially refused to visit the scene of the *Valdez* oil spill, he sent the message that he had more important things to do than show concern for environmental damage. And when Exxon resisted the offer of help from other oil companies, the federal government, and local fishermen, it not only said, "We're big enough to handle it ourselves," but gave the impression of enormous arrogance. Exxon's corporate culture was criticized for assigning too little weight to environmental values, which later included concern about global warming. It remains to be seen whether investor activists will be able to change that culture.

Because the public looks to a company's behavior during a crisis as a revelation of its true nature, last-minute efforts to shore up the corporate image seem artificial. For example, feature stories in organizational communication media about corporate social responsibility or a new theme for a corporate image program will simply be ineffective. Mattel's ad that, as promised, they had been busy testing and retesting toys before they left factories simply appeared too late to authentically represent its true culture.

A deep-seated corporate culture is difficult to change. Management must identify the roots of its culture, decide what kind of culture it wants, and then make that culture explicit in all it does.[964] This is the task of organization development and organization transformation efforts. Two aspects of corporate culture, however, are particularly relevant in crises of skewed values: its ideological foundations and how new values, such as environmental ones, are integrated.

Realign Business Ideology

Broadly speaking, business ideology falls into two creeds. One is the classical creed which holds that management's responsibility is wholly or primarily to serve in a fiduciary capacity to protect the interest of stockholders. The other is the managerial creed that requires management to serve the interests of all of its stakeholders—all those who contribute to an organization or are affected by it. Exxon mainly professes the first creed, which might be called "pipeline vision." Its value system was so narrowly concentrated on maximizing return on investment for stockholders that it failed to meet broader social expectations of protecting the environment. For many years it refused to accept the possibility of global warming caused by human activity. However, it engages in many other social responsibility programs, such as providing netting for people in malaria-prone areas.

In shunning the broader managerial creed, some business executives argue that even if a corporation wants to be socially responsible, pressures from institutional investors and, sometimes, potential acquirers, leave them little choice but to think in terms of financial performance in the short term.

By accepting the alternative managerial creed, a company redresses the balance between financial performance and social performance. While the goal of earning satisfactory and competitively attractive profits must remain an undisputed motivating force for management and a measurement of performance, this goal must be tempered with other values that modern society imposes on business. The bottom line is now a "double bottom line," one financial and the other social.[965] Some add a third bottom line to refer specifically to environmental performance.

Strengthen Corporate Governance

The central question of corporate governance with respect to crises of skewed values is whether the managerial creed is reflected in the membership and thinking of the board of directors. One possibility is to include special interest representation, such as employees or consumers on boards. Except for special situations, that approach has not been accepted in the United States. An early case was Chrysler's appointment of the president of the United Automobile Workers (UAW) when the company faced bankruptcy and needed a strong case (and voice) for a government bailout. Another case was Exxon's 1989 appointment of John M. Steele, a scientist, to represent environmental interests in the aftermath of the Exxon Valdez spill. In Europe, the structure of codetermination is used in some countries. In Germany, for example, the law requires companies in such industries as steel to have almost half of its board represented by labor.

In the United States, some corporations have ancillary structures, such as a public policy committee, that allow a wide range of voices to be heard. This follows Peter Drucker's recommendation that a board needed a "public and community relations" organ.[966] Exxon created a Public Issues Committee, again in response to the oil spill. But it trailed by 20 years General Motors' notable decision in September 1970 to form a Public Policy Committee.[967] GM did so after Ralph Nader's Project on Corporate Responsibility included a proposal for the formation of a Committee for Corporate Responsibility in his highly publicized proxy resolution "Campaign GM."

The role of public policy committees is continuing to be examined more closely. S. Prakash Sethi, director of the Center for Research in Business and Social Policy at the University of Texas in Dallas, who studied their role in the life insurance industry, said that to be effective as an agent for social change, these committees must generate issues and not merely respond to issues formulated by other social groups. Too often these committees have addressed legally mandated issues, such as equal employment opportunity or pollution standards, and issues that are noncontroversial or have reached a high degree of public visibility. They have also overseen well-established activities such as charitable giving. More emphasis, he says, should be placed on "issue development," forecasting, and long-range planning.

Nonprofit organizations have also strengthened their boards. The American Red Cross's Board of Governors decided to reduce its board from 50 members to between 12 and 25 members by 2009, and 12 to 20 members by 2012. Three categories of board members were reduced to one, to be elected by the full board. It also created a Red Cross Cabinet Advisory Council and the establishment of an Office of the Ombudsman to provide annual reports to Congress.[968]

Institute Social Accounting

Social accounting and the accompanying idea of a social audit support the double bottom line concept and the managerial creed in that they endeavor to measure the social benefits and social costs created by an organization in the production and consumption of its products and services. A social audit reports on the social performance of a corporation, just as a financial audit reports on revenues, costs, and profits or losses.[969] Exxon was one of the first companies that published the third type of report. In 1971, when the company was still called Standard Oil Company (New Jersey), it published a 56-page Social Action report "on evolving programs to meet the social responsibilities of the corporation in the world of the 1970s."

Social reports became popular in the 1980s and 1990s. According to Pamela Buxton, a design expert, more firms were publishing social as well as financial reports at the turn of the century.[970] They know they are being judged on social and environmental issues. She suggests that such reports disclose full facts, not just what's mandatory; obtain independent verification of hard facts; and put social reporting in context as part of the business strategy. Many organizations conduct employee and customer surveys to determine their satisfaction with organizational policies and practices. The results can be used in their social reports. Most Fortune 500 companies now include their social reports in their websites.

Conclusions

The central feature of strategies for managing crises of skewed values is that they focus on top management goals, direction, and effectiveness.[971] The very essence of the organization must be examined: what is its purpose for existing besides making money? Management must assess both its external opportunities and threats and internal strengths and weaknesses. On that basis it defines the organization's overall mission and official goals and then selects operative goals and strategies. Appropriate organizational design follows, including the ones discussed in this chapter: corporate culture, organizational structure, corporate governance, and interorganizational and societal linkages, e.g., by means of a system of social accountancy.

However, when management blames others for its difficulties, it is less likely to institute the changes discussed in this chapter. Managers cannot absolve themselves of responsibilities that are ultimately theirs. Mattel may delegate responsibility for providing safe toys to its Chinese suppliers. But, as in all delegation of responsibility, the delegator does not surrender ultimate responsibility. What the act of delegation should mean is that a special relationship is established. Some companies work so closely with their suppliers, for example, that they have virtually made them a part of the organization.

Management does not, however, carry the entire environmental burden. All stakeholders, including the general public, must be willing to accept one of the basic tenets of social accountancy: namely, a willingness to recognize and pay for the full social costs in the price of goods and services offered in the marketplace.

Chapter 12

Crises of Deception

The deliberate practice of deceiving investors, customers, and other stakeholders is another subtype of crises of management failure. This occurs when management conceals or misrepresents information about itself and its products in its dealings with others. It knows, but does not tell; or worse, it states a falsehood about such matters as products, finances, and environmental compliance.

Companies engage in deception for a variety of reasons. The harshest critics of business assert that these companies are more interested in profits than in safety—that they display the flaw of skewed values, discussed in the previous chapter. Another reason is that they take advantage of consumers' ignorance of information about complex products, such as drugs, medical devices, and financial securities. By taking advantage of this lack of symmetry in knowledge, companies indirectly but knowingly engage in deception. They may argue, as pharmaceutical companies generally do, that information must be interpreted by intermediaries, such as doctors, who possess the knowledge to understand a company's messages. This rationale is undermined, however, when companies fail even to inform intermediaries or use financial incentives to bias their recommendations. The simple fact is that companies that engage in deception fail to acknowledge the consumer's and public's right to know about matters of concern to them.

Managers also deceive themselves. In the consumer product field, they may engage in minimum and insufficient product testing; they may draw conveniently optimistic research conclusions; they may ignore negative research findings; and they may actually engage in misconduct by faking evidence. These practices are most likely to occur when products such as medical devices are unregulated or when government follows laissez faire policies.

If the drug and medical industries are criticized for not making information comprehensible for the average person, the housing and banking industries deserve that criticism even more so. The problem has been excessive risk-taking and lack of transparency. Even investors and bankers with considerable experience have purchased securities that are undecipherable and later become known as "toxic." The failure to adequately assess risk and disclose it to others in the market is tantamount to deception.

Cases of Management Deception

The two cases of deception that follow reflect the new nature of the economy—one that reflects "innovations" in how business is conducted. Enron made more money through trading than through physical outputs. It is a case that focuses on how a company's accounting system no longer reflects its true value. The banking industry invented new securities that enabled it to command a greater portion of the gross domestic product (GDP). Here too the invention of abstractions blurs the line between what is true and what is false.

Enron's Mighty Fall

On December 2, 2001, Enron, the seventh-largest company in the United States, filed for Chapter 11 bankruptcy. The collapse came at a shocking speed. There were lots of signs, including those from previous scandals, but the game was too attractive and those who saw the warning signs weren't listened to. Enron's bankruptcy was not sudden, but as *The Economist* said, "took place in slow motion."[972]

Enron was in the business of selling products and services in the natural gas, electricity, and communications industries to wholesale and retail customers. "Enron had the biggest and strongest energy-trading business in North America," said Harvey Padewer of Duke Energy, an American utility that was a big rival of Enron's.[973] The company accounted for 15 to 20 percent of gas and power trading in the region and was the biggest energy trader in the world. Its reported revenues in 2000 were about $100 billion and over $130 billion in the first three quarters of 2001, which, however, turned out to be more imagined than real.[974]

Forewarnings Ignored

Enron was aware by at least May 2001 that its portfolio of foreign assets had lost as much as half of the $6.15 billion value shown on its books at the time. Typically, such a big drop would be shown by taking write-downs, but company filings with the Securities and Exchange Commission in 2001 don't show them because they were controversial "off-balance-sheet" vehicles—in other words, important financial information is not disclosed.[975]

As early as 1999, Vince Kaminski, who headed a research group at Enron and did analysis for Enron's vast and sophisticated risk-control and trading operations, warned top Enron executives that the partnership arrangement—called special-purpose entities (SPEs)—had gone from being merely "stupid" for Enron and its shareholders to being fraudulent.[976] Only days earlier, its bonds had been downgraded to junk and Dynergy, a smaller energy-trading rival, had pulled out of a planned takeover.[977] Investors lost confidence in the integrity of the company when they learned that Enron had been using partnerships to conceal its losses.

Fallout

As stated in The Houghton Mifflin Guide to the Enron Crisis, "Since the collapse of the Enron Corporation, the term Enron has conjured up images and buzzwords not often encountered in the world of personal finance—greed, incompetence, arrogance, negligence, fraud, insider trading, and financial chicanery, to name but a few."[978] This perspective was quite different from Kenneth Lay's, the former chairman and CEO of Enron, who described the company in glowing terms:

> One of our great successes at Enron was creating a culture, an environment, where people could try to achieve their God-given potential. But certainly I wanted it to be a highly moral and highly ethical environment. I have done the best job I can of following that everywhere I have been.[979]

It was either a blatant lie or a case of self-delusion. Chuck Watson, the CEO of rival company Dynergy, thought otherwise: "Enron never understood that business is not just about numbers and the balance sheet: It's about your brand, and the confidence you inspire."[980]

Enron's approach to building its reputation was to tout company stocks to investors. It followed a risky master plan. Jeffrey Skilling, then president, "vowed to skyrocket past ExxonMobil to become the world's leading energy firm. . . ."[981] Yet, only days earlier, its bonds had been downgraded to junk and Dynergy had pulled out of a planned takeover.[982] Nevertheless, John Martin, an economist at Baylor University, thought that the internal risk management of the trading business was basically sound.

Deception: Corruption of the Financial Information Infrastructure

Enron engaged in deception through its fraudulent financial reporting: "By forming numerous off-the-books partnerships and transferring debt-laden and risky assets to them, Enron's executives created a favorable but false image of their company's profitability."[983] Widespread trust dissipated nearly overnight when an "accounting error" led to a $1.2 billion reduction in the company's net worth, which wiped out nearly $600 million of profits, about a fifth of the total.[984] More deception followed, for "even as Enron's prospects began to erode, senior executives were urging investors to buy more stock, were restricting the ability of lower-level Enron employees to sell their stock, and, at the same time, were hastily selling off much of the stock they themselves owned."[985]

Besides false financial reporting, Enron's corporate officers corrupted the financial information infrastructure upon which the efficient and ethical function of the economic system depends. This infrastructure comprises seven components: (1) corporate accountants; (2) auditors; (3) lawyers; (4) boards of directors; (5) security analysts and investment bankers; (6) stock exchanges; and (7) the Securities and Exchange Commission (SEC).

Corporate accountants provided questionable information and had poor internal control systems. Regarding "off books" partnerships, two of Enron's former senior officials, Jeffrey Skilling and Kenneth Lay, testified during congressional hearings that they did not know the details of several questionable partnerships.

The company's auditors, Arthur Anderson, colluded with Enron rather than conducting an objective and professional audit. Although Anderson officials noted Enron's "aggressive" accounting practices and potential conflicts of interest, they decided to retain Enron as a client. Their rationale was that "it appeared that we had the appropriate people and processes in place to serve Enron and manage our engagement risks." (Shortly after Enron's collapse, the accounting firm went out of business.)

Lawyers were to come to the rescue of those who felt uncomfortable with the accounting firm. Sherron Watkins, an Enron vice president and a former Andersen employee, wrote anonymously to chairman and CEO Kenneth Lay in August 2001 with concerns about potential conflicts of interest and accounting practices. But in fall, Enron's law firm Vinson & Elkins, after conducting a preliminary investigation into Watkins's charges, concluded that "the facts disclosed through our preliminary investigation do not, in our judgment, warrant a further widespread investigation by independent counsel and auditors."[986] Vinson & Elkins is one of the country's most powerful law firms, with some 850 lawyers in nine cities.

Again, after Watkins warned Lay in summer 2002 of "accounting scandals," Enron asked the law firm to investigate. It agreed to limit the inquiry's scope and in mid-October, just before Enron unraveled, sent a nine-page report that raised no serious alarms. Although lawyers sometimes objected to ever-more-complex deals for the big energy and trading company, saying the deals posed conflicts of interest or weren't in Enron's best interests, the lawyers never blew the whistle.[987] The law firm has remained in the spotlight since Enron's fall and was named in lawsuits by Enron shareholders and employees.

Enron's board of directors was negligent and its audit committee failed. Although several Enron board directors professed ignorance of Enron Corp.'s questionable accounting practices, documents showed that David Duncan, a senior Arthur Anderson LLP auditor, warned them about the maneuvers more than three years prior to the bankruptcy.[988] Board members, however, remained complacent and didn't want to be seen as party-spoilers as long as the company was making profit and its stockholders were satisfied. Enron's corporate governance had failed.

Security analysts, investment bankers and stock exchanges were silent about Enron. Analysts later said they never understood Enron's books and deliberately gave wrong advice. They wanted high, million dollar incomes and knew how to get it. Neither did large banks and financial institutions curb Enron's behavior or seem to care about customers. "They let all of us down," said a guest on the Lehrer News Show.[989]

The SEC also failed. There was a revolving door between the SEC and accounting firms; e.g., the SEC's chairman Pitt had previously worked for accounting firms who were his clients.

Enron's Compensation System

Enron followed the practice of rewarding top executives with millions of dollars a year, much of it in stock options. The theory was that by linking executives' and shareholders' interests, executives would benefit if they managed companies in a way that lifted share prices. But it didn't work as advertised. As Gordon Gekko said in a speech to shareholders in the 1987 movie *Wall Street*, "Greed is all we have left, but greed is also what made America great. It's normal. It's healthy and it's what keeps the system going."[990]

The incentives inherent in this compensation system allegedly encouraged Enron's top managers to present misleading financial information to shareholders to inflate the stock price so they could cash in and walk away with millions. Enron reportedly paid about $681 million in cash and stock to its 140 senior managers, including at least $67.4 million to former chairman and CEO Lay in the year up to December 2, 2001 when it filed for bankruptcy-court protection.[991] A report filed in federal bankruptcy court valued payments to Lay at $104 million. In addition, he exercised stock options valued at $34.4 million, and received restricted stock valued at $14.7 million.[992]

Ethical Lapses

Business school professors have latched upon Enron as a major case study of ethics. They find revelations about the maneuverings of Enron's executives too tempting to pass up.[993] The company tolerated rule bending in many dimensions of business practice. The exuberance of the 1990s is blamed for the loss of executives' ethical moorings. "A stock-market bubble magnified changes in business mores and brought trends that had been building for years to a climax."[994] Some, like the Business Roundtable and President Bush, believed it was just a problem of a few bad apples, but the number admitting fault seemed to grow week after week. The *Wall Street Journal* listed 18 big companies that faced serious questions about their business practices, including Global Crossing, Halliburton, ImClone Systems, Kmart, Lucent Tecnologies, Qwest Communications, Tyco International, WorldCom, and Xerox.[995]

Summary

Although Enron predominantly manifests the characteristics of a crisis of deception, some elements of skewed values and misconduct also played a role. Enron's top echelon of managers cared mainly about enriching themselves and ignored the interests of employees and other stakeholders. It deceived its primary stakeholders—its business partners, customers, investors, and employees—about the firm's profitability. It also failed to meet its obligations to the outside community with the notable exception of supporting the Enron Field for the Houston Astros."[996] One form of misconduct was insider trading; for example, Lay sold close to $175 million in Enron stock between 1999 and 2001.[997]

The Banking Crisis of 2008—Public and Self-Deception

The financial crisis of 2008 constitutes a colossal, comprehensive crisis of management failure, which is appropriately labeled a crisis of deception. The failure affected the banking industry, businesses that depend on bank credit, the public, and the economic system as a whole. The definition of a crisis as an event that could threaten an organization's survival was realized when two major banks, Bear Stearns and Lehman Brothers, failed and brought on the crisis—the crisis threshold was reached.

Evolution of the Crisis

A cascade of events followed as one big bank's problems affected all the others, much as in a nuclear plant where a problem in one part of the system leads to the failure of the entire plant. It was a systemic failure. When Bear Stearns, one of Wall Street's major investment banks, faced difficulties, all the other big financial institutions were affected. Retrospectively, crisis managers can identify the warning signals that were ignored and how the vulnerabilities of specific financial institutions grew the banking crisis to the financial crisis.

House Prices Fall

At the bottom of the financial crisis was the falling price of houses, with too many of them supported by subprime mortgages whose amounts exceeded the value of the houses in the real estate market. Thanks to government encouragement of home ownership in what was heralded as an ownership society, even poor people were able to buy houses. Abetted by the Fed's policy of low interest rates and bank teaser-rate mortgages, home ownership looked attractive. Rising house prices even made it possible to use houses as ATMs to support consumer purchases.

The peak in housing prices was reached in 2005 and early 2006. By late 2006, however, prices began to fall. The highly regarded Case-Shiller 20-city home price index showed that prices fell 7.7 percent in November 2006 from the year before and that average house prices fell by 9 percent in 2007.[998] At the time, it was estimated that for about 8.8 million mortgage holders, 17 percent of the total, home loans were greater than the house value.[999]

Falling house prices represented the first early warning signal of an impending financial crisis. Sheila Blair, head of the Federal Deposit Insurance

Corporation (FDIC), was among the first to recognize potential problems among banks. She gave warnings as early as 2002 about sloppy mortgage-lending and lax regulation.[1000] But troublesome facts were largely ignored even in 2006.[1001] By February 2008, subprime losses hit the $100 billion mark.[1002] One economist estimated that banks and other financial institutions would suffer about $200 billion in real estate losses and would cut their lending by $2 trillion.[1003]

Fall of Bear Stearns

Bear Stearns was highly vulnerable because it was a major holder of derivatives—often called "toxic assets"—much of which were based on subprime loans. As early as 2002, Warren Buffet called derivatives "weapons of mass destruction."[1004] An excerpt from Kate Kelly's book, *Street Fighters: The Last 72 Hours of Bear Stearns, the Toughest Firm on Wall Street*, details the fall of the venerable 85-year-old Wall Street firm.[1005]

On Thursday, March 13, 2008, CEO Allan Schwartz and CFO Sam Molinaro came to the shocking realization that they didn't have enough money on hand to open for business the following day. Appeals to the Federal Reserve Bank and secretary of the treasury for funds were fruitless because, upon examining the books, they found the situation hopeless. By Sunday, March 16, Bear Stearns ceased to exist as a shotgun marriage was arranged with JPMorgan Chase.[1006] A $30 share was now worth only $2 (the price was later raised to $10) and Bear Stearns was gone as an independent entity. The bank had dug a hole for itself through exposure to credit default swaps (CDSS) and other complex instruments whose risk they didn't fully understand.

The cascade continued and, by April, the rating services were forced to downgrade thousands of mortgage-related investments after their initial calls about the U.S. housing market proved too optimistic in the last 18 months.[1007] Standard & Poors downgraded or threatened to downgrade more than 80,000 mortgage investments. A widening array of financial institutions would ultimately face mortgage-securities losses totaling more than $265 billion.[1008]

Fannie Mae and Freddie Mac

Throughout the summer of 2008, toxic stocks took their toll, even as Secretary of the Treasury Hank Paulson proclaimed confidence in Wall Street. The next casualties after Bear Stearns were the privately held and publicly traded mortgage giants Fannie Mae and Freddie Mac, which were seized on September 8, 2008.[1009] Fannie Mae was founded as a government corporation in 1938 and privatized by President Lyndon B. Johnson in 1968.[1010] Although investors nevertheless assumed they were backed up by the government, they lost 60 percent of their value at the onset of the financial crisis. Now the prospect of their possible failure sent shock waves throughout the economy, because if they failed anyone could. Realizing that their failure would signal a systemic risk, Paulson announced plans in September to replace the companies' chief executives and put the two companies under a conservatorship, giving management control to their regulator, the Federal Housing Finance Agency (FHFA).[1011]

A Run on Lending Institutions

It is difficult to know when pessimism seized the market and skeptical investors acted simultaneously and started to withdraw funds. One of the first lending institution casualties was Countrywide Financial Corp., the largest U.S. mortgage lender and the source of many bad loans. It was sold to the Bank of America.[1012] Angelo Mozilo, its founder and CEO, had pocketed nearly $400 million in the six years of the housing boom and bust. Even after its sale, he stood to take home around $100 million, plus country club fees.[1013]

Two other casualties were IndyMac and Washington Mutual (WaMu). Indy-Mac was seized by regulators on July 13, 2008, but the failing thrift was immediately reopened under federal control. A senior investigator for the Center for Responsible Lending commented, "There was a culture of top-down pressure to push through as many loans as possible—and to ignore the problems."[1014] In September 2008, WaMu, America's largest savings-and-loan institution, was seized by the FDIC, constituting the largest U.S. banking failure in history.

WaMu was vulnerable because it was known as a national mortgage-and-consumer-lending giant that had overextended subprime mortgages. Its customers began withdrawing billions in deposits. Its mortgage losses were mounting and its stock price was plunging.[1015] Photos of depositors lining up outside of these banks carried the Wall Street crisis to Main Street and confirmed the reality that a crisis existed. WaMu's branches and deposits were sold to JPMorgan Chase, in a deal brokered by Sheila Bair, head of FDIC.[1016]

Fall of Lehman Brothers and Merrill Lynch

In "The Weekend That Wall Street Died," the *Wall Street Journal* described the chaotic days of September 12 to 14, 2008 when two prominent investment banks failed. At the country's oldest investment bank, Lehman Brothers, stock prices were declining every day. It was a huge player in the mortgage finance business.[1017] Its president Dick Fuld was a Wall Street fixture and known as an arrogant, aggressive trader. Fuld tried to sell the bank but had no takers and when Ben Bernanke, head of the Federal Reserve Bank, and Paulson declined to bail it out, Fuld had no alternative but to file for bankruptcy. At a House committee, Lehman was described as "a financial firm that operated like a casino run by greedy executives." Just days before it collapsed, Lehman agreed to pay a total of more than $23 million to three executives leaving the securities firm. Fuld pocketed roughly $480 million in pay since 2000.[1018] During that week Merrill Lynch, another big player in derivatives, sold itself to the Bank of America, and two Wall Street giants, Morgan Stanley and Goldman Sachs, barely survived.[1019]

Insurer AIG in Trouble

Another part of the financial system that was severely impacted was American International Group (AIG), one of the world's biggest insurers. AIG did business with virtually every bank, resulting in tens of billions of obligations connected with the housing market. It was swamped with CDOs of banks, which they had insured, but lacked sufficient funds to support its commitments to firms like Lehman Brothers. Bernanke and Paulson decided that AIG was too interconnected with the financial system to let it fail. On September 16, 2008, the government seized control of AIG, in an $895 billion deal, giving the government a 79.9 percent equity stake in the insurer.[1020]

The Financial System Falls Apart—The Bubble Bursts

These events caused an even greater erosion of confidence than Paulson had imagined. Not only individual banks, but the whole banking and financial system seemed to be falling apart. The stock markets plunged, interbank lending stopped, and credit markets for car loans and loans to small businesses froze. The contagions spread from investment banks to commercial banks, and even the safest companies in the world were unable to borrow money. Underscoring the global reach of the crisis, Iceland went bankrupt because of its overexposure to derivatives.

The study of bubbles summarizes what went wrong in the banking industry, say Princeton economists Harrison Hong and Justin Lahart.[1021] A bubble usually originates from a development with far-reaching effects, like the Internet in the 1990s or the growth of China and India. Bubbles grow when valuations become disconnected from fundamentals and financial bubbles are marked by huge increases in trading (making them easier to identify). Two most important characteristics of bubble formation is that people pay a crazy price and people trade like crazy. The bubble pops only at a moment when investors become skeptical and act simultaneously, the timing of which, however, is impossible to predict.

The Government Bailout

As the cascade of banking failures continued, Paulson and Bernanke concluded that a full-scale bailout of the financial system was needed and that they would seek bailout money from Congress. The idea of a government bailout was anathema to many politicians and defenders of the free-market system. Furthermore, there was fear in abandoning the concept of moral hazard—that government assistance would encourage further risk-taking. But these misgivings were abandoned in the face of the risk of a general economic failure. Although conservatives in Congress were outraged, on September 29, 2008, the House voted on a bailout bill, called the Troubled Assets Recovery Plan (TARP).

Showing the need for TARP, when the bill initially failed in the House, the Dow fell 500 points. By the end of the week, a revised bill cleared the house, providing $700 billion bailout money, $350 billion of which was spent before the end of the Bush administration in January 2009. The idea was to inject billions into ailing banks to restore confidence. Investment banks showed their agility in obtaining TARP funds by converting to a commercial bank status, which the federal government required to control them. On October 14, 2008, Treasury announced plans to inject $125 billion into eight banks, including $25 billion into Citigroup.[1022]

The Many Faces of Deception—What Went Wrong?

All along the chain of events leading to the banking crisis, aspects of deception were apparent and undermining the reputation of banks and trust in general. Trust is particularly important in the banking industry because it represents the intangible asset of goodwill. Banking deals with money and its instruments, which is not backed up by a pile of gold in Fort Knox but by the faith people place in the government as the creator of money and in banking institutions as its handlers. Meaning is given to the inscription on the dollar bill, "In God We Trust." As became evident, trust is the foundation of the banking industry.

Trust is created by the open flow of accurate and reliable information. The disclosure of "full and timely" information promoted by the SEC, establishes the trust needed in our financial transactions. The need for transparency was one of the lessons learned from the collapse of Enron. There we learned that trust is supported by a financial information infrastructure that upholds the accuracy of information.

But the lessons of the collapse of Enron were ignored by the financial industry. In his column, "The Game," Dennis K. Berman concludes that the "post-Enron crackdown appears not only to have failed to stop flagrant corporate risk-taking, but to have lulled Washington to sleep."[1023] The law gives executives wide latitude to run their business, no matter how terrible their decisions; for example, Fuld pushed Lehman into real estate as the boom was reaching a climactic end. All the admonitions about greater transparency and better regulatory oversight were forgotten as the continuing race for bigger economic opportunities spawned another crisis. Herd psychology rode over these cautions: everybody was making money and it appeared foolish to stay away from the game.

Trust was severely undermined by financial institutions in a variety of both simple and sophisticated forms of deception: through borrower or investor ignorance and incompetence; the practice of securitization; and corruption of rating agencies.

Deception Through Ignorance and Incompetence

The first deception is that the loan amount of a mortgage was overvalued relative to the market value of a house and often issued to borrowers that lacked sufficient income. Mortgage lenders could take advantage of the recipients' lack of background to understand financial information. It's an aspect of general public economic illiteracy. Many applicants of subprime mortgages had low-income and were poorly educated. They couldn't be expected to understand complex legal documents.

Sometimes borrowers weren't even employed, leading to the term "Ninja" loans: "no income, no jobs or assets."[1024] Information on mortgage applications was often falsified by mortgage originators. They were selling and giving borrowers insufficient or false information. Borrowers were offered "teaser interest rates"—low beginning rates that would later jump to high rates that might double monthly payments. Borrowers expected that rising house prices would compensate for higher payments or that their homes would serve as collateral for further loans. Homes became ATMs.[1025]

Traditionally, home mortgages were issued by local banks that could best appraise the credit-worthiness of mortgage applicants and knew the local real estate market. Banks required a down payment so that borrowers would retain some risk and responsibility. The banks retained the balance of the risk and held the mortgages until maturity. This remains the basic system in Canada, where risky subprime loans were largely avoided and loans tended to be safer because mortgages generally require 20 percent down payments.[1026]

The subprime mortgage deception arose with the replacement of the traditional banker with a slew of fee-collecting middlemen—from mortgage brokers to bankers and security dealers to hedge fund traders.[1027] Many were fastbuck con artists, reminiscent of the savings and loan scandal in the 1980s.[1028] Information-giving was subordinate to promoting mortgage sales. The originators could build their commissions by concentrating on the quantity rather than the quality of loans, while the risk was passed on to other financial institutions. They seemingly didn't care about the risks to the borrower or ultimate holders of mortgages on overvalued houses. They were able to repeat the lending cycle again and again through the innovation of securitization, which enabled the mortgage originators to pass the mortgages on to other institutions, thereby incentivizing them to issue loans to uncreditworthy borrowers.[1029]

Deception Through Securitization

The second source of deception was securitization. This "innovation" enabled banks and other mortgage originators to unload mortgages to the larger financial market. But the main problem was that securitization obscured the true value of a security. Investment firms like Bear Stearns were able to "slice and dice" mortgages along with bonds and other securities in novel ways. The process was akin to a butcher shop that mixes a variety of meats to make delectable sausages without providing a meaningful label of ingredients. As Joseph Stiglitz described it, "Bankers—and the rating agencies—believed in financial alchemy. They thought that financial innovations could somehow turn bad mortgages into good securities, meriting AAA ratings."[1030]

Many bankers and investors were incompetent in assessing the products of securitization.[1031] Charles R. Morris reports in his book, *The Trillion Dollar Meltdown*, that even Citigroup's chief financial officer "did not know how to value his holdings."[1032] A report by the SEC inspector general also criticized Bear Stearns management as having a dearth of risk-management skills to match the business."[1033] As Jack and Suzy Welch said in their *BusinessWeek* column, banks are one of the culprits "for selling products they didn't understand while enjoying outsized profits."[1034] Robert J. Shiller, author of *The Subprime Solution*, commented, "many people who bought securitized mortgages had little access to financial advice that might have warned them how risky these instruments really were."[1035]

In retrospect it is amazing that intelligent individuals, the "masters of the universe" at Wall Street, could not realize that the selling of subprime mortgages and their reselling as "safe" securities on the world market could not go on forever. When home prices stopped rising and teaser interest rates started in after about two years, homeowners would inevitably default on their mortgage payments and the house of cards would collapse. Yet bankers excuse their failure with comments like "no one could have predicted the problems."

Deception by Rating Agencies

The third source of deception was the failure of rating agencies—Moody's, Standard & Poor's, and Fitch. They were one of the most egregious wrongdoers in the financial community. When information is complex, as with the products of securitization, reliable analysts are needed to confirm their degree of risk. The financial analysts of rating agencies are expected to have the requisite professional knowledge and independence to make scientific assessments of the value of a security. Yet they generally gave triple-A ratings to the many new and complex securities—later called "toxic securities." Moody's alone rated about 94 percent of the $190 billion in mortgage-related and other structured-finance CDOs issues in 2007.[1036] Moody's structured-finance group accounted for 3 percent of the company's revenues in 2006, up from 28 percent in 1998. It now had more revenue from structured finance, $881 million—than its entire revenue had been in 2001.

What had happened at rating agencies is that profit maximization easily dominated professional values. They no longer followed the precept of keeping an arm's length separation from the firms whose securities they were rating. The "Chinese wall" about which so much was said during the mergers and acquisitions boom of the 1980s had disappeared. In the past, John Moody, the president of Moody's (from 1989 to 1996), told recruits that Moody's was a "special business where 'you can't go out for beers' with friends who worked for investment banks." That distance assured that rational analysis would not be contaminated by personal relationships.

In a break with conservative tradition, Brian Clarkson, the new head of Moody's, stressed the importance of promoting relationships, telling his staff that it was important to socialize. He hired customer-service coaches to give sessions on improving relationships with bond issuers and investors. He encouraged his people to be more responsive—to pick up the phone when in the office and find ways deals could get done within Moody's "methodologies."[1037] In many cases, analysts who disagreed with new rating firm policies were fired or transferred, sometimes at the request of clients. Rating firms became "accreditors"—endorsers—of misinformation, as this instant-message exchange by two employees at S&P revealed: "but that deal is ridiculous," and a colleague replied: "it could be structured by cows and we would rate it."[1038]

At a House hearing in October 2008, Rep (D., Calif.) Henry Waxman, chairman of the House Committee, said, "The story of the credit-rating agencies is a story of colossal failure,"[1039] and Senator Charles Schumer (D., N.Y.) said, "There has to be a lot more done about conflicts of interest" at rating companies.[1040] The hearing revealed that the CEO of Moody's had told directors in 2007 that the firm's push to increase profitability posed a "risk" to the quality of the rating process—but apparently no action was taken at the time.

Professional groups and institutions that process, interpret, and judge information in today's complex financial marketplace also failed to live up to their standards. Players in the financial infrastructure—bank accountants, auditors, lawyers, boards of directors, investment banks, and rating agencies—provided meager or erroneous information and were often complicit.[1041] These watchdogs were asleep and sounded no early warning.

Enabling Factors

The three forms of deception were made possible by several enabling factors: laissez faire government, failure of the financial media, absence of ethics and social responsibility, and the arcane language of securitization.

Laissez Faire Government

Led by the then Federal Reserve Bank chairman Alan Greenspan, the government placed complete faith in the wisdom of the market. With a shrug of his shoulders he lectured lawmakers, ". . . we're not smart enough as people. We just cannot see events that far in advance."[1042] Although he had the power to regulate the excesses of the free market, he refused to do so, being a believer in Ayn Rand's doctrine of libertarianism as reflected in *Atlas Shrugged*. More affirmatively, Greenspan boasted that "increasingly complex financial instruments have contributed to the development of a far more flexible, efficient, and hence resilient financial system than the one that existed just a quarter-century ago." He believed that the market knew best and that government regulation and oversight were unnecessary.[1043]

Speaking in his typical arcane, Delphic manner, in October 2004, he reassured the public, "While local economies may experience significant speculative price imbalances, a national severe price distortion seems most unlikely in the United States, given its size and diversity." Yet two years earlier, in November 2002, he said at a Fed meeting, "It's hard to escape the conclusion that at some point our extraordinary housing boom . . . cannot continue indefinitely into the future."

The resulting absence of regulatory oversight allowed deception to go unchecked. The function of government regulation in the financial sphere is to establish rules that require full and timely disclosure of material facts and establish a fair, competitive marketplace. Bankers, however, sought lax enforcement of existing regulations and maximum deregulation. The SEC failed in its oversight responsibilities. Its 2006 report on Bear Stearns "identified precisely the types of risks that evolved into the subprime crisis in the U.S." but it did nothing to influence corrective action by Bear Stearns.[1044]

A major victory of deregulation was the dropping of the Glass Steagall Act in 1989.[1045] The law was enacted during the depression to keep commercial banks apart from the risk-taking investment banks. With the removal of this restriction, investment banks could now use depositors' money to invest in risky securities and enterprises. A further attempt to deregulate financial markets was most recently expressed in Basel II discussions. The original Basel I, named after the Swiss city where bankers met, was crafted in 1988, sought to overcome the variety of bank regulations from country to country. In 2008, Citibank and others lobbied for looser, European style "Basel II" guidelines saying, "Banks should be given more freedom to decide for themselves how much financial risk they should take on, since they are in a better position than regulators to make that call."[1046] Again, there was no appetite for government interference.

Two areas where banks sought looser restrictions were in bank reserve and collateral requirements. Banks are required to keep a percentage of their deposits and other obligations in ready cash to cover withdrawals and possible losses. However, by keeping such reserves at a minimum, Citigroup held only $80 billion in core capital on its balance sheet to protect against its $1.1 trillion in assets of questionable value. Banks holding esoteric securities were consequently unable to meet their obligations and, after unsuccessfully scurrying around for fresh money, defaulted. Banks no longer trusted each other and were unwilling to lend to one another, as shown in the jump in the interbank loan rate known as Libor. Cries of "help" were resounding everywhere and the mortgage crisis metastasized into a full-blown banking crisis.

Similarly, loosened collateral requirements allowed banks to command large amounts of assets with a minimum investment of their own money.

Homeowners who take out mortgages are familiar with this feature, enabling them to command a house worth considerably more than his or her down payment, for example, $50,000 could purchase a $500,000 house. This 1 to 10 ratio was far exceeded by bankers. Starting at about 1 to 15, they raised the ratio 1 to 30, and in a few instances 1 to 70. Goldman's gross leverage ratio jumped from 18.7 times assets in 2003 to 26.2 by 2007; Morgan Stanley's topped 32. Such leveraging ratios result in bountiful profits when the market goes up, but are disastrous when the market falls.

The loosening of regulations was accompanied by poor oversight by the three main regulatory bodies, the FRB, SEC, and Commodity Futures Trading Commission. As the highly respected economist Allan H. Meltzer, who has little faith in the FRB, stated: "History shows that the Federal Reserve is a poor supervisor and regulator. The Fed's Board ignored warnings about the risky housing loans that banks were keeping off their balance sheets." He believes that "Investment banks don't need the Fed to regulate them. Some clear rules on capitalization would suffice."[1047]

Failure of the Financial Media

The financial media must take blame for failing in its watchdog function, says David Folkenflik in his National Public Radio article, "Where Were the Media As Wall Street Imploded?"[1048] Although some articles described some of the new securities and even hinted at trouble ahead, none of those cautionary stories landed on page 1. There just wasn't "much appetite for speculative stories about complicated issues in most newrooms," said Martha M. Hamilton in "What We Learned in the Meltdown."[1049] Stephen J. Adler, editor-in-chief of *Business Week*, admitted, "It's true that collectively we failed to predict the horror of the financial crisis the world now faces."[1050] The explanation, he says is that so many variables were interacting with so much complexity—"including the ever-mysterious x-factor of human psychology and behavior."[1051]

Among the exceptions to media neglect were articles by *Business Week* economics editor Peter Coy who wrote about "synthetic collateralized debt obligations," and Pulizer Prize-winning business columnist for the *New York Times* Gretchen Morgenson who wrote many articles about the new esoteric financial instruments.[1052] At the same time, syndicated columnists, stock pickers, and authors of personal finance best-sellers, and TV personalities were promoting stock purchases. In his celebrated interview with Jim Cramer, a CNBC superstar of the "Daily Show," John Stewart accusingly said, "Listen, you knew what the banks were doing and yet were touting it for months and months." Although initially defensive, Cramer was forthright in confessing his errors and limitations when he said, "I'm not Eric Sevareid. I'm not Edward R. Murrow. I'm a guy trying to do an entertainment show about business for people to watch."[1053] As people know, however, entertainment is a poor instrument for communicating serious information.

A few financial journalists expressed some caution. *Wall Street Journal* reporters Mark Whitehouse and Greg Ip wrote a front-page piece in November 2005 titled "Awash in Cash: Cheap Money, Growing Risks."[1054] But these articles weren't common and weren't heeded by most readers. Only a few stories were written about such financial institutions as Bear Stearns, Citigroup, Goldman Sachs, J.P.Morgan, Merrill Lynch, and Morgan Stanley that later imploded. None of these articles would have alerted readers to the grave risks the firms were taking in absorbing so many mortgage-backed investments, says Folkenflik.[1055] He thought journalists didn't really understand how the credit market worked and readers didn't want to hear about risks at a time when the housing market boomed and stock prices rose. However, Coy acknowledged that the press should have sought more ways to get people to listen. That conclusion was reinforced by former *Wall Street Journal* reporter Dean Starkman who complained to Coy, "You didn't tell us, or you didn't tell us nearly enough."[1056]

Absence of Ethics and Social Responsibility

Acceptance of social responsibility and a code of ethics can to some degree substitute for regulation. Many mortgage originators of subprime mortgages seemed to show neither. Some were pure salespersons eager to earn commissions and turned a blind eye to the ability of borrowers to meet their monthly payments. As stated earlier, they were not "financial professionals" whose ethical code is to give priority to client interests.

Lack of ethics was reflected in false statements by Lehman Brothers executives shortly before it went bankrupt. In a conference call for investors held on September 10, 2008, CEO Richard Fuld said the planned restructuring "will create a very clean, liquid balance sheet," and "We are on the right track to put these last two quarters behind us."[1057] A *Wall Street Journal* article described the lengths Lehman went to conceal its deteriorating financial condition in its last week. On September 15, Lehman filed for bankruptcy, which many regard as the beginning of the banking crisis.[1058] Lawmakers at an October 2008 meeting pointed to an internal Lehman document from June that questioned how the firm had allowed itself to become so exposed to the real estate market but didn't allocate enough capital.

Another example of ethical lapse was when Mertin Sullivan, a former AIG CEO, told investors in December 2008 that AIG was "confident in our marks and the reasonableness of our valuation methods." Yet, less than a week before, AIG's outside auditor had warned Sullivan on November 29 that the giant insurer "could have a material weakness in its risk management."[1059] Sullivan's public statement did not represent the true situation.

Reflecting a sense of social responsibility, John Moody, one of the inventors of credit ratings, was certainly motivated by money, but he also cared about people. Believing in financial democracy, he wanted to provide the average investor with careful information that would prevent financial misfortune.[1060]

He was obsessed with ethical behavior and refused to accept money under terms that would bias his ratings. Shiller likewise believes that we need to think more about how to help investment professionals with a bent to communicate good and honest information to make a decent living serving the broad public.

The Arcane Mathematics of Securitization

The bundling of mortgages with other loans was guided by financial models designed by mathematicians and physicists. These "'wizards' claimed their esoteric models had magically eliminated risk and uncertainty."[1061] They were encouraged by the previous initial success of the hedge fund Long-Term Capital Management (LTCM). For four years in the mid-1990s this fund boasted extraordinary profits based on supposedly flawless computer formulas devised by a team that included two Nobel laureates. But in the summer of 1998, after losing more than $4 billion in a few months, this fund had to succumb to a federally organized rescue, and later shut down altogether.

This lesson was ignored as financiers continued to be enamored by computer formulas. Commenting on these formulas, Emanuel Derman and Paul Wilmott, authors of books on financial models, said, "Financial theory had tried hard to emulate physics and discover its own elegant, universal laws."[1062] They concluded, however, that "a model, however beautiful, is an artifice. To confuse the model with the world is to embrace a future disaster in the belief that humans obey mathematical principles."[1063] But these models inevitably masked risk rather than exposed it. As Henry T. Hu, a corporate law professor at the University of Texas, characterized these "rocket scientists," they have a knack for neglecting low-probability, catastrophic events. As seen in technological crises, this is a frequent neglect that causes serious crises.

Other Aspects of Management Failure

Although the financial crisis is predominantly one of deception, other aspects of management failure are also present.

Skewed Values

Wall Street's top executives reflected plain avarice—a good biblical term—in their pursuit of personal gain. Their concern for stockholders appeared secondary to maximizing their salaries and bonuses. The poster figure was John Thain, Merrill Lynch's CEO. The media described his purchase of corporate jets and his extravagant lifestyle: how he took a one-week skiing vacation in Vail, Colorado, during the time when the deal with BOA was in jeopardy and his $1.5 million office renovation, including the purchase of a $1,400 wastebasket.[1064] Even after being rescued by the government and acquired by Bank of America he had the audacity to distribute $4 billion in bonuses to employees. This decision was considered so serious by New York State Attorney General

Andrew Cuomo that he issued a subpoena to Chairman and Chief Executive Kenneth Lewis to explain the matter.[1065]

Outrage over bonuses reached a peak with the disclosure that AIG made bonus payments of about $365 million for roughly 418 current and former employees at a business unit that lost $40.5 billion in 2008 the year earlier. When Edward Liddy, the government-appointed chief executive, appeared before a U.S. House committee to explain the bonuses, he explained that the contracts predated his hiring and that he would urge recipients to return the bonuses, which some of them agreed to do. Meanwhile, an organized protest reflected that "a high point of public anger," as Liddy perceived it, had been reached.[1066]

Skewed values were evident in the lack of consideration given by Wall Street executives to the "public interest." The courts long ago upheld the primacy of the public interest over property rights, as shown in the 1971 case of Munn v. People. Here the United States Supreme Court introduced the doctrine that when private property is "affected with a public interest, it ceases to be *juris privai* only." The Court added that property becomes clothed with a public interest and subject to public regulation "when used in a manner to make it of public consequence, and affect the community at large." Bankers implicitly acknowledged this view when they pleaded for a government bailout on the basis that "they were too important for the economy to fail."

Deception Becomes Misconduct

Some aspects of deception spilled over into misconduct. Prosecutors started to examine evidence of insider trading, which is prohibited by the SEC, and the possibility that deception amounted to fraud, e.g., that Wall Street firms may have improperly mispriced mortgage securities.[1067] Federal criminal prosecutors in New York were investigating whether UBS AG, one of the banks involved in the subprime mortgage mess, misled investors by booking inflated prices of mortgage bonds it held despite knowledge that the valuations had dropped. The SEC upgraded its probe of Merrill Lynch to a formal investigation into the bank's practices in the wake of the subprime slide.[1068]

Malevolent acts may also have been committed. The SEC ordered more than two dozen hedge funds to turn over trading information as it investigates whether traders were spreading rumors to manipulate shares, such as false information about Lehman Brothers regarding takeover talks and the possibility of government financing.[1069]

Response Strategies to Crises of Management Failure

Full and Honest Disclosure

The initial core problem of subprime loans could have been avoided if mortgage lenders had not falsified applications and if they had disclosed mortgage terms truthfully and understandably. Similarly, the securitization process required more transparency so that lenders could better determine the asset value of a particular bundle of securities. The proliferation of arcane terms to describe securities made such determination difficult—so difficult that even top-level bankers did not understand them. Transparency is hardly possible under such conditions and knowledge is replaced by blind faith. Furthermore, business journalists cannot report on imponderable transactions.

Bankers did not attempt to explain the banking crisis. They were strangely silent even after their firms announced billions of dollars of write-downs and top management changes. They never apologized. It can be argued, however, that a drowning person doesn't apologize when all energies must be devoted to survival. Red ink looks like a bloody affair, but couldn't bankers at least exclaim, "Oh my God, I'm wounded!" No, they were invisible, silent, and inhuman. They appeared totally disconnected from society. As Klaus Schwab, founder and executive chairman of the World Economic Forum, stated, the fundamental question is "whether we can adopt a more communitarian spirit or whether we will fall back into old habits and excesses, thereby undermining social peace."[1070]

An exception was Robert Rubin, senior counselor and a director at Citigroup who said the bank's problems were due to the buckling financial system, not its own mistakes and that his role was peripheral to the bank's main operations. "Nobody was prepared for this."[1071] But he acknowledged that he was involved in a board decision to ramp up risk-taking in 2004 and 2005, even though he was warning publicly that investors were taking too much risk. The problem, he said, was that the plan was improperly executed. He was one of Wall Street's highest-paid officials, having received $115 million in pay since 1999.

Only when summoned to congressional hearings were bankers made visible and heard, although from carefully scripted comments. At a House oversight committee meeting, Rep. John Mica (R., Fla.) told Fuld, former head of Merrill Lynch: "If you haven't discovered your role, you are the villain today." And Rep Henry Waxman (D., N.Y.), who headed the panel, said that internal documents "portray a company in which there was no accountability for failure."[1072]

Opinion of Communication Professionals

As stated by Mary Ellen Podmolik in *B to B*, "Wall Street's blue-chip brands have not put themselves in front of a microphone to fully explain the mess, apologize or detail how they plan to stabilize their businesses. They haven't taken out full-page ads."[1073] She said, "Unlike other public relations crises affecting top-tier brands, the complexity of the issue, shareholder lawsuits, regulatory inquiries and leadership changes at Merrill Lynch and Citicorp call for more than a mea culpa, say branding and PR experts. Strong brand equity has bought the sector some time, but it only lasts so long; and prolonged silence leads to speculation that more bad news is ahead. . . ."

Ron Culp, senior vice president-managing director at Ketchum Midwest, said, "They should have responded quicker. . . . There's sometimes operational paralysis on the communications front. In this kind of thing you're required to have a public hanging. The question is how long do you leave the body hanging?" PR experts recommended these crisis steps:

- Develop an internal communication program, not only to boost executive retention and boost the confidence of front-line employees, but also so they can reiterate the continued strength of the company and its brand to customers.
- Reach out to journalists to help frame their stories and be ready to answer the difficult questions that will arise. (Graham Hales, chief communications officer at Interbrand)
- Focus on the business, not the angst. (Sallie Gaines, senior vice-president at Hill & Knowlton)

There's some dissent from this mostly conventional advice. Branding consultant Lynn Upshaw advises banks not to move into damage-control mode because the headlines continue to report more bad news. "You have to be sure all the bleeding is done and all the messages are out there . . . Ads in the Journal aren't going to do it until you've got a firm grip on things." The simple platitude and apologies that b-to-c companies often rely on in crises won't work Gaines of H&K agreed: "It's smarter to say nothing than gloat that you're OK, and then two weeks later say, 'Ooops,'"[1074]

Apologize—and Be Humble

The management decisions of Wall Street banks surely caused enormous damage to their investors, the entire banking system, and the economy as a whole, including the entire world. When a wrong or harm is publicly identified, the top person of the involved organization must apologize. As discussed in crisis communication, the offending person or organization seeks the benefit of public forgiveness. It's a way of swiping the slate clean. The millions of employees who lost their jobs, homeowners who were evicted after foreclosure, and businesses facing bankruptcy expect and deserve an apology.

Bankers may explain that the banking failure was a market failure that could not have been foreseen. They could argue that there was no intentional "wrongdoing," just wrong judgments about risk-taking. But their blindness to the inevitable risks of subprime mortgages, overconfidence in being able to insure against risk, and unwillingness to listen to warnings do not leave bankers innocent. Their apology should explain what correctiveness measures would be taken in the future.

Reform Corporate Governance and Compensation Policies

Structural changes may be needed in corporate governance, including replacement of members of the board of directors and revisions in executive compensations. Nell Minow, editor and co-founder of The Corporate library, an independent firm respected for its research on corporate governance and compensation, blames compensation committees 100 percent. Her focus in reform is the ability of boards to replace directors who do a bad job. "Without that, as long as you still have this very dozy interlocked system of having CEOs control who is on their boards, you're going to have no incentive for directors to say no to bad pay."[1075] She states, "With regard to the subprime mess, compensation was structured so that people were paid based on the number of transactions rather than the quality of transaction."[1076] Executives could increase their bonuses by making risky decisions, knowing that investors would ultimately pay for poor risks.

Business leaders had been taking excessive risks in the quest to increase next quarter's profits, because compensation plans paid them handsomely for taking on risks today that would only be realized later. The crisis stimulated new thinking about the role of risk managers who, until the subprime losses, were midlevel functionaries lacking clout and usually reporting to the head of trading. When John Thain became the new CEO of Merrill Lynch before its collapse, he created two high-profile risk-management positions reporting directly to him. Morgan Stanley took similar measures, naming Thomas Daula the new chief risk officer reporting to the CFO. At Citigroup, the new CEO, Vikram Pandit, vows he'll be a "hands-on-participant" in risk management.[1077] There is agreement that risk assessment must be improved and better managed, particularly at credit rating firms.

At a meeting of high-level business leaders at the Aspen Institute, there was an unprecedented consensus: "Short-term thinking had become endemic in business and investment, and it posed a grave threat to the U.S. economy." Banks and finance companies had become increasingly focused on a single, short-term goal of raising share price. "Rather than focusing on producing quality products and services, they have become consumed with earnings management, 'financial engineering,' and moving risk off their balance sheets." They also recommend that top executives who receive equity-based compensation should be prohibited from using derivatives and other hedging techniques to offload the risk that goes along with equity compensation, and instead be required to continue holding a significant portion of their equity for a period beyond their tenure."[1078]

Another needed change in corporate governance is the removal of the universal or integrated banking model. For example, UBS announced that its wealth-management and asset-management division would become stand-alone entities. The purpose of this change was to stop its investment banking arm from funding itself with inexpensive capital thrown off by the wealth-management arm.

Whether such changes in banking models succeed, however, depends on management.[1079]

Some bank CEOs voluntarily reduced their compensation. CEO Pandit said he would get $1 a year until Citigroup returns to profitability.[1080]

Replace Problem Executives

Replacing executives is a common response in extreme cases of management misconduct. It is also an appropriate remedy, as in the banking crisis, when people lose confidence in the competence and integrity of managers. New leaders are more likely to be able to restore social equilibrium. After the bailout, the government installed new CEOs at AIG, Fannie Mae, and Freddy Mac, and at Citigroup, an experienced leader familiar with crisis management, Robert T. Rubin, was appointed.

At Moody's Investors Service, Brian Clarkson, the controversial president and chief operating officer, retired voluntarily, effective at the end of July 2009. Commenting on this retirement, Moody's spokesman Greg Jonas, said, "Brian Clarkson concluded that in such an environment [rating agencies being subject to a lot of criticism] it was a good time to turn the leadership over to someone new."[1081] Arguing against the replacement of too many top managers was Edward Liddy, the government-appointed head of AIG, saying that they had the expertise needed to rescue their companies. His comment was made in response to congressional outrage at the bonuses made by AIG to their top managers after receiving bailout money.

Changes in top management help restore public confidence. People don't trust the former "masters of the universe" and feel the government has been coddling them. Email protests, for example, called for the replacement of Lewis of Bank of America. Simon Johnson, an M.I.T School of Management professor, says that replacement should extend to other "elites" who brought about the crisis, arguing that the power of the erring and arrogant elites must be broken. The policy of being nice to banks, he said is wrong, recognizing that political contributions played a role.

Reform Organizational Culture

As stated by *The Economist*, "the best defence against 'infectious greed' is a healthy corporate culture."[1082] At the best companies, the way managers interact helps to set the tone. At Moody's rating agency, Clarkson changed the culture from one of caution to one of increasing "market share." As Senator Charles Schumer commented, "There has to be a lot more done about conflicts of interest" at rating companies.[1083] Cultures are also influenced by the sort of people a company recruits. Enron, for example, had a policy of recruiting fast-track MBA "talent" into the culture of an electric utility.

Organizations should also create an organizational culture that discourages groupthink and welcomes dissenting information and opinions. The former internal AIG auditor, Joseph St. Dennis, stated that he had early on raised concerns about being excluded from conversations about the valuation of the derivatives in the last week of September 2007. The unit's head, Joseph Cassano, said he had "deliberately excluded" him "because I was concerned that you would pollute the process."[1084]

A glaring omission in the banking culture is conscious consideration for the "public interest." A temporary arrangement in financial institutions that received bailout money is the presence of a government representative who in effect represents the public interest.

Accept Government Regulation and Public Oversight

A regulatory system that gave bankers unfettered freedom greatly contributed to the financial crisis. The SEC, the FRB, the Treasury Department, and Congress are considering regulations in several areas:

- Restore the wall between commercial banks and investment banks so that depositors are protected again investment risks.
- Require sufficient capital reserve by banks as a cushion against risks.
- Require transparency of all securities and a public exchange for CDOs and other instruments.
- Remove the conflict of interest at rating agencies. In December 2008, the SEC tightened rules for ratings firms, largely by prohibiting certain forms of conflicts of interest: rating firms could no longer rate debt they helped structure and analysts involved in ratings can't participate in fee negotiations.[1085]
- Outlaw certain types of "hazardous" and opaque mortgages and securities.
- Tighten regulation of Fannie Mae and Freddie Mac.
- Stop the selling of mortgages to people who cannot afford them.
- Change compensation policies that encourage executives to take excessive risk.
- Create a new consumer products regulator.

Curb Excessive Lobbying

Financial institutions are expected to lobby against some regulations, but they should not be blind to public outrage and the public interest. For example, AIG, which had received a government emergency loan, continued to lobby to soften new controls on the mortgage industry. New rules imposed by Congress in its sweeping housing industry rescue package hold originators accountable if they engaged in the sort of improper or fraudulent lending that ultimately contributed to AIG's downfall.[1086] Kenneth Gross, a Washington attorney who advises lobbyists, said, "I would think it would be difficult to justify a sustained lobby budget of that magnitude ($3 million in the second quarter of 2008) in a bailout mode."[1087]

Troubled financial institutions continued to spend heavily on lobbying Congress while accepting billions of dollars in U.S. government money. Bankers say they can't afford not to lobby. Bank of America spent $4.1 million in 2008, nearly a million more than in 2007.[1088] Merrill Lynch spent at least $1.5million on lobbying between July 1 and September 30, 2008, defending its action by saying, financial services is "a heavily regulated space, and there is a tremendous amount of activity that the Congress and the next administration is going to undertake."[1089]

Restore Public Confidence

A herculean task of financial institutions was to restore public confidence in themselves and the economy in face of constant flow of bad news of more fore-closures, bank closings, rising unpaid credit card debt, business bankruptcies, and employee layoffs. In his book, *Prosperity and Depression*, Gottfried Haberler wrote about the powerful psychological impact of waves of pessimism and opti-mism on the economy.[1090] Both government and the private sector are aware of the importance of raising public confidence to prevent the recession from turning into a depression.

To help restore public confidence, President Barack Obama and his key economic advisers, including treasury secretary Timothy Geithner, announced their faith that a variety of plans to rid the financial system of toxic securities and to stimulate the economy would get banks and business back on their feet. They were careful not to raise expectations too much and stressed that the cor-rection would take time. They decided that efforts to stimulate consumption were sounder under the circumstances than urging people to become more prudent and save more. While thrift is beneficial to private individuals, it would hamper recovery.

Provide Marketing and Public Relations Support

Banks have traditionally engaged in marketing campaigns to win new custom-ers and convince existing ones to remain customers and to expand their use of services. The strategy of customer relationship marketing (CRM), which has won advocates throughout business started with the banking industry. Accord-ingly J.P.Morgan, which took over failed WaMu, pursued a direct marketing approach to persuade WaMu customers to switch to them. Bank of America continued its print, TV, radio and online advertising during the crisis. They referred to the funding of $50 billion in home loans, extended $35 billion in new credit lines to nearly six million credit-card customers, and helping peo-ple to stay in their homes.[1091] Nevertheless, commenting on such efforts, Beth Snyder Bulik of *Advertising Age* said bank marketers have failed to reassure "wary and befuddled customers."[1092]

Jonah Bloom argues in *Advertising Age* that AIG's public relations and advertising should "explain to the press and public exactly what went wrong, offer full apologies and start to outline what steps the company is taking to rebuild business and create some value for the American people."[1093] AIG did in fact, as reported in *PRWeek*, hire Kekst & Co. and BursonMarsteller to help. MSNBC's Rachel Maddow questioned this choice of PR representation, but Bloom says that the serious information vacuum, which was being filled by anger, fear and speculation, requires more rather than less communication and that PR people are needed who will put the "emphasis on the 'public' in public relations."[1094]

Advertising was getting close scrutiny by congressmen who question whether TARP recipients should spend money on marketing—implying that advertising and other forms of marketing are discretionary and frivolous expenditures. ABC News on February 2, 2009 referred to the Bank of America's sponsorship of the Super Bowl as a "carnival-like event."[1095] Bank marketers must prove the effectiveness of their campaigns more than ever before.

Good banks face the danger that they might be associated with bad banks, so good banks launched campaigns to differentiate themselves by publicizing their soundness. For example, in full-page ads in the *Wall Street Journal*, Citi Smith Barney and Citi Private Bank used the theme of "Where we stand" and enumerated seven strengths, including two financial measures: "We stand with over $1 trillion in assets. . . and the strength of over $750 billion in deposits worldwide"; and "We stand with a Tier 1 capital ratio of over 14 percent—an important measure of balance sheet and capital strength."[1096]

Conclusions

The banking crisis of 2008 led to the collapse of several financial institutions and created a ripple effect that endangered many organizations and the general public. It was caused by the same kind of deception that led to Enron's demise earlier in the decade. Despite passage of the Sarbanes-Oxley Act, the banking system lacked transparency. Banks traded in securities that became increasingly arcane and not adequately understood by its buyers. Low bank reserve requirements and high leveraging raised risk-taking to unsustainable levels. Rating agencies, the SEC and FRB, and the financial media fell down on their job of protecting the integrity of financial transactions.

A controversial government bailout helped the large investment banks, like Goldman Sachs, JPMorgan Chase, and Bank of America, survive. They were mostly defensive and did not apologize for their excessive risk-taking. They lobbied to ward off greater government regulation and oversight, which are needed to prevent a future crisis. The further strategies of reforming corporate governance and organizational cultures are needed, but few changes have taken place. The big challenge is to restore public confidence in individual financial institutions and the system as a whole.

Appendix to Chapter 12: Risk as Seen by Behavioral Economics

The financial crisis involves a knowledge of economics, especially such subjects as risk and uncertainty.[1097] As Olivier Blanchard, the International Monetary Funds' (IMF) chief economist wisely states: "Crises feed uncertainty. And uncertainty affects behaviour, which feeds the crisis."[1098] With this emphasis on how people behave, the financial crisis has become the coming-out party for behavioral economics, which integrates insights from psychology into economics. The insights of cognitive psychologists help us to analyze human judgment and decision-making in economic matters. Most economists make the typical assumption that people act like *homo economicus*—like human calculating machines. They make an economic decision by listing all the alternatives and then choosing the one that minimizes costs and maximizes benefits.

Rational Behavior Questioned

What is most fascinating about the rise of behavioral economics is that it reminds us that "conventional" academic economics somehow became sundered from human nature. Seventeen years before he published *The Wealth of Nations*, Adam Smith published *The Theory of Moral Sentiments* in which he never imagined that humans were rational calculating machines. Similarly, the greatest economists of the 20th century—von Mises, Hayek, Schumpeter and Keynes—all regarded *homo economicus* as a nonsense.

Keynes was the odd man out, however, because he believed in an even more fanciful construct—*homo politicus*—a brilliant individual motivated solely by the public good. But behavioral economics explains that in many situations people are not guided by rationality but instead are ruled by emotions. As a *Washington Post* article suggests, "Behavioral economics shows that when it comes to investing, people aren't that smart."[1099]

Meaning of Behavioral Economics

Behavioral economics melds psychology, finance and emotion. As the Swedes put it, behavioral economics integrates "insights from psychology into economics, thereby laying the foundation for a new field of research." It seeks to explain, and sometimes exploit, why we do what we do when it comes to investing.[1100] A popular book by Dan Ariely, *Predictably Irrational*, reports his findings from experiments on his students that expose their propensity for irrationality when under the influence of pleasure, arousal and pain.

Princeton University psychologist Daniel Kahneman is credited with laying the foundation for this new field of research, for which he was awarded the Nobel Prize in Economics in 2002. Among his key insights is that people suffer from various cognitive illusions, which affect their decisions and their behavior.[1101]

Role of Overconfidence

Kahneman blames people's overconfidence in their own judgment for making some wrong [financial] decisions, saying that "the idea that you know better than the market . . . is a very strange idea."[1102] His behavioral explanation is that we have no way of thinking properly about what we don't know. "What we do is we give weight to what we know and then we add a margin of uncertainty. You act on what you think will happen," Kahneman added, "In fact, in most situations what you don't know is so overwhelmingly more important than what you do know that you have no business acting on what you know. Oops."[1103]

Loss Aversion

We like to make decisions that support our overconfidence. It explains why we would want to hold on to losers when we trade in the financial market. When we sell losers, we have to admit we have lost. Instead we sell winners because that makes us feel better and feeds our overconfidence. Rationally, if we sold losers we could get a tax write-off, but that would cause us to admit we have lost, so we do something that makes us feel better, i.e., well the winners, which feeds our overconfidence.[1104] Overall, however, Kahneman thinks investors "trade too much": "they think they know things and they don't."[1105]

"Loss aversion" is a form of irrationality. Kahneman's example is that if people are offered a deal such as I toss a coin and if it's heads, you will win $200, but if it's tails you will lose $100, the majority of people will refuse to take the bet. The pain of losing $100 outweighs the pleasure of winning $200. Losses are given a weight of 2:1 compared with gains. This kind of decision can also be seen in terms of "narrow framing," considering decisions one at a time; we focus on how much we can lose or gain from one decision, instead of a series of decisions. People also misperceive the possibility of rare events, which explains why the eventual failure of subprime mortgages was not widely recognized.

Short-Term Time Perspective

Another insight is that people give greater weight to the present than to the future. When offered the option of receiving five dollars today rather than waiting for six dollars tomorrow, most people take the five dollars. However, when it comes to equivalent trade-offs far away in the future, we seem to be more indifferent so that EUR 5 in ten years versus EUR 6 in ten years and one day is seen as less of a trade-off.[1106]

Herd Instinct

Behavioral economics explains the herd instinct. As described by Michael S. Rosenwald, "When a group of frogs senses they are about to be visited by the dreaded snake, they do not hop in separate directions. They bunch up together. And they fight to get in the middle, taking comfort in being further from being eaten by the bad guy."[1107]

Chapter 13

Crises of Management Misconduct

Of four kinds of management failure, misconduct or wrongdoing lies at the core of morality—ideas about what is right and wrong. It refers to conduct that violates prevailing laws, professional standards, and social norms. Incidences of bribery, kickbacks, fraud and accounting irregularities are frequent examples. Within professional societies, infractions of codes of ethics and conduct are not given enough serious attention.

Management misconduct is more likely to lead to crises than the previous ones of mismanagement, skewed values and deception, mainly because they are more likely to be exposed. Furthermore, the word scandal applies to violations of social norms as well as more egregious forms of organizational conduct. A scandal is always newsworthy. As Suzanne Garment states in *Scandal: The Culture of Mistrust in American Politics*, the raw material of a scandal is a wrongful act that has no redeeming aspect.[1108] It is the public revelation of the wrongful act that causes a scandal. The public is highly sensitive to any violations of society's values, resulting in widespread publicity and gossip. When the public perceives misconduct as a scandal, the crisis facing an organization is particularly severe because it is unavoidably harmful and difficult to manage.[1109] Even when scandals occur in an organizational context, they are committed by specific individuals and thus possess a personal dimension, which makes them especially attractive subjects for the news media.

In today's society, the likelihood of revelations about the wrongdoing of individuals is vastly increased because of the presence of various "investigatory bodies" and the willingness of many individuals to step forward as "whistle-blowers." Besides news organizations, alarms are set off by the attorney general's office, members of the huge staffs of congressmen, and a galaxy of public interest groups, competing firms, disgruntled employees, and individuals or groups who feel they have been harmed. Blogs, Twitter and other forms of social networking on the Internet, as well as exposure through email, have accelerated and amplified the broadcasting of misconduct by individuals and organizations.

The recent so-called Liechtenstein Affair shows how digital information makes disclosure easy. In Germany's biggest-ever tax fraud case, tax inspectors paid EUR4.2 million for a DVD stolen from LGT Group, a firm owned by Liechtenstein's ruling dynasty, which "tells investigations everything they need to know about hundreds of Germans who established 'foundations' in Liechtenstein to manage their money without disclosing their identities." It incriminated Klaus Zumwinkel, boss of Deutsche Post.[1110]

In addition to some of the major cases of misconduct discussed in this chapter, many others have received media attention. Two South Korean companies were implicated in corrupt activities. One was Hyundai Motor Co. Its chairman Chung Mong Koo was arrested in April 2006 on charges of creating a $100 million slush fund to bribe officials. Poor corporate governance was blamed for allowing his "concentrated power and the intragroup dealing."[1111] Koo was also charged with embezzlement and breach of trust, e.g., he "inflicted damage of more than $400 million on the group through irregular deals aimed at enriching his family."[1112] One of the "sweet deals" for a family member was with its affiliate Glovis Co., Hyundai's auto-shipping arm. Investors were concerned about the company's ownership structure whereby an investment of just over $5 million in 2001 to become the sole shareholders of Glovis mushroomed to $1.6 billion in April 2006. *Business Week* said the Chung family's gain on the investment was $1.2 billion.[1113]

Another company charged with misconduct was Samsung Electronics Co., which had a $200 million political slush fund that it used regularly to bribe prosecutors and judges. Some of the fund was also used by the chairman's wife to buy expensive works of art from abroad. Samsung Group Chairman Lee Kun-hee explained, "This is all due to my carelessness. I am responsible for everything and must take responsibility."[1114]

In the United States there were several violations of the U.S. Foreign Corruption Practices Act. Alcoa allegedly overcharged Aluminum Bahrain (known as Alba) for alulmina, a precursor to aluminum used in smelting, and used the fund to make improper payments to a senior Bahrain government official. Another company, Chiquita, the world's largest banana company with sales of $4.5 billion in 2006, admitted it made illegal payments to a violent Colombian group that the U.S. branded as terrorists. The company was faced with the moral dilemma of whether to break the law or prevent harm to employees. The paramilitary organization had threatened to kidnap or kill employees.[1115] Chiquita's new CEO, Fernando Aguirre, decided to stop payments immediately upon his appointment in January 2004.

Management misconduct is pervasive and affects all types of organizations in society: business, nonprofit, and government. The Ethics Resource Center has observed more instances of fraud and lying to stakeholders accompanying the growth, in both number and size, of nonprofits. Revenues in the nonprofit sector grew to $1.4 trillion in 2004 from $678 billion in 1994.[1116] Charities may be losing as much as $40 billion to fraud, according to a study of 58 charity fraud cases from the Certified Fraud Examiners Association 2004 database. A study by Marion Fremont-Smith of Harvard University's Hauser Center for

Nonprofit Organizations listed 152 incidents of misconduct by U.S. nonprofits between 1995 and 2002, including 104 cases of criminal activity. She notes that as non-governmental organizations (NGOs) now operate more like businesses, the need for tighter rules and enforcement will grow.[1117]

Universities are among the nonprofits that have been blemished in connection with student loan programs. University loan officers placed certain loan companies on recommended lists to students. The officers benefitted from a lack of clear rules that prohibit loan companies from offering gifts, travel and other inducements. Johns Hopkins University's financial aid director had received $65,000 in payments from a lender.[1118]

Governments continue to face ethics crises, said Patricia Harned, president of the Ethics Resource Center. A survey released in January 2008 stated that six out of ten local, state and federal government employees have witnessed misconduct on the job in the last year.[1119] Of the 774 survey government respondents, only 10 percent said there was an "ethical culture" at the office. Almost half said they encountered situations that "invited" misconduct by making them feel the need to commit an ethics or compliance violation in order to do their jobs. However, the rates of illegal behavior, such as discrimination, stealing, bribery, sexual harassment, and alteration of documents have decreased.

Major Cases of Misconduct

The Madoff Swindle

Money manager Bernard I. Madoff was arrested on December 11, 2008, accused of a $50 billion fraud—the largest ever on Wall Street.[1120] He blew the whistle on himself after he realized that his game had reached a dead end. Although the fraud was based on massive deception, the case is mainly one of misconduct because the scheme was blatantly illegal. When he gave himself up he claimed he was the sole perpetrator of the fraud and that others, including his wife and two sons, were uninvolved. It turned out that for over three decades he ran "a giant Ponzi scheme"—a scheme which is able to pay an attractive return to early and ongoing investors from funds received from new investors. It was a massive deception that is illegal. The scheme is credited to Charles Ponzi who was arrested in 1920. He promised 50 percent investment returns in 45 days, which tempted about 40,000 people to invest.[1121]

Madoff was a notable figure, a former chairman of the Nasdaq Stock Market and well-known on Wall Street. He thus had credibility, which garnered client trust. His asset-management business firm made him a wealthy man. A 1986 report in *Financial World* listed him as one of the highest paid people on Wall Street who owned three homes and kept a yacht moored in the Bahamas. His New York City apartment on Manhattan's Upper East Side was valued at more than 5 million.

His investors enjoyed steady monthly returns ranging from zero to 2 percent.[1122] They were mostly wealthy private investors, many Jewish, but also included international banks, hedge funds, universities, and U.S. foundations.[1123] An embarrassingly large number, says *The Economist*, were supposed to have been highly sophisticated.[1124] As Greenspan said: "I've been extraordinarily distressed by how badly the most sophisticated people in the business handled risk management. But the question is: If, protecting their own resources, they can't do it, who's going to do it better?"[1125] Almost daily for several weeks after his arrest the media reported new victims.

One of Madoff's methods was to recruit investors from social networks in Dallas, Chicago, Boston, and Minneapolis. His largest cluster was in Florida, mainly through the Palm Beach Club. Investors were recommended by many informal agents and from "fund of hedge funds" type of firms, e.g., Fairfield Greenwich and Tremont Capital Management.[1126] The scheme worked because even sophisticated investors trusted Madoff, ignoring the adage that if something sounds too good to be true, then it's not.

Robert Cialdini, a psychology professor and author of *Influence: Science and Practice*, identifies the strategy as "a triple-threat combination."[1127] One component is the "murkiness" of a hedge fund, which makes investors feel that it is "the inherent domain of people who know more than we do." A second component is social proof—"evidence that other people we trust have already decided to invest." The third component is exclusivity—"You can't get in unless you're invited, which shifts investors' fears from the risk that they might lose money to the risk they might lose out on making money." If you were invited to join the club of "sophisticated investors" it would almost seem an "insult" to do any further investigation. "Due diligence" just wasn't done. In retrospect, Stephen McMenamin of the Greenwich Roundtable says, due diligence is the art of asking good questions. "It's also the art of not taking answers on faith.[1128]

Some of Madoff's middlemen operated in Europe. For example, Banco Santander funneled billions from wealthy Spaniards and Latin Americans. Access International invested $1.5 billion with Madoff, mostly from wealthy Europeans.[1129] The aristocratic Frenchman, Rene-Thierry Magon de la Villehuchet, who operated the firm, was so distressed that he committed suicide in his office.[1130] One of the sophisticated clients was Swiss bank Union Bancaire Privee (UBP), which kept about $700 million dollars of its wealthy clients' money in Madoff-related investments through its funds-of-funds and client portfolio.

After the Madoff disclosure, UBP told clients it was the victim of a "massive fraud" and claimed that it had conducted due diligence, which included visits with Madoff.[1131] The officers who approved the investment, however, didn't heed the warnings of their own research department. Its former deputy head, Gideon Nieuwoudt, reported that he was worried about the lack of even basic information such as what assets Madoff had, how many feeder funds there were, and how the investment strategy worked. "It all seems very opaque," wrote Nieuwoudt, who had talked with more than 100 funds that invested or had invested with Madoff.[1132] None of them could explain how the strategy produced such consistent returns. UBP officers took comfort from such meager facts that Madoff's firm was registered with the SEC.

After being on house arrest in his luxury apartment, Madoff was sent to a federal prison in Butner, North Carolina, where he is serving a 150-year sentence. In December 2009 he was transferred to the facility's medical center.[1133]

Bribery and Corruption Scandal at Siemens

In November 2006, German police raided Siemens' offices across Germany in response to allegations of bribery and corruption.[1134] Siemens, Europe's largest engineering company by revenue, was charged by the U.S. Justice Department and the SEC with engaging in bribery. The SEC claimed Siemens made at least 4,283 bribe payments totaling $1.4 billion alone between March 2001 and September 2007.[1135] It was reckoned that Siemens illegally spent about E1.3 billion ($2.5 billion) illegally around the world in the past few years to beat the competition. Authorities said misconduct was "systematic" and involved employees at all levels of the company, including former senior management.

The bribes were made to government officials in ten countries. They included payment to supply transit systems in Venezuela, medical equipment in China, Vietnam and Russia, power equipment in Iraq and Israel, refineries in Mexico, and telecommunications equipment in Nigeria and Bangladesh. Among the methods Siemens used to conceal bribes, besides the usual sham consulting contracts, were "removable Post-It Notes" with affixed signatures to obscure audit trails, a "cash desk" where employees could fill an "empty suitcase" with as much as E1 million ($1.3 million) to pay bribes, and giving clients airline tickets which they could exchange for cash.[1136]

Siemens' permissive culture allowed the use of bribes and slush funds to win contracts, but the company denies that the problem was "systemic."[1137] The SEC accused the company's former chief financial officer, Heinz-Joachim Neuburger, of taking insufficient action in 2003 after auditors flagged suspicious payment and of misleading the company's nonexecutive supervisory board on other compliance matters.[1138]

The U.S. Justice Department fined the company $800,000, much lower than the $2.7 billion in criminal damages it could have sought. It was the largest penalty ever imposed under the U.S. Foreign Corrupt Practices Act. In addition, Siemens would pay an additional E395 million ($528 million) in Germany to settle criminal investigations there.[1139] Three former company managers received suspended court sentences and Munich prosecutors were continuing investigations of about 300 suspects, including former management board members. One board member was Johannes Feldmayer, who was handed a two-year suspended prison sentence.[1140] In addition, more than ten countries are continuing the investigation.

Company responses

Siemens failed to take anticorruption laws seriously until it was ensnared in a scandal. When that happened, Siemens' CEO Klaus Kleinfeld took the minimum measure of promising to investigate it. He hired a leading anticorruption expert, Michael J. Hershman, a onetime investigator for the Senate Watergate Committee, to advise the management board and the audit committee of its supervisory board. In return, Hershman stated that Kleinfeld was committed to stamping out illegal practices.[1141]

Responding to criticism of its corporate culture, Kleinfeld said he recognized the need to change it so that "managers do not fall back into easy, and illegal, patterns of behavior."[1142] He admonished his employees, "If you, in your mind, get it wrong and think, 'I just have to beat the competition,' you are fundamentally doing something wrong."[1143] He said the company would steer clear of some countries, e.g., Sudan because of concerns about human rights abuses in the Darfu region. Kleinfeld implied that bribes were not necessary for a company that anticipates growing demand for power turbines in the fast-growing cities in the developing world and medical scanners for aging populations in advanced industrial nations.

Satyam Computer Services Ltd.

Satyam Computer Systems Ltd., founded in 1987, is one of India's largest technology-outsourcing companies, owned by the Raju family and led by Satyam's founder and chairman, B. Ramalinga Raju. Satyam also controls two other companies: Maytas Properties Ltd., which is run by Raju's son B. Rama Raju, and Maytas Infra Ltd. The crisis was precipitated when, on December 16, 2008, Raju persuaded Satyam's board to purchase the two companies for a total of $1.6 billion.[1144] It was this decision that triggered the crisis for the company and the two brothers. A review of minutes from the meeting showed that the purchase was a last-ditch attempt to cover up the discrepancies in the company's balance sheet.[1145] At least three directors asked questions about the acquisitions, including questions about the ties between the Raju family and Maytas.

In retrospect, the board should have been involved earlier, said one independent director, Krishna Palepu, a Harvard Business School professor of corporate governance, who participated in the meeting by phone conference. He later explained, "There should be complete transparency and justification for the [valuation] methodology to be adopted." He also identified two complicated aspects of the proposal: "unrelated diversification, and related party transactions." Nevertheless, along with other directors, he voted unanimously to approve the purchase. He resigned from the board saying that to get the company back on its feet, board members would have to spend much more time in the country for meetings, to which he could not commit. When

Satyam's shareholders resisted the board's decision, it was reversed and disclosures were forced.[1146]

B. Ramalinga Raju resigned after he admitted he had fudged books for several years by exaggerating the company's financial health and creating a fictitious cash balance of more than $1 billion. He and his brother, Rama Raju, the company's former managing director, were arrested on January 9, 2009, on complaints of cheating, forgery, breach of trust and other charges. The government investigation was widened to eight other companies linked to Satyam and the Raju family.[1147] Investigators have since learned that account-balance statements and letters of confirmation of account balances at several banks—HSBC Holdings PLC of the U.K., Citigroup Inc of the United States, and HDFC Bank and ICICI Bank Ltd. of India—were forgeries.[1148]

Reforms

Satyam's board was replaced by a government-appointed board. The fraud focused attention on India's weak corporate governance and investors in Indian shares lost faith in corporations across the board. The Confederation of Indian Industry accordingly set up a special task force to look at corporate governance issues.[1149] The new board also replaced the firm's auditor PricewaterhouseCoopers, that had worked with company for about eight years, with new independent accountants.

Parmalat's Brazen Fraud

The collapse of Parmalat, Italy's dairy giant, was the largest corporate bankruptcy ever in Europe. More than 100,000 private investors lost their savings. Parmalat was the jewel of Italian capitalism. It was one of Europe's largest and most global companies. It did $3.3 billion in business in North America alone. Its shares traded in New York where it sold more than $1.5 billion in bonds to U.S. investors. Calisto Tanzi started the company when he was in his early 20s. Milk, particularly long-life milk, was always at the heart of the business. It also expanded into the marketing of yoghurts, fruit juices and other foodstuffs, and by 2000, it was employing 36,000 people in 31 countries.

In December 2003, Parmalat went bankrupt after it defaulted on a $185 million bond payment in mid-November. After more than a decade of deceiving investors, regulators, auditors, bankers, and even many of the company's other managers, Tanzi and other executives were unable to cover their tracks.[1150] They had systematically looted the company, leaving an $18 billion hole in its books. Assets of between $8.5 billion to 12 billion vanished.[1151] Or, as Tanzi later said, "No money disappeared, [there were] just nonexistent assets."[1152] The Italian dairy-foods giant Parmalat became Europe's equivalent of Enron, WorldCom, and Tyco International.

Methodology of Fraud

Investigators were astonished at the simplicity and amateurishness of the affair. Parmalat created a new subsidiary in the Cayman Islands called Bonlat, through which most of Parmalat's myriad offshore operations and allegedly fraudulent financial transactions were channeled.[1153] An account that supposedly held $4.8 billion in a Bank of America account, some 38 percent of Parmalat's assets, simply didn't exist. Managers had invented the assets to offset up to $16.2 billion in liabilities and falsified accounts over a 15-year period.[1154]

An episode shows the auditors' sloppiness. They supposedly sent and received replies from a state-owned Cuban importer saying that $620 million of powdered milk, which would produce the equivalent of 2.5 billion quarts, was purchased and listed as a credit on Bonlat's balance sheet. The letter was forged on a Bank of America letterhead with a signature from an old letter obtained by a data processor who knew nothing about it.[1155] As prosecutors later commented, the transaction was obviously a fake, for if the figures were true "we would be swimming in milk."[1156]

Prosecutors arrested two top executives of the Italian arm of Grant Thornton, Lorenzo Penca, chairman, and Maurizio Bianchi, a partner in the firm's Milan office, on charges that their actions contributed to Parmalat's bankruptcy. The arrest warrant accused them of suggesting ways that Parmalat executives could "falsify the balance sheet" of a subsidiary and then have it "falsely certified" on the financial statement.[1157]

Failure of Auditors and Regulators

The case alarmingly revealed the lack of transparency of corporate accounts and the inability—or incompetence—of the auditors to uncover the fraud. The failure of accounting firms became the big story. Grant Thornton International, one of the largest of the so-called second-tier U.S. accounting firms, was Parmalat's accounting firm from 1990–99, followed by Deloitte Touche Tohmatsu.[1158] Italian markets became suspicious of Parmalat after it was unable to provide Grant Thornton with a value on one of the investments, known as Epicurum, and Deloitte subsequently had to "qualify" Parmalat's third quarter results.[1159]

Regulators also failed, albeit making corporate governance and regulatory supervision more difficult was that Parmalat was family-controlled through a chain of holding companies. Parmalat's board of directors was stuffed with family members and local cronies. Its non-executive directors lacked independence. Furthermore, Tanzi was both the chairman and the chief executive of the group, which enlarged his control. *The Economist* stated that Italy has a reputation for poor corporate governance and shameless exploitation of minority shareholders, but adds that the same is true of other European countries, such as France, the Netherlands and Switzerland.[1160] The Italian Parliament was

expected to propose a new financial market watchdog modeled on Britain's
Financial Services Authority.[1161]

Arrests and Convictions

Tanzi, his son, a brother, his former Chief Financial Officer Fausto Tonna,
and some 16 other individuals, including former board members and even
the company's lawyers were investigated. Tanzi was arrested on December 27
on suspicion of fraud, embezzlement, false accounting, and misleading investors. He confessed to misappropriating some $620 million to cover losses in
other family-owned companies.[1162] Umberto Mosette, a law professor, said that
the main legal issues were "false accounting, insufficient disclosure and the
provision of misleading information to investors."[1163]

In December 2008, Calisto Tanzi was sentenced to ten years in prison,
accused of market-rigging, false accounting and obstructing market oversight.
Fauso Tonna, his former CFO, accused of weaving a web of offshore subsidiaries to disguise the group's true cash flow, got a two-and-a-half-year sentence.
Seven other people, including three former Bank of America employees, were
acquitted.[1164]

Sanlu Baby Formula Scandal

China's reputation for food safety was severely undermined by the tainted milk
scandal in the late summer and fall of 2008, especially its use in baby formula.
Six infants died and over 54,000 suffered from severe kidney failure, with the
possibility of permanent kidney damage.[1165] In addition, 294,000 children
under three years of age were sickened.[1166] Farmers and milk traders had knowingly added melamine to milk, which makes protein-deficient or diluted milk
appear to contain more protein and thereby pass quality testing.[1167]

Tainting of milk was an open secret in China. One farmer frankly admitted,
"It is true milk farmers add water to raw milk when the purchasing price is
too low."[1168] It was a cheap way to help the milk of undernourished cows fool
dairy companies' quality checks. Milk manufacturers who collected milk from
traders were negligent in their quality control. The reputation of the Chinese
milk industry, as well as China's nation brand, was damaged.

Twenty-two Chinese manufacturers were linked to the baby formula scandal, including some of the country's biggest dairy companies.[1169] China's dairy
industry had been prospering, growing to $17.9 billion in 2007 from $8.8 billion
in 2003. During the same period, milk formula sales rose to $3.1 billion from
$1.4 billion. The Shijazhuang Sanlu Group received most media attention, but
others such as Mengniu Dairy Co., one of China's largest dairy producers, were
also implicated. Sanlu bought milk from many sources, including milk traders who buy raw milk from small farmers and mix it together before reselling
it. Sanlu had been a trusted brand, but as one mother who had taken her

one-year-old son to hospital said, "I will never believe in domestic brands."[1170] Some of the mothers filed lawsuits.[1171]

The problem of tainted milk became a major crisis for the Sanlu Group, the industry's largest producer. Its response to the problem was one of denial and coverup. An early warning was a complaint to the company by the father of a 13-year-old girl who reported that his daughter's urine became turbid with granule after drinking Sanlu milk powder. On May 20 he also posted his concern on Tianya.cn, China's biggest online forum, blaming Sanlu Group's milk powder.

Sanlu's response to the complaint was to try to keep the whole matter quiet. Wang was told to mail two packages of his milk powder for lab testing. Although the results of the test were never shared with Wang, a representative of Sanlu visited him and offered to replace the milk powder, which Wang refused. The initial offer was increased and ultimately the company offered four cartons of milk powder whose value exceeded Wang's purchase 25 times. Wang accepted this offer and even deleted his posts, saying the milk powder he previously bought was "counterfeit." Nevertheless, he continued to report the problem to quality supervision authorities, but with no success. Sanlu was accused by sina.com on September 13 of trying to cut a deal with Baidu.com, China's largest search engine, to filter out negative news about the company. Baidu.com, after confirming that it twice received a proposal, issued a statement saying they rejected it because "it's a violation of the company's principle of letting users collect objective information easily."[1172]

The traditional media were slow to report on tainted milk. *Changjiang Shang Bao* of Hubei province first reported in late August that infants in at least six Chinese provinces were diagnosed with kidney stones and all had used formula from "the same company." Ironically, China's Central Television program on September 2 praised Sanlu Group's quality control process, stating at the end of the program, "I wish China will have more companies like Sanlu to cherish the quality of their products."[1173] It wasn't until September 11 that a Shanghai newspaper, *Dngfang Azo Bao*, made the connection with milk powder products of the Sanlu Group.

Sanlu and New Zealand Investor Ponder Announcement

Sanlu started receiving reports of sickened babies in March 2008, but its investigations supposedly revealed no problems.[1174] In May a child died of kidney problems, but officials only later connected the death to the tainted formula. In July after a second child died, Sanlu tests revealed melamine contamination.

It wasn't until August 2, just six days before the opening of the Beijing Olympics, that Sanlu directors were informed of the problem at a board meeting. Among them were directors from the Fonterra Co-operative Group Ltd., a New Zealand dairy company, which owned 43 percent of Sanlu. At the meeting, Andrew Ferrier, Fonterra's chief executive urged disclosure: "We encouraged Sanlu, we encouraged the authorities, to go public." Ferrier did not, however, insist on disclosure because after some "soul searching," he decided that Fonterra would not to make a public statement on its own but let Sanlu exercise "their own judgment."[1175] This was a highly questionable decision. *Newsweek* asked: Should differences in Chinese and U.S. political systems be taken into account? Should the cultural admonition not to let their Chinese partners get offended or "lose face" be a factor?[1176]

Ferrier defended his decision by saying that to reveal the problem before Chinese officials did would have been "totally irresponsible."[1177] He claimed that local Chinese authorities misled the company into thinking central health authorities in Beijing had been notified.[1178] Following the August 2 board meeting, Sanlu limited its actions to informing local health officials. These officials told the company not to make a public announcement but to quietly remove tainted product from store shelves.[1179] Accordingly, on August 6 Sanlu asked distributors to recall all formula made before that date and removed more than 8,000 tons of products in supermarkets, schools and Starbucks outlets across China.[1180]

By following this procedure and not making a public announcement, Sanlu broke the rules of corporate social responsibility and ethical behavior. Sanlu's paramount concern should be public health and safety, but, instead, it delayed action. Furthermore, had the company really been serious about disclosing the facts to consumers, local health officials would be the worst ones to depend on, for they said they were not in a position to make a public announcement. They were afraid that central government would be displeased with such a disclosure just days before the opening of the Olympics, knowing that China's central government had made order and social stability the number one priority. In effect, Sanlu cooperated with the government in giving the nation-building goal of the Olympics precedence over the health and safety of infants. The decision was short-sighted for when the crisis occurred China's nation-brand as well as the reputation of the Chinese milk industry were damaged. The milk scandal may have destroyed the China brand as much as the Olympics improved it.

Product Recall

Over a month passed before Fonterra on September 5 took further action by informing its government in New Zealand of the tainted milk. Prime Minister Helen Clark consequently ordered her ambassador in Beijing to notify authorities there, which was done on September 9. She claimed that Fonterra had previously tried "for weeks" to persuade local officials to allow a public recall, but to no avail.[1181] On September 11, the Chinese central government publicly linked infant kidney problems to Sanlu's formula. Sanlu then issued a public recall of remaining formula on the market and, in its struggle to restore confidence in the safety of China's food supply, the Chinese government also ordered stores across the country to pull all milk products made before September 14 from their shelves until milk passed safety tests.[1182]

Reflecting the globalization of business, the recall had worldwide repercussions. Nestlé recalled its line of milk in Hong Kong, Cadbury pulled 11 products made at its Beijing plant from stores in Asia, and Unilever Hong Kong recalled four batches of Lipton milk-tea powder in Hong Kong and Macau. White Rabbit Creamy Candy, made famous when Chinese premier Zhou Enlai presented it to President Nixon during his visit to China in 1972,[1183] also lost face when Tesco PLC said it recalled the candy as a precautionary measure from its stores in the U.K., China and Malaysia.[1184]

Some companies disassociated themselves from the baby formula problem. Groupe Danone SA's International Nutrition Co. units said it uses only imported milk for the baby formula it makes in China. Nestlé SA said it buys milk from local farmers who are supervised daily by its own agricultural officers.[1185]

The Sanlu case cuts across all three of the specific types of crises of management failure. It is included in this chapter on misconduct because the government took the deception so seriously that it executed two of the violators. Elements of skewed values also played a role as the welfare of consumers was sacrificed in favor of producer profitability. The milk industry apparently did not engage in issues monitoring for it seemed unaware of the pet food scandal in spring 2007 that killed about 4,500 animals after melamine and cyanuric acid were added to the food.[1186] The farmers said that they themselves became victims when they were forced to pour their milk into rivers because of lack of buyers.[1187]

Strategies for Handling Management Misconduct

Relationships are damaged by management misconduct. Thus the immediate strategy is to try to repair the damage. Another early strategy is to replace errant managers and deficient accounting firms. Longer term and more difficult efforts must be undertaken to reinforce organizational culture with ethics and to reform corporate governance.

Repair Damaged Relationships

In the Satyam crisis, a major concern of the new management was the retention of clients and employees. Incidents that create customer mistrust often spell the end for businesses. "When we have seen this kind of massive breach of trust case in US firms there has been a huge flight of customers." He added. "If I was a CIO and a competitor of (Satyam) called me I would definitely talk to them."[1188] To this end, the head of Satyam's division for banking and financial-services clients went to New York to meet each of Satyam's largest banking customers. He had also been on the phone almost constantly since the news broke.

In addition, the company's hundreds of "relationship managers" were talking to customers and offering to let them talk directly to the new board of directors. Satyam's employees received daily emails reassuring them that the contracts were safe. But some clients such as State Farm Insurance of the United States quit, and others were reviewing their relationship. A Citi-group representative, however, said they were retaining their relationship.[1189] Customers and employees were both concerned about the company's cash-flow problems.

For Sanlu to repair damaged relationships, it had to show that necessary reforms were being undertaken. These include improving risk analysis, rebuilding supply chains, and instituting quality control. The Chinese government also became involved through the setting of standards and institution of inspections.

Willingly Make Public Disclosure and Apologize

If management misconduct seriously endangers public health and safety, as with Sanlu, the universal crisis rule must be followed immediately by thoroughly investigating a complaint and, if the complaint is justified, taking quick remedial action. When this accommodative strategy is used, appropriate apologies are made, including providing financial payment to victims. Should the complaint be unjustified, the defensive strategy would be used and wrongdoing would be denied, following the lawyers' approach in seeking to lower the risks of litigation. As shown, Sanlu did not follow either prescription. It engaged in denial and coverup. Only after pressure from the government and exposure by the media did it take action.

Replace Errant Managers and Unprofessional Accounting Firms

In all of the major cases in this chapter, the leadership of the companies was changed. The wrongs were too enormous and it was too late to apply image restoration strategies. Siemens replaced its entire top leadership, including the chairman of the supervisory board, its chief executive officer, its general counsel, the head of internal audit and the chief compliance officer.[1190] Although Kleinfeld said he had no plans to step down, he was replaced in July 2007 by Peter Löscher who was brought into Siemens to lead one of the biggest corporate cleanups in history. He was familiar with various cultures, having studied at the Chinese University in Hong Kong and Harvard Business School and being married to a Spanish wife. He appointed legal officers to each of the sprawling engineering group's divisions to emphasize that obeying the law is a vital aspect of every operational decision. In another step, he sent a letter over Christmas 2007 to top managers saying that ignorance and loyalty were no excuse for having broken the law. He offered an amnesty until January 31—later extended by a month—to encourage them to disclose all, which 110 did.[1191]

Siemens decided to cooperate with government authorities, thereby reducing the fine imposed by the Justice Department and SEC. It hired a New York law firm Debevoise & Plimpton LLP that filed frequent reports with U.S. authorities. Siemens paid the law firm and the accounting firm Delotte & Touche more than $850 million in fees and expenses[1192]

At Satyam, the board named a new chief executive, A. S. Murty, a 15-year company veteran. He would be assisted by special pro-bono advisers, along with the Boston Consulting Group. The board also named the law firm of Wachtell, Lipton, Rosen & Katz to represent the company in two purported class-action suits filed against it in the U.S. Several companies have expressed interest in buying Satyam.[1193]

Accounting firms were shown in an unfavorable light in all of the cases in this chapter. They did not meet the standards of a profession. Madoff's outside auditor, David Friehling, pleaded guilty to signing off on sham audits, filing false tax returns for Madoff and other Madoff investors, and fraud, although he denied knowing about the Ponzi scheme.[1194] The firm's outside auditor Siemens, Satyam, and Parmalat hired new accounting firms. Commenting on the scope of accounting problems, SEC Chairman Christopher Cox said in front of a startled business community that public companies were facing a "pandemic of crooked accounting practices."[1195] One of his examples was the backdating of stock options, which is questionable if not outright fraudulent. The practice erased more than $5 billion in company earnings. Sixty senior officers and directors—including 18 chief executives—were forced out of office.

Reinforce Organizational Culture with Ethics

As stated in the introduction of Part IV, the focus in crises of management failure is on immoral managers and organizational culture as well as weak corporate governance and the absence of vigilant external accountancy reviews. One of the solutions is to reinforce organizational culture with ethics.

The culture of an organization strongly affects ethical behavior by employees. Unfortunately, an April 2008 survey released by the Ethics Resource Center and the Society for Human Resource Management found that nearly half of HR professionals believe ethical conduct is not rewarded in business today, with the implication that organizational cultures are unsupportive of ethical behavior.[1196] Many employees believe that sometimes cutting corners really does get them somewhere. The most common types of misconduct, said survey respondents, are misrepresenting hours worked; lying to supervisors, employees, vendors, customers or the public; misusing organizational assets; and lying about or falsifying records. The study shows that standards of conduct need to be addressed day to day and that a culture of ethics needs to be constant. To this end, most companies want a code of ethics in place.

A study of ethics in marketing also supports this view, saying that "top management actions" were the single best predictor of managers' perception of ethical problems, especially when top management reprimands unethical behavior.[1197] In marketing management, corporate or industry codes are not enough because they seem feeble and unrelated to the extent of unethical problems in marketing management. At best they produce uniformity of ethical values. According to a survey of 1076 marketing professionals of the American Marketing Association, bribery is the most often mentioned ethical problem faced by marketers.[1198] Other top ones are fairness, honesty, pricing strategy, product strategy, and personnel decisions. Most marketing managers do not believe that unethical behaviors in general lead to success, with only 26 percent agreeing that "in order to succeed in my company, it is often necessary to compromise one's ethics." They acknowledge, however, that successful marketing managers do engage in certain specific unethical behaviors: 48 percent take credit for the ideas and accomplishments of others; 43 percent withhold information that is detrimental to their self-interest; 32 percent look for a "scapegoat" when they feel they may be associated with failure; and 29 percent make rivals look bad in the eyes of important people in their company.

Reform Corporate Governance

Weaknesses in corporate governance continue to contribute to crises of misconduct. Most egregious is Parmalat, whose board largely consisted of family members and other insiders that were not inclined to take their oversight responsibilities seriously. Satyam's board was also derelict, having approved a deal that exposed corruption. A sound system of accountancy should accurately record financial transactions and identify any fraud and other misconduct and unethical behavior.

The Satyam fraud focused attention on India's weak corporate governance, which led investors in Indian shares to lose faith in corporations across the board. The Confederation of Indian Industry accordingly set up a special task force to look at corporate governance issues.[1199] The new board also replaced the firm's auditor PricewaterhouseCoopers, that worked with the company for about eight years. The accounting firm, often implicated in inadequate auditing, defended its procedures with the defensive statement, "The audits were conducted by Pricewaterhouse in accordance with applicable auditing standards and were supported by appropriate audit evidence."[1200] Later, Indian police arrested two partners of the Indian arm of the auditing firm on charges of criminal conspiracy and cheating. The company's former chief financial officer, Srinivas Vadlamani, was also arrested on charges of forgery, cheating and breach of trust.[1201]

In the Parmalat case, the accounting firm of Grant Thornton was replaced. Grant Thornton's defense was that it too was a "victim," but as others in the accounting profession said, claiming harm to itself isn't an excuse. An auditor's job is to catch malfeasance at the companies they oversee. Grant Thornton fell down on the job. Douglas Carmichael, the Public Company Accounting

Oversight Board's chief auditor, explained in a speech that when an auditor fails to detect a major fraud, "a proper professional response for the head of the firm involved is not to invoke the tired litany that an auditor is not responsible for detecting all fraud and that the firm fully adhered to all professional standards, even though it failed to find that most of the income was false."[1202]

In many European countries there is no enforcement of accounting standards at all, something that the international Accounting Standards Board (UIASB) is attempting to change. One proposal is for each EU member state to set up a national accountancy overseer, similar to America's Public Company Accounting Oversight Board, established by the Sarbanes-Oxley act.[1203]

Strengthen Government Oversight

As seen in the Madoff case, SEC oversight failed abysmally. Madoff Investment Securities LLC had been examined at least eight times in 16 years by the SEC and other regulators who did not detect any fraud. Madoff deceived regulators by saying he managed accounts for hedge funds and wasn't running an investment-advisory business. When his trading practices were questioned he outlined new procedures to address the findings. SEC staffers lacked sufficient expertise and were no match for Madoff's knowledge and experience.[1204] An additional safeguard had failed: Madoff's books were audited by a virtually unknown accounting firm, said financial columnist James B. Stewart. His advice is never to invest in hedge fund, partnership, mutual fund, or anything else whose books aren't audited by a recognized accounting firm with a strong reputation.[1205]

In the Sanlu case, after provincial authorities informed the central government of the problem on September 8 after the Olympics ended, the central government arrested several suppliers and sacked several local officials, including the head of a local food-and-drug agency. On September 17, it detained for questioning Sanlu's former chairwoman, Tian Wenhua, who was fired within the week. Along with three other executives she was charged with "manufacturing and selling counterfeit commodities." They and 17 other people appeared in court in December. After giving tearful testimony in court, Wenhua pleaded guilty and faces a possible life sentence.[1206] The government hopes these trials will restore trust.[1207] In the meanwhile, Sanlu ceased operations and filed for bankruptcy.[1208]

Chinese authorities on September 13 offered free treatment to all children sickened by tainted dairy products. This offer was followed up by an announcement by China's Dairy Industry Association that its 22 Chinese dairy companies would make one-time cash payments to the families of the children sickened by the contaminated milk products.[1209]

To restore confidence in the dairy industry, Prime Minister Wan Jiabao announced that his government would fix the domestic dairy industry.[1210] This need was recognized by an analyst for Sealand Securities in Shenzhen who said

that if Chinese dairy companies want to avoid being overtaken by foreign coun-
terparts they would have to rebuild their supply chains and practice better corporation responsibility. This is an endemic problem in China, which has often
diffuse and poorly regulated supply chains for foods, pharmaceutical and other
products. This was illustrated by the recent crisis involving the anticlotting drug
Heparin, which was linked to more than 80 deaths in the United States.[1211]

Government instituted several remedial measures: (1) government inspectors were posted to monitor dairy companies; (2) imposed rules to improve
accountability among milk suppliers; (3) required additives to be registered with
quality-supervision departments; (4) made sure exports comply with standards
of import nations; and (5) moved to expand the number of state-certified independent testing labs to test products for impurities.[1212]

Conclusions

Crises of misconduct are a report card on the free-market system and suggest
that some enterprises abuse the freedom they are given. Some have engaged in
unethical and illegal actions that impugn their reputations and endanger others. They have undermined the integrity of the accounting profession, whose
member firms are supposed to certify that transactions are accurately recorded.
They have corrupted organizational cultures.

Main responsibility for reducing misconduct lies with the board of directors. Too often they have been co-opted by the CEO and fail in their oversight
responsibility. The result is that the seeds of a crisis are planted and slowly
simmer until a crisis threshold is reached and misconduct is disclosed. Apologies and other techniques of image restoration cannot be expected to save the
offenders. It is then too late to sermonize about ethics. Top managers face
the personal crises of being disgraced and losing their jobs. All enterprises are
affected when government campaigns for greater regulation.

Part V

Conclusions

Chapter 14

Learning from Crises

Crises are signs of strain, disruption, and malfunctioning—in managers, organizations, and society. The precipitous rise in the number, variety, and intensity of crises from year to year indicates that the pressures and demands on organizations are outstripping their ability to cope with them. Therefore, not only has the subject of crisis management risen in importance, but its relevance to general management has become more pronounced and urgent. More and more "everyday" decisions now require a crisis management perspective.

This has come about because problems and decisions contain higher levels of risk and uncertainty arising from a variety of sources: a more crowded world living in unsuitable areas; scarcer resources that must be extracted from more remote and deeper places; more complex, intertwined and sometimes unfamiliar technologies; societies with rising expectations and relentless demands; multiplying number and variety of diverse groups, often with strong differences in goals and values; fierce competition among groups, organizations, and countries, for economic and political supremacy; increasing pressure on managers to accomplish their missions and achieve successful results; and a loss of a sense of community with common purposes, norms, and bonds.

The different types of crises discussed in this book reflect the challenges and problems that arise from these sources of risk and uncertainty. The physical environment represents the realities of nature and technology. Humankind must recognize and adjust to those natural forces—earthquakes, hurricanes, floods, storms, fires—the occurrence of which it has no control over, although political and business leaders are held accountable for their forecasting and response to them. Environmental reports on the "state of the world" suggest that crises stemming from the physical environment will escalate.[1213] The looming problem of global warming is the single, most urgent challenge.

In efforts to mitigate nature's effects, crisis managers apply technology by building sea walls, emergency shelters, dams, and spillways. But as Hurricane Katrina's devastation of much of New Orleans showed, public policy questions arise about the wisdom of allowing people to build and live in flood-prone areas. In addition to applying emergency management skills, crisis managers will have to become more adept as players in the public policy process.

While attempting to reduce the impact of natural forces through technology and disaster control measures, humankind has added to the store of potential crises by inventing and using more complex and dangerous technologies, such as biotechnology, to satisfy mounting human demands. To various degrees, each technology contains risks and uncertainties that must be weighed against the added human benefits and worthiness of a mission. The Chernobyl disaster raised serious questions about the safety of nuclear power, and the *Challenger* explosion about whether manned space missions are necessary.

Besides dealing with the physical environment, crisis managers face an intensified human climate. Activist groups confront their targeted organizations, insisting that their demands be addressed and their social grievances satisfied. Some groups with extreme agendas or tactics escalate confrontational crises into crises of malevolence, which must be treated differently.

The American public seeks empowerment on issues that affect its welfare, such as dangerous chemicals manufactured or stored in factories and warehouses and the location of toxic waste sites and nuclear power facilities. Interest groups formed by the public also seek to advance their social agendas.

The "dark mirror"[1214] of crises of malevolence shows that some groups, like the Animal Liberation Front (ALF), are so arrogant and angry that they will resort to extreme measures, including breakins, kidnappings, and sending of mail bombs, to achieve their aims. Other individuals and groups, such as extortionists or industrial spies, place self-interest ahead of any sense of fair play. And still others, like computer hackers, simply enjoy the thrill of outsmarting society without considering the harm caused. These more or less random attacks create a high degree of uncertainty for managers over which there is little or no control.

Pressures from the external environment, however, are not the only sources of crises. An increasing number of crises are self-imposed, as seen in the four types of crises of management failure described in this book: crises of mismanagement, crises of skewed values, crises of deception, and crises of misconduct. Managers must look inward and ask what they are doing wrong. Concentrating almost exclusively on the bottom line interests of investors creates stakeholder asymmetry, which the slighted stakeholders—consumers, community citizens, affirmative action groups, environmentalists and others—will attempt to correct. Stakeholders on the lose side of a win–lose equation seek changed corporate cultures that acknowledge their interests, a more representative corporate governance structure, and some form of social accountability. Consumer stakeholders in particular insist on "full and timely disclosure" of product information as a safeguard against such abuses as asbestos deaths, injury from silicone breast implants, and other health and safety menaces. And the victims of corporate misdeeds seek adherence to ethical standards and laws.

Crisis managers who have endured the crucible of coping with a crisis have seen the soul of their organizations, and of their own, exposed for better and for worse. They know what weaknesses need attention and what strengths to build upon.

Lessons Learned from Crises

In distilling their experience in dealing with crises, crisis managers have learned the following lessons:

Assess Personal and Organizational Vulnerability

If risk lurks, it is prudent to acknowledge its existence and identify it. Denial of threats is the most common and serious flaw in crisis management. Because denial is self-defeating and costly, crisis management begins in the pre-crisis phase with risk assessment and contingency planning. An all-out effort must be made to identify everything that could possibly go wrong, extending that thinking into worst scenario situations.

Crisis managers have learned that certain institutional characteristics may add to their organization's vulnerability. For example, when a company is classified as a "public corporation" and is perceived as the industry leader, it is more vulnerable because it is more likely to be targeted by government, pressure groups, and the media than are other companies. Similarly, on an individual level, a manager who works for one of these companies is more likely to become a victim of malevolence, such as being kidnapped. Furthermore, some industries using complex technologies like nuclear power or bioengineering have a reputation for being more risky and, therefore, vulnerable.

Considering the risks and uncertainties faced by the modern organization, crisis managers have learned to make decisions on the basis of incomplete and ambiguous information and to accommodate for unplanned events or unexpected shocks. They overcome the limitations and deficiencies of the former ideal type of organization known as bureaucracy, which conveniently assumes that the external environment is stable. In a bureaucracy there are no surprises; every type of expected event has been classified and assigned to specified bureaucrats. These traditional managers handle an event in a prescribed fashion, which focuses on certain facts and is tailored to specified organizational values. Non-routine happenings that might portend a crisis, therefore, tend to be ignored or mishandled.

Bureaucratic managers find it difficult, if not impossible to work under conditions of ambiguity and uncertainty. In contrast, the crisis manager differentiates between routine and uncommon types of decisions. When necessary, he or she is ready to engage in innovative thinking and vigilant problem solving (which are discussed below).

Look for Ways to Reduce Vulnerability

Staying out of harm's way is an obvious response to dangerous situations. People and organizations can decide not to locate in geographical areas vulnerable to natural disasters, although the search for scarce resources provides counter-motivations. By shunning or abandoning risky products lines, vulnerability is avoided.

Skewing risk analysis decisions toward lower risk solutions is another proven way to reduce vulnerability. In the infamous Pinto case, Ford's decision to keep a dangerous fuel tank design and to invest some of the saved money into a legal defense fund to pay for the claims of car-crash victims is now seen as irresponsible and foolhardy.[1215] Similarly, use of double-hulled oil tankers—at least in sensitive areas like Valdez, Alaska—is a way to reduce potential environmental damage. Weighing benefits against costs is a complex calculation.

When companies venture into risky areas, they must recognize the dangers and look for ways to make operations and products as safe as possible. Under the heading of "Responsible Care," the chemical industry has been taking many initiatives in this direction by designing closed-loop systems to minimize leakage of dangerous substances, storing smaller inventories, and installing more and better safety devices. In the event of an accident, contingency plans indicate what emergency resources are available and what procedures are to be used.

Public policies are often needed in the absence of adequate company policies. To prevent an overflowing population in Bhopal to live close to Union Carbide's factory, the local government should have imposed land use regulations. If floods are a periodic menace, the construction of dams, dikes, spillways and other suitable infrastructure must be undertaken. As San Francisco, Los Angeles, and Kobe, Japan, have learned, highways and buildings must be redesigned and, sometimes, retrofitted to reduce deaths, injuries and damage caused by earthquakes. Finally, vulnerability can be reduced through contingency plans that provide advance warning and evacuation from an impending disaster.

Exercise Constant Vigilance and Establish Monitoring Systems

Just as people listen to early morning news or scan their computers for the latest news to find out what's going on—and probably to see if there is anything to worry about—organizations must establish monitoring systems. The objective is twofold: to keep them apprized of threats and opportunities in the external environment and to audit critical organizational decisions and behavior.

Crisis managers have learned the importance of detecting and responding to "weak signals" that foretell "big trouble." They have established issues management systems to monitor events, issues and trends in the external environment that might impinge upon them. These systems involve staff units such as public relations, public affairs, law, purchasing, marketing, and human resources because of their "boundary-spanning" function. Even more important, crisis managers involve operating managers because their daily decisions cause or contribute to crises and their cooperation and involvement is needed to implement sound corporate public policy initiatives.

Communicate With and Relate to a
Wide Range of Stakeholders

In their contingency planning and decision-making, crisis managers should include a wide range of stakeholders and not only employees shown on the organizational chart. Their concerns, views, ideas, and reactions are important kinds of information. Within the organization, he or she seeks the counsel of colleagues and staff experts. Outside the organization, he or she communicates with and involves an ever-expanding number and variety of stakeholder groups: the financial community, consumers, special interest groups, government officials, politicians, social agencies, and community citizens and groups.

In dealing with stakeholders, managers are slowly learning to look for shared purposes and interests. They no longer close their minds to the views of others while single-mindedly seeking to gain acceptance of their own. Managers are learning to listen to the concerns of stakeholders and are ready to modify their own position when necessary and possible.

Communications

Management often acknowledges the importance of the public belatedly, after a crisis occurs, for a consequence of a crisis is that the organization is placed on the public stage and scrutinized. Managers give the news media highest priority because they have no choice—the media intrude themselves upon a crisis situation. A crisis manager is also aware that the special role accorded the news media in our society is to serve as a watchdog and, sometimes, reformer. Other publics, however, such as government officials, employees, stockholders, suppliers, and dealers must be given information during a crisis because they have a need to know. How these stakeholders are treated during a crisis is the test of the sincerity and soundness of the relationships and sets the foundation for future dealings.

Managers of large enterprises, whether they embrace the stakeholder concept or not, have been forced to "go public" and spend between a quarter and half of their time communicating. Crash courses in telecommunications have become a necessity. Executives learn how to outwit their media interviewers and to appear humane and convincing. They become "bilingual" in a special way—by understanding not only the cold language of economics but the warm language of human feelings. And they know that in today's media environment, images are as important as words.

They are also sharpening their skills in presenting their organization's position in a convincing manner to their various audiences—whether to their own employees or to lawmakers. A crisis manager knows that there is often a conflict between competing claims among stakeholders, especially in crises of confrontation and crises of management failure.[1216] The ethical prescription for business is to achieve a more equitable balance between corporate self-interest and the interests of others in society and, increasingly important, to safeguard the environment. Furthermore, the principle is recognized that all economic transactions also involve moral relationships.[1217] The marketplace focus on transactions or exchanges cannot displace the sociological concept that a relationship is also involved. At a minimum, managers must consider the basic moral question: Is anybody likely to get hurt from this transaction? This dimension is part of a manager's definition of job responsibilities.

Developing Relationships

An important lesson learned from crisis management is that an organization's regular stakeholders, including environmental groups, must be dealt with on a continuing basis. As public relations professionals advise, organizations must establish a relationship with relevant stakeholders.

To make a relationship meaningful, all involved parties must recognize one another's legitimacy and make an effort to understand the others' interests and views. Second, two-way communication must prevail. This means that an organization should to the extent possible provide "full and timely disclosure" of all information relevant to the other persons or groups. This is a lesson particularly drawn from corporate deception cases, such as the Enron and banking crisis cases.

The exchange of information for the purpose of gaining mutual understanding is a precursor to mutual accommodation that recognizes the principle of mutual benefit. An organization must be willing to discuss all matters of mutual interest with the aim of achieving a consensus. This is done by using such processes as public consultation, collaborative planning, and stakeholder negotiations.

One occasion for such public participation is the drafting of a contingency plan. Being willing to share decision-making with others, however, requires willingness by all parties to listen to the arguments of others and to change one's views and behavior. For example, if dependence on dangerous technology is to be lessened or harm to the environment reduced, customers must be willing to modify their wants. Some customers have already begun to cooperate with utility companies that encourage the use of energy efficient appliances and lighting fixtures.

Finally, the definition of a relationship must recognize its continuing, long-term nature. The consequences of management decisions and actions over time must be envisioned and responsibility extended into the future. One manifestation of this lengthened time perspective is product stewardship whereby a company takes customer product guarantees seriously and, when necessary, monitors the responsible use of a product.

Speed Up and Broaden the Decision-Making Process

Traditional industrial organizations are based on the principles of specialization and authority. Organizational tasks are divided up into specialist areas that are assigned to individuals who limit their authority to their sphere. The modern, "reinvented" and "reengineered" organization, however, places higher priority on the connection of specialists—that they consider the consequences of their actions beyond their own borders and endeavor to integrate their efforts.[1218] During a crisis this need is most evident. A crisis manager knows that an ever-widening spectrum of information is required for modern decision-making and that ways must be found to put it all together in a meaningful manner.

To cope with the large volume of data that must be absorbed and not succumb to the stress of information overload, managers must acquire new skills in selecting information, assigning weights, and synthesizing a wide range of variables. The danger of information overload and confusion must be avoided. As psychologists suggest, the process of selective perception must be applied so that people can sort out relevant from irrelevant information. A way to accomplish this difficult task is essentially to emulate the way computerized database software stores and retrieves information. However, participants in what has been called "The Information Age" must not forget a warning by public relations consultant Philip Lesly: ". . . information is not intelligence, it's only raw material." He adds, "Information merely feeds judgment, imagination, creatively and disciplined thinking." Thus he suggests that we call this "The Intelligence Age."[1219]

The crisis manager recognizes the importance and value of new decision-making approaches: innovative thinking, vigilant problem solving, and organizational learning. Traditional managers are adept at "maintenance learning," which is a type of learning designed to uphold an existing system. With such learning, managers acquire the fixed outlooks, methods and rules for dealing with known and recurring situations. When events overwhelm them, "shock learning" results.[1220] But even this kind of learning is inadequate because it produces solutions that are still made within the limits of expert knowledge or technical competence and designed for known conditions.

Management theorists, therefore, are proposing a more powerful type of learning, which Warren Bennis calls "innovative learning." Its principle components, he says, are anticipation and participation. Anticipation requires managers to be active and imaginative rather than passive and habitual, and to learn by listening to others. Contingency planning is an application of the anticipation aspect of innovative learning. The other aspect, participation, asks managers to shape events, rather than being shaped by them.[1221] The "shaping" strategy is a fundamental aspect of stakeholder management and issues management.[1222]

Stated another way by David A. Garvin, the need is for "building a learning organization," one that is "skilled at creating, acquiring, and transferring knowledge, and at modifying its behavior to reflect new knowledge and insights."[1223] Besides creating new ideas, the way work gets done must also be changed. Garvin says that learning organizations are skilled at five main activities: "systematic problem solving, experimentation with new approaches, learning from their own experience and past history, learning from the experiences and best practices of others, and transferring knowledge quickly."[1224] In addition, managers must cultivate the art of open, attentive listening and a willingness to be open to criticism.

Suggesting an innovative way in which organizations can make decisions when an event or problem overwhelms routine decision-making and exposes its inadequacy, Irving Janis proposes the system of "vigilant problem solving."[1225] The system is applicable to the non-routine decisions of both organizational policy making and crisis management. Vigilant problem solving must be used sparingly, however, because its rigorous approach requires more work and uses more resources than routine approaches. But because the quality of resultant decisions is higher, vigilant problem solving is justified when the stakes are high, such as crisis situations.

Once a challenge in the form of a threat or opportunity is recognized, a manager applying the vigilant problem-solving approach must undertake four basic steps:

1. Formulate the problem. Ask what requirements should be met—averting certain dangers, attaining certain goals, and keeping certain costs to tolerable levels. Also ask what the best direction for the solution seems to be, something that can be done by engaging in a top-of the-head survey of alternatives.

2. Use information resources. Ask what prior information can be recalled or retrieved, and what new information can be obtained from experts' forecasts, intelligence reports and analyses.

3. Analyze and reformulate. Ask whether there are any additions or changes in the requirements of Step 1; any additional alternatives; any additional information that might reduce uncertainties.

4. Evaluate and select by asking:

   • What are the pros and cons for each alternative?
   • Which alternative appears to be best?
   • Are any requirements unmet?
   • How can potential costs and risks be minimized?
   • What additional plans are needed for implementation, monitoring, and contingencies.[1226]

During a crisis, decisions must be made quickly and decisively so Janis's vigilant problem-solving process can only serve as guide and an inspiration to break out of the mould of traditional decision-making.

Apply a Variable Time Perspective

The risk of a crisis increases when managers use a short-term time perspective, which is often a year or less because it is based on the requirements of issuing quarterly financial statements. Instead of allowing a single, arbitrary time perspective to dominate, the crisis manager is flexible and able to examine immediate, short-term, and long-term impacts.

Managers must view a crisis from a long-term time perspective even though the compelling need is to make immediate decisions during a crisis to limit damage and regain control over events. The short-term view—expressed by some as why worry about the distant future when it might not have any relevance unless the immediate problem is solved—must be tempered by consideration of long-term consequences on organizational reputation and the effect on stakeholder relationships. Johnson & Johnson's handling of the Tylenol crisis established its future reputation and thereby enhanced its entire range of products. As some managers have bitterly learned, another reason why long-term implications cannot be avoided is because some crises are of an evolving nature. In these cases, managers must be able to sense weak signal and recognize their potential for escalating to a crisis threshold.

Consumers and consumerists take economists seriously when they conceive of a product as a stream of future services rather than a thing. Environmentalists think in terms of exceedingly long-term impacts, such as the destruction of the Earth's ozone layer, fears of the "roasting of plants and people," and of "spaceship earth" possessing only finite resources. As they recognize the endangered state of the Earth's ecology, managers, too, are beginning to think about long-term concepts such as product stewardship, tree farming (instead of "mining"), and recycling of resources.

Recognize the Importance of the Corporate Culture and its Supporting Structures

Corporate culture is a central concept of crisis management, as evident in the frequent reference made to it throughout the book. It determines how the external environment is perceived and how managers respond to it; it also permeates all aspects of managerial behavior. The corporate culture describes the inner soul of an organization. Because information has to be rapidly processed when a crisis strikes, a manager cannot wait until such time to try to figure out its mission and core values. Johnson & Johnson knew what its credo was and was guided by it. Sanlu floundered when its milk products were implicated in children's deaths; it forgot the importance of a corporate culture that stood for product quality and safety.

Many companies are now trying to decide on their attitude toward the environment—whether reluctantly to comply with the law and whether to subscribe to some provisions of such environmental codes as the Coalition for Environmentally Responsible Economies (Ceres), the Global Environmental Management Initiative (GEMI), or the Chemical Manufacturers Association's "Responsible Care." To avoid another *Exxon Valdez* crisis or other crisis of skewed values, companies must be clear on where they stand.

Ethical codes are an integral part of corporate culture, determining how fairly others will be treated and, more broadly, a company's willingness to go beyond profitmaking and be socially responsible. Ethical blindness is especially responsible for most crises of misconduct.

An organization's structure and reward systems must be compatible with, and re-enforce corporate values in general and ethical codes in particular. Starting with corporate governance on the top, the composition of the board of directors should include members who have responsibility for public policy issues. Depending on the industry, an organizational structure might include a vice president for health, safety, and the environment and/or a vice president for consumer affairs. Their authority and responsibility should be backed up by adequate internal reporting mechanisms and, where deemed appropriate, external social reports, such as the increased trend toward environmental annual reports.[1227] In large banks that have a large economic and social impact, consideration should be given to having public interest members on bank boards.

An organization's reward system must reflect and be consonant with its ethical code. If salaries, bonuses, and promotions are solely based on high sales performance, the temptation is high to ignore restrictions of an ethical code. And if performance and bonuses of top-level bankers is measured by reaching ever-higher profit levels, then they will be encouraged to take excessive risks at the expense of the public.

Organizational Renewal in the Aftermath of a Crisis

In the aftermath of a crisis when an organization reviews why things went wrong and seeks corrective solutions, the time is particularly opportune to start the transformational development process. Management consultants in this area have been crafting new skills and coining new concepts in a frantic effort to help organizations adapt to rapidly changing technologies and environments. Specific methodologies such as risk assessment, cost/benefit analysis, operations research, and systems approach help in solving specific problems as well as to understand interrelationships among them. The process known as organizational transformation explains how necessary changes in organizational goals, values, and behavior can be achieved.

Organizational Transformation

Organizational transformation (TD) is a process that seeks fundamental changes in the purpose, strategy, structure, and culture of an entire organization.[1228] TD asserts that no simple linear extrapolation from past behavior or incremental change associated with the related field of organizational development (OD) is adequate because of discontinuities in the pattern of events and trends. For this reason, OD is considered inadequate. Both OD and TD use powerful intervention techniques to address problems by individuals, groups, and the entire organization. TD, however, focuses more on large-scale change that "demands new ways of perceiving, thinking, and behaving."[1229]

OT requires consensus and commitment among members of an organization to succeed, so that it will not become just another program. In reviewing transformations that have succeeded and failed, Ralph Kilmann and Joyce Covin conclude: "Starting a transformation in advance of a crisis and without sufficient top management consensus about impending problems . . . raises the likelihood that it will become just another program."[1230] Mere programs and words transmitted in classes, memoranda, speeches, and glossy booklets are bound to fail. While these programs are attractive because they do not threaten the power of top managers, they fail to accomplish change. Furthermore, leaders must be able to translate the new external demands into real employee commitment to change by putting them in touch with creative realities and finding a theme with which people can identify, e.g., quality.

The burdens of executives who must manage their organizations in competitive marketplaces and volatile environments are enormous. They must expand their traditional repertories to include the insights obtained from the accumulating record of crises. Unless executives incorporate the additional modes of crisis management problem solving in their lexicon of competencies both they and their organizations will falter. But if executives adopt new perspectives and acquire new skills in dealing with expanded external environments, they will become leaders and their organizations will excel.

Organizations don't have to wait for a crisis to recognize the desirability of transforming their organizational cultures. Georgia Power Company initiated change to address two workplace issues of concern to it: that many workers would be retiring by 2020 and that recent Supreme Court decisions provided broader protection to employee claims of retaliation, discrimination and harassment.[1231] It followed a five-step process of cultural transformation that addressed both business and human capital needs for change:

- cultural analysis, focusing on priorities;
- leadership strategy and commitment;
- management buy-in, education and training;
- accountability;
- employee communications.[1232]

In its cultural analysis, Georgia Power identified management behaviors, especially those perceived as retaliatory, as a growing concern and a potential liability. J.R. Hipple and Felix Verdigets who participated in the program concluded: "By emphasizing core values of trust and inclusion, companies can help create a culture that is collaborative and effective."[1233]

Harmonizing Business and Society

An additional level has been added to OT: the relationship of an organization to society. As proposed by John D. Adams in *Transforming Work*, "OT will help a given organization explore its purpose and charter in relation to the larger environment and facilitate the necessary fundamental realignments."[1234] The objective is to make the interests of an organization congruent with the public interest. Having blind faith that free market forces will automatically do it through the operation of the invisible hand is unrealistic. It certainly has not worked in the financial industry. Neither is the practice of corporate social responsibility tantamount to upholding the public interest. The term free-market system has come to imply lax attitudes of laissez faire.

Even conservative economist Friedrich Hayek agreed that the economic system requires societal rule setting and guidance in which the government's fundamental role is twofold: to establish the "rule of law" that provides a reliable legal framework for business transactions, and, second, to enforce regulations within which markets can function efficiently.[1235] Conservative economist Milton Friedman also saw this need, warning, however, that government involvement in the economy should be kept at a minimum.[1236]

Include Civil Society

Government should not be the only arbiter of what is in the public interest. A healthier situation is to encourage and enable institutions in civil society, such as professional associations, to play a larger role in representing the public interest. Professional associations are delegated this right by government bodies, but as seen in crises of deception and misconduct they have egregiously violated that trust. One solution is to weaken the financial dependence on the very organizations they are intended to judge and to fortify the sanctions imposed by the professions. Business must be willing to surrender its virtual monopoly to define what is for the public good. A correction is now needed: The word "free" should be qualified to allow a larger role for government and civil society. Competition should be operative among all institutions of society.

As both Hayek and Friedman recognize, the free-market system needs a suitable infrastructure of supporting institutions. They say that one way government can help is to create an institutional structure that extends beyond the public sector through the development of private enterprise and organizations of civil society. Included among the latter are employers' organizations, industry associations, commercial associations, independent labor unions, employee groups, and professional associations. Also included are independent policy and advisory groups; a free press, television, and radio; gender, language, religious, and other social-interest groups; and community and neighborhood groups.

Public Affairs and Public Relations

The function of public affairs and public relations is to relate an organization to its external environment and to all the stakeholders who are connected to it. Public affairs specifically deals with government and the many civil society groups that make demands on the organization. Public relations engages in the larger task of managing the communications and relationships with all stakeholder groups and with the media, both mass media and social media. In the best practice of public relations, the goal is to build and maintain effective and healthy two-way symmetrical relationships.

There has been a tendency, especially in the management literature, to equate public relations solely with publicity. What is forgotten is that the modern concept of stakeholder relations is entirely patterned after the function of public relations. Regardless of the terminology used, the basic idea is that an organization recognizes its obligation to relate to the larger society. Community relations programs are illustrative of the many ways an organization works with local civil society organizations.

Corporate social responsibility, commonly referred to by its acronym CSR, is a laudable endeavor associated with public relations that relates an organization to the larger society. CSR engages in philanthropic endeavors that support artistic, educational and other charitable organizations and activities. CSR also requires an organization to reduce the social costs it imposes on society and to join government and civil society to help solve social problems. In its fullest meaning, CSR seeks to improve the lot of humankind. Despite these beneficial objectives, CSR by itself is only part of the larger mission of an organization to harmonize with society.

Don't Waste a Crisis!

A crisis is a turning point—in terms of medicine as well as in the life of an executive and that of an organization. The crisis literature emphasizes what has gone or can go wrong. Through its focus on dangers it neglects the opportunity that a crisis creates for renewal. People and organizations can learn from their failures and discover strengths that will triumph over weaknesses—that a renewed life will ensue, energized by a discovery of latent resources and new growth possibilities. A crisis should not be wasted.

Crises focus on hazards and risks. Its positive aspect is that mitigation efforts will be undertaken; the negative aspect is that too many risks may be avoided. The fear of losing, however, does not prevent the possibility of gaining. And by doing nothing, opportunities may be missed or squandered.[1237] The lesson of crisis management is to face up to risks and manage them carefully, just as the model Swedish athlete does by wearing all available safety gear.

Notes

1 Stephen Power, "Political Alliances Shift in Fight Over Climate Bill," Wall Street Journal, October 5, 2009, p. A6.
2 The term "human climate" is borrowed from Philip Lesly's newsletter, Managing the Human Climate, a bimonthly supplement of the weekly pr reporter (Exeter, N.H.).
3 Irving L. Janis, *Crucial Decisions: Leadership in Policymaking and Crisis Management* (New York: The Free Press, 1989), p. 45.
4 Rajdeep Grewal, Jean L. Johnson and Suprateek Sarker, "Crises in Business Markets: Implications for Interfirm Linkages," *Journal of the Academic Marketing Science*, Vol. 35, 2007, pp. 398–416.
5 Mark Sappenfield, "Cut Undersea Internet Cables Slow India's Connectivity," *Christian Science Monitor*, February 4, 2008, p. 4.
6 Ben Worthen, Cari Tuna and Justin Scheck, "Companies More Prone to Go 'Vertical," *Wall Street Journal*, November 30, 2009, pp. 1, 16.
7 Catherine Bolgar, "Corporate Resilience Comes From Planning, Flexibility and the Creative Management of Risk," *Wall Street Journal*, May 2, 2007, p. A12.
8 Peter Sanders, "Boeing Takes Control of Plant," *Wall Street Journal*, December 23, 2009, p. B2.
9 "Annual ICM Crisis Report," Institute for Crisis Management, March 2008, p. 2.
10 Ronald Alsop, "Institutions Engage More on Confronting Scandals," *Wall Street Journal*, April 17, 2007, p. B9.
11 Ibid.
12 David W. Guth, "Organizational Crisis Experience and Public Relations Roles," *Public Relations Review*, Vol. 21, Summer 1995, pp. 132–133.
13 Thierry C. Pauchant and Ian I. Mitroff, *Transforming the Crisis-Prone Organization: Preventing Individual, Organizational, and Environmental Tragedies* (San Francisco: Jossey-Bass, 1992), p. 12.
14 The sources of these crisis features are: M.W. Seeger, T. L. Sellnow and R. R. Ulmer, "Communication, Organization and Crisis," in M.E. Roloff (ed.) *Communication Yearbook*, Vol. 21 (Thousand Oaks, C.A.: Sage, 1998), pp. 231–275; Robert Billings, Thomas W. Milburn, and Mary Lou Schaalman, "A Model of Crisis Perception: A Theoretical and Empirical Analysis," *Administrative Science Quarterly*, Vol. 25, June, 1980, p. 301; Charles. F. Hermann, "Some Consequences of Crisis Which Limit the Viability of Organizations," *Administrative Science Quarterly*, Vol. 8, No. 1, pp. 61–82. Also see his "Some Issues in the Study of International Crises," in C. F. Hermann (ed.) *International Crises: Insights from Behavioral Research* (New York: The Free Press, 1972), pp. 3–17.
15 *Impact*, a newsletter of The Public Affairs Council, Washington, D.C., June 2007, p. 2.

16 Charles J. Fombrun and Naomi A. Gardberg, "The Reputation Quotient: Why and How to Measure Corporate Reputation," Vol. 4, No. 2 (May 2001), p. 24.

17 Ibid.

18 Bart J. Mindszenthy, T.A.G. Watson and William J. Koch, *No Surprises: The Crisis Communications Management System* (Toronto, Canada: Bedford House Communications Limited, 1988).

19 James I. Lukaszewski, *Crisis Communication Plan Components and Models* (White Plains, N.Y.: The Lukaszewski Group Inc., 2008).

20 "When Issues 'Go From Zero to 60' overnight, CEO Involvement Is Vital," *Impact*, a publication of the Public Affairs Council, December 2007, p. 3.

21 "Smouldering Crises," Annual ICM Crisis Report, May 2009, p. 4.

22 A prominent example of denial occurred when Toshiba top management ignored early warnings of an imminent crisis caused by one of its subsidiaries that sold military-sensitive machine tools to the former Soviet Union, in violation of the Coordinating Committee for Multilateral Export Controls (COCOM) agreement.

23 Pete Smuddle, "Issue Crisis: A Rose by Any Other name," *Public Relations Quarterly*, Vol. 46, Winter 2001.

24 "When Issues 'Go From Zero to 60' overnight, CEO Involvement Is Vital," *Impact*, a publication of the Public Affairs Council, December 2007, p. 3.

25 This factor is discussed in Richard L. Dahl, *Organization Theory and Design*, Third Edition (New York: West Publishing Company, 1989), pp. 196–197.

26 Patrick Lagadec, *Preventing Chaos in a Crisis: Strategies for Prevention, Control, and Damage Limitation*, trans., Jocelyn M. Phelps (London; New York: McGraw-Hill, 1993), pp. 32–33.

27 Ibid., pp. 65–67.

28 Christine M. Pearson and Judith A. Clair, "Reframing Crisis Management," *Academy of Management Review*, Vol. 23, No. 1, 1998, p. 62.

29 Ibid.

30 Ibid. Reference to T. Pauchant and I. Mitroff is found in their book, *Transforming the Crisis-Prone Organization* (San Francisco: Jossey-Bass, 1992).

31 Ibid., p. 63.

32 Joel Brockner and Erika Hayes James, "Toward an Understanding of When Executives See Crisis as Opportunity," *The Journal of Applied Behavioral Science*, Vol. 44, March 2008, p. 95.

33 Ibid., p. 104.

34 Ibid., p. 106.

35 Robert A. Guth and Keven J. Delaney, "Sky-High Search Wars," *Wall Street Journal*, May 24, 2005, p. B1.

36 "Crisis Group Opens," *PR Week* (US), July 14, 2008, p. 2, "Burson-Marsteller Launch New Practice," *PR Week* (US), January 19, 2009, p. 2.

37 www.wilson-group.com

38 "Managing Distress," *Business Wire*, August 20, 2001.

39 Charles B. Clayman (ed.) American Medical Association, *Family Medical Guide*, Third Edition (New York: Random House, 1994).

40 Ibid., pp. 86, 597.

41 W. Timothy Coombs, *Ongoing Crisis Communication: Planning, Managing, and Responding* (Thousand Island, C.A.,: Sage, 1999), p. 61.

42 See book review by Christopher Farrell, "Skirting the Disaster Ahead," *BusinessWeek*, December 20, 2004, p. 26.

43 "Pope Benedcit Assails 'Insatiable Consumption,'" *Wall Street Journal*, July 18, 2008, p. A6.

44 "Hurricanes: Storm Surge," *The Economist*, September 17, 2005, p. 81.

45 "We Have the Power. Do We Have the Wisdom?" the *Guardian* (London), January 1, 1999, p. 19.

46 Ibid.

47 Christopher Farrell, "Skirting the Disaster Ahead," a book review, *BusinessWeek*, December 20, 2004, p. 26.

48 Roger E. Kasperson and K. David Pijawka, "Societal Response to Hazards and Major Hazard Events: Comparing Natural and Technological Hazards," *Public Administration Review*, Special Issue 1985, p. 7. They reported that in the United States, geophysical hazards accounted for fewer than 1,000 fatalities per year, while the threat from technological development and application rose.

49 See Charles Perrow, *Normal Accidents: Living with High Risk Technologies* (New York: Basic Books, 1984).

50 With some technologies, such as nuclear power, there is an insufficient degree of slack or buffer between each component and sub-system to prevent the whole system from being affected and possibly running out of control. That is what almost happened at Three Mile Island when, over a 33-hour period, the famous hydrogen bubble appeared. The accident started in the secondary cooling system, which in turn was activated when, it is surmised, a leaky seal from the polishing system, contaminated a turbine and tripped (stopped) it. The flow of water was blocked because valves in the emergency feedwater pumps were mistakenly closed during maintenance two days before. In the control room, the operators did not see the indicator of the closed values because a repair tag obscured it. The general lesson is that failure of any part of the system could cause other malfunctions in unanticipated ways.

51 For a summary of the rise in government regulation see Rogene A. Buchholz, *Business Environment and Public Policy: Implications for Management and Strategy Formulation*, Second Edition (Englewood Cliffs, N.J.: Prentice-Hall, 1986), Chapter 8, pp. 171–203.

52 See Foundation for Public Affairs, Public Interest Profiles, 1992–1993 (Washington, D.C.: Congressional Quarterly, Inc., 1992).

53 Christine M. Pearson and Judith A. Clair, "Reframing Crisis Communication," *Academy of Management Review*, Vol. 23, No. 1, 1998, p. 68.

54 Mark A. Hofmann, "Interest in Enterprise Risk Management Is Growing," *Business Insurance*, May 4, 2009.

55 Shivan S. Subramaniam, "Management Trends . . . Keep It Simple: Getting Your Arms Around Enterprise Risk Management," *Executive Action Series*, No. 165 (New York: The Conference Board, October 2005), p. 1.

56 Douglas W. Hubbard, *The Failure of Risk Management: Why It's Broken and How to Fix It* (Hoboken, N.J.: John Wiley & Sons, Inc., 2009), p. 10.

57 Ibid., p. 11.

58 Ibid., p. 26.

59 Ibid., p. 27.

60 Ibid., p. 10.

61 Kenneth N. Myers, *Total Contingency Planning for Disasters: Managing Risk—Minimizing Loss—Ensuring Business Continuity* (New York: John Wiley & Sons, Inc., 1993).

62 Ibid., p. 147.

63 These are quantitative analysts with degrees such as Master of Science in Financial Engineering, Master of Science in Financial Math, and Master in Mathematical Finance. See "The Top 10 Quant Schools, According to the Street," *Wall Street & Technology*, August 1, 2008, p. 32.

64 "Survey of Quants Finds Risk Management Is Larger Part of Role," TECHWEB, August 10, 2009

65 Hubbard, op. cit., p. 3.

66 Ibid., p. 6. His long definition of risk is "The probability and magnitude of a loss, disaster, or other undesirable event."

67 Amy Jacques, "Domino's Delivers During Crisis," *The Strategist*, Vol. 15, Summer 2009, pp. 6–10.

68 Stephanie Clifford, "Video Prank At Domino's Taints Brand, *New York Times*, April 16, 2009, p. B1

69 Jacques, op. cit., p. 9.

70 Ibid. p. 88.

71 Ibid., p. 9.

72 "Message to Domino's: Contingency Planning Still Rules the Roost," press release by Nicolazzo & Associates, April 16, 2009.

73 Jacques, op. cit., p. 9.

74 Ibid.

75 Ibid.

76 Heather Martin, "Crisis Communication Plan—The Next Best Thing to Avoiding a Crisis; The Importance of Crisis Management Is Magnified Every Time a Crisis Ocurs," *New York Construction*, December 1, 2007, *The Bottom Line*, Vol. 55, No. 5, p. 109.

77 Ibid, pp. 3–4.

78 "BU Emergency Response," email dated May 15, 2007.

79 I.I. Mitroff and M.C. Alpaslan, "Preparing for Evil," *Harvard Business Review*, Vol. 81 (4) 2003, pp. 109–115. Mentioned by Carmeli and Schaubroeck (see below, Note 86), p. 180.

80 T. McCollum, "Multinationals Aren't Planning for Crisis Events", *The Internal Auditor*, Vol. 64, February 2007, pp. 13–14.

81 Ben Worthen, "Disaster-Plan Study Finds Firms Less Prepared Than They Think," *Wall Street Journal*, September 18, 2007, p. B3.

82 Ibid., p. B3.

83 "H1N1 Swine Flu Preparedness Uncertainty Results in Higher Business Disruption Risk; Crisis Communication Experts Provide Readiness Plan to Help Companies Plan for Possible Pandemic," PR Newswire, New York: September 10, 2009.

84 Thierry C. Pauchant and Ian I. Mitroff, *Transforming the Crisis-Prone Organization: Preventing Individual, Organizational, and Environmental Tragedies* (San Francisco: Jossey-Bass, 1992), p. 69.

85 The author performed this function at the Potdevin Machine Co. in Brooklyn, N.Y.

86 Abraham Carmeli and John Schaubroeck, "Organisational Crisis-Preparedness: The Importance of Learning from Failures," *Long Range Planning*, Vol. 41, 2008, p. 180.

87 "From Risk Management to Risk Strategy," The Conference Board, p. 4.

88 "Managing Business Risk in 2006 and Beyond" (www.protectingvalue.com). NA-based companies allocate more than half their risk management budget to risk control (loss prevention) rather than risk transfer (buying insurance).

89 Lublin and Tuna, op. cit.

90 Joann S. Lublin and Cari Tuna, "Anticipating Corporate Crises," *Wall Street Journal*, September 22, 2008, p. B5.

91 Joann S. Lublin and Erin White, "More Outside Directors Taking Lead in Crises," *Wall Street Journal*, March 19, 2007, pp. B1, B3.

92 Stuart Z. Goldstein, "Information Preparedness: Harnessing Technology," in Lloyd B. Dennis (ed.) *Practical Public Affairs in an Era of Change* (Lanham, N.Y.: University Press of America, Inc., 1995), pp. 329–346.

93 For a discussion of organizational responses to uncertainty see Richard L. Daft,

Organization Theory and Design, Fourth Edition (New York: West Publishing Company, 1992), pp. 84–89.

94 See www.crisisexperts.com/vulnerability

95 "Annual ICM Crisis Report," —2008 (Louisville, Kentucky: Institute for Crisis Management, May 2009), p. 3.

96 Two useful books are Laurence Barton's *Crisis in Organizations: Managing and Communicating in the Heat of Chaos* (Cincinnati, Ohio: South-Western Publishing Co., 1993) and Jack A. Gottschalk's *Crisis Response: Inside Stories on Managing Image Under Siege* (Detroit, M.I.: Visible Ink Press, a division of Gale Research Inc., 1993).

97 Ian I. Mitroff, *Why Some Companies Emerge Stronger and Better from a Crisis: 7 Essential Lessons for Surviving Disaster* (New York: AMACOM, 2005), p. 98.

98 This is one of four perspectives of completeness in risk assessment. Hubbard, op. cit., p. 48.

99 This classification is based on Exxon Chemical's Emergency Response External Communications Guidelines, 1990.

100 David Ignatius, "The Death of 'National Man'," *Washington Post,* February 8, 2009, p. B07. Also see Hubbard, op. cit., pp. 247–248.

101 Adolf A. Berle, Jr. and Gardner C. Means, *The Modern Corporation and Private Property* (New York: Macmillan, 1932), p. 46.

102 Robert S. Greenberger, "Eminent Domain to Get a Review," *Wall Street Journal,* September 29, 2004, p. A6.

103 "An American's Home is Still Her Castle," *The Economist,* November 25, 2006, p. 36.

104 A point made by Thierry C. Pauchant and Ian I. Mitroff, op. cit., in Chapter 2, "When People and Systems Fail: Lessons from Bhopal," op. cit., p. 34.

105 Dan Keeney, "In the Eye of the Storm: Ten PR Lessons Learned from Hurricane Ike," *Tactics,* a publication of the Public Relations Society of America, November 2008, p. 9.

106 Charles Perrow, *Normal Accidents: Living with High Risk Technology* (New York: Basic Books, 1984), p. 20.

107 Carmeli and Schaubroeck, op. cit., p. 178.

108 For a list of who is represented on a crisis management team and percentage of respondents who mention each position, see Pauchant and Mitroff, op. cit., p. 110.

109 This is a point emphasized by David W. Guth in "Organizational Crisis Experience and Public Relations Roles," *Public Relations Review,* Vol. 21, No. 2, 1995, p. 127.

110 Laura Wetherell, "Crisis Management: Dealing With a Disaster—Bad News Has Become Big Business. Now two leading PR Firms Are Launching All-In Services Ready for the Next Crisis to Erupt," *PR Week,* June 28, 1990.

111 Kyra Auffermann, "'It Still Chokes Me Up'—Responding to a Deadly Campus Shooting at Northern Illinois University," *The Strategist,* Vol. 15, Summer 2009, p. 14.

112 Suggestion by Chris Mundy, "Crisis Simulation—Coping with the Unexpected," *Petroleum Economist,* Vol. 60, October, 1993, p. 66.

113 Cheryl Fenelle, "Lessons Learned: The Response to TWA Flight 800," *Risk Management,* November 11966, Vol. 43, No. 11, p. 58(1).

114 Om P. Kharbanda and Ernest A. Stallworthy, "Planning for Emergencies—Lessons from the Chemical Industry," *Long Range Planning,* Vol. 22, February 1989, p. 88.

115 Stacy Shapiro, "Spotlight Report: International Risk and Benefit Management; Many Multinationals Are Failing to Plan for All Contingencies; All Too

Often, Planning for Crisis Takes Backseat to Other Priorities," *Business Insurance*, November 6, 1995, p. 3.

116 Gonzalez-Herrero Alfonso and Ruiz de Valbuena Miguel, "Trends in Online Media Relations: Web-Based Corporate Press Rooms in Leading International Companies," *Public Relations Review*, Vol. 32, No. 3, 2006, pp. 267–275.

117 Gerald Baron and John Philbin, "Social Media in Crisis Communication: Start with a Drill," *Tactics*, April 2009, p. 12.

118 Ibid.

119 Alfonso and Miguel, op. cit., p. 268.

120 "The End of Newsrooms?" www.prsa.org.

121 Ibrey Woodall, "From Old Media to Social Media: Survey Reveals the Essential Elements for Today's Online Newsroom," *Tactics*, June 2009, p. 17. The 2009 survey can be found at: www.tekgroup.com/research

122 Ibid.

123 Carmeli and Schaubroeck, op. cit., p. 189.

124 Ibid., p. 190.

125 "Psychology's Ambassador to Economics. The Father of Behavioural Economics Daniel Kahneman talks to Vikram Khanna About Cognitive Illusions, Investor Irrationality and Measures of Well-Being," *The Business Times* (Singapore), July 12, 2008.

126 Carmeli and Schaubroeck, op. cit., p. 182.

127 Joel Brockner and Erika Hayes James, "Toward an Understanding of When Executives See Crisis as Opportunity," *The Journal of Applied Behavioral Science*, Vol. 44, March 2008, p. 181.

128 Carmeli and Schaubroeck, op. cit., p. 181.

129 This case is reviewed in the original edition of this book, Otto Lerbinger, *The Crisis Manager: Facing Risk and Responsibility* (Mahwah, N.J.: Lawrence Erlbaum Associates, Publishers, 1997), pp. 192–194.

130 Yukari Twatani Kane, "Sony Apologizes for Battery Recall," *Wall Street Journal*, October 25, 2006, p. B2.

131 Melissa K. Flynn, "First Response: The Importance of Acting Within Minutes, Not Hours," *Tactics*, April 2009, p. 13.

132 James E. Lukaszewski, *Crisis Communication Plan Components and Models* (White Plains, N.Y.: The Lukaszewski Group Inc., 2008).

133 Flynn, op. cit.

134 "The New Crisis Landscape," *PR Week*, February 19, 2007, p. 12.

135 Ibid.

136 This case is partly based on a term paper by Kristie Volante, "Crisis Report: The Sinking of the Russian Submarine—Kursk," November 8, 2000, written for graduate course on crisis management at Boston University's College of Communication.

137 Daniel Williams, "Russian Sub Stranded at Sea Bottom," *Washington Post* Foreign Service, August 15, 2000, p. 1.

138 Yevgenia Borisova, "A Nation Asks: Has Enough Been Done?" *The Moscow Times*, August 18, 2000, p. 1.

139 David Filipov, "Letter From Deep Revives Sub Tragedy," *Boston Globe*, October 27, 2000, p. A1.

140 CNN.com "Anger Grows Amid Vigils for the Kursk Crew," August 18, 2000, p. 2.

141 Foreign Desk Staff, "Putin Flies to Moscow As Relatives Shun Ceremonies," *The Irish Times*, August 24, 2000, p. 2.

142 Much background information was provided by C. Nina Handoko in a paper for a crisis management course at Boston University's College of

Communication, "Understanding and Managing Crisis of Clergy Sexual Misconduct in the Roman Catholic Church," November 8, 2000.

143 Some articles by Jason Berry are "Church Strikes Back At Priests' Accusers," *The
Atlanta Journal and Constitution*, May 1, 1994; "Listening to the Survivors: Voices of
People of God," *America*, November 13, 1993, p. 6.

144 Geoghan was convicted in January 2002 and faces scores of lawsuits that charge
he sexually abused 130 children over the three decades he served as a priest in
several Massachusetts parishes. Daniel J. Wakin, "Facing a Sin Of the Fathers,"
New York Times, February 17, 2002, p. WK5.

145 See Carl M. Cannon's "The Priest Scandal" in the May 2002 issue of *American
Journalism Review*.

146 "Sex and the Catholic Church: Wolves in the Flock," *The Economist*, March 30,
2002, p. 12.

147 For more information, see Cannon, op. cit.

148 Laurie Goodstein, "A Time to Bend," *New York Times*, June 16, 2002, p. NE1

149 From an interview with Susan Gibbs, "The Decentralized Network of the Catholic Church Underscores the Role of Leadership, Structure in Crisis," *pr reporter*,
April 8, 2002.

150 Ibid.

151 Ibid.

152 Ibid.

153 Andrew Higgins, "How Muslim Clerics Stirred Arab World Against Denmark,"
Wall Street Journal, February 2, 2006, p. A1.

154 John G. Knight, Bradley S. Mitchell and Hongzhi Gao, "Riding Out the Muhammad Cartoons Crisis: Contrasting Strategies and Outcomes," *Long Range Planning*,
Vol. 42 (2009), p. 9.

155 Ibid., p. 13.

156 Lukaszewski, op. cit.

157 Ibid.

158 George S. Lowman, "The Calnev Pipeline Fire," in Jack A. Gottschalk, *Crisis
Response: Inside Stories on Managing Image Under Siege* (Detroit, M.I.: Visible Ink Press,
1993), pp. 263–276.

159 Chester Burger, "How to Meet the Press," *Harvard Business Review*, Vol. 53, July–
August 1975, pp. 62–70.

160 Cincinnati Microwave Inc. did this. After being visited by a *Business Week* reporter
who asked some sensitive questions, company officials in painstaking detail shared
some of their responses in a national news release. The company listed a number
of rumors and allegations that were not even raised by the reporters, e.g., that the
company didn't pay taxes and inflated sales projections to boost its stock. Matt
Murray, "Journalism 101: First You Read Story, Then You Comment on It,"
Wall Street Journal, September 28, 1995, p. B1.

161 Greg Efthimiou, "Balance of Power," *The Public Relations Strategist*, Vol. 14, No. 2,
2008, p. 47.

162 Ibid., p. 46.

163 Ibid., p. 47.

164 Lukaszewski, op. cit.

165 Mentioned in Lagadec, op. cit., p. 188.

166 Ibid., p. 105.

167 Many of these questions are suggested by Alan B. Bernstein, *The Emergency Public
Relations Manual* (New Brunswick, N.J.: PASE Inc., 1981), pp. 32–33.

168 Matthew Rose discusses this selection in "CEO as Crisis Spokesperson? Think
Again," *The Strategist*, Vol. 14, Fall, 2008, pp. 16–19.

169 Quote in Lagadec, op. cit., p. 109. Original source is Sharon M. Friedman,

"TMI: The Media Story," in Lynne Masel Walters, Lee Wilkins and Tim Walters (eds.), *Bad Tidings: Communication and Catastrophes* (Hillsdale, N.J.: Lawrence Erlbaum Associates, Publishers, 1989), pp. 63–83.

170 These events and quotations are from Richard Hyde, "Meltdown on Three Mile Island," in Jack A. Gottschalk, *Crisis Response: Inside Stories on Managing Image Under Siege* (Detroit, M.I.: Visible Ink Press, 1993), pp. 114–117.

171 Jessica E. Vascellaro and Amol Sharma, "BlackBerry Users Stew in Wake of Outage," *Wall Street Journal*, April 20, 2007, p.B4.

172 Case is described in Otto Lerbinger, *The Crisis Manager: Facing Risk and Responsibility* (Mahwah, N.J.: Lawrence Erlbaum Associates, Publishers, 1997), p. 42.

173 Doughty, op. cit., p. 351. After USAir's Flight 427 crashed near Pittsburgh, Pennsylvania, on September 8, 1994, airline employees carefully followed prescribed rules in referring to the passenger manifest. Showing extreme sensitivity to the family and friends, employees were told not to say to callers, "Yes, sir. She was on the plane." Instead, they said, "Yes, sir. Her name is on the list." The rationale is: why falsely alarm someone if perchance a passenger didn't make the flight or someone else used the ticket. Julie Schmit and Del Jones, "The First 24 Hours — How USAir Coped with the Crash," *USA Today*, September 12, 1994, p. 1B.

174 This case is discussed in Otto Lerbinger, *Corporate Public Affairs: Interacting With Interest Groups, Media, and Government* (Mahwah, N.J.: Lawrence Erlbaum Associates, Publishers, 2006), pp. 102–103.

175 Lukaszewski, op. cit.

176 For example, W. L. Benoit, *Accounts, Excuses, and Apologies: A Theory of Image Restorations* (Albany, NY: SUNY Press, 1995), and Keith Michael Hearit, *Crisis Management by Apology* (Mahwah, N.J.: Erlbaum, 2006).

177 Hearit, op. cit., p. 4.

178 Ibid., pp. 15–17.

179 Ibid., p. 17.

180 Ibid., pp. 17–18.

181 Benoit, op. cit.

182 Hearit, op. cit.

183 W. T. Coombs, Ongoing Crisis Communication (Thousand Oaks, C.A.: Sage, 1999).

184 Ibid., p. 126.

185 Coombs, op. cit., p. 123.

186 Hearit, op. cit.

187 Aaron Lazare, *On Apology* (Oxford, N.Y.: Oxford University Press, 2004).

188 Ibid., p. 263.

189 Ibid., p. 1.

190 Barbara Kellerman, "When Should a Leader Apologize and When Not?" *Harvard Business Review*, Vol. 84, April 2006, pp. 73–81.

191 Laurent Belsie, "The Rise of the Corporate Apology," *Christian Science Monitor*, September 13, 2000, p. 1.

192 Hearit, op. cit., pp. 19–39.

193 Phred Dvorak, "Japanese Dairy Pour on the Apologies," *Wall Street Journal*, July 12, 2000, p. A21.

194 Alan Murray, "JetBlue: Now Just Another Airline in a Lousy Business," *Wall Street Journal*, February 21, 2007, p. A13.

195 Maria Bartiromo, "Neeleman Explains Himself," *BusinessWeek*, March 5, 2007, p. 90.

196 Susan Carey, "Changing the Course of JetBlue," *Wall Street Journal*, June 21, 2007, p. B1.

197 "Jonathan Russell Asks Is It Too Much to Expect An Apology?" *The Daily Telegraph* (London), February 9, 2009, p. 4.

198 Ibid.

199 Ibid.

200 Liam Christopher, "We're Profoundly Sorry, Say Bail-Out Banks Ex-Bosses; Regret As RBS Reveals Plan to Axe 2,300 jobs," *Daily Post* (Liverpool), February 11, 2009, pp. 4, 11.

201 *The Daily Star* was particularly severe in its judgment, as its story's headline indicated: Tom Savage, "Sorry . . . But We're Keeping Our Dosh & Sacking 2,300; Bankers Get a Grilling," *The Daily Star*, February 11, 2009, p.4.

202 Ibid.

203 "Economic Reflections; Bailouts, Stimulus Carry Ugly Long-Term Costs," *USA Today*, February 13, 2009, p. 8A.

204 Liam Pleven, "Congress Grills Former AIG Chiefs," *Wall Street Journal*, October 8, 2008, p. A3.

205 Monica Langley and David Enrich, "Citigroup Chafes under U.S. Overseers," *Wall Street Journal*, February 25, 2009, p. A12.

206 Alfred A. Marcus and Robert S. Goodman "Victims and Shareholders: The Dilemmas of Presenting Corporate Policy During a Crisis," *Academy of Management Journal*, Vol. 34, No. 2, 1991, pp. 281–305.

207 Ibid., p. 284.

208 Ibid.

209 Ibid., p. 291.

210 Ibid., p. 282.

211 Ibid., p. 291.

212 Kai Ryssdal, "Author Paul Slansky Discusses His Book *My Bad: 25 Years of Public Apologies* on 'Marketplace'," Minnesota Public Radio, May 10, 2006.

213 Hearit, op. cit., pp. 134, 146. Ford announced a recall of 47,000 of its Year-2002 Explorer and Mercury Mountaineer SUVs. Joseph B. White, Timothy Appel and Clare Ansberry, "Ford Plans to Recall 47,000 Year-2002 SUVs," *Wall Street Journal*, May 21, 2001, p. A3. As stated earlier, the simmering crisis boiled over with *USA Today*'s August 7th story.

214 Hearit, ibid., p. 134.

215 "Ford, A Crisis of confidence," *BusinessWeek*, September 18, 2000, pp. 40–42.

216 "Ford Put Profit Ahead of Safety in Explorer Design," *Los Angeles Times*, September 10, 1990, p. C2.

217 Anthony Flint, "Firestone Fighting to Preserve Image With Recall, Company Implements Strategy to Minimize Damage," *Boston Globe*, August 11, 2000, p. C1.

218 Caroline Mayer and James V. Grimaldi, "Tires Linked to 80 Deaths; NHTSA Asks About Ford Policy Abroad," *Washington Post*, August 31, 2000, p. E01.

219 Kellerman, op. cit.

220 James v. Grimaldi, "Firestone CEO Says Apology Wasn't Admission of Fault," *Washington Post*, October 10, 2000, p. E02.

221 Hearit, op. cit., p. 141.

222 Miki Tanikawa, "Bridgestone President Admits Tire Quality-Control Problems," *New York Times*, September 12, 2000, p. C12.

223 Frank Swoboda, "CEO Nasser, Not Chairman Ford, in Front Seat for Crisis," *Washington Post*, September 10, 2000, p. H01.

224 "Internal PR Efforts at Ford Keep Employees Informed," *PR Week*, October 2, 2000, p. 2.

225 "Hummer Picks New Ad Agency," *Automotive News*, October 16, 2000, p. 1.

226 Robert L. Simson, "For Ford CO Nasser Damage Control Is the New 'Job One,'"

Wall Street Journal, September 11, 2000, p. A1. Also see Ford's press release, "Statement of Jac Nasser, Chief Executive Officer of Ford Motor Company, September 6, 2000."

227 Robert L. Simison, "Ford Pressures Firestone to Release Recall Statistics; Auto Maker Annoyed with Tire Company's Handling of Massive Plan," The Globe and Mail (Canada), August 14, 2000, p. B6.

228 Kathryn Kranhold, "Bridgestone Turns to Ketchum to Redo Image After Tire Recall," Wall Street Journal, September 12, 2000, p. A4.

229 Ibid.

230 Todd Zaun, "Bridgestone Lets Firestone Be Firestone," Wall Street Journal, May 24, 2001, p. A14.

231 Marie Szaniszlo and Eric Convey, "Contrition—Law's Apology Draws Mixed Reaction From Faithful," The Boston Herald, March 10, 2002, p. 001.

232 Rose Moss, "A Clergy Ill Prepared to Deal With Scandal," New York Times, February 16, 2002, p. A19.

233 See "Title III: The Right to Know, the Need to Plan," Chemecology, March 1987, p. 2.

234 Philip Shabecoff, "Industry to Give Vast New Data on Toxic Perils," New York Times, February 14, 1988, p. 38; also see p. 1.

235 David L. Schultz, "Toxic Chemical Disclosure: Companies Tackle the Challenge," Public Relations Journal, Vol. 45, January 1989, pp. 13–20.

236 Terry McDermott and Carol M. Ostrom, "Face Facts: Living Is a Risky Business," The Seattle Times, February 9, 1993, p. A1.

237 Irving Lerch, "Risk and Fear," New Scientist, Vol. 85, January 3, 1980, pp. 8–11.

238 The public is also more concerned about toxic waste dumps and underground storage tanks than it is about indoor air pollution and pesticide residues, which pose greater health risks. See "Public and Experts See Risks Differently," Chemecology, Vol. 19, February 1990, p. 9.

239 William W. Lowrance, Of Acceptable Risk: Science and the Determination of Safety (Los Altos, C.A.: Kaufmann, 1976), p. 87.

240 Ann E. Przybyla, "Risk: How to Talk About It," Food Engineering, January 1990, pp. 73ff.

241 Albert H. Cantril (ed.) Polling on the Issues (Washington, D.C.: Seven Locks Press, 1980), p. 82.

242 Robert L. DuPont, "The Nuclear Power Phobia," BusinessWeek, September 7, 1981, p. 14.

243 Ibid.

244 Paul Slovic, "Perception of Risk," Science, Vol. 236, April 17, 1987, pp. 280–285.

245 Robert L. DuPont, "The Nuclear Power Phobia," Business Week, September 7, 1981, p. 14. Also see Billie Jo Hance, Caron Chese, and Peter M. Sandman, "Improving Dialogue with Communities: A Risk Communication Manual for Government" (Trenton, N.J.: Division of Science and Research Risk Communication Unit, New Jersey Department of Environmental Protection, 1988).

246 Gregg Easterbrook, "The Sky Is Falling," The Atlantic Monthly, June 2008, pp. 74–84.

247 Michio Kaku, "Russia Takes Aim at Asteroids," Wall Street Journal, January 6, 2009, p. A13.

248 Ibid., p. 78.

249 Ray Kurzweil, The Singularity Is Near: When Humans Transcend Biology (New York: Penguin Group, 2005), pp. 405–406.

250 Among those making this distinction is Robert Tickner, "Reducing the Risk of Chaos After Natural Disasters," The Canberra Times, October 10, 2007, p. A15.

251 Marja Eurgenia Ibarraran, Matthias Ruth, Sanjana Ahma, and Marisa

London, "Climate Change and Natural Disasters: Macroeconomic Performance and Distributional Impacts," *Environment Development and Sustainability*, Vol. 11, 2009, pp. 549–579. The authors define disasters as events that have natural causes and lead to 10 or more fatalities, affect 100 or more people, or result in a call for international assistance or the declaration of a state of emergency.

252 Ibid.

253 Joorn Birkmann and Korinna von Teichman, "Integrating Disaster Risk Reduction and Climate Change Adaptation: Key Challenges,—Scales, Knowledge, and Norms," *Sustainability Science*, Vol. 5, Issue 2, July 2010, p. 17.

254 Betty Kotevski, "Flooding Puts Pressure on Australian Investors," *Investor and Pension Asia*, January 14, 2011.

255 Caroline McDonald, "Munich Re Initiates Climate Change Debate As Global Summit Begins," *National Underwriter Property & Casualty/Risk & Benefits Management*, December 1, 2010, News Section No. 12.

256 Anisya Thomas and Lynn Fritz, "Disaster Relief, Inc.," *Harvard Business Review*, Vol. 83, November 2006, pp. 114–122.

257 Byron Scott, "Tsunami Coverage: Slow to Start, Left Us Wanting More," *The Global Journalist*, First Quarter 2005, p. 15.

258 Frances D'Emilio, "Aid Teams Head to Countries Devastated by Tidal Waves," Associated Press Worldstream, December 26, 2004, International News.

259 "Asia's Devastation—Asia's Devastation; the Tsunami," *The Economist*, January 1, 2005, p. 9

260 Jackie Calmes, Ann Carrns, and Jeff D. Opdyke, "New Architecture: As Gulf Prepares to Rebuild, Tensions Mount Over Control," *Wall Street Journal*, September 15, 2005, p. A1.

261 Ibid.

262 Joel Kotkin, *The City: A Global History* (Modern Library, 2005)

263 "New Orleans," *Wall Street Journal*, September 1, 2005, p. A10.

264 Loretta Chao, "In China, Stranded for the Holidays," *Wall Street Journal*, February 1, 2008, p. A6.

265 Jake Hooker and Jim Yardley, "Powerful Quake Ravages China, Killing Thousands," *New York Times*, May 13, 2008, p. 1.

266 "Quake Expert Warns of Aftershocks in Southwest China," BBC Monitoring Asia Pacific –Political, May 12, 2008.

267 "Premier Keeps Promise with Beichuan Students," *Chinadaily.com.cn*, September 2, 2008.

268 Jose de Cordoba and David Luhnow, "Ferocious Earthquake Rocks Haiti," *Wall Street Journal*, January 13, 2010, p. A1. The casualty figure was estimated later.

269 Jose de Cordoba, "Haiti Needs $11.5 Billion, Report Says," *Wall Street Journal*, March 16, 2010, A12.

270 Miriam Jordan, "In Haiti's Tent Cities, Social Order Emerges," *Wall Street Journal*, March 8, 2010, p. A17.

271 "Dionne Searcey and Kevin Noblet, "Time running Out for Haiti Survivors," *Wall Street Journal*, January 16–17, 2010, pp. A1, A6.

272 Christine Kenneally, "The Inferno," *The New Yorker*, October 26, 2009, pp. 46–53. "Australia's Wildfires: The Burning Bush," *The Economist*, February 14, 2009, p. 49.

273 Geoffrey Rogow and Gavin Lower, "Waterlogged Brisbane Begins Cleanup," *Wall Street Journal*, January 15–16, 2011, p. A11.

274 Enda Curran, "Deadly Floods Slam Australian Region," *Wall Street Journal*, January 12, 2011, p. A8.

275 Geofrey Rogow and David Fickling, "Australia's Flood Exact Economic Toll," *Wall Street Journal*, January 6, 2011, p. A13.

276 David Fickling, Enda Curran, and Rachel Pannett, "Australia Floods Peak Woes Rise," *Wall Street Journal*, January 13, 2011, p. A9.

277 Kotevski, op. cit.

278 Audrey E. Kramer, "Russian Villages Ravaged by Wildfires; Thousands Are Homeless and Dozens Are Killed as Heat Wave Sweeps Region," *International Herald Tribune*, July 31, 2010, p. 3.

279 "Floods in Pakistan: After the Deluge," *The Economist*, August 21, 2010, p. 10; Zahid Hussain, "Millions of Children Face Cholera Risk Amid Floods," *Wall Street Journal*, August 17, 2010, p. A9.

280 This section is inspired by Roger E. Kasperson and K. David Pijawka, "Societal Response to Hazards and Major Hazard Events: Comparing Natural and Technological Hazards," *Public Administration Review*, Special Issue, Vol. 45, January 1985, pp. 7–28. Also see entire issue, which is titled "Emergency Management: A Challenge for Public Administration," edited by William J. Petak.

281 Ibid.

282 Robert Block, "Hearings to Shape FEMA's Future," *Wall Street Journal*, September 15, 2005, p. A12.

283 Based on summary by Waugh and Hy, ibid., pp. 2–3.

284 Sian Powell, "Extreme Disasters on the Rise," *The Australian*, All-round Country Edition, August 21, 2007, p.8.

285 Kotevski, op. cit.

286 Waugh and Hy, op. cit., p. 66.

287 Michael Corkery and Ann Carrns, "Supersizing the Levees," *Wall Street Journal*, September 21, 2005, p. A15.

288 Robert Block, Amy Schatz, Gary Fields, and Christopher Cooper, "Power Failure: Behind Poor Katrina Response, a Long Chain of Weak Links," *Wall Street Journal*, September 6, 2005, p. A1.

289 Ann Zimmerman and Valerie Bauerlein, "At Wal-Mart, Emergency Plan Has Big Payoff," *Wall Street Journal*, September 12, 2005, pp. B1, B3.

290 Unfortunately, some communities lack local media. When a train derailment released a toxic cloud of anhydrous ammonia in the small North Dakota city of Minot, local police were unable to broadcast an alert because the six local commercial radio stations were owned by radio giant Clear Channel Communications, which was piping in music and news talk from a remote location. See Will Harper, "Rethinking the Media Monopoly," *East Bay Express* (California), July 7, 2004, in news and features section.

291 Dan Keeney, "In the Eye of the Storm: Ten PR Lessons Learned from Hurricane Ike," *Tactics*, a publication of the Public Relations Society of America, November 2008, p. 9.

292 Joe Hagan and Joseph T. Hallinan, "Why Levee Breaches in New Orleans Were Late-Breaking News," *Wall Street Journal*, September 12, 2005, p. B1.

293 Ibid., p. B4.

294 Ibid.

295 Ibid.

296 Andi Djatmiko, "Death Toll from Tidal Waves mounts to Around 44,000," The Associated Press, December 28, 2004, International News.

297 Patrick Barta and Yayu Yuniar, "Rising Indonesia Tsunami Toll Exposes Flaws in Alert System," *Wall Street Journal*, October 29, 2010, p. A12.

298 Ibid.

299 Mei Fong, "Technology Helped News Spread Quickly," *Wall Street Journal*, May 13, 2008, p. A14.

300 Ibid.

301 "Tsunami Warnings: Run Like the Wind," *The Economist*, January 1, 2005, p. 18.

302 "Escape Snafus: U.S. Power Plants Have Fouled Up Disaster Drills," *Wall Street Journal*, May 9, 1986, p. 8.

303 See Patrick Lagadec, *Preventing Chaos in a Crisis: Strategies for Prevention, Control and Damage Limitation*, translated by Jocelyn M. Phelps (London: McGraw-Hill Book Company, 1993), pp. 305, 337–338.

304 Corey Boles, "Clearing Emergency Radio Waves," *Wall Street Journal*, August 7, 2007, p. A4.

305 Kenneally, op. cit., p. 46.

306 "Chinese President Visits Quake-Hit People in Beichuan County, Sichuan 16 May," BBC Monitoring Asia Pacific—Political.

307 Shai Oster, "Rescue Effort Overwhelms China," *Wall Street Journal*, May 15, 2008, p. A1.

308 Robert Block, Amy Schatz and Gary Fields, "Power Failure: Behind Poor Katrina Response, a Long Chain of Weak Links," *Wall Street Journal*, September 6, 2005, p. A1.

309 Robert Block, "U.S. Had Plan for Crisis Like Katrina," *Wall Street Journal*, September 19, 2005, p. A3.

310 Robert Block, "FEMA Points to Flaws, Blubs in Terror Drill," *Wall Street Journal*, October 31, 2003, p. B1.

311 Alternative: Rowan Callick, "Beijing at Best in Response to Crisis—China Quake," *The Australian*, May 14, 2008, p. 22.

312 James T. Areddy, "China Tries to Help Its Homeless," *Wall Street Journal*, May 21, 2008, p. A15.

313 Ibid.

314 Chad Terihune, "Along Battered Gulf, Katrina Aid Stirs Unintended Rivalry," *Wall Street Journal*, 9/29/05, pp. A1 & A8.

315 Alan Murray, "The Profit Motive Has a Limit: Tragedy," *Wall Street Journal*, Sept. 7, 2005, p. 12.

316 Ad in *Wall Street Journal*, September 7, 2005, p. A13.

317 Murray, op. cit.

318 Susan Warren, "Employers Struggle to Pick Up Pieces," *Wall Street Journal*, September 1, 2005, p. A6.

319 Michelle Krupa, "Report: N.O. Is Poised to Bounce Back; But Post-Katrina Data Not All Favorable," *Times-Picayune*, August 4, 2010, p. B01.

320 Kevin McGill, "Post-Katrina Report a Mixed Bag for New Orleans," The Associated Press State & Local Wire, August 4, 2010.

321 Michael M. Phillips and Cynthia Crossen, "Will New Orleans Rebound?" *Wall Street Journal*, Sept. 1, 2005, pp. B1, B7.

322 Michael Corkery and Ann Carrns, "Supersizing the Levees," *Wall Street Journal*, September 21, 2005, p. A15.

323 From John Carey, Lorraine Woellert, Eamon Javers, and Otis Port, "Let That Be a Warning," *BusinessWeek*, September 12, 2005, pp. 42–43.

324 Alex Frangos, "Can Rebuilding New Orleans Solve Its Old Problems," *Wall Street Journal*, September 8, 2005, p. B1.

325 Tony Freemantle, "Katrina's Aftermath; New Orleans' Revival; Recapturing the City's Flavor Is Not a Given," *The Houston Chronicle*, September 4, 2005, p. A1.

326 "After the Tsunami: The Rebuilding Starts," *The Economist*, February 5, 2005, p. 42. *The Economist* compiled a chart listing the amounts showing government pledges and private donations. See "The Tsunami: After the Deluge," *The Economist*, January 8, 2005, p. 24.

327 "Tourism and Asia's Tsunami: Back to the Beach?" *The Economist*, January 8, 2005, p. 54.

328 Gordon Fairclough and Matt Pottinger, "Tourists Return to Damaged Coasts," *Wall Street Journal*, January 4, 2005, p. D1.
329 Ron Lieber, "Airlines and Hotels Offer Refunds," *Wall Street Journal*, January 4, 2005, p. D5.
330 "Tsunami-Hit Areas Ask West not to Warn Off Vacationers," *Wall Street Journal*, January 26, 2005, p. D5.
331 Bruce Stanley and John Larking, "Tourism Industry Treads Carefully," *Wall Street Journal*, December 31, 2005, p. A5.
332 Members of the Air Force team, the 621st Contingency Response Wing, thought they should have been sent earlier and could have avoided the flight freeze the day before. Dionne Searcey and Kevin Noblet, op. cit., p. 6.
333 Ibid.
334 Dave Yates and Scott Paquette, "Emergency Knowledge Management and Social Media Technologies; A Case Study of the 2010 Haiti Earthquake," *International Journal of Information Management*, Vol. 31, Issue 1, February 2011, pp. 6–13.
335 Jacob Goldstein and Avery Johnson, "Survivors Face Threat of Outbreak of Disease," *Wall Street Journal*, January 15, 2010, p. A11.
336 Robert Greenhill, "The Corporate Response to Haiti," *Wall Street Journal*, July 17–18, 2010, p. A11. A report, "Innovations in Corporate Global Citizenship: Responding to the Haiti Earthquake," will be published by the World Economic Forum.
337 Ianthe Jeanne Dugan and Corey Dade, "Health Risks Grow Among Survivors," *Wall Street Journal*, January 21, 2010, p. A12.
338 "Haiti"s Ongoing Disaster; Earthquake Recovery Efforts Have Stalled Amid Poor Planning, Slow Delivery of Aid and Corruption," Editorial Desk, *Los Angeles Times*, July 19, 2010, p. A16.
339 Inbrid Arnesen and Mike Esterl, "Haiti Struggles to Contain Cholera," *Wall Street Journal*, October 28, 2010, p. A13; Jose de Cordoba, "Aid Spawns Backlash in Haiti," *Wall Street Journal*, November 13–14, 2010, pp. A1, A10.
340 Tarini Parti, "Haiti Earthquake: Six Months Later, Are Relief Efforts Dragging?" *Christian Science Monitor*, July 12, 2010.
341 "Haiti at Six Months," *New York Times*, July 17, 2010, editorial section, p. A18. Also, "Rebuilding Haiti: Dreaming Beyond the Rubble," *The Economist*, April 17, 2010, p. 41.
342 Jose De Cordoba, "Planned Haitian Textile Park Provides Hope for Jobs," *Wall Street Journal*, January 11, 2011, p. A12.
343 Gordon Fairclough, "China Sets Mourning Period as Rescues Continue," *Wall Street Journal*, May 19, 2008 (Online).
344 James T. Areddy and Miho Inada, "China to 'Allow Foreign Help' as Death Toll Is Raised," *Wall Street Journal*, May 16, 2008.
345 Hugo Gurdon, "Why They Left Her to Weep in the Rubble; The Plight of Kobe's Earthquake Victims Was Worsened by the Incompetence of the Authorities," *The Daily Telegraph*, January 27, 1995, p. 19.
346 Norihiko Shirouzu and Michael Williams, "Rescue, Relief Efforts Criticized by Many in Japanese Quake Zone," *Wall Street Journal*, January 19, 1995 p. A15.
347 James Sterngold, "Gang in Kobe Organizes Aid for People in Quake," *New York Times*, January 22, 1995, p. 9.
348 Wall Street Journal News Roundup, "Myanmar Cyclone Death Toll Climbs Into Thousands," *Wall Street Journal*, May 6, 2008, p. A10.
349 "Burman Warned a Week Ago," *The Nation* (Thailand), May 7, 2008.
350 "Myanmar After the Cyclone: A Modest Opening," *The Economist*, May 24, 2008, p. 58.

351 Patrick Barta, "Myanmar Regime Takes Control of U.N. Shipment," *Wall Street Journal*, May 10–11, 2008, p. A5.

352 "Myanmar's Cyclone: The Regime Is Satisfied," *The Economist*, May 17, 2008, p. 52.

353 "The UN and Humanitarian Intervention: To Project Sovereignty, Or to Protect Lives?" *The Economist*, May 17, 2008, p. 73.

354 James Hookway, "Myanmar Urges Vote Amid Crisis," *Wall Street Journal*, May 10–11, 2008, p. A5.

355 "Myanmar After the Cyclone," op. cit.

356 Block, op. cit.

357 Robert Block, Greg Hitt, and Jess Bravin, "Aid for Asia Rises Amid Daunting Needs, Logistics," *Wall Street Journal*, December 29, 2005, p. A1.

358 "The World's Response: More Generous Than Thou," *The Economist*, January 8, 2005, p. 27.

359 Ibid., p. 29

360 Thomas and Fritz, op. cit., p. 114.

361 Guy Gaylor, "U.S. Firms Contribute $80 Million," *Washington Times*, December 31, 2004, p. A01.

362 Kelley Holland, "New Corporate Path To Disaster Relief," *New York Times*, December 23, 2007, Section 3, p. 14.

363 Ibid.

364 Thomas and Fritz, op. cit., pp. 117–119.

365 Phil Turner, "Companies Seek Better Disaster Response," CUP, May 12, 2005.

366 Glenn R. Simpson, "Just in Time: In Year of Disasters, Experts Bring Order to Chaos of Relief," *Wall Street Journal*, November 22, 2005, p. A1.

367 Ibid., p. A12.

368 James Hookway, "Aid Groups Were Ready to Respond," *Wall Street Journal*, October 2, 2009, p. A8.

369 Larry Brilliant, "The Age of Pandemics," *Wall Street Journal*, May 2–3, 2009, p. W1.

370 Herb Schreier, "Don't Be Blinded by the Human Genome Project," *San Francisco Chronicle*, September 18, 2000, p. A17.

371 Robin Cook, "Plague: A New Thriller of the Coming Pandemic," *Foreign Affairs*, November/December, 2009, p. 62.

372 The Black Death is described by Emily Anthes, "What a Pest: Why the Black Death Still Won't Die," *Foreign Policy*, November/December 2009, p. 67.

373 Brilliant, op. cit., p. W2.

374 Dale Keiger, "Farmacology," Johns Hopkins Magazine (http://www.jhu.edu/jhumag/0609web/ farm.html).

375 Ibid., p. 2

376 Mitchell J. Schwaber and Yehuda Carmeli, "Don't Forget the Bacterial Threat," *Wall Street Journal*, August 12, 2009, p. A15.

377 Bryson, op. cit., p. 314. He states the discomforting fact that the average healthy person has a herd of about one trillion bacteria grazing on the skin—see p. 302.

378 Lawrence K. Altman, "Is This a Pandemic? Define 'Pandemic'," *New York Times*, June 9, 2009, p. 1.

379 Betsy McKay, "Swine-Flu Report Details Number of Potential Cases," *Wall Street Journal*, August 25, 2009, p. A3.

380 Betsy McKay, "About 1 in 6 Americans Hit With Swine Flu," *Wall Street Journal*, December 11, 2009, p. A6.

381 Bill Bryson, *A Short History of Nearly Everything* (New York: Broadway Books, a division of Random House, 2003), p. 319.

382 "AIDS: WHO's Counting," *The Economist*, November 24, 2007, p.65.

383 David Ballingrud, "African Dust May Bring Disease to U.S.; Wind Sweeping Bacteria, Fungi Across the Atlantic," *Chicago Sun-Times*, September 6, 2000, p. 42.
384 David P. Fidler, *SARS, Governance and the Globalization of Disease* (New York: Palgrave Macmillan, 2004), p. 13.
385 Matt Pottinger, Elena Cherney, Gautam Naik, and Michael Waldholz, "Cellular Sleuths: How Global Effort Found SARS Virus in Matter of Weeks," *Wall Street Journal*, April 16, 2003, p. A1.
386 "Epidemics & Economics," *BusinessWeek*, April 28, 2003, p. 44. For a comprehensive review of SARS see David P. Fidler, *SARS, Governance and the Globalization of Disease* (New York: Palgrave Macmillan, 2004).
387 "Global Health: Preparing for the Worst," *The Economist*, May 9, 2009, p. 83.
388 Bryson, op. cit., p. 316.
389 Fidler, op. cit., pp. 71–72.
390 Ibid., p. 5.
391 Ibid., p. 6.
392 Ibid.
393 Arthur Kleinman and James L. Watson (eds.) *SARS in China: Prelude to Pandemic?* (Stanford, C.A.: Stanford University Press, 2006), p. 3.
394 Fidler, op. cit., p. 107 ff.
395 Ibid., p. 121.
396 Ibid., p. 74.
397 Ibid., pp. 74–75.
398 Ibid., pp. 1, 76, 82, 187.
399 Ibid., p. 77.
400 Lawrence K. Altman, "Sound the Alarm? A Swine Flu Bind," *New York Times*, April 28, 2009, p. D1.
401 Fidler, op. cit., p. 79.
402 Ibid., p. 93.
403 Ibid.
404 Ibid., p. 95.
405 Viewpoint of Fidler, ibid., p. 95.
406 Ibid., pp. 96–97.
407 "Cracks in the Wall. . . ." *Wall Street Journal*, April 21, 2003, p. A1.
408 Ibid.
409 Fidler, op. cit., p. 99.
410 Ibid., p. 104.
411 Kleinman and Watson, op. cit., p. 5.
412 "Standing Guard: How a Big Factory Is Keeping SARS Out," *BusinessWeek*, May 5, 2003, p. 46.
413 Fidler, op. cit., p. 103.
414 Fidler, p. 118.
415 WHO, *Severe Acute Respiratory Syndrome (SARS): Status of the Outbreak and Lessons for the Immediate Future* (Geneva: WHO, 2003), p. 8
416 Jose de Cordoba and Ana Compoy, "Mexico Closes Schools as Virus Spreads Widely," *Wall Street Journal*, April 28, 2009, p. A5.
417 Marc Lacey and Elisabeth Malkin, "Mexico Takes Emergency Powers to Track and Isolate Cases of a Deadly Flu," *New York Times*, April 26, 2009, p. 6; Betsy McKay and David Luhnow, "Mexico Races to Stop Deadly Flu Virus," *Wall Street Journal*, April 25/26, 2009, p. A1.
418 Henry I. Miller, "Understanding Swine Flu," *Wall Street Journal*, April 28, 2009, p. A13. Also see "The Origin of Swine Flu: Putting the Pieces Together," *The Economist*, May 30, 2009, p. 82.

419 Peter Stein and Gordon Fairclough, "Asian Nations Move Quickly to Check Virus," *Wall Street Journal*, April 28, 2009, p. A4.
420 Jonathan Weisman, "Biden's Remarks Derail President's Temperate Message," *Wall Street Journal*, May 1, 2009, p. A10.
421 Betsy McKay, "New Strain of Flu Virus Spreads to 18 Countries," *Wall Street Journal*, May 4, 2009, p. A14.
422 Andrew Browne, "China Forces Dozens of Mexican Travelers Into Quarantine," *Wall Street Journal*, May 4, 2009, p. A14. Wenran Jiang, "Hard Lessons of SARS Crisis Explain China's Tough Action; In Beijing's View, Quarantining Canadians and Banning Alberta Pork Are Sensible Precautions," *Toronto Star*, May 6, 2009, p. A21.
423 Betsy McKay, "New Strain of Flu Virus Spreads to 18 Countries, *Wall Street Journal*, May 4, 2009, p. A14.
424 Shai Oster and Patricia Jialyi Ho, "China Clashes With Canada as Mexicans Depart," *Wall Street Journal*, May 6, 2009, p. A10.
425 Betsy McKay, "Flu Fears Spur Global Triage," *Wall Street Journal*, April 27, 2009, p. A1.
426 *Wall Street Journal*, May 6, 2009, p. A5.
427 "Birth of a Disaster," *The Economist*, March 14, 1998, p.22.
428 Richard Rhodes, *Deadly Feasts: Tracking the Secrets of a Terrifying New Plague* (New York: Simon & Shuster, 1997), pp. 171–172.
429 Ibid., p. 244.
430 Paula Dwyer, Julia Flynn and Heidi Dawley, "Mad Cows-and Mad Politicians," *BusinessWeek*, April 8, 1996.
431 Rhodes, op. cit., pp. 180–181.
432 Ibid., p. 185.
433 Ibid., p. 212; "Of Secrecy and Madness," *The Economist*, October 28, 2000, p. 53.
434 Fred Barbash, "Mad Cow Disease Fears," *The Washington Post*, March 26, 1996, p. A9.
435 www.bseinquiry.gov.uk
436 http://news.bbc.co.uk/hi/english/sttic/in_depth/health/2000/bse/bse_cases
437 *USA Today*, December 14, 2000, p. 25A.
438 "Mad Cow Rules Are Justified," *The Gazette* (Montreal), July 13, 2007, p. A18.
439 Patrick van Zuanenberg, *BSE: Risk, Science, and Governance* (Oxford: Oxford University Press, 2005), p. 236.
440 Ibid, pp. 231–232.
441 David Brooks, "Globalism Goes Viral," *New York Times*, April 28, 2009, p. A23.
442 "AIDS: WHO's Counting," *The Economist*, November 24, 2007, p.65.
443 Henry I. Miller, "Understanding Swine Flu," *Wall Street Journal*, April 28, 2009, p. A13.
444 Ron Winslow and Avery Johnson, "Deadlier Strain Would Overwhelm Health Systems," *Wall Street Journal*, May 1, 2009, p. A10.
445 Jeanne Whalen and Gautam Naik, "Officials Face a Tough Decision Over Ordering Vaccine," *Wall Street Journal*, April 30, 2009, p. A5.
446 Ibid.
447 Scott Gottlieb, "Why You Can't Get the Swine Flu Vaccine," *Wall Street Journal*, October 28, 2009, p. A21.
448 Nicholas Winning and Laurence Norman, "U.K. Ramps Up Flu Preparation," *Wall Street Journal*, July 21, 2009, p. A11.
449 Donald G. McNeil Jr., "Officials Point to Swine Flu in New York," *New York Times*, April 26, 2009, p. 19.

450 Betsy McKay and Jeanne Whalen, "Delay Undercuts H1N1 Vaccine Campaign," *Wall Street Journal*, October 17–18, 2009, p A4.
451 Flavelle, op. cit.
452 Ibid.
453 Carole Gorney, "Are You Ready for H1N1? The Unique Challenges of Pandemic Preparedness Planning," *Tactics*, a publication of the Public Relations Society of America, September 2009, p. 10.
454 Cam Simpson and Betsy McKay, "Swine Flu Threat to Business Prompts a Call for Readiness," *Wall Street Journal*, August 20, 2009, p. A3.
455 Some of these recommendations and others are mentioned by David Howell, principal of The Pandemic 101 Corp., an emergency preparedness consultancy based in Mississauga in Dana Flavelle, "Corporate Watch Begins on Swine Flu; Preparedness Planners Say They're Advising Firms Not to Overreact Until We Get more information," *Toronto Star*, April 28, 2009, p. B3.
456 "Pandemic Planning: Flu Fighters," *The Economist*, October 6, 2007, p. 88.
457 "University of Toronto Joint Center for Bioethics; Medical Ethics Experts Identify, Address Key Issues in H1N1 Pandemic," *Drug Week*, October 9, 2009, p. 1863.
458 *The Economist*, May 9, 2009, p. 38.
459 Betsy McKay and Cam Simpson, "Fighting Flu Without Big Gun," *Wall Street Journal*, September 9, 2009, p. A3.
460 Emily Steel, "Soap Makers, Others Hitch Ads to Swine Flu," *Wall Street Journal*, April 30, 2009, p. B1.
461 Jennifer Corbett Dooren, "FDA Gives Advice on Divulging Risks," *Wall Street Journal*, May 27, 2009, p. B6.
462 Evan Ramstad, "Korea's Beef With the U.S.," *Wall Street Journal*, June 6, 2008, p. A11.
463 Michael Hansen, "Stop the Madness," *New York Times*, June 20, 2008, p. 21
464 "China's Latest Virus: Better Safe Than Sorry," *The Economist*, May 10, 2008, p. 52.
465 "Global Health: A Shot of Transparency," *The Economist*, August 12, 2006, p. 65.
466 Gautam Naik, "Transmission of Virus a Puzzle for Scientists," *Wall Street Journal*, May 4, 2009, p. A14.
467 Peter A. Singer, "Grading a Pandemic; It's Now Been a Fortnight Since Swine Flu Hit Us. How Have We Handled It, and What Have We Learned?" *National Post* (from *The Financial Post*) (Canada), May 11, 2009, p. A14.
468 Betsy McKay, "New Strain of Flu Virus Spreads to 18 Countries, *Wall Street Journal*, May 4, 2009, p. A14.
469 "New America Media; NAM Launches Emergency Network System That Will Deliver Disaster Alerts and Health Warnings to Ethnic Communities," *Drug Week*, p. 1922.
470 "Google Site Lets Users Follow Flu Outbreaks," *Wall Street Journal*, Nov 12, 2008, p. D16.
471 David Barstow, David Rohde and Stephanie Saul, "Deepwater Horizon's Final Hours," *New York Times*, December 26, 2010, p. 1.
472 Margaret Nelson Brinkhaus, Eve Conant and Andrew Romano, "Death on the Mississippi," *Newsweek*, August 13, 2007, pp. 41–43.
473 Eric Scigliano, "10 Technology Disasters," *Technology Review*, Vol. 105, No. 3, June 2002, pp. 49–50.
474 See Charles Perrow, *Normal Accidents: Living with High-Risk Technologies* (New York: Basic Books, 1984).
475 Alexei Breus, "Chernobyl 22 years later: Reactors Defueled, Sarcophagus Stabilized," *Nucleonics Week*, Vol. 49, May 1, 2008, p. 7; Jane Armstrong, "Nature Lover

Discover Chernobyl," *The Globe and Mail* (Canada), October 5, 2007, p. A22; Guy Fugliotta, "Putting a Lid on Chernobyl," *Washington Post* national *Weekly Edition*, January 6–12, 2003, p. 18.

476 "Russian Authorities Hush Up Chernobyl Disaster Consequences," BBC Monitoring Former Soviet Union—Political, April 26, 2009.

477 Terry Macalister and Helen Carter, "National: Hundreds of Farms Still Restricted by Fallout from Chernobyl," The *Guardian* (London), May 13, 2009, p. 9.

478 Ray Kurzweil, *The Singularity Is Near: When Humans Transcend Biology* (New York: Viking Press, 2005), p. 50.

479 *Questions and Answers on the Singularity*, distributed by Viking Press, p. 3. Kurzweil's book identifies three great overlapping revolutions: genetics, nanotechnology, and robotics—using the acronym GNR. Technology has always been a mixed blessing. Despite its dangers, it will extend life and free us from physical and mental drudgery. The technology of gene engineering "has the potential to bypass evolutionary protections by suddenly introducing new pathogens for which we have no protection, natural or technological." For this reason, some scientists believe that it's better not to carry out certain technologies to avoid possible disastrous outcomes. Opposition to genetically modified organisms (GMOs)—often resulting in crises of confrontation and, sometimes, malevolence—is one consequence of this attitude. Furthermore, GNR can be employed by a bioterrorist "to create a bioengineered biological virus that combines ease of transmission, deadliness, and stealthiness. . . ."

480 "Public and Experts See Risks Differently," *Chemecology*, Vol. 19, February 1990, p. 9.

481 For a further discussion of this topic, see first edition of this book, pp. 272–274.

482 Jeffrey Ball, "Disaster Invokes the Specter of Valdez," *Wall Street Journal*, May 3, 2010, p. A4.

483 Ben Casselman, Russell Gold and Angel Gonzalez, "Blast Jolts Oil World," *Wall Street Journal*, April 22, 2010, p. A4.

484 Guy Chazan, "Final Seal for Well In Gulf Is Delayed," *Wall Street Journal*, August 20, 2010, p. A2. Also see Siobhan Hughes, "Spill Fix Doomed to Fail," *Wall Street Journal*, November 23, 2010, p. A3.

485 Harry R. Weber, "'Bottom Kill' Complete, Engineers Test Gulf Well," *Washington Post*, September 19, 2010, p. A10.

486 Cassandra Sweet, "Spill Uncorked 4.9 Million Barrels," *Wall Street Journal*, August 3, 2010, p. A7.

487 Ann Zimmerman, "Big Skimmer Hindered By Weather; Oil Hits Texas," *Wall Street Journal*, July 6, 2010, p. A14.

488 Chazan, op. cit.

489 Jared Favole and Stephen Power, "Obama to Name Panel to Probe Disasters," *Wall Street Journal*, May 18, 2010, p. A7.

490 Robert Lee Hotz, "Oil Plume From Spill Persists, Data Show," *Wall Street Journal*, August 20, 2010, p. A1, A2. Also see Jeffrey Ball, "Strong Evidence Emerges of BP Oil on Seafloor," *Wall Street Journal*, December 9, 2010, p. A20.

491 Some mishaps occurred, such as when a powerful storm capsized a huge Norwegian oil rig in 1980 that killed all 123 workers aboard. Also, in 1998, a fire aboard a U.K. North Sea platform killed 167 people.

492 Cory Dade, "Containment Structure Near Seafloor," *Wall Street Journal*, May 8–9, 2010, p. A5.

493 Guy Chazan, "New Drilling rules Imperil Some Rig Operators," *Wall Street Journal*, August 3, 2010, p. A6.

494 Sam Fletcher, "Deep Water, Deep Drilling Stimulate Gulf of Mexico," *Oil & Gas*

Journal, June 11, 2007, Vol. 105, Iss 22, pp. 20–24. Also see Bryant Urstadt, "The Oil Frontier," *Technology Review,* Vol. 109, July/August 2006.

495 Russell Gold and Ben Casselman, "Far Offshore, a Rash of Close Calls," *Wall Street Journal,* December 9, 2010, p. A1.

496 Ben Casselman and Guy Chazan, "Disaster Plans Lacking at Deep Rigs," *Wall Street Journal,* May 18, 2010, p. A6.

497 Peter N. Spotts, "Gulf Oil Spill: Why Is it So Hard to Stop?" *Christian Science Monitor,* June 8, 2010.

498 Ed Crooks, "Crisis Exposes Risks of the Deep," *Financial Times,* May 4, 2010, p. 2.; Tom Bower, "Drilling Down: A Troubled Legacy in Oil," *Wall Street Journal,* May 1–2, 2010, p. W3.

499 Spotts, op. cit.

500 Philip Sherwell, Alex Hannaford, James Quinn, "BP: From Bad to Disastrous," *The Sunday Telegraph* (London), June 20, 2010, p. 27.

501 Ulrich Beck, "Comment: No More BPs: We Must Turn Our Deserts into Solar Power: The Deepwater Horizon Disaster Should Make Us Look to the Sun, and Start a Revolution in How We Meet Our Energy Needs," The *Guardian* (London), July 6, 2010, p. 28.

502 Ben Casselman and Siobhan Hughes, "Contractor Accused of Flawed Job on Rig," *Wall Street Journal,* October 29, 2010, p. A1.

503 Ben Casselman, "Industry Weights New Safeguards for Offshore Drilling," *Wall Street Journal,* May 21, 2010, p. A6.

504 Stephen Power and Guy Chazan, "Navy Joins Oil Spill Fight," *Wall Street Journal,* April 30, 2010, p. A6.

505 Tim Webb and Ed Pilkington, "BP Faces $34 Bn in Fines as Senate Smashes Estimates," The *Guardian,* pp. 10, 18.

506 BP's poor corporate culture is mentioned in "Briefing: BP and the Oil Spill: The Oil Well and the Damage Done," *The Economist,* June 19, 2010, p. 66. Also see Guy Chazan, Benoit Faucon, and Ben Casselman, "BP's Fatal Culture Clash: Cost vs. Safety," *The Australian,* July 1, 2010, p. 26.

507 Paul Sonne, "In Crisis, Hayward Struggled to Find Right Tone," *Wall Street Journal,* July 26, 2010, p. A7.

508 Spotts, op. cit.

509 "BP to Invest $1-Billion Upgrades to Texas City; Company Could Face Criminal Charges Over Refinery Blast," *Platts Oilgram Price Report,* December 12, 2005, Vol. 83, No. 238, p. 1.

510 Steven Greenhouse, "BP Incurs Record Fine for Plant Safety Violation; Failure to Correct Hazards at Texas Refinery Costs Company $50.6 Million," *International Herald Tribune,* August 14, 2010, p. 9.

511 Bower, op. cit. Also see Cassandra Sweet and Guy Chazan, "BP Faces New Hit Over Spill in Alaska," *Wall Street Journal,* November 20–21, 2010, p. B1.

512 Jan Urbana, Justin Gillis and Clifford Kramer, "On Defensive, BP Tests Ideas to Stem Leaks," *New York Times,* May 4, 2010, p. A1. Guy Chazan and Neil King, "BP's Preparedness for Major Crisis Is Questioned," *Wall Street Journal,* May 10, 2010, p. A6.

513 Laurent Belsie, "Six Lessons from the BP Oil Spill; What the Tragedy of the BP Oil Spill Has Taught Us About Regulations, Technology, and How Our Energy Diet Must Change," *Christian Science Monitor,* July 10, 2010, np.

514 Ben Casselman and Guy Chazan, "Disaster Plans Lacking at Deep Rigs," *Wall Street Journal,* May 18, 2010, p. A1.

515 Chazan and King, op. cit.

516 Angel Gonzalez and Brian Baskin, "'Static Kill' Begins, Raising New Hopes,"

Wall Street Journal, August 4, 2010, p. A4. Also see Guy Chazan, "BP Nears Final Steps on Well," *Wall Street Journal*, August 5, 2010, p. A4.

517 Guy Chazan, "Experts Question Why BP Delayed Cap," *Wall Street Journal*, July 22, 2010, p. A6.

518 Russell Gold and Ben Casselman, "Alarm Was Disabled Before BP Blast," *Wall Street Journal*, July 24–25, 2010, p. A1. Jacqui Goddard, "Alarms 'Were Silenced' Before BP Oil Well Blast," *The Times* (London), July 23, 2010, p. 7.

519 "Briefing: BP and the Oil Spill," op. cit., p. 67.

520 "Nuclear Power; Bursting Point," *The Economist*, August 14, 2004, p. 54.

521 Mihama Yamaguchi, "Accident at Japanese Nuclear Plant Kills at Least Four, Raises Worries About Reactor Safety," The Associated Press, August 10, 2004.

522 Peter Landers, "Diary of Nuclear Accident: Japan Wasn't Ready," *Wall Street Journal*, October 8, 1999, p. A17.

523 Stecklow, op. cit., p. A7.

524 Eric Scigliano, "10 Technology Disasters," *Technology Review*, Vol. 105, No. 3, June 2002, pp. 49–50. He explains the 1965 blackout as one of faulty design; "Lights Out: Huge Power Failure Hits Major Cities in U.S. and Canada," *Wall Street Journal*, August 15, 2003, p. A1. Rebecca Smith, "Report Sheds Light on Blackout," *Wall Street Journal*, October 20, 2003, p. A6.

525 "Business and Terrorism: Homeland Insecurities," *The Economist*, August 23, 2003, p. 49.

526 Eleeena de Lisser and Mielikki Org, "After Blackout, Hotels Rethink Disaster Plans," *Wall Street Journal*, August 20, 2003, p. D1.

527 "Homeland Insecurities," *The Economist*, August 23, 2003, p. 49; "Lights Out: Huge Power Failure Hits Major Cities in U.S. and Canada," a news roundup, *Wall Street Journal*, August 15, 2003, p. A1.

528 Rebecca Smith and Jospeh T. Hallinan, "Splintered Midwest Grid Helped Outage Spread," *Wall Street Journal*, August 19, 2003, p. A3.

529 Rebecca Smith, "Blackout Could Have Been Avoided," *Wall Street Journal*, April 6, 2004, p. A6.

530 Ibid.

531 Jason Pontin, editor of *Technology Review*, July/August 2010, p. 10.

532 See Jay Stuller, "The Balance of Terror on Main Street, USA," *Across the Board*, Vol. 24, February 1987, pp. 37–41.

533 Rebecca Smith, "The New Nukes," *Wall Street Journal*, September 8, 2009, p. R3. *Backgrounder* Even in NASA's space explorations, the desirability of using alternative technology has been proposed. Why risk humans when unmanned robots or research on earth can achieve the same results?

534 Hearing was held on May 11, 2010, and shown on C-span.

535 Belsie, op. cit.

536 Discussed in Irving L. Janis, *Crucial Decisions: Leadership in Policymaking and Crisis Management* (New York: The Free Press, 1989), pp. 145–147.

537 Barry Meier and Terence Toth, "Union Carbide Says Site Lacked New Safety Gear," *Wall Street Journal*, August 13, 1985, p. 3.

538 See first edition of *The Crisis Manager: Facing Risks and Responsibility* (Mahwah, N.J.: Lawrence Erlbaum Associates, 1997), p. 43.

539 Belsie, op. cit.

540 Laurent Belsie, "Six Lessons from the BP Oil Spill; What the Tragedy of the BP Oil Spill Has Taught Us About Regulations, Technology, and How Our Energy Diet Must Change," *Christian Science Monitor*, July 10, 2010, np.

541 Guy Chazan and Neil King, "BP's Preparedness for Major Crisis Is Questioned," *Wall Street Journal*, May 10, 2010, p. A6.

542   Tim Webb, Ed Pilkington, "BP Accused of Oil Spill Lies to Congress," *The Guardian*, June 21, 2010, p. 16.
543   Rowena Mason, "BP 'Told of Safety Device Fault Weeks Before Rig Explosion,'" *The Daily Telegraph*," June 22, 2010, p. B1.
544   Ben Casselman and Russell Gold, "Federal Probe Extends to 2 BP Managers," *Wall Street Journal*, July 23, 2010, p. A4.
545   Tom Bower, "Drilling Down: A Troubled Legacy in Oil," *Wall Street Journal*, May 1–2, 2010, p. W3. The blame game would continue in anticipation of lawsuits. Two BP executives, who declined to be publicly identified, claimed that Transocean's own documents specify that its workers aboard the Deepwater Horizon rig were in charge of operations and monitoring the oil well. Russell Gold and Guy Chazan, "BP Tries to Shift Blame to Transocean," *Wall Street Journal*, May 22–23, 2010, p. A4
546   Stephen Power and John R. Emshwiller, "Investigators Focus on Failed Device," *Wall Street Journal*, May 6, 2010, p. A5.
547   Ibid.
548   Ad appeared in the *Wall Street Journal*, September 28, 2010, p. A22.
549   Belsie, op cit.
550   Jeffrey Ball, "Oil-spill Dispersants Get Scrutiny," *Wall Street Journal*, August 2, 2010, p. A3.
551   Jeffrey Ball, "Success on Surface, Questions Below," *Wall Street Journal*, August 4, 2010, p. A4. Also see Jeffrey Ball, "Strong Evidence Emerges of BP Oil on Seafloor," *Wall Street Journal*, December 9, 2010, p. A20.
552   Belsie, op. cit.
553   Angel Gonzalez, "Oil Firms Plan Rapid-Response Force," *Wall Street Journal*, July 22, 2010, pp. A1, A6.
554   Ibid.
555   Howard W. French, "Question for Japan," *New York Times*, October 3, 1999, p. NE8.
556   "Operator Blamed for Nuclear Leak at Japanese Plan," *Wall Street Journal*, October 13, 1999, p A25.
557   Landers, op. cit.
558   "Electricity in America; How to Keep the Lights On," *The Economist*, August 23, 2003, p. 10.
559   Peter Coy, "Political Power Overload," *BusinessWeek*, September 1, 2003, p. 28.
560   Jeffrey Ball, "Energizing Off-Grid Power," *Wall Street Journal*, August 18, 2003, p. B1.
561   John J. Fialka, "Power Industry Sets Campaign to Upgrade Grid," *Wall Street Journal*, August 25, 2003, p. A3.
562   Rebecca Smith, "Overloaded Circuits: Outage Signals Major Weaknesses in U.S. Power Grid," *Wall Street Journal*, August 18, 2003, p. A8; Rebecca Smith, "Blackout Probe Focuses on Ohio," *Wall Street Journal*, August 18, 2008, p. A3.
563   Jacob M. Schlesinger, "New Pressure Arises for Energy Bill," *Wall Street Journal*, August 18, 2003, p. A6.
564   Erica Herrero-Martinez, "Fuel Fight: Patrick Moore Believes in Nuclear Power—to the Disbelief of Former Greenpeace Colleagues," *Wall Street Journal*, February 12, 2007, p. R11.
565   Guy Chazan, "Sweden Set to Overturn Ban on Nuclear Power," *Wall Street Journal*, February 6, 2009, p. A7.
566   Mariko Sanchanta, Chester Dawson and Juro Osawa, "Quake, Tsunami Slam Japan," *Wall Street Journal*, March 12—13, 2011, p. A1; Jhred Dvorak, Joro Osawa and Yka Hayashi, "Japanese Crisis Is Ranked Alongside Chernobyl," *Wall Street Journal*, April 21, 2011, p. A1.

567   Chester Dawson and Yka Hayashi, "Fateful Move Exposed Japan Plant," *Wall Street Journal*, July 12, 2011, p. A6.
568   When the Steam Clears, *The Economist*, March 26, 2011, p. 79.
569   Matt Moffett, Anthony Esposito and Carolina Pica, "Chile's Rescue Formula: '75% Science, 25% Miracle,'" *Wall Street Journal*, October 14, 2010, p. A1, 17.
570   Peggy Noonan, "Viva Chile! They Left No Man Behind," *Wall Street Journal*, October 16–17, 2010, p. A17.
571   http://intranet.bnl.gov/newsclips/
572   Anne Trafton, "Nanotech on the Farm," *Technology Review*, Vol. 113, July/August 2010, p. M17.
573   Patti Waldmeir, "The Brave New Risks of Nanotechnology," *Financial Times* (London, USA Edition), September 19, 2007, p. 14.
574   Stephen Baker and Adam Aston, "Why the Old Rules Don't Apply," *Business-Week*, February 14, 2005, p. 68.
575   Stephen Baker and Adam Aston, "The Business of Nanotech," *BusinessWeek*, February 14, 2005, pp. 64–71.
576   Alex Scott, "Nanotechnology; Chalking Up Success in the Downturn," *Chemical Week*, August 3, 2009–August 10, 2009, p. 20.
577   James Brewer, "Small Matter Which Could turn Hugely Nasty," *Lloyd's List*, May 12, 2004, p. 2.
578   Ibid.
579   Waldmeir, op. cit.
580   Mandavilli, op. cit., p. 84.
581   Waldmeir, op. cit.
582   This happened when consumers sympathetic to the grape boycott organized by Cesar Chavez's United Farm Workers in 1968 picketed supermarkets to have grapes from California producers removed from stores.
583   Richard Ettenson, N. Craig Smith, Jull Klein and Andrew John, "Rethinking Consumer Boycotts," *MIT Sloan Management Review*, Vol. 47, Summer 2006, p. 6.
584   Ibid.
585   James H. Dowling, "Public Relations in the Year 2000," *Public Relations Journal*, Vol. 46, January 1990, p.6.
586   Frank Den Hond and Frank G. A. DeBakker, "Ideologically Motivated Activism: How Activist Groups Influence Corporate Social Change Activities," *Academy of Management Review*, Vol. 32, July 2007, p. 901.
587   This process is mentioned by Frank G. A. de Bakker and Frank den Hond, "Activists. Influence Tactics and Corporate Policies," *Business Communication Quarterly*, Vol. 71, March 2008, p. 107.
588   Manny Fernandez and Petula Dvorak, "Without IMF, Protesters Giving Peace A Chance," *Washington Post*, September 28, 2001, p. B01.
589   This vulnerability is mentioned in many crisis management articles, e.g., Frank Den Hond and Frank G. A. De Bakker, op. cit., p. 902.
590   Michael J. Lenox, Charles E. Eesley, "Private Environmental Activism and the Selection and Response of Firm Targets," *Journal of Economics & Management Strategy*, Vol. 18, Spring 2009, p. 45.
591   Harry C. Boyte, *The Backyard Revolution; Understanding the New Citizen Movement* (Philadelphia: Temple University Press, 1980), p. 51. See Saul D. Alinsky, *Rules for Radicals; A Practical Primer for Realistic Radicals* (New York: Random House/Vintage Books, 1971).
592   Berry, op. cit., pp. 243–250.
593   Maureen Taylor, Michael L. Kent, and William J. White, "How Activist Organizations Are Using the Internet to Build Relationships," *Public Relations Review*, Vol. 27, Fall 2001, pp. 263–284.

594 Ibid.
595 Tom Horton, "The Green Giant," *Rolling Stone*, September 1993, p. 112.
596 Andrew Higgins, "How Muslim Clerics Stirred Arab World Against Denmark," *Wall Street Journal*, February 2, 2006, p. A1.
597 Ibid.
598 Adam Jones and William Wallis, "Middle East Boycott of Danish Goods Hits Hard; Commercial Impact," *Financial Times* (London), February 4, 2006, p. A6.
599 Raphael Minder and Annukka Oksannen, "Denmark Warns on Saudi Arabia Trips," *Financial Times* (London), January 31, 2006, p. A9.
600 Anthony Shadid and Kevin Sullivan, "Anatomy of the Cartoon Protest Movement; Opposing Certainties Widen Gap Between West and Muslim World," *Washington Post*, February 16, 2006, Final ed., p. A-1.
601 "The Cartoons That Shook the World," *Wall Street Journal*, February 11–12, 2006, p. A7.
602 Stephen Castle, "Europe: Mohamed Cartoons Provoke Bomb Threats Against Paper," *The Independent* (London), February 1, 2006, p. 18.
603 Robert Z. Nemeth, "If You Say 'Sorry' Do It by the Book," *Sunday Telegram*, June 25, 2006, p. C2. The article refers to Aaron Lazare's book, *On Apology* (Oxford, New York: Oxford University Press, 2004). For an article on the ingredients of a sincere apology, see Barbara Kellerman, "When Should a Leader Apologize and When Not?" *Harvard Business Review*, Vol. 85, April 2006.
604 Eric Pfanner, "Danish Companies Endure Snub by Muslim Consumers," *New York Times*, February 27, 2006, late ed—Final. Sec. C-2.
605 Andrew Higgins, "Danish Businesses Struggle With Big Dilemma," *Wall Street Journal*, February 10, 2006, p. A4.
606 Pfanner, op. cit.
607 "Arla Looks to Rebuild Markets," *Daily Farmer*, April 25, 2006, p. 2.
608 "Arla Attempts a Comeback in the Middle East," March 20, 2006; "The Middle Eastern Boycott Is Slowly Lifting," March 29, 2006; and "Breakthrough for Arla in the Middle East," April 6, 2006, www.arlafoods.com, downloaded April 29, 2006.
609 Gary Younge, "The Right to Be Offended," *The Nation*, February 27, 2006, p. 5.
610 Diana Brady, "Pepsi: Repairing a Poisoned Reputation in India," *BusinessWeek*, June 11, 2007, p. 48.
611 "Top 100 Global Thinkers," *Foreign Affairs*, January 2010, p. 74.
612 Brady, op. cit.
613 Ibid., pp. 50, 54.
614 "Perspective 2000: The Year of Global Protest Against Globalization," *Business World* (Philippines), December 26, 2000.
615 "After Seattle: A Global Disaster," *The Economist*, December 11, 1999, p. 19.
616 "$127 M grant from NIG, National Biocontainment Laboratory to be built at BMC," *B.U. Bridge*, Boston University Community's Weekly Newspaper, October 2003, p. 1.
617 Judith Miller, "New Biolabs Stir a Debate Over Secrecy and Safety," *New York Times*, February 10, 2004, p. F1.
618 Frank Propp, "The BU Biowapons Project: Ground Zero for Boston," *Alternative Views* (a nonprofit publication of Newton Dialogues on Peace and War, Newton, M.A.) March 25, 2004, p.1.
619 Christine MacDonald, "Opponents Vow Fight Against BU BIOLAB," *Boston Globe*, February 17, 2005, p. B8.
620 Propp, op. cit.
621 Miller, op. cit.
622 Jia-Rui Chong, "Research Into Potent Bioagents Increases the Risk; Hundreds

of Universities and Labs Have Joined the Study of Toxic Microbes," *Los Angeles Times*, October 3, 2007, p. A1.

623 "Safety Risk posed by BU Lab," *Green News*, a newsletter of the Green Decade Coalition, in Newton, M.A., p. 3.

624 Miller, op. cit.

625 Ibid.

626 Stephen Smith, "Ruling May Stall Opening of Biolab," *Boston Globe*, December 14, 2007, p. B1.

627 Stephen Smith, "US Review of BU Biolab Inadequate, Panel Finds Scientists Point to Safety Issues," *Boston Globe*, November 30, 2007, p. A1.

628 Elizabeth Becker, "Group Says It Will Begin a Boycott Against KFC," *New York Times*, January 6, 2003, p. A12.

629 Kerry Capell, "Animal-Rights Activism Turns Rabid," *BusinessWeek*, August 30, 2004, p. 64.

630 Daniel S. Levine, "Animal Rights 'Terror' Rattles Biotechs' Cage," *San Francisco Business Times*, February 6, 2004, p. 1.

631 Richard Alleyne, "He Got Off Lightly, Says Militant Who Began 'Liberation Struggle,'" *The Daily Telegraph* (London), February 24, 2001.

632 Kim Jennings, "Case Study: Huntingdon Life Sciences v. Animal Rights Campaign and 'Stop Huntingdon Animal Cruelty,'" a class report, Boston University, College of Communication, September 27, 2001.

633 Alleyne, op. cit.

634 "Big Mac Under Attack," *The Gazette* (Montreal), October 17, 1999, p. A5.

635 Richard Tomkins, "When Global Leaders Become Global Targets," *Financial Times*, October 15, 1999, p. 15.

636 Foundation for Public Affairs, op. cit., p. 555.

637 Foundation for Public Affairs, Public Interest Profiles 1992–1993 (Washington, D.C., Congressional Quarterly Inc. 1992, p. 558.

638 Massachusetts Society for Medical Research (Waltham, M.A.), *MSMR News*, September 1990, p. 1.

639 "Animal Rights Extremists: Four Legs Good, Two Legs Bad," *The Economist*, August 27, 2005, p. 45.

640 Jeanne Whalen, "Animal Activists Expand Corporate Attacks," *Wall Street Journal*, August 7, 2009, p. B1.

641 Institute for Crisis Management—2007, p. 4.

642 Steven Greenhouse, "In America Labor Has An Unusually Long Fuse," Week in Review, *New York Times*, April 5, 2009, p. 3.

643 Greenhouse, op. cit.

644 Kent Jackson, "Strikes Becoming Less Common," www.standardspeaker.com

645 These benefits included: finding three alternatives jobs within Danone for every downsized worker or jobs in other firms; also to pay all relocation costs for such workers, paying indemnities to workers or their spouses who suffered a loss of salary in moving, and offering to finance up to two trips for employees and their families to cities where a job was open and paying for training for displaced spouses, and offering to evaluate and finance self-employment projects for employees who decided to leave the company.

646 Greenhouse, op. cit.

647 David Jolly, "Taking the Boss Hostage? In France, It's a Labor Tactic," *New York Times*, April 3, 2009, p. B5. The other companies were PPR, the group that owns Gucci, a 3M plant, and Sony.

648 Foundation for Public Affairs, Public Interest Profiles 1992–1993 (Washington, D.C.: Congressional Quarterly, Inc., 1992).

649 De Bakker and den Hond, op. cit., p. 110.

650 Michael M. Phillips and Yaroslav Trofimov, "Trading Places: Police Go Undercover To Thwart Protesters Against Globalization," *Wall Street Journal*, September 11, 2001, p. A1.
651 597 Paul Magnusson, "Meet Free Traders. Worst Nightmare," *BusinessWeek*, March 20, 2000, pp. 113–116.
652 Michael J. Lenox, Charles E. Eesley, "Private Environmental Activism and the Selection and Response of Firm Targets," *Journal of Economics & Management Strategy*, Vol. 18, Spring 2009, p. 45.
653 Monroe Friedman, "Consumer Boycotts: A Conceptual Framework and Research Agenda," *Journal of Social Issues*, Vol. 47, 1991, pp. 149–168.
654 See Friedman, op. cit.
655 Jason Gay, "Trade Winds: November's World Trade Organization Summit in Seattle Is Shaping Up to Be the Mother of All Political Demonstrations," *The Boston Phoenix*, October 7–14, 1999.
656 Bob Davis, "Economic Forum Focuses on Conflict," *Wall Street Journal*, January 29, 2002, p A13.
657 Roger Thurow and Vanessa Fuhrmans, "This Swiss Ski Village Is in Unlikely Company As a World Trouble Spot," *Wall Street Journal*, January 25, 2001, p. A1.
658 Jim Carlton, "Protests May Be Toned Down at WTO's Meeting in Cancun," *Wall Street Journal*, September 9, 2003, p. A10.
659 Mark Hunter, Marc LeMenestrel, Henri-Claude de Bettignies, "Beyond Control: Crisis Strategies and Stakeholder Media In the Danone Boycott of 2001," Corporate Reputation Review, Vol. 11, No. 4, Winter 2008, pp.335–350.
660 Ibid.
661 Ibid., p. 32.
662 Hal Bernton, "Environmental Advocates Have Links to Corporations," *The Oregonian*, November 30, 1999.
663 Pui-wing Tam, "Turning Videocams Into Weapons," *Wall Street Journal*, September 11, 2001, p. B1.
664 Daniel D. Cook, "Labor's Last Resort," *Industry Week*, Vol. 189, June 28, 1976, p. 31.
665 Roger Thurow and Vanessa Fuhrmans, "This Swiss Ski Village Is in Unlikely Company As a World Trouble Spot," *Wall Street Journal*, January 25, 2001, p. A1.
666 Neil King Jr. and Scott Miller, "Shipping News: Post-Iraq Influence of U.S. Faces Test at New Trade Talks," *Wall Street Journal*, September 3, 2003, p. A10.
667 John Giuffo, "Smoke Gets In Our Eyes," Columbia Journalism Review, Vol. 40, No. 3, September/October 2001, pp. 14–17.
668 Yaroslav Trofimov and Ian Johnson, "Law and Disorder: G-8 Protesters in Italy Describe Police Attack on Group in a School," *Wall Street Journal*, August 6, 2001, p. A1.
669 Sandra Laville, "National: Policing: Specialist Protest Squads at Centre of Investigations Into Police Violence: Territorial Support Teams, Used at Demonstrations and Marches, Involved in Controversy Before," *The Guardian* (London), April 16, 2009, p.7; Paul Lewis, "Caught on Film: Campaigner Who Asked for Police Identification," *The Guardian*, June 22, 2009, p. 1.
670 Diane Feen, "Anti-global Activist Groups Master Art of Grassroots PR," O'Dwyer's PR Services Report, June 2001, p. 33.
671 Alan Marsh, "The New Matrix of Political Action," *Futures*, 11, April 1979, p. 98.
672 *pr reporter*, May 29, 1978, insert from Managing the Human Climate, May–June 1978.

673   Feen, op. cit., "Anti-global Activists Groups Master Art of Grassroots PR," O'Dwyer's PR Services Report, June 2001, pp. 1, 32–35.

674   "The Rise of the 'Three Rs," *New Scientist,* July 20, 2002, p. 15.

675   Lawrence Susskind and Patrick Field, *Dealing with an Angry Public: The Mutual Gains Approach to Resolving Disputes* (New York: Free Press, 1996).

676   Roger Fisher and William Ury, *Getting to Yes: Negotiating Agreement Without Giving In* (Boston: Houghton Mifflin, 1981).

677   Adam Sage, Suzy Jagger and Rory Watson, "Unions fight to 'Stay French' as Kraft Bid for Danone Biscuits," *The Times* (London), July 3, 2007.

678   Mark Hunter, Marc LeMenestrel, Henri-Claude de Bettignies, "Beyond Control: Crisis Strategies and Stakeholder Media In the Danone Boycott of 2001," Insead: Faculty & Research Working Paper. Http://www.insead.edu/facultyresasrch/ research/doc.cfm?did=19242

679   Fidler, Stephen, "Inside Track: Opening UP to Criticism," *Financial Times* (London), September 22, 2000, p. 15.

680   Ibid.

681   "Lessons from the World Bank," *pr reporter*, February 4, 2002, pp. 2–3.

682   A table in Edward F. Mickolous' book, *Transnational Terrorism: A Chronology of Events, 1968–1979* (London: Aldwych Press, 1980), p. xxi lists these terrorist methods: kidnapping; barricade-hostage; occupation; letter bombing; incendiary bombing; explosive bombing; missile attack; armed attack; aerial hijacking; non-aerial takeover; assassination or murder; sabotage; exotic pollution; nuclear weapons; threat; theft or break-in; conspiracy; hoax; sniping; shootout with police; arms struggle; other actions.

683   In book review by Paul Johnson, "The Meagre Harvest of Mayhem," *Times Literary Supplement*, August 29, 1986, p. 929.

684   Ibid.

685   David W. Balsiger, "Terrorism: Freedom Held Hostage," Terrorism Edition, *Family Protection Scoreboard* (A BNS-Mott Media Publication), p. 4.

686   "We Have Some Planes," *New York Times,* June 19, 2004, p. A16.

687   Charles A. Russell, Leon J. Banker, Jr., Bowman H. Miller, "Out-Inventing the Terrorist," in Yonah Alexander, David Carlton, and Paul Wilkinson (eds.) *Terrorism: Theory and Practice* (Boulder, C.O.: Westview Press, 1979), p. 12

688   "Terror in Mumbai: India Under Attack," *The Economist*, November 29, 2008, p. 45; Geeta Ahand and Arlene Chang, "Mumbai Marks Year Anniversary of Attacks," *Wall Street Journal*, November 27, 2009, p. A12.

689   Eric Bellman, "A Traumatized Mumbai Seeks to Protect Itself," *Wall Street Journal*, December 18, 2008, p. A12.

690   Michelle Leder, "Perks: Now Available: The Bodyguard Bill," *BusinessWeek*, May 14, 2007, p. 16.

691   Jacob M. Schlesinger and Thaddeus Herrick, "Delayed Reaction; Chemical Manufacturers Elude Crackdown on Toxic Materials," *Wall Street Journal*, May 21, 2003, pp. A1, A10.

692   Evan Perez, Siobhan Gorman, Susan Schmidt and Elizabeth Williamson, "FBI's Anthrax Case Relies on Spores Discovered on a Flask," *Wall Street Journal*, August 6, 2008, p. A3.

693   "Bioterroristm: A Mystery Unravelled," *The Economist*, August 9, 2008, p. 30.

694   Tara Parker-Pope, "How to Distinguish Anthrax Symptoms From Common Illnesses," *Wall Street Journal*, November 2, 2001, p. B1.

695   Jonathan Eig, "Will Local Officials Know Anthrax When They See It?" *Wall Street Journal*, November 2, 2001, p. B1.

696   Catherine Arnst and William C. Symonds, "The Next Phase: Bioterrorism?" *BusinessWeek*, October 1, 2001, p. 58.

697 Ibid.
698 Book review by Catherine Arnst, "Bio-Terrorism under the Microscope," *Business Week*, October 15, 2001.
699 Jonathan Eig, "Will Local Officials Know Anthrax When They See It?" *Wall Street Journal*, November 2, 2001, p. B1. OR Tom Post, "Doomsday Cults: 'Only the Beginning'," *Newsweek*, April 3, 1995, p. 40.
700 Susan W. Brenner, "The Council of Europe's Convention on Cybercrime," in Jack M. Balking, et. al, *Cybercrime: Digital Cops in a Networked Environment* (New York: New York University Press, 2006), p. 107.
701 Ibid., p. 219.
702 Siobhan Gorman, "Arrest in Epic Cyber Swindle," *Wall Street Journal*, August 18, 2009, p. A1.
703 "Cyber Crimes Continue to Plague Businesses and Keep Security Software Spending High," *Chemical Week*, June 20, 2007, p. 29. The survey was conducted among participants in the Computer Security Institute (CSI; San Francisco) and San Francisco Federal Bureau of Investigation (FBI).
704 Siobhan Gorman, "U.S. Fears Threat of Cyberspying at Olympics," *Wall Street Journal*, July 17, 2008, p. A6.
705 Joseph Pereira, "Breaking the Code: How Credit-Card Data Went Out Wireless Door," *Wall Street Journal*, May 4, 2007, p. A1.
706 Cassell Bryan-Low, "Turkish Police Hold Data-Theft Suspect," *Wall Street Journal*, August 10, 2007, pp. A6, A12.
707 W. J. Hennigan, "TJX to Pay for Breach of Data," *Los Angeles Times*, June 24, 2009, pp. B5, B12.
708 Ibid.
709 L. Gordon, "Internet Attacks Are a Real and Growing Problem," *Wall Street Journal*, December 18, 2008, p.A17.
710 Keith Epstein and Ben Elgin, "The Taking of NASA's Secrets," *Business Week*, December 1, 2008, pp.73–78.
711 Ibid., p.73.
712 "Cyberwarfare: Newly Nasty," *The Economist*, May 26, 2007, p. 63.
713 Reid Goldsborough, "Hide and Seek: The Implications of Anonymous Blogging and Commenting," *Tactics*, November 2009, p. 16.
714 "Workplace Violence," *Risk Management*, Vol. 40, June 1993, pp. 76–77.
715 Katestone Lombardi, "Efforts to Stem Violence in the Workplace," *New York Times*, February 13, 1994, Section 13WC, p. 1.
716 Roberto Ceniceros, "Stricter Company Policies Help Lower Number of Homicides in Workplace: Training, Early Intervention Can Keep Violence from Escalating," *Business Insurance*, June 16, 2008, p. 11.
717 W. Barry Nixon, "Assessing Workplace Violence Risk to the Business," *Security*, May 2009, p. 30.
718 Ibid., p. 32.
719 Nancy Lampen and Nellie Brown, "Thinking About the Unthinkable: Workplace Crisis Management," *Perspectives on Work*, Vol. 6, No. 1, 2002, pp. 16–18.
720 For an excellent analysis of this and other workplace violence incidents, see Kathleen Fearn-Banks, *Crisis Communications: A Casebook Approach* (Mahwah, N.J.: Lawrence Erlbaum Associates, 1996), pp. 213–239.
721 Ibid., p. 223.
722 Ibid., pp. 215, 221–226.
723 An excellent summary of the event appeared as a Special Report, Evan Thomas, et al., "Making of a Massacre," *Newsweek*, April 30, 2007, pp. 22–47.
724 Ibid., p. 24. See review by Vincent Carroll, "A Nightmare Re-Examined," *Wall*

Street Journal, April 18–19, 2009, p. W8, of two books on the events: Jeff Kass, *Columbine: A True Crime Story*, and Dave Cullen, *Columbine*.

725 "The Virginia Tech Massacre: In the University of Death," *The Economist*, April 21, 2007, p. 27.

726 Natasha Altamirano, "Shooting Report 'Critical' of Tech Response; Steger Defends Actions; Kaine Rejects Calls for Firing," *The Washington Times*, August 31, 2007, p. B01.

727 See Jerry Adler, "Story of a Gun," *Newsweek*, April 30, 2007, p. 36 ff.

728 Burt Helm and Paula Lehman, "Media: Buying Clicks to a Tragedy," *Business-Week*, May 7, 2007, p. 42.

729 Stephanie Ebbert, "Colleges Reviewing Security Policies; Shootings Prompt Questions from Student Prospects," *Boston Globe*, February 16, 2008, p. B1.

730 Kyra Auffermann, "'It Still Chokes Me Up'—Responding to a Deadly Campus Shooting at Northern Illinois University," *The Strategist*, Vol. 15, Summer 2009, pp. 12–16. Susan Saulny and Monica Davey, "Gunman Slays Five in Illinois at University," *New York Times*, February 15, 2008, p. A1.

731 "The Virginia Tech Massacre: Curbing Guns, But Not Too Much," *The Economist*, April 19, 2008, pp. 42–43.

732 Stephanie Ebbert, op. cit.

733 "The Virginia Tech Massacre: In the University of Death," *The Economist*, April 21, 2007, p. 27.

734 "Portrait of a Killer," *Express*, a publication of *The Washington Post*, April 18, 2007, p. 1.

735 Ibid.

736 Donna Leinwand, "State Report Criticizes Va. Tech Response; Panel: Cho Long Showed Signs of Mental Illness," *USA Today*, August 30, 2007, p. 3A.

737 Evan Thomas, op. cit., p. 28.

738 Elizabeth Bernstein, "Delicate Balance: Colleges. Culture of Privacy Often Overshadows Safety," *Wall Street Journal*, April 27, 2007, p. A1.

739 The *in loco parentis* doctrine, which required schools to take on the responsibility of parents, was replaced by the Family Educational Rights and privacy Act (FERPA) in 1974. Ibid., A13.

740 Bernstein, op. cit.

741 Otto Lerbinger, *The Crisis Manager: Facing Risk and Responsibility* (Mahwah, N.J.: Lawrence Erlbaum Associates, 1997), pp. 160–161.

742 Michael Doan, "Businesses Fight Back Against 'Cybersmears'," *Kiplinger Business Forecasts*, Vol. 2002, May 6, 2002.

743 "Where Does Apple Go From Here?" *TECHWEB*, February 21, 2009.

744 Marina Emmanuel, "New Samsung Plant May Offer 2,000 Jobs Here," *New Straits Times* (Malaysia), February 3, 2009, p. 1.

745 Fionola Meredith, "A Boom Time for the Rumour Mill," *The Irish Times*, December 5, 2008, p. 17.

746 Richard Weiner, *The Gossip Book* (not yet published in July 2011).

747 Leonard M. Fuld, *The Secret Language of Competitive Intelligence: How to See Through and Stay Ahead of Business Disruptions, Distortions, Rumors, and Smoke Screens* (New York: Crown Publishing Group, a division of Random House, 2006), pp. 181–183.

748 Richard L. Hudson, "London Exchange Probes 'Suspicious Dealings' In Stocks that May Have Been Bear Raid Targets," *Wall Street Journal*, November 7, 1990, p. C12.

749 Case is largely based on A. Berenson, "On Hair-Trigger Wall Street, A Stock Plunges on Fake News," *New York Times*, August 26, 2000, pp. A1 and B, and Karina Khodorkovsky's crisis management class paper, "Emulex and the Fake Press Release," Boston University, College of Communication, November 7, 2000.

750 Dan Thomasson, "Taking Stock of a Hoax," *The Washington Times*, September 4,2000, p. A14; "Swift IR Limits Bogus Release Damage," *Investor Relations Business*, September 11, 2000.
751 "Bankruptcy Rumours Denied, But Countrywide Stock Slides," *The Toronto Star*, January 9, 2008.
752 Steven Mufson and Peter Whoriskey, "Chrysler and Fiat Strike an Alliance," *The Washington Post*, January 21, 2009, p. D1.
753 W. Barry Nixon, "Seven Steps to Implementing a Workplace Violence Crisis Response Plan," LP Magazine, online.
754 Ibid.
755 See Brooks McClure, Chapter 6, "Corporate Vulnerability—and How to Assess It," in Yonah Alexander and Robert A. Kilmarx, *Political Terrorism and Business: The Threat and Response* (New York: Praeger, 1979), pp. 79–96.
756 See the supplement, "Securing the Cloud: A Survey of Digital Security," *The Economist*, October 26, 2002.
757 Peter Day's interview with Mark Anderson on BBC Worldservice, January 2010.
758 "Cyber Crimes Continue to Plague Businesses and Keep Security Software Spending High," *Chemical Week*, June 20, 2007, p. 29.
759 Ibid.
760 Hennigan, op. cit., p. 64.
761 Many books mention this fact. One source is Ernest R. Hilgard, *Introduction to Psychology* (New York: Harcourt, Brace and Company, 1953), p. 184.
762 Russell, Banker, and Miller, op. cit. p. 32. One typology lists groups that are (1) nationalistic/ethnic/separatist, (2) ideological, (3) nihilist, (4) issue-oriented. Nationalistic terrorists are particularly ubiquitous. For example, Shiite Muslims are centered in Iran; Libyans, although not Shiites, are sympathetic to the Palestinians and have a strong hatred of Israel and the United States. The Red Brigades in Italy and the Baader-Meinhof group in Germany are neo-fascist groups that are also known as urban guerrillas. Their particular form of terrorism has a random quality, as evidenced in the bombing of the railroad station in Bologna, which killed more than 80 people.
763 Art Jahnke, "Banking on Terror," *Boston Magazine*, Vol. 78, December 1986, pp. 191–193, 253–256.
764 Peter Merkl, "In the Minds of Terrorists," *The Center Magazine*, Vol. 19, March–April 1986, pp. 18–24. Peter Merkl found that terrorists are typically young, in their early twenties, or younger. Terrorist movements often start with students and then spread to other classes, especially the lower middle class, and sometimes working people. It is assumed that the student milieu combines the element of youth with a preoccupation with cultural issues. The formation of a terrorist group often starts with people who tend to be more intellectual than others and who agonize a good deal. On the other hand, terrorists have often led aimless lives before they became terrorists; some were drop-outs from school or on drugs. One personality feature is a willingness to do something physical. When a division of labor exists, at least some must be willing to "slug somebody" while others are preoccupied with ideology. Once an organization is established and becomes known for its violent deeds, a lot of people jump on board who have no qualms about using violence. Persons who are highly valued are those who have knowledge about the use of weapons or explosives. Also see Charles Mohr, "A Pride of Hesitant Scholars Investigates the Emerging Discipline of Terrorism," *New York Times*, May 27, 1979, p. E8.
765 Jack Honomichl, "Now's the Time to Know a Good Lawyer," *Marketing News*, Oct. 29, 1990, p. 13.

766 Agis Salpukas, "Working Abroad in Terror's Shadow," *New York Times*, April 13, 1986, p. F8.
767 John Markoff, "Ex-Student Faces Trial Over Computer Chaos," *New York Times*, January 7, 1990, p. 18.
768 Mark Lewyn, "Hackers: Is a Cure Worse Than the Disease," *BusinessWeek*, December 4, 1989, p. 37.
769 Ned Barnett, "The PR Response to Virginia Tech and Beyond," *Communication World*, Vol. 24, July/August 2007, pp. 14–15.
770 Greg Toppo, "College on the Alert in Low-Tech Ways, Too; Loudspeakers, Sirens Join High-Tech Devices in schools. Arsenals Against Emergencies," *USA Today*, April 15, 2008, p. 4D.
771 "Community Colleges Improve Crisis Communications with e2Campus Emergency Notification System," PR Newswire, New York: April 14, 2009.
772 Evan Perez, Siobhan Gorman, Susan Schmidt and Elizabeth Williamson, op. cit.
773 David Stipp, "Virus Verdict Likely to Have Limited Impact," *Wall Street Journal*, February 24, 1990, p. B7. Evidence of limited impact is found in the trial of Robert T. Morris, one of the young men who was apprehended. His lawyer argued that Morris was guilty of a mistake, not a crime. One witness described Morris's virus as "neat," and "purely an intellectual experiment."
774 Omar El Akkad, "Hams Recalled After Syringes Found; Casing Discovered in Ontario Pork Processing Plant," *The Globe and Mail* (Canada), November 8, 2006, p. A14.
775 Daryl Passmore and Kellie Cameron, "Blade, Needles in Food," *Sunday Herald Sun* (Australia), May 28, 2006, p. 1.
776 Kurt T. Dirks, Roy J. Lewicki, and Akbar Zaheer, "Repairing Relationships Within and Between Organizations: Building a Conceptual Foundation," *Academy of Management Review*, Vol. 34, No. 1, January 2009, pp. 68–84.
777 Ibid., p. 75.
778 Ibid., p.72.
779 Ibid.
780 As James E. Post states, "Modern management is awash, perhaps drowning, in ethical issues." "Fighting the Ethics Pandemic," *Builders & Leaders*, March 2007, p. 36.
781 Ronald E. Berenbeim and Jeffrey M. Kaplan, "Ethics Programs: The Role of the Board; a Global Study" (New York: The Conference Board, February 17, 2004), p. 4.
782 Archie B. Carroll, "In Search of the Moral Manager," *Business Horizons*, Vol. 30, March–April 1987, pp. 7–15. Unless otherwise noted, the examples in this section are all from Carroll.
783 Toffler, op. cit.
784 As quoted by James O'Toole and Warren Bennis, "What's Needed Next: A Culture of Candor," *Harvard Business Review*, June 2009, Vol. 87, June 2009, op. cit, p. 59.
785 See Barbara Ley Toffler, *Tough Choices: Managers Talk Ethics* (New York: John Wiley & Sons, 1986), pp. 17–18. Competing claims are one of four elements of ethical situations.
786 Committee for Economic Development, Social Responsibilities of Business Corporations (New York: Committee for Economic Development, June 1971), p. 15.
787 Chester I. Barnard, *The Functions of the Executive* (Cambridge, M.A.: Harvard University Press, 1938).
788 Kenneth E. Goodpaster, "Can a Corporation Have an Environmental Conscience?" in W. Michael Hoffman, Robert Frederick, and Edward S. Petry,

Jr. (eds.), *The Corporation, Ethics, and the Environment* (New York: Quorum Books, 1990), Chapter 3, pp. 25–38.

789 Ibid., p. 26.

790 Kurt T. Dirks, Roy J. Lewicki, and Akbar Zaheer, "Repairing Relationships Within and Between Organizations: Building a Conceptual Foundation," *Academy of Management Review*, Vol. 34, No. 1, January 2009, pp. 68–84.

791 "Business Ethics and the Bottom Line," *Christian Science Monitor*, February 21, 2007, editorial, p. 8.

792 Christine M. Pearson and Judith A. Clair, "Reframing Crisis Management," *Academy of Management Review*, Vol. 23, No. 1, 1998, p. 60.

793 Ibid., p. 68.

794 Using these criteria, Pearson and Clair give a low grade to Exxon's handling of the *Exxon Valdez* incident: "Exxon failed: warning signals were ignored; plans and preparations for such an event were substandard, and public statements made by Exxon's CEO Rawl riled stakeholders." Exxon was also generally unwilling to learn from the crisis. Ibid., p. 61.

795 Peter F. Drucker, *Management: Tasks, Responsibilities, Practices* (New York: Harper & Row, Publishers, 1973), pp. 494–505.

796 James O'Toole and Warren Bennis, "What's Needed Next: A Culture of Candor," *Harvard Business Review*, June 2009, Vol. 87, June 2009, p. 56.

797 Ibid., p. 57.

798 Ibid., p. 60.

799 Stephen Power and Ben Casselman, "White House Probe Blames BP, Industry in Gulf Blast," *Wall Street Journal*, January 6, 2011, p. A2.

800 Examples of faulty decision-making were reported by the *Wall Street Journal* based on BP internal documents along with public testimony before a joint Coast Guard and Interior Department panel. See Russell Gold and Ben Casselman, "On Doomed Rig's Last Day, A Divisive Change of Plan," *Wall Street Journal*, August 26, 2010, pp. A1, 16.

801 Gold and Casselman, op. cit., p. 25.

802 Ben Casselman, "Supervisor Says Flaw Was Found in Key Safety Device," *Wall Street Journal*, July 21, 2010, p. A7.

803 Ben Casselman, "Rig Owner Had Rising Tally of Accidents," *Wall Street Journal*, May 10, 2010, p. A6. In June 2000, BP issued a "notice of default" letter to Transocean over problems with a blowout preventer made by Cameron and another company, Hybrid. Moreover, according to a 2008 lawsuit, both companies used defective blowout preventer equipment resulting in leakage in 2007 from an offshore Louisiana well.

804 Ben Casselman and Siobhan Hughes, "Contractor Accused of Flawed Job on Rig," *Wall Street Journal*, October 29, 2010, p. A16; "Blame and Shame; The Deepwater Horizon Report," *The Economist*, January 8, 2011.

805 Robin Pagnamenta and Robert Lea, *The Times*, notes, pp. 10–11.

806 Stephanie Kirchgaessner, "BP Accused of 'Falling Short' on Data," *Financial Times*, May 21, 2010, p. 8.

807 Patrik Jonsson, "Enter the No-Spin Zone of the Deep: the BP Live Feed," *The Christian Science Monitor*, June 5, 2010. After yielding to congressional pressure, however, it was surprised to reap some unexpected plaudits.

808 The White House also blundered in its public communication when its environmental policy czar Carol Browner and Jane Lubchenco, administrator of the National Oceanic and Atmospheric Administration (NOAA), released a study that nearly 75 percent of the 4.09 million barrels spilled from BP's well in the Gulf had been dispersed, evaporated, or collected in cleanup operations. "Oil Plume From Spill Persists, Data Show," *Wall Street Journal*, August 20, 2010, p. A2.

809 Sherwell, Hannaford and Quinn, op. cit.

810 Monica Langley, "Hayward Defends Tenure, BP's Spill Response," *Wall Street Journal*, July 30, 2010, p. A5.

811 Sonne, op. cit. "In Crisis, Hayward Struggled to Find Right Tone," *Wall Street Journal*, July 26, 2010, p. A7.

812 Daniel Goleman, *Emotional Intelligence: Why It Can Matter More Than IQ* (New York: Bantam Books, 1995).

813 David Teather, "Bosses Who Take Holiday at the Wrong Time Can Find Themselves Sailing Into the Sunset," *The Observer* (London), June 27, 2010, p. 44.

814 Ibid.

815 Jad Mouawad and Clifford Krauss, "Another Torrent BP Works to Stem—Its C.E.O.," *New York Times*, June 4, 2010, p. A1.

816 Robin Pagnamenta, Robert Lea, "BP's Next Great Battle Is Already Under Way—to Salvage Its Battered Reputation," *The Times* (London), June 19 2010, pp. 74, 75.

817 Jack Neff, "What's Ailing J&J–and Why Isn't Its Rep Hurting?" *Advertising Age*, May 10, 2010, p. 0004.

818 Jonathan D Rockoff and Jennifer Corbett Dooren, "FDA Ties Recall of Tylenol to Contaminated Materials," *Wall Street Journal*, August 24, 2010, p. B7.

819 Jonathan D. Rockoff and Jon Kamp, "J&J Contact Lenses Recalled," *Wall Street Journal*, August 24, 2010, p. B7.

820 Jonathan D. Rockoff and Jon Kamp, "For J&J, Latest Recall Is Hip Implants," *Wall Street Journal*, August 27, 2010, p. B1.

821 "NcNeil Recalls Hurt Brand 'Credibility' in OTC Medications," *Supermarket News*, December 20, 2010, p. 17. Also see "House Panel Asks for Names of J&J Employees Involved in 'Phantom Recall,'" *Drug Industry Daily*, Vol. 9, June 2, 2010.

822 Gardiner Harris and Duff Wilson, "U.K. Giant Sets Payout Over Sales of Risky Drugs; $750 million Settlement Includes $96 Million Cut for a Whistle-Blower," *International Herald Tribune*, October 27, 2010, p. 1.

823 Gordon Fairclough, "How a Heparin Maker in China Tackles Risks," *Wall Street Journal*, March 10, 2008, pp. B1, B5.

824 Alicia Mundy and Bill Tomson, "Senate Acts on Food Safety," *Wall Street Journal*, December 1, 2010, p. A3.

825 Jane Zhang and Janet Adamy, "Salmonella Outbreak Exposes Food-Safety Flaws," *Wall Street Journal*, July 23, 2008, p. A2.

826 "Cookie Dough at Nestlé Plant Yield Positive Test for E. Coli," *New York Times*, June 30, 2009, p. A14.

827 "Topps Calls It Quits; Cargill Recalls Patties," *Refrigerate Transporter*, April 1, 2008, p. 13.

828 Jane Zhang, "Salmonella in Peanut Butter Linked to Other U.S. Cases," *Wall Street Journal*, January 13, 2009, p. A2.

829 Michael M. Phillips and Jane Zhang, "Peanut Butter Suspected in Salmonella Outbreak," *Wall Street Journal*, January 12, 2009, p. A3.

830 Julie Schmit, "Broken System Hid Peanut Plants' Risk; Case Reveals Every Link in Food-Safety Chain Failed," *USA Today*, April 27, 2009, p.1B.

831 Ibid.

832 Jane Zhang, "Meatpacker Admits Ailing Cattle Used at Slaughterhouse," *Wall Street Journal*, March 13, 2008, p. B1.

833 Andrew Martin, "Humane Society Sues U.S. in Cattle Case," *New York Times*, February 28, 2008, A16.

834 "USDA Expands Beef Recall, Says Plant Fell Short," *New York Times*, August 15, 2008, p. A3.

835 Gardiner Harris, "E. Coli Kills 2 and Sickens Many Others, Focus on Beef," *New York Times*, November. 3, 2009, p. 12.

836 Timothy W. Martin, "Egg Firms Reassure Customers in Wake of Recall," *Wall Street Journal*, August 20, 2010, p. A3.

837 Alicia Mundy and Bill Tomson, "Egg Inspectors Failed to Raise Alarms," *Wall Street Journal*, September 10, 2010, p. A4.

838 Alicia Mundy and Bill Tomson, "Allegations Fly in Recall of Eggs," *Wall Street Journal*, September 1, 2010, p. A4, and Alica Mundy and Bill Tomson, "Egg Probe Tracks Tainted Feed," *Wall Street Journal*, September 17, 2010, p. A5.

839 Jean Guerrero, "Cracking California's Eggs Rules," *Wall Street Journal*, August 19, 2010, p. A3.

840 Richard Tomkins, "A Spillage of Goodwill," *Financial Times*, June 14, 1999, p. 25.

841 Andy Pasztor, "Airline Safety Gap Cited in Crash Probe," *Wall Street Journal*, May 15, 2009, p. A3.

842 Andy Pasztor, "Crash Probe Examines Pilot Fatigue," *Wall Street Journal*, May 14, 2009, p. A3.

843 Andy Pasztor, "Captain's Training Faulted in Air Crash That Killed 50," *Wall Street Journal*, May 11, 2009, p. A1. Also see Deborah A. Silverman, "A Community Comes Together: The Crash of Continental Flight 3407," *The Strategist*, Summer 2009, pp. 22–24.

844 Andy Pasztor, "Doomed Pilots Talked of Inexperience," *Wall Street Journal*, May 15, 2009, p. A1.

845 Robert D. McFadden, "All 155 Aboard Safe as Crippled Jet Crash-Lands in Hudson," *New York Times*, January 16, 2009, p. A1.

846 Andy Pasztor and Daniel Michaels, "Qantas Drama Fuels Cockpit Lessons," *Wall Street Journal*, December 4–5, 2010, p. B4.

847 Andy Pasztor and Susan Carey, "Pilots Allege That Gulfstream Falsified Work-Hour Records," *Wall Street Journal*, May 29, 2009, p. A5.

848 Andy Pasztor, "Laptops Cited for Pilot Inattention," *Wall Street Journal*, October 27, 2009, p. A3.

849 Cam Simpson and Andy Pasztor, "FAA Reacted Slowly to Errant Jet," *Wall Street Journal*, October 29, 2009, p. A2.

850 Jonathan D. Rockoff, "J&J, Bruised by Recalls, Aims Higher," *Wall Street Journal*, August 19, 2010, p. B10.

851 "Johnson & Johnson Fights for Its Integrity: Consumer Brand Giant CEO Announces Plans to Overhaul Manufacturing Hierarchy, Create New Quality-Control Officer Positions," *Bulldog Reporter's Daily Dog*, August 19, 2010.

852 Suzanne Vranica, "Public Relations Learned the Hard Way," *Wall Street Journal*, December 30, 2010, p. B6.

853 "FSK Responds to 60 Minutes," Google.com

854 Schmit, op. cit.

855 Ibid.

856 "American Meat Institute Elects New Officers," States News Service, October 29, 2009.

857 Ben Worthen, Cari Tuna and Justin Scheck, "Companies More Prone to Go 'Vertical,'" *Wall Street Journal*, November 30, 2009, p. A16; Peter Sanders and Doug Cameron, "Boeing Again Delays 787 Delivery," *Wall Street Journal*, January 19, 2011, p. B3.

858 Ibid., p. A1.

859 Shawn Rhea, "The Rise of Foreign Agents; Drugs and Other Medical Products from Offshore Suppliers Can Offer Tremendous Savings, but Safety Has Become an Increasing Concern," *Modern Healthcare*, Special Report, May 26, 2008, p. 28.

860 Ibid.
861 Matthew Daly, "BP Ad Spending Since Spill: $5 Million a Week," *The Washington Post*, September 2, 2010, p. A21.
862 Steve McClellan, "BP's 'Apology' Ad Not a Complete Disaster," *Adweek*, June 8, 2010.
863 Ad appeared in *Wall Street Journal*, May 22–23, 2010, p. A9.
864 *Wall Street Journal*, July 30, 2010, p. A14.
865 Mouawad and Krauss, op. cit.
866 Jeff Casale, "BP Spill Response Tars Reputation," *Business Insurance*, May 31, 2010, p. 0001.
867 Brian Morrissey, "BP Gets Aggressive," *AdWeek.Com*, June 21, 2010. Also Jaimy Lee, "Oglivy Counsels BP on Social Media Strategy," *PR Week* (US), July 6, 2010, p. 6.
868 Robin Pagnamenta, Robert Lea, "BP's Next Great Battle is Already under Way—to Salvage Its battered Reputation," *The Times* (London), June 19, 2010, pp. 74, 75.
869 Angel Gonzalez and Russell Gold, "BP Puts American Face on Crucial U.S. Market," *Wall Street Journal*, July 26, 2010, p. A6.
870 Bruce Orwall, Monica Langley, and James Herron, "Embattled BP Chief to Exit," *Wall Street Journal*, July 26, 2010, p. A1.
871 Chazan, August 5, 2010, op cit.
872 Guy Chazan, "BP Reveals Comeback Plan," *Wall Street Journal*, July 28, 2010, p. A1. Also see "Briefing: BP and the Oil Spill," op. cit., p. 66.
873 Jad Mouawad and Clifford Krauss, "BP Details $30 Billion Plan to Pay for Spill," *New York Times*, July 28, 2010, p. B1.
874 Karla Cook, "Peanut Recall's Ripples Feel Like a Tidal Wave For Some Companies," *New York Times*, February 26, 2009, p. B6.
875 Julie Schmit, "Broken System Hid Peanut Plants' Risk; Case Reveals Every Link in Food-Safety Chain Failed," *USA Today*, April 27, 2009, p.1B.
876 Zhang and Adamy, op. cit.
877 Jane Zhang, "Hoping to Make Food Safer, States Decide to Go it Alone," *Wall Street Journal*, May 12, 2009, p. A13.
878 Jane Zhang, "FDA Warns on Pistachios Amid Salmonella Probe," *Wall Street Journal*, March 31, 2009, p. A2.
879 Jared A. Favole, "FDA Requires Faster Food-Safety Alerts," *Wall Street Journal*, September 9, 2009, p. A3.
880 Mundy and Tomson, op. cit.
881 Ibid.
882 Russell Gold, Ben Casselman and Maurice Tamman, "Permit Snafus on BP's Oil Well," *Wall Street Journal*, June 1, 2010, p. A8.
883 Russell Gold and Stephen Power, "Regulator Ceded Oversight of Rig Safety to Oil Drillers," *Wall Street Journal*, May 7, 2010, p. A4. For example, offshore oil workers in the United States in the past five years were more than four times as likely to be killed than a worker in European waters. At least one company complained about the inadequacy of the agency's safety investigations.
884 Ibid.
885 Andy Pasztor, "Flight Plan: How China Turned Around A Dismal Air Safety Record," *Wall Street Journal*, October 10, 2007, p. A1.
886 Ibid., p. A18.
887 Ibid.
888 These are some of the "essential lessons" discussed in Ian I. Mitroff., *Why Some Companies Emerge Stronger and Better from a Crisis: 7 Essential Lessons for Surviving Disaster* (New York: AMACOM, 2005), p. xiii.

889 John A. Byrne, "The Making of a Corporate Tough Guy," *Business Week*, January 15, 1996, p. 61. In less than two years after his arrival at Scott, the company's stock rose 225 percent, adding $6.3 billion in value to the company. Sacrificed, however, were more than 11,000 laid-off employees—71 percent of headquarters staff, 50 percent of the managers, and 20 percent of hourly workers. Also eliminated were all corporate gifts to charities, including reneging on the final $50,000 payment of a $250,000 pledge to the Philadelphia Museum of Art. Managers were even forbade from becoming involved in community activities because that would take away from their business duties.

890 James O'Toole, *Vanguard Management: Redesigning the Corporate Future* (Garden City, N.Y.: Doubleday & Company, Inc., 1985), pp. 42–49.

891 Ian I. Mitroff and Thierry C. Pauchant, *"We're So Big and Powerful Nothing Bad Can Happen to Us"* (New York: A Birch Lane Press Book by Carol Publishing Group, 1990), p. xv.

892 Christine M. Pearson and Judith A. Clair, "Reframing Crisis Management," *Academy of Management Review*, Vol. 23, No. 1, 1998, p. 61.

893 Peter Maass, "Scenes from the Violent Twilight of Oil," *Foreign Policy*, Vol. 174, September/October 2009, p. 114.

894 Russell Gold, "Exxon's CEO Gets Raise," *Wall Street Journal*, April 14, 2009, p. B3.

895 Staunch environmentalists refer to gallons rather than barrels: 11,000,000 gallons makes the spill sound much worse than 240,000 barrels. Also, Prince Edward Sound would be described as "pristine."

896 Alaric Nightingale and Tony Hopfinger, "Exxon Sailing Solo Against Push for Safer Tankers," *The Age* (Melbourne, Australia), March 26, 2009, p. 2.

897 Christopher Reddy, "Let's Not Forget Exxon Valdez," *Boston Globe*, March 24, 2009, p. A15.

898 Gerald Karey, "After 20 Years, Valdez Spill Impact Persists," *Platts Oilgram News*, March 23, 2009, p. 9.

899 "Supreme Court Overturns ExxonValdez $2.5 billion punitive damages aware," *Oil & Gas Journal*, July 7, 2008, p. 39.

900 "Campaign for New, Modern Chairman at ExxonMobil Gathers Weight," *The Times* (London), May 21, 2008, p. 57.

901 Gold, op. cit.

902 Russell Gold, "In Strategy Shift, Exxon Plans $600 Million Biofuels Venture," *Wall Street Journal*, July 15, 2009, p. B4.

903 Ann Davis, Matthew Dalton and Guy Chazan, "BP Moves to Clean Up Troubles," *Wall Street Journal*, October 24, 2007, p. A3.

904 Chip Cummins, Carrick Mollenkamp, Aaron G. Patrick and Guy Chazan, "Scandal, Crises Hasten Exit for British Icon," *Wall Street Journal*, May 2, 2007, p. A1.

905 Jeffrey Sonnenfeld, "The Real Scandal at BP," *BusinessWeek*, May 14, 2007.

906 Chip Cummins, Carrick Mollenkamp, Aaron O. Patrick and Guy Chazan, "Scandal, Crises Hasten Exit for British Icon," *Wall Street Journal*, May 2, 2007, p. A1.

907 Davis, Dalton and Chazan, op. cit.

908 From press release from Ann Pryor at McGraw-Hill for Michael Levine, *Guerrilla PR Wired: Waging a Great Publicity Campaign On-Line, Off-Line, and Everywhere in Between* (New York: McGraw-Hill, 2002).

909 Nicholas Casey, "Mattel Issues Third Major Recall," *Wall Street Journal*, September 5, 2007, p. A3.

910 Bloomberg News, "Mattel to Pay $2.3 Million Penalty for Lead in Toys," *New York Times*, June 6, 2009, p. B2.

911 Jane Spencer and Nicholas Casey, "Toy Recall Shows Challenge China Poses to Partners," *Wall Street Journal*, August 3, 2007, p. A1.

912 Bob Eckhart, "In Defense of Mattel," *Wall Street Journal*, September 11, 2007, p. A19.

913 Bob Dart, "Mattel CEO Defends toy Manufacturing Operations in China," Cox News Service, September 12, 2007, Washington General News section.

914 Emily Parker, "Made in China," *Wall Street Journal*, July 12, 2007, p. A15.

915 Ibid.

916 Andrew Batson and Lauren Etter, "Safety Becomes a Hot Trade Issue," *Wall Street Journal*, July 16, 2007, p. A4.

917 Neil King Jr. and Rebecca Blumenstein, "On message: China Launches Public Response to Safety Outcry," *Wall Street Journal*, June 30/July 1, 2007, p. A1. Also see Chapter 10 on lobbying by China.

918 Nicholas Zamiska, *Wall Street Journal*, June 28, 2007, p. A8.

919 Nicholas Zamiska, "China Sets Arrests over Product Safety," *Wall Street Journal*, October 30, 2007, p. 8; also "China Takes Aim at U.S. on Quality Control," *Wall Street Journal*, October 10, 2007, p. B1.

920 Nicholas Casey, Nicholas Zamiska and Andy Pasztor, "Mattel Seeks to Placate China With Apology," *Wall Street Journal*, September 22–23, 2007, p. A1. Also see "Chinese Manufacturing: Plenty of Blame to Go Around," *The Economist*, September 29, 2007, p. 68.

921 Ibid., p. 7.

922 Ibid.

923 Ibid.

924 Jason Leow "U.S. Pushes China on Safety," *Wall Street Journal*, August 1, 2007, p. A8.

925 Martinez, Anna Wilde Mathews, Joann S. Lublin and Ron Winslow, "Expiration Date: Merck Pulls Vioxx From Market After Link to Heart Problems," *Wall Street Journal*, October 1, 2004, p. A1.

926 Eric J. Topol, M.D., "Failing the Public Health—Rofecoxib, Merck, and the FDA," *New England Journal of Medicine*, Vol. 3351, October 21, 2004, pp. 1707.

927 Ibid.

928 Martinez, op. cit., p. A12.

929 "The Sick Need More Than Just Healthy Profits," *Financial Times*, November 23, 2004, p. 19. Nexis.

930 Topol, op. cit., p. 1708.

931 Alex Berenson, Gardiner Harris, Barry Meier and Andrew Pollack, "Despite Warnings, Drug Giant Took Long Path to Vioxx Recall," *New York Times*, November 14, 2004, p. 1. Nexis.

932 Testimony by David J. Graham, Associate Director for Science and Medicine in the Federal Drug Administration's Office of Drug Safety before the Congressional Committee on Senate Finance, Federal Document Clearing House Congressional Testimony, "Withdrawal from the Market of Vioxx Arthritis Pain Medication," November 18, 2004. Nexis.

933 Jeanne Whalen, "Study of Vioxx Critic Links Drug to Extra Coronary Cases," *Wall Street Journal*, January 25, 2005, p. D3.

934 Ibid.

934 Max H. Bazerman and Michael D. Watkins, *Predictable Surprises: The Disasters You Should Have Seen Coming and How to Prevent Them* (Boston, M.A.: Harvard Business School Press, 2004).

936 Topol, op. cit., p. 1707.

937 Berenson, op. cit.

938 Ibid., pp. 1707–1708 and Alex Berenson, Gardiner Harris, Barry Meier and

Andrew Pollack, "Despite Warnings, Drug Giant Took Long Path to Vioxx Recall," *New York Times*, November 14, 2004, Section 1, p. 1.
939 Anna Wilde Mathews, "Did FDA Staff Minimize Vioxx's Red Flags?" *Wall Street Journal*, October 10, 2004, p. B1.
940 Topol, op. cit., p. 1708.
941 Brian Steinberg, "Celebrex Moratorium Threatens to Chill Some Drug Marketing," *Wall Street Journal*, December 21, 2004, p. B4.
942 Scott Hensley, "In Switch, J&J Gives Straight Talk on Drug Risks in New Ads," *Wall Street Journal*, March 21, 2005, p. B6.
943 Diedtra Henderson, "Kennedy Raps Drug Firms' Sales Tactics," *The Boston Globe*, March 4, 2005, p. C3.
944 Ron Winslow, "What Makes a Drug Too Risky? There's No Easy Answer," *Wall Street Journal*, February 16, 2005, p. B1.
945 John Carey, "Side Effects of the Drug Scares," *BusinessWeek*, March 7, 2005, p. 42.
946 Amy Barrett, "Pharmaceuticals: Will Drugmakers Back Off the Hard Sell?" *BusinessWeek*, March 7, 2005, p. 44.
947 Hensley, op. cit.
948 Ibid.
949 Berenson, op. cit.
950 Topol, op. cit., p. 1709.
951 Graham testimony, op. cit.
952 Barbara Martinez, "Vioxx Lawsuits May Focus on FDA Warning in 2001," *Wall Street Journal*, October 5, 2004, p. B1.
953 Barbara Martinez, "Embattled Merck Touts Cost Cuts, Drug Pipeline," *Wall Street Journal*, December 15, 2004, p. A6.
954 Berenson, op. cit.
955 Scott Hensley, "Merck Faces Twin Vioxx Inquiries," *Wall Street Journal*, November 9, 2004, p. A3.; also *International Herald Tribune*, November 15, 2004.
956 Anna Wilde Mathews and Leila Abboud, "FDA Establishes Board to Review Approved Drugs," *Wall Street Journal*, February 16, 2005, p. A1.
957 John Carey, "The Vioxx Fallout on the Hill," *BusinessWeek*, February 7, 2005, p. 47.
958 Alex Berenson, "Chief Executive Quits at Merck; Insider Steps Up," *New York Times*, May 6, 2005, p. 1.
959 Martinez, op. cit.
960 Amy Barrett, "Merck: How Much Misery After Vioxx?" *Wall Street Journal*, November 22, 2004, p. 48, 50.
961 Barbara Martinez, "A Vioxx Comeback Could Tilt Balance in Merck Litigation," *Wall Street Journal*, February 22, 2005, p. B1.
962 Case is discussed in greater detail in Otto Lerbinger, *The Crisis Manager: Facing Risk and Responsibility* (Mahwah, N.J.: Lawrence Erlbaum Associates, 1997), p. 131.
963 John Carey, "Getting Business to Think about the Unthinkable," *BusinessWeek*, June 24, 1991, p. 104.
964 In analyzing an organization's culture, an excellent reference book is Edgar H. Schein, *Organizational Culture and Leadership*, Second Edition (Jossey-Bass Management Series, 1992).
965 One of the first public relations counselors to recognize this need was Carlton E. Spitzer, *Raising the Bottom Line: Business Leadership in a Changing Society* (New York: Longman, 1982).
966 Peter F. Drucker, *Management: Tasks, Responsibilities, Practices* (New York: Harper & Row, Publishers, 1973), p. 632.

967 Ian H. Wilson, "One Company's Experience with Restructuring the Governing Board," *Journal of Contemporary Business*, Vol. 8, No. 1, 1979, pp. 71–81.

968 Paul Clolery and Mark Hrywna, "Red Cross Audit Comes Up Clean," *The Non-Profit Times*, January 1, 2008, pp. 8, 9.

969 An influential book was by Howard R. Bowen, *Social Responsibilities of the Business-man* (New York: Harper & Brothers, 1953). In it he described the social audit as follows: "Just as businesses subject themselves to audits of their accounts by independent public-accountant firms, they might also subject themselves to periodic examination by independent outside experts who would evaluate the performance of the business from the social point of view." p. 155.

970 Pamela Buxton, "Design: Companies with a Social Conscience," *Marketing*, April 27, 2000.

971 For a full discussion of this subject, see Chapter 2, "Top Management Direction, Goals, and Effectiveness," in Richard L. Daft, *Organization Theory and Design*, Fourth Edition (New York: West Publishing Company, 1992), pp. 36–68.

972 *The Economist*, February 16, 2002, p. 57.

973 *The Economist*, December 8, 2001, p. 62.

974 "The Ship That Sank Quietly," *The Economist*, February 16, 2002, p. 57.

975 Rebecca Smith and Kathryn Kranhold, "Enron Knew Foreign Portfolio Had Lost Value," *Wall Street Journal*, May 6, 2002, p. C1.

976 John R. Emshwiller, "Enron Official Gave Warnings as Early as '99," *Wall Street Journal*, March 18, 2002, p. A3.

977 "Wasted Energy," *The Economist*, Dec. 8, 2001, p. 13.

978 E. Thomas Garman and Raymond E. Forgue, "The Enron Crisis from the Perspective of Personal Finance," *The Houghton Mifflin Guide to the Enron Crisis*, an uncorrected proof (Boston, M.A.: Houghton Mifflin, 2003), p. 7.

979 Bryan Gruley and Rebecca Smith, "Anatomy of a Fall: Keys to Success Left Kenneth Lay Open to Disaster," *Wall Street Journal*, April 26, 2002, p. A1.

980 "The Amazing Disintegrating Firm," *The Economist*, December 8, 2001, p. 62.

981 Ibid., p. 61.

982 "Wasted Energy," *The Economist*, December 8, 2001, p. 13.

983 William Sigismond, "The Enron Case from a Legal Perspective," op. cit., p. 11.

984 "The Amazing Disintegrating Firm," op. cit.

985 David Wessel, "Venal Sins: Why the Bad Guys of the Boardroom Emerged en Mass," *Wall Street Journal*, June 20, 2002, p. A1.

986 Steve Liesman, Jonathan Weil and Scot Paltrow, "When Rules Keep Debt Off the Books," *Wall Street Journal*, January 18, 2002, p. C1.

987 Ellen Joan Pollock, "Limited Partners: Lawyers for Enron Faulted Its Deals, Didn't Force Issue," *Wall Street Journal*, May 22, 2002, p. A1.

988 Michael Schroeder, "Enron's Board Was Warned in '99 on Accounting," *Wall Street Journal*, May 8, 2002, p. A2.

989 Lehrer News Show, January 1, 2002.

990 Vincent Canby "Film; Stone's 'Wall Street,'" *New York Times*, December 11, 1987, p. C3.

991 Kathryn Kranhold and Mitchell Pacelle, "Enron Paid Top Managers $681 Million, Even as Stock Slid," *Wall Street Journal*, June 17, 2002, p. B1.

992 Mitchell Pacelle, "Enron's Disclosure of Awards to Top Officials Draws Outrage," *Wall Street Journal*, June 18, 2002, p. C18.

993 Sana Siwolop, "Enron's Many Strands: A Case Study; Enron Is Grist for Business School Courses," *New York Times*, February 16, 2002, p. C8.

994 David Wessel, "Venal Sins: Why the Bad Guys of the Boardroom Emerged en Mass," *Wall Street Journal*, June 20, 2002, p. A1.

995 Ibid, p. A6.

996 Debbite Thorne Mcalister, "Enron and Beyond: Corporate Citizenship as a Business Imperative," op. cit., p. 27.

997 Kathryn Kranhold, Rick Wartzman and John R. Wilke, "Following the Trail: As Enron Inquiry Intensifies, Midlevel Players Face Spotlight," *Wall Street Journal*, April 30, 2002, p. A12.

998 Peter Coy, "Housing Meltdown," *BusinessWeek*, February 11, 2006, p. 41.

999 "Foreclosures in America: Searching for Plan B," *The Economist*, March 1, 2008, p. 77

1000 "Face Value: The Bailiff," *The Economist*, October 11, 2008, p. 90.

1001 One of the few exceptions in the financial sector was John Paulson, founder of Paulson & Co.'s hedge fund, who saw "overvalued" credit markets in 2006 and made $15 billion in 2007 shorting subprime securities.

1002 Jessica Silver-Greenberg, "Banking: More Muscle for Risk Managers," *Business-Week*, February 25, 2008, p. 062.

1003 Damian Paletta and Alistair MacDonald, "Mortgage Fallout Exposes Holes in New Bank-Risk Rules," *Wall Street Journal*, March 4, 2008, p. A1.

1004 David Henry, "None So Blind . . . How Regulators, Investors, and Lenders Failed to See a Crisis Coming," *BusinessWeek*, March 31, 2008, p. 44.

1005 Kate Kelly, "Excerpt: Inside the Fall of Bear Stearns," *Wall Street Journal*, May 9–10, 2009, p. W3.

1006 "The Captain of the Street," *Newsweek*, September 29, 2008, p. 26. "Bear Stearns: No Picnic," *The Economist*, March 29, 2008, p. 95.

1007 Aaron Lucchetti and Kara Scannell, "SEC Is Urged to Step Up Policing of Rating Firms," *Wall Street Journal*, April 16, 2008, p. C6.

1008 Aaron Lucchetti, "S&P Ramps Up Mortgage Downgrades," *Wall Street Journal*, January 31, 2008, p. A3.

1009 James R. Hagerty, Ruth Simon and Damian Paletta, "U.S. Seizes Mortgage Giants," *Wall Street Journal*, September 8, 2008, p. A1.

1010 Nick Timiros, "Fannie, Freddie Losses May Hit U.S.," *Wall Street Journal*, January 22, 2010, p. A6.

1011 Hagerty, Simon and Paletta, op. cit.

1012 James R. Hagerty and Joann S. Lublin, "Regulatory-Crackdown Fear Drove Countrywide," *Wall Street Journal*, January 29, 2008, p. A3.

1013 Roben Farzad, "Fair Value: In Search of a Subprime Villain," *BusinessWeek*, February 4, 2008, p. 77.

1014 "Why Did IndyMac Implode," *BSW*, August 4, 2008, p. 24.; Damian Paletta, Lingling Wei, and Ruth Simon, "IndyMac Reopens, Halts Foreclosure on Its Loans," *Wall Street Journal*, July 15, 2008, p. C1.

1015 Robin Sidel, David Enrich, and Dan Fitzpatrick, "WaMu Is Seized, Sold Off to J.P. Morgan, In Largest Failure in U.S. Banking History," *Wall Street Journal*, September 28, 2008, pp. A1, A14.

1016 "Face Value: The Bailiff," *The Economist*, October 11, 2008, p. 90.

1017 Paul M. Barrett, "Wall Street Staggers," *BusinessWeek*, September 29, 2008, p. 35.

1018 Susanne Craig, "Lawmakers Lay into Lehman CEO," *Wall Street Journal*, October 7, 2008, p. A3.

1019 Susanne Craig, Jeffrey McCracken, Aaron Lucchetti, and Kate Kelly, "The Weekend That Wall Street Died," *Wall Street Journal*, December 29, 2008, p. A1. Also see Gretchen Morgenson, "How the Thundering Herd Faltered and Fell," *New York Times*, November 9, 2008, p. BU9.

1020 Matthew Karnitschnig, Deborah Solomon, Liam Pleven and Jon E. Hilsenrath, "U.S. to Take Over AIG in $85 Billion Bailout; Central Banks Inject Cash as Credit Drys Up," *Wall Street Journal*, September 17, 2008, p. A1.

1021 Harrison Hong and Justin Lahart, "Bernanke's Bubble Laboratory," *Wall Street Journal*, May 16, 2008, p. A1.

1022 Monica Langley and David Enrich, "Citigroup Chafes Under U.S. Overseers," *Wall Street Journal*, February 25, 2009, p. A12.

1023 Dennis K. Berman, "Post-Enron Crackdown Comes up Woefully Short," *Wall Street Journal*, October 20, 2008 p. C2.

1024 Kevin Phillips, *Bad Money: Reckless Finance, Failed Politics, and the Global Crisis of American Capitalism* (New York: Viking, 2008), p. 4.

1025 Many owners obtained home equity loans that turned wealth into spending money, amounted to $700 billion in the third quarter of 2007. Damian Paletta and Alistair MacDonald, "Mortgage Fallout Exposes Holes in New Bank-Risk Rules," *Wall Street Journal*, March 4, 2008, p. A42.

1026 "O, Canada: Banks Look Healthier," *Wall Street Journal*, March 7–8, 2009, p. B10.

1027 David Henry, "None So Blind . . . How Regulators, Investors, and Lenders Failed to See a Crisis Coming," *BSU*, March 31, 2008, p. 44.

1028 Case is discussed in Otto Lerbinger, *The Crisis Manager: Facing Risk and Responsibility* (Mahwah, N.J.: Lawrence Erlbaum Associations, 1997), pp. 252–254.

1029 "Economics Focus; Chain of Fools," *The Economist*, February 9, 2008, p. 84.

1030 Joseph Stiglitz, "Central Banks Cannot Act Only After Horse Bolts," *Business Day* (South Africa), February 5, 2008, p. 9.

1031 Robert J. Shiller states that "many people who bought securitized mortgages had little access to financial advice that might have warned them how risky these instruments really were." "Good Financial Information Matters More Than Ever," *Wall Street Journal*, August 9, 2008, p. A17.

1032 Mentioned in a book review by Barry Gewen "Bad Money Reckless Finance, Failed Politics, and the Global Crisis of American Capitalism," *The International Herald Tribune*, April 23, 2008, p. 5.

1033 Kara Scannell, "SEC Faulted for Missing Red Flags at Bear Stearns," *Wall Street Journal*, September 27–28, 2008, p. A3. Only a few financiers exercised their knowledge to foresee the looming crisis. *BusinessWeek*'s David Henry listed four: Warren Buffett, John Paulson, founder of Paulson & Co, Laurence Fink, CEO of BlackRock, and Lloyd Blankfein, CEO of Goldman Sachs. The latter bet against housing and netted $4 billion in 2007. At Goldman, traders flagged their concerns to the firm's top executives who apparently listened; BlackRock had technology "that X-rayed complex collateralized debt obligations, exposing flaws in the underlying securities." But the prescience of these few was not widely shared.

1034 "The Welchway: Murder on the Financial Express," *BusinessWeek*, October 6, 2008, p. 84.

1035 Robert J. Shiller, "Good Financial Information Matters More Than Ever," *Wall Street Journal*, August 9, 2008, p. A17.

1036 Aaron Lucchetti, "Rating Game: As Housing Boomed, Moody's Opened Up," *Wall Street Journal*, April 11, 2008, pp. A1, A15.

1037 Ibid.

1038 Aaron Lucchetti and Judith Burns, "Moody's CEO Warned Profit Push Posed a Risk to Quality of Ratings," *Wall Street Journal*, October 23, 2008, p. A4.

1039 Ibid.

1040 Aaron Lucchetti and Kara Scannell, "SEC Is Urged to Step Up Policing of Rating Firms," *Wall Street Journal*, April 16, 2008, p. C6.

1041 Otto Lerbinger, *Corporate Public Affairs: Interacting With Interest Groups, Media, and Government* (Mahwah, N.J.: Lawrence Erlbaum Associates, 2006), p. 388

1042 Kara Scannell and Sudeep Reddy, "Greenspan Admits Errors to Hostile House Panel," *Wall Street Journal*, October 24, 2008, p. A15.

1043 "The Financial System, What Went Wrong," *The Economist*, March 22, 2008, p. 79.

1044 Kara Scannell, "SEC Faulted for Missing Red Flats at Bear Stearns," *Wall Street Journal*, September 27–28, 2008, p. A3.

1045 Phil Gramm, "Deregulation and the Financial Panic," *Wall Street Journal*, [no date] with the passage of the Financial Services Modernization Act.

1046 Damian Paletta and Alstair MacDonald, "Mortgage Fallout Exposes Holes in New Bank-Risk Rules," *Wall Street Journal*, March 4, 2008, p. A1.

1047 Allan H. Meltzer, "Keep the Fed Away From Investment Banks," *Wall Street Journal*, July 16, 2008, p. A17.

1048 David Folkenflik, "Where Were The Media As Wall Street Imploded?" from Planet Money, National Public Radio, March 9, 2009.

1049 Martha M. Hamilton, "What We Learned In the Meltdown," *Columbia Journalism Review*, January/February 2009, p. 36.

1050 Stephen J. Adler, "Editor's Memo: Beware Groupthink on the Economy," *BusinessWeek*, February 16, 2009, p. 016,

1051 Ibid.

1052 Folkenflik, op. cit.

1053 Thomas Frank, "Financial Journalists Fail Upward," *Wall Street Journal*, March 18, 2009, p. A13.

1054 Folkenflik, op. cit.

1055 Folkenflik, op. cit.

1056 Ibid.

1057 Carrick Mollenkamp, Susanne Craig, Jeffrey McCracken and Jon Hilsenrath, "The Two Faces of Lehman's Fall," *Wall Street Journal*, October 6, 2008, p. A1, A15.

1058 David Enrich and Damian Paletta, "Finance Reform Falters as Shock of '08 Fades," *Wall Street Journal*, September 9, 2009, p. A1.

1059 Liam Pleven and Susanne Craig, "Congress Grills Former AIG Chiefs," *Wall Street Journal*, October 8, 2008, p. A3.

1060 Robert J. Shiller, "Good Financial Information Matters More Than Ever," *Wall Street Journal*, August 9, 2008, p. A17.

1061 Paul M. Barrett, "Wall St. Staggers," *BusinessWeek*, September 29, 2008, p. 31.

1062 Emanuel Derman and Paul Wilmott, "Perfect Models, Imperfect World," *BusinessWeek*, January 12, 2009, p. 59.

1063 Ibid., p. 60.

1064 Maria Bartiromo, "FACETIME: Nell Minow on Outrageous CEO Pay—and Who's to Blame," *BusinessWeek*, March 2, 2009, p. 15.

1065 Susanne Craig and Dan Fitzpatrick, "BofA's Lewis Subpoenaed Over Merrill; Thain Talks," *Wall Street Journal*, February 20, 2009, p. C1.

1066 Michael M. Phillips, "Outrage Overflows on Capitol Hill as Lawmakrs Denounce Bonuses," *Wall Street Journal*, March 11, 2009, p. A4; Randall Smith and Liam Pleven, "Some Will Pay Back AIG Bonuses," *Wall Street Journal*, March 11, 2009, pp. A1, A4.

1067 Kara Scannell, Anita Raghavan and Amir Efrati, "The Subprime Cleanup Intensifies," *Wall Street Journal*, February 2–3, 2008, p. B1.

1068 Amir Efrati, Susan Pulliam, Kara Scannell and Craig Karmin, "Prosecutors Widen Probes Into Subprime," *Wall Street Journal*, Februrary 8, 2008, p. C1.

1069 Kara Scannell, "SEC Presses Hedge Funds," *Wall Street Journal*, September 29, 2008, p. A3.

1070 Klaus Schwab, "Bank Bonus and the Communitarian Spirit," *Wall Street Journal*, January 15, 2010, p. A19.

1071 Ken Brown and David Enrich, "Rubin, Under Fire, Defends His Role at Citi," *Wall Street Journal*, November 29–30, 2008, p. A1.
1072 Ibid., Susanne Craig, "Lawmakers Lay into Lehman CEO," *Wall Street Journal*, October 7, 2008, p. A3.
1073 Mary Ellen Podmolik, "Financial Industry Mum on Crisis," *B to B*, November 12, 2007, p. 1.
1074 Ibid.
1075 Maria Bartiromo, "FACETIME: Nell Minow on Outrageous CEO Pay—and Who's to Blame," *BusinessWeek*, March 2, 2009, p. 16.
1076 Ibid.
1077 Jessica Silver-Greenberg, "Banking: More Muscle for Risk Managers," *Business-Week*, February 25, 2008, p. 062.
1078 Judith F. Samuelson and Lynn A. Stout, "Are Executives Paid Too Much?" *Wall Street Journal*, February 26, 2009, p. A13.
1079 "Bank Strategies: No Size Fits All," *The Economist*, August 16, 2008, p. 13.
1080 Monica Langley and David Erich, op. cit.
1081 "Moody's President Will Step Down at End of July," *New York Times*, February 20, 2009.
1082 "Corporate Culture: When Something Is Rotten," *The Economist*, July 27, 2002, pp. 53–54.
1083 Aaron Lucchetti, "S&P Ramps Up Mortgage Downgrades," *Wall Street Journal*, January 31, 2008, p. A3.
1084 Liam Pleven and Amir Efrati, "Documents Show AIG Knew of Problems With Valuations," *Wall Street Journal*, October 11–12, 2008, p. B1.
1085 Kara Scannell and Aaron Lucchetti, "SEC Tightens rules for Ratings Firms," *Wall Street Journal*, December 4, 2008, p. C3.
1086 Elizabeth Williamson, "AIG Still Lobbies to Relax Oversight Rules," *Wall Street Journal*, October 16, 2008, p. A6. The mortgage-broker oversight law is known as the SAFE Act, short for the Secure and Fair Enforcement for Mortgage Licensing Act of 2008. Also see Elizabeth Williamson and Louise Radnofsky, "Banks Keep Up Lobbying Efforts," *Wall Street Journal*, October 20, 20008, p. A3. Note: American Financial Services Association.
1087 Ibid.
1088 Elizabeth Williamson and Brody Mullins, "Firms Keep Lobbying As They Get TARP Cash," *Wall Street Journal*, January 23, 2009, p. A4. In the auto industry, GM spent $3.3 million In the 4th quarter of 2008; in all of 2008, it spent $13.1 million on lobbying, down, however, from $14.3 million in 2007.
1089 Elizabeth Williamson and Louis Radnofsky, "Banks Keep Up Lobbying Efforts," *Wall Street Journal*, October 20, 20008, p. A3.
1090 Gottfried Haberler, *Prosperity and Depression: A Theoretical Analysis of Cyclical Movements* (New York: Atheneum, 1963). (Originally published by Harvard University Press.)
1091 The specifics of these ads are: (1) "The mortgage industry may be uncertain, but that doesn't mean you have to be . . ." "We think that buying or refinancing a home should be within reach of every individual who meets the requirements." It also says, "In fact, in the past three months alone, we've funded more than $50 billion in home loans, financing over 250,000 home, sweet homes." (*Wall Street Journal*, November 14, 2008,p. A7; December 1, 2008, p. A11.) (2) "Giving America the credit it deserves," which said, "That's why in 2008, we extended $35 billion in new credit lines to nearly 6 million credit card customers." "Last year alone, we worked together with our customers to modify nearly 850,000 consumer credit card loans by reducing interest rates, reducing/forgiving fees or working out new

payment plans." (*Wall Street Journal*, February 20, 2009, p. A9.) (3) "We're working to help people stay in their homes, not just buy them." (*Wall Street Journal*, January 28, 2009, p. A16.)

1092 Beth Snyder Bulik, "Bank Marketing Fails to Reassure Wary and Befuddled Customers," *Advertising Age*, Vol. 80, March 2, 2009.

1093 Jonah Bloom, "AIG Misses Chance to Prove Value of Honest Communication," *Advertising Age*, Vol. 80, March 23, 2009, p. 20.

1094 Ibid.

1095 Jack Neff, "Public Floggery for Bailed Out Marketers," *Advertising Age*, Vol. 80, No. 5, p. 1.

1096 Ad appeared on November 26, 2008, p. A7. Other banks pursued these themes: (1) "Citi's commitment to helping our clients and customers find solutions that will drive their financial success." (*Wall Street Journal*, November 24, 2008, p. A13.) (2) Bank of America's "the mortgage industry may be uncertain, but that doesn't mean you have to be . . . We think that buying or refinancing a home should be within reach of every individual who meets the requirements. . . . In fact, in the past three months alone, we've funded more than $50 billion in home loans, financing over 250,000 home, sweet homes." (*Wall Street Journal*, November 14, 2008, p. A7; December 1, 2008, p. A11.)

1097 See Frank H. Knight, *Risk, Uncertainty & Profit* (New York: Harper & Row: Harper Torchbooks, 1921). He was a Chicago University economist.

1098 "Economics Focus (Nearly) Nothing to Fear But Fear Itself," *The Economist*, January 31, 2009, p. 84.

1099 Michael S. Rosenwald, "How Thinking Costs You; Behavioral Economics Shows That When It Comes to Investing, People Aren't That Smart," *Washington Post*, May 25, 2008, p. F01.

1100 Ibid.

1101 "Psychology's Ambassador To Economics; the Father of Behavioural Economics Daniel Kahneman Talks to Vikram Khanna about Cognitive Illusions, Investor Irrationality and Measures of Well-Being," *The Business Times* (Singapore), July 12, 2008, section "Raffles Conversation."

1102 Rosenwald, op. cit.

1103 Ibid.

1104 Katherine Penaloza, "How Behavioural Economics Is Shaking Our Beliefs," *The Business Times* (Singapore), June 13, 2008, Book section.

1105 Ibid.

1106 Peter Foster, "The Dangers of Behavioural Economics" *Financial Post* (Canada), November 26, 2008, p. FP1.

1107 Rosenwald, op. cit.

1108 Suzanne Garment, *Scandal: The Culture of Mistrust in American Politics*, (New York: Times Books, a division of Random House, Inc., 1991), p.14.

1109 A point made by Hiroshige Seko, "Scandal Management," a Master of Science thesis, Boston University, College of Communication, May 1992.

1110 "German Tax Scandals: The Disgrace of Germany AG," *The Economist*, February 23, 2008, p. 68.

1111 "Crisis Management: Hyundai's 'We're Sunk' Defense," *BusinessWeek*, June 19, 2006, p.13.

1112 Moon Ihlwan, "South Korea: A Smoother Ride Minus the Big Wheel?" *Business-Week*, May 25, 2006, p. 48.

1113 Moon Ihlwan, "A Scratch on Hyundai's Paint Job," *BusinessWeek*, April 17, 2006, p. 82.

1114 "Samsung Chairman Takes Responsibility for Scandal," *Wall Street Journal*, April 7, 2008, p. B7.

1115   Laurie P. Cohen, "Chiquita Under the Gun," *Wall Street Journal*, August 2, 2007, p. A1.

1116   Christopher Farrell, "Do-Gooders Doing Mischief," *BusinessWeek*, April 21, 2008, p. 18.

1117   Rana Foroohar, "The $1.6 Trillion Non-Profit Sector Behaves (or Misbehaves) More and More Like Big Business," *Newsweek*, Atlantic (Algeria) Editions, September 5, 2005, p. 30.

1118   Anne Marie Chaker and John Hechinger, "Cuomo Assails Lack of Student-Loan Oversight," *Wall Street Journal*, April 28, 2007, p. A6.

1119   Jennifer Harper, "Government in 'an Ethics Crisis,' Survey Finds; Workplace Said to Breed Misconduct," *Washington Times*, January 30, 2008, p. A5.

1120   Amir Efriti, Tom Lauricella and Dionne Secrecy, "Top Broker Accused of $50 Billion Fraud," *Wall Street Journal*, December 12, 2008, p. A1.

1121   Steve Stecklow, "In Echoes of Madoff, Ponzi Cases Proliferate," *Wall Street Journal*, pp A1, A12.

1122   Ibid, p. 14.

1123   Robert Frank, Peter Lattman, Dionne Searcey and Aaron Lacchetti, "Fund Fraud Hits Big Names," *Wall Street Journal*, December 13–14, 2008, p. A7.

1124   "The Madoff Scandal; Follow the Feeders," *The Economist*, January 3, 2009, p. 55.

1125   Paul M. Barrett, et al., "Wall St. Staggers," *BusinessWeek*, September 29, 2008, p. 28.

1126   Robert Frank, Peter Lattman, Dionne Searcey and Aaron Lacchetti, "Fund Fraud Hits Big Names," *Wall Street Journal*, December 13–14, 2008, p. A7.

1127   Jason Zweig, "How Bernie Madoff Made Smart Folks Look Dumb," *Wall Street Journal*, December 13–14, 2008, p. B1.

1128   Ibid.

1129   Jane J. Kim, "Burned Investors Won't Find Strong Safety Net," *Wall Street Journal*, December 17, 2008, p. A8.

1130   Dionne Searcey and David Gauthier-Villars, "Big Madoff Investor Found Dead," *Wall Street Journal*, December 24, 2008, p. A1.

1131   Cassell Bryan-Low, "Inside a Swiss Bank, Madoff Winnings," *Wall Street Journal*, January 14, 2009, p. C1.

1132   Ibid.

1133   Amir Efrati and Dionne Searcey, "Madoff Is Moved to Medical Facility," *Wall Street Journal*, December 24, 2009, p. C1.

1134   "Face Value: Stopping the Rot," *The Economist*, March 8, 2008, p. 76.

1135   Mike Esterl and David Crawford, "Siemens to Pay Huge Fine in Bribery Inquiry," *Wall Street Journal*, December 15, 2008, p. B1.

1136   Ibid.

1137   "Face Value: Stopping the Rot," op. cit.

1138   Mike Esterl and David Crawford, "Siemens to Pay Huge Fine in Bribery Inquiry," *Wall Street Journal*, December 15, 2008, p. B5.

1139   David Crawford and Mike Esterl, "Siemens Pays Record Fine in Probe," *Wall Street Journal*, December 16, 2008, p. B2.

1140   Mike Esterl, "Ex-Siemens Manager Sentenced," *Wall Street Journal*, November 25, 2008, p. B2.

1141   Mark Landlere and Carter Dougherty "Scandal at Siemens Tarnishes Promising Results," *New York Times*, February 28, 2007, p. C1.

1142   Ibid.

1143   Ibid.

1144   Eric Bellman, "Satyam Investigators to Look at Maytas Companies," *Wall Street Journal*, January 12, 2009, p. B3.

1145 Niraj Sheth and Jackie Range, "Satyam Minutes Show Directors Raised Questions," *Wall Street Journal,* January 16, 2009, p. B1.
1146 Ibid.
1147 Eric Bellman and John Satish Kumar, "Founder Arrested, Board Out at Satyam," *Wall Street Journal,* January 10–11, 2009, p. B1.
1148 Geeta Anand and Romit Guha, "Satyam Bank Documents at Issue," *Wall Street Journal,* January 20, 2009, p. B3.
1149 Eric Bellman and Jackie Range, "Satyam to Hire New Auditor," *Wall Street Journal,* January 13, 2009, p. B3.
1150 Alessandra Galloni, David Reilly, and Carrick Mollenkamp, "Skimmed Off: Parmalat Inquiry Finds Basic Ruses At Heart of Scandal," *Wall Street Journal,* December 31, 2007, p. A1.
1151 Gail Edmondson and Laura Cohn, "Italy: How Parmalat Went Sour: Here's the Skinny on Europe's Enormous Financial Scandal," *BusinessWeek,* January 12, 2004, p. 46.
1152 Alessandra Gdalloni, Carick Molenkamp, and Darren McDermott, "Scandal at Parmalat Broadens; Staff may Have Destroyed Files," *Wall Street Journal,* December 29, 2003, p. A2.
1153 Ibid.
1154 Gail Edmondson and Laura Cohn, op. cit.; "Special Report: Europe's Corporate Governance; Parma Splat," *The Economist,* January 17, 2004, pp. 59–61; Alessandra Galloni, Carrick Molenkamp and Darren McDermott, "Scandal at Parmalat Broadens; Staff May Have Destroyed Files," *Wall Street Journal,* December 29, 2003, p. A2.
1155 Gail Edmondson and Laura Cohn, "Italy: How Parmalat Went Sour: Here's the Skinny on Europe's Enormous Financial Scandal," *BusinessWeek,* January 12, 2004, p. 47.
1156 Alessandra Galloni, David Reilly, and Carrick Mollenkamp, op. cit., p. A4.
1157 David Reilly, Jonathan Weil, and Alessandra Galloni, "Grant Thornton Is Likely to Face Skepticism It Was Ever a Victim," *Wall Street Journal,* December 29, 2003, p. A2.
1158 Edmonson and Cohn, "Italy: How Parmalat Went Sour," op. cit., p. 46.
1159 Alessandra Galloni, David Reilly, and Carrick Mollenkamp, "Skimmed Off: Parmalat Inquiry Finds Basic Ruses At Heart of Scandal," *Wall Street Journal,* December 31, 2007, p. A4.
1160 Gail Edmondson and Laura Cohn, "Special Report: Europe's Corporate Governance; Parma Splat," *The Economist,* January 17, 2004, p. 60.
1161 Edmonson and Cohn, "Italy: How Parmalat Went Sour," op. cit., p. 48.
1162 Ibid.
1163 "Parma Splat," *The Economist,* op. cit., p. 60.
1164 John Hooper, "Parmalat Founder Gets 10 Years. Prison For Market Rigging," *The Guardian* (London), December 19, 2008.
1165 Loretta Chao, "More Firms Tied to Tainted Formula," *Wall Street Journal,* September 17, 2008, p. A23; Gordon Fairclough, "Tainting of Milk Is Open Secret in China," *Wall Street Journal,* November 3, 2008, p. A1. Also see Chao's "More Countries Ban Chinese Products Amid Milk Scandal," *Wall Street Journal,* September 25, 2008, p. A12.
1166 Gordon Fairclough, "Tainting of Milk Is Open Secret in China," *Wall Street Journal,* November 3, 2008, p. A1. Also Loretta Chao, "Ex-Executive Pleads Guilty in China's Tainted-Milk Case," *Wall Street Journal,* January 2, 2009, p. A4.
1167 Gordon Fairclough and Loretta Chao, "Chinese Formula Maker Hid Toxic Danger for Weeks," *Wall Street Journal,* September 18, 2008, p. A15.

1168 Ibid.
1169 Loretta Chao, "Chinese Dairies Face a Worsening Crisis," *Wall Street Journal*, September 19, 2008, p. B1.
1170 Ibid.
1171 Sky Canaves and Juliet Ye, "Chinese Parents File Milk Lawsuit," *Wall Street Journal*, October 1, 2008, p. A21.
1172 Robert Chang, "Tainted," *Global Journalist*, Vol. 14, Winter 2008, p.15.
1173 Ibid.
1174 Fairclough, op.cit.
1175 Gordon Fairclough and Loretta Chao, op. cit.
1176 "China: Saving Face Goes Sour," *Newsweek*, October 6, 2008, p. 7.
1177 Shai Oster and Loretta Chao, "China Arrests 2 in Milk Scandal as Number of Sick Infants Rises," *Wall Street Journal*, September 16, 2008, p. A16.
1178 Shai Oster, Loretta Chao, Jason Leow, and Jane Zhang, "FDA Warns of Products in U.S. Tied to Tainted Milk," *Wall Street Journal*, September 27–28, 2008, p. A14.
1179 Chao, op. cit., January 2, 2009, p. A4.
1180 Sky Canaves and Juliet Ye, "Chinese Parents File Milk Lawsuit," *Wall Street Journal*, October 10, 2008, A21; also Loretta Chao and Jason Leow, "Chinese Tainting Scandal Pulls Milk Off Shelves," *Wall Street Journal*, September 20–21, 2008, p. A10.
1181 "China's Baby-Milk Scandal: Formula for Disaster," *The Economist*, September 20, 2008 p. 57.
1182 Gordon Fairclough, "China Orders Wide Milk-Product Tests in Effort to Restore Public Confidence," *Wall Street Journal*, October 15, 2008, p. A15.
1183 Bill Savadove, "Sales of White Rabbit Candy Halted Over Melamine Scare; Sweet's Maker Takes Action While Awaiting Test Results," *South China Morning Post*, September 27, 2008, p. 7.
1184 Loretta Chao, "More Countries Ban Chinese Products Amid Milk Scandal," *Wall Street Journal*, September 25, 2008, p. A12.
1185 Fairlough and Chao, op. cit.
1186 "Food and Pet Food: Not On the Label," *The Economist*, September 6, 2008, p. 97. Also see Marion Nestle, *Pet Food Politics: The Chihuahua in the Coal Mine*, University of California Press.
1187 David Barboza, "Squeezed by Milk Scandal, China's Dairy Farmers Say They Are Victims," *New York Times*, October 4, 2008, p. A5.
1188 Karl Finders, "Satyam Fraud a PR Disaster for India," *Computer Weekly*, January 13–19, 2009, p. 8.
1189 "Satyam Funds Allegedly Tapped," *Wall Street Journal*, January 23, 2009, p. B5.
1190 Anonymous, *International Financial Law Review*, London, July/August 2009.
1191 "Face Value: Stopping the Rot," op. cit.
1192 David Drawford and Mike Esterl, "Siemens Pays Record Fine in Probe," *Wall Street Journal*, December 16, 2008, p. B2.
1193 Romit Guha and John Satish Kumar, "Satyam Appoints an Insider As New CEO, Secures Funding," *Wall Street Journal*, February 6, 2009, p. B2.
1194 Chad Bray, "Madoff Auditor Says He Was Duped, Too," *Wall Street Journal*, November 4, 2009, p. C3. Amir Afrati, "Madoff Auditor Plea May Signal Other Probe," *Wall Street Journal*, December 10, 2009, p. C3.
1195 James E. Post, "Fighting the Ethics Pandemic. Can We Turn Things Around?" *Builders and Leaders*, DATE?, p. 36.
1196 Amy Joyce, "Rising Pressure and Falling Standards; A New Survey Shows Human Resources Units Feel Caught in an Ethics Bind," *The Washington Post*, May 4, 2003, p. F6.

1197 Lawrence B. Chonko and Shelby D. Hunt, "Ethics and Marketing Management: A Retrospective and Prospective Commentary," *Journal of Business Research*, Vol. 50, December 2000, p. 235.
1198 Ibid.
1199 Eric Bellman and Jackie Range, "Satyam to Hire New Auditor," *Wall Street Journal*, January 13, 2009, p. B3.
1200 Ibid.
1201 Jackie Range, "Accountants for Satyam Arrested by Indian Police," *Wall Street Journal*, January 26, 2009, p. B3.
1202 Ibid.
1203 "Special Report—Europe's Corporate Governance," op. cit., p. 61.
1204 Kara Scannell, "Madoff Chasers Dug for Years, to No Avail," *Wall Street Journal*, January 5, 2009, p. C1.
1205 James B. Stewart: "The Lessons to Be Learned From the Madoff Scandal," *Wall Street Journal*, December 31, 2008, p. D1.
1206 Chao, January 2, 2009, op. cit.
1207 Gordon Fairclough, "China Hopes Melamine Trials Will Restore Trust," *Wall Street Journal*, December 27–28, 2008, p. A4.
1208 Loretta Chao, "Ex-Dairy Executive Is Set for Trial in China's Milk Scandal," *Wall Street Journal*, December 31, 2008, p. A4.
1209 Loretta Chao, "Tainted-Milk Victims to Get Payments," *Wall Street Journal*, December 29, 2008, p. A4.
1210 Sky Canaves and Juliet Ye, op. cit.
1211 Loretta Chao and Jason Leow, "Chinese Tainting Scandal Pulls Milk Off Shelves," op. cit.
1212 Loretta Chao, "China Bolsters Dairy-Supply Oversight In Effort to Rebound From Scandal," *Wall Street Journal*, January 21, 2008.
1213 See such publications as Lester R. Brown, *State of the World 1995* (New York: W.W. Norton & Company, 1995).
1214 An apt phrase borrowed from the title of Richard Clark Sterne's book, *Dark Mirror: The Sense of Injustice in Modern European and American Literature* (New York: Fordham University Press, 1994).
1215 For a discussion of this decision, see Thierry C. Pauchant and Ian I. Mitroff, *Transforming the Crisis-Prone Organization: Preventing Individual, Organizational, and Environmental Tragedies* (San Francisco: Jossey-Bass Publishers, 1992), p. 117.
1216 See Barbara Ley Toffler, *Tough Choices: Managers Talk Ethics* (New York: John Wiley & Sons, 1986), pp. 17–18. Competing claims are one of four elements of ethical situations.
1217 Archie B. Carroll, "In Search of the Moral Manager," *Business Horizons*, Vol. 30, March–April 1987, p. 13.
1218 See the section on "Integrative Action Versus Segmentalism: Keys to Innovation" in Rosabeth Moss Kanter, *The Change Masters: Innovation and Entrepreneurship in the American Corporation* (New York: Simon & Schuster, Inc., A Touchstone book, 1983), pp. 27–36.
1219 From Philip Lesly's newsletter, *Managing the Human Climate*, No. 156, January–February, 1996.
1220 Warren Bennis, *On Becoming a Leader* (Reading, M.A.: Addison-Wesley Publishing Company, Inc., 1989), p. 75.
1221 Ibid., pp. 76–77. For shaping applied to public affairs, see John F. Mahon, "Corporate Political Strategy," *Business in the Contemporary World*, Vol. 2, Autumn 1989, pp. 50–62.
1222 See John F. Mahon, op cit.

1223 David A. Garvin, "Building a Learning Organization," *Harvard Business Review*, Vol. 71, July–August 1993, p. 80.

1224 Ibid., p. 81. The article discusses and illustrates each of the five steps.

1225 See Irving L. Janis, *Crucial Decisions: Leadership in Policymaking and Crisis Management* (New York: The Free Press, a division of Macmillan, 1989), Chapter 5, pp. 89–117.

1226 Ibid., p. 91.

1227 See section on environmental annual reports in Bob Frause and Julie Colehour, *The Environmental Marketing Imperative: Strategies for Transforming Environmental Commitment Into a Competitive Advantage* (Chicago, I.L.: Probus Publishing Company, 1994), pp. 159–163.

1228 Ralph H. Kilmann, Teresa Joyce Covin, and Associates, *Corporate Transformation* (San Francisco: Jossey-Bass Publishers, 1988), p. xiii. They state: "Corporate transformation is a new phenomenon. Never before in the history of the world have so many organizations had to question their very purpose, strategy, structure, and culture as they have had to do in the 1980s."

1229 Ibid., p. xiv.

1230 Kilmann and Covin, op. cit., p. 27.

1231 J.R. Hipple and Felix Verdigets, "Transformers: The Five Elements of Transforming Corporate Culture," *The Public Relations Strategist*, Vol. 14, No. 2, 2008, p. 16.

1232 Ibid.

1233 Ibid., p. 19.

1234 John D. Adams, *Transforming Work* (Alexandria, V.A.: Miles River Press, 1984), p. vii.

1235 See Friedrich A. Hayek, *Individualism and Economic Order* (London: Routledge & Kegan Paul Ltd, 1949), and *The Road to Serfdom* (London: George Routledge & Sons Ltd, 1944).

1236 See Milton Friedman, *Capitalism and Freedom* (New York: Harcourt Brace Javanovich, 1962).

1237 As Leda Karabela, a management coach, observes: Decisions imply consequences. Consequences imply risks. Risks imply possibilities of loss. Does this mean that the fear of losing—however we perceive loss—will prevent us from the possibility of gaining? And what happens when you do nothing? At best, nothing will change.

Index

Abu Laban, A. 164
acceptability of risk 81
accidents 66
accommodative strategies 62–3, 67, 68–9, 181–2
accounting firms 255, 256; replacement of unprofessional accountants 294
achievement of immediate goals, unwillingness to impede 4
acoustic switch 146
activist groups 16, 20, 157; engaging 180–3; see also confrontation crises
Adams, J.D. 312
advance arrangements (emergency plans) 39–40, 96
advertising: banks 276–7; BP 229; misleading by Merck 243–5
aerial photography 15
aggression 202
AIB International 227
aid: foreign 106–8; private sector 108–9
AIDS/HIV 113, 124
AIG 65, 261, 268, 274–5, 275, 277
Airbus 233
airlines 225–6; safety reforms in China's airlines 232–3
Alaskan pipelines 137
Alcoa 282
alert responsibility 37–8
alert systems 204–5
algae-based biofuels 237
Alinsky, S. 162
Allen, K. 169
Allen, T. 148
alternative technologies 143, 145–6
American Meat Institute (AMI) 227
American Red Cross 100, 250

Amoco Texas City refinery 137
amorality 209–10
Animal Liberation Front (ALF) 172–3, 302
animal–human disease transmission 111–13
animal rights 171–3, 181
anthrax 187, 205
antibiotic resistance 112
anticipation 307
anti-globalization protests 161–2, 167–8, 175–6, 178, 181
antiviral drugs 125
anxiety 12–13
apologies 63–6; BP 218; by the Catholic Church 73–4; crises of deception 272; criteria of a sincere apology 70; misconduct 293
Apple 197
approvals, advance 39–40
Archdiocese of Washington 48–9
Arla Foods 50–1, 159, 164–6, 176
ascertaining the reality of a crisis 53
asteroid collision 83
attack 62
auditors 255, 256, 288, 295–6
Australia: fires 88–9, 97–8, 99; Queensland flooding 89
avian flu 111

baby formula scandal 289–92, 293, 296–7
Bam earthquake, Iran 108, 110
Bank of America 276, 277
banking crisis see financial crisis of 2008
banks 6, 7, 36; apologies for the financial crisis 64–6
banning products/services 142–3

Baptist Church 175
Bartlett, D. 197
Basel II guidelines 266
Baxter International 220
Bea, R. 144
"bear" rumors 198
Bear Sterns 258, 259
beef, recall of 222
behavioral economics 278–80
Belgium 223–5
Benedict, Pope 18–19
Bennis, W. 215–16, 307
Benoit, W.L. 62
Berle, A.A. 35
Bernanke, B. 261
Berry, J. 47
Bhopal gas leak 37, 67
Biden, J. 121
biological crises 19, 77–83, 111–30;
    characteristics of biological
    diseases 111–14; mad cow
    disease 122–4, 128; SARS 6–7,
    114–19; similarities with natural
    disasters 113–14; strategies for
    dealing with 124–30; swine flu
    112–13, 120–2, 125–6, 128;
    transmission of diseases between
    animals and humans 111–13
biotechnology 90, 133, 172
bioterrorism 168–70, 187–8
bishops, Catholic 48
Black Death 111, 114
Blackberry 56
Blair, S. 258–9
blame game 223, 247
Blanchard, K. 11
blogging, defamation in 191
Bloomberg News 199
blowout preventer (BOP) 217
boards of directors 310; BP and
    reputational damage 230; crises
    of deception 273; Enron 255,
    256; involvement and crisis
    preparedness 31–2; PCA's
    dysfunctional board 231;
    strengthening corporate
    governance 249
Boeing 7, 228, 233
Bonlat 288
bonuses 269–70
Boston Globe 74
Boston Phoenix 48
Boston University 29, 179; National

Biocontainment Laboratory 168–70;
    rape case 192–3
bovine spongiform encephalopathy (BSE)
    (mad cow disease) 122–4, 128
boycotts 176–7
Boyden, S. 69
BP 232; Deepwater Horizon
    oil spill 131, 134–9, 216–19;
    mismanagement 216–19; poor
    application of hazard management
    measures 145–8; repairing
    reputational damage 228–30; skewed
    values 137, 237–8
bribery 285–6
Bridgestone 70–1, 72
British Airways 38
broadcasting stations 36
Brockner, J. 14
Browne, Lord J. 229, 237, 238
bubbles 261
Buffett, W. 9
building codes 92
Bureau of Ocean Energy, Regulation and
    Enforcement 148, 232
bureaucracy 106–7; bureaucratic
    managers 303
Burger, C. 52
Burston-Marsteller 16
business ideology 248–9
business schools 212

Cabrera, A. 7
California's Proposition 2 223
Campbell's Soup 247
Canada 121, 140–1
Carlton, K. 193
Carmeli, A. 43
Carroll, A.B. 209–10
Caterpillar 109
Catholic Church sexual abuse
    scandal 47–50, 73–4
Celebrex 244, 246, 247
Centers for Disease Control and
    Prevention (CDC) 187
Centre for Science and Environment
    (CSE) 166
Ceres 237
Chemical Emergency Preparedness
    Plan 40–1
chemical industry 33, 304
Chemical Security Act 186
Chernobyl disaster 78, 132
Chertoff, M. 94

chief executive officers (CEOs) 55; costs of protecting 186; replacing problem executives 274
Chilean miners rescue 151
China 92, 128–9; baby formula scandal 289–92, 293, 296–7; Lunar New Year snow storm 87, 95; Mattel recall of toys made in China 238–42, 247–8; safety reforms in the airline industry 232–3; SARS crisis 114–19; Sichuan earthquake 18, 87, 95, 98, 99–100, 106; swine flu and diplomatic row with Mexico 121
Chiquita 282
Cho, S.-H. 194, 195–6
cholera 105
Chrysler 67, 199, 249
Chung Mong Koo 282
Cialdini, R. 284
Cincinnati Microwave Inc. 321
Citigroup 65
civil society 160, 312; see also confrontation crises
Clair, J.A. 13, 212–13, 236
Clark, H. 291
Clark, J. 182–3
Clarkson, B. 265, 274
classification of crises 17–22
climate change 85; see also global warming
cloud computing 201
Coca-Cola 108; tainted in Europe 223–5; water problems in India 166–7
cognitive illusions 278–80
cognitive theory 13
Cohen, L. 191
Colgan Air crash 225
collateral requirements 266–7
Columbine High School shooting 193–4
communication 1, 15, 45–59, 305–6; BP's blunders 218–19; complicated by foreign ownership 70–1; crises of communication failure 46–51; crises of deception 270–2; crises of malevolence 193; emergency alert systems 204–5; essentials of 51–3; guidelines for 53–9; image restoration strategies see image restoration strategies; media and reputational damage 45–6; public communication channels 96; risk communication 78–9

competitive intelligence (CI) 190
Computer Emergency Response Team (CERT) 204
concern, and risk perception 81
confrontation crises 20, 155–7, 159–83, 302; animal rights 171–3, 181; anti-globalization protests 161–2, 167–8, 175–6, 178, 181; Boston University's National Biocontainment Laboratory 168–70; Danish cartoon crisis 50–1, 159, 164–6, 176; dynamics of confrontations 160–4; labor disputes 173–4; managing 174–83; Pepsi's water problems 166–7
construction industry 28–9
consumer movement 161
containment dome 137–8
Continental Airlines 225
contingency planning 26, 33–42, 44, 247–8; activating contingency plans 98–9; advance arrangements 39–40; assignment of crisis alert responsibility 37–8; background press materials 41–2; biological crises 126; contingency media plans 97; crisis communication center 38–9; crisis management team 38–9; crisis media list 41; designation and training of spokespersons 42; establishment of crisis thresholds 36–7; identification of areas of vulnerability 33–6; identification and prioritization of publics to be informed 40–1; objectives 33
Cook, R. 111
Coombs, W.T. 17–18, 62–3
Coors beer 178
corporate culture see organizational culture
corporate governance 249–50, 273–4, 295–6
corporate social responsibility (CSR) 235, 313
corrective action 63, 71–2
cost-cutting 137
Council for Responsible Genetics (CRG) 169
Countrywide Financial Corp. 199, 260
Coy, P. 267, 268
Cramer, J. 267
Creutzfeldt-Jakob Disease (CJD) 122–4

crises 5–23; characteristics 10–14; criteria of a successful outcome 22; effect on managers 10–13; formal definitions 9–10; guidelines for analyzing 23; as opportunities 14; public exposure 15–17; recognizing 8–10; severity 8, 34; trends promoting 6–7; typologies 17–22, 66–7
crisis alert responsibility 37–8
crisis communication see communication
crisis communications center 38–9, 54
crisis event 26
crisis industry, growth of 16–17
Crisis Management Exercise Program 39
crisis management team 38–9; activation of 53–4
crisis media center 54
crisis mentality 22
crisis preparedness see preparedness
crisis-provoking tactics 160, 162–3
crisis task forces 38, 39
crisis thresholds 36–7
critical response time 46
Culp, R. 272
customer relationship management (CRM) 72, 211
customer relationship marketing (CRM) 276
cybercrime 188–91
cybersecurity 201–2
Cyclone Nargis 107–8

Dalles, The 188
Danish cartoons crisis 50–1, 159, 164–6, 176
Danone 173–4, 179, 182, 292
data theft 189–90
Davos 178, 180
Debrowski, T.A. 241
decentralization 49–50
deception, crises of 21, 207–13, 253–80; Enron 6, 254–8; financial crisis see financial crisis of 2008; response strategies 270–7
decision-making: ethics and 212; involving public interest groups in 182–3; speeding up and broadening 306–8
deep sea drilling technology 135–7, 137–8
Deepwater Horizon oil rig 131, 134–9, 145–8, 216–19, 228–30

defensive strategies 62–3, 66, 67, 68–9, 205–6
Dell 45–6
Delta Works project 92
denial 10, 316; China and the SARS crisis 115–17; mad cow disease 122–3; strategy 62, 68
derivatives 259
developing countries 144
DHL 110
Diamond, J. 19
diplomatic crisis 241–2
direct-to-consumer advertising (DTC) 243–5
disclosure 56–7, 293; crises of management failure 270–2
Disney Corp. 175
distributed denial of service (DDOS) attacks 190–1, 202
Domino's Pizza video prank 27–8
double-loop learning 43, 44
Dow Chemical 79
Dow Corning 207
downer cows 222
downstream measures 142, 144–5; BP's poor application 147–8
Doyle, P. 27, 28
Doyne, K. 46
dread risks 82
Dreamliner jet 7, 228
Drucker, P.F. 215
Drug Safety Oversight Board 246
drugs 242–6, 247
Dudley, R. 230
Dunlap, A.J. 235
Dyhes, R. 97
Dynergy 254, 255

E. coli 221
e2Campus 205
early warning signals: gagging 66; ignored by Enron 254; ignored in Ford/Firestone case 69; ignored by Merck 243
early warning systems 93–5
earthquakes: Haiti 87–8, 103–5; Iran 108, 110; Kashmir 110; Kobe 106–7; Sichuan 5, 87, 95, 98
Easterbrook, G. 83
Eckard, C. 220
Eckart, B. 239
ecological damage 18–19, 86–7
economic relationships 211

Efthimiou, G. 52
Egeland, J. 108
egg industry 222–3
ego defenses 3–4
Electric Power Research Institute
    149–50
electricity industry: blackouts 140–1,
    149–50; need for technological
    overhaul 149–50; *see also* nuclear
    power
Ellis, M. 57–8
emergency alert systems 204–5
emergency planning/plans 39–40, 96
Emergency Planning and Community-
    Right-to-Know Act (Title III) 16, 79
employee awareness and education
    programs 203–4
employees: direct communication 58;
    organization's preparedness and
    biological crises 126
Emulex 198–9
engaging opposition groups 180–3
Enron 6, 254–8
Entenmann's 200
enterovirus 128–9
enterprise risk management (ERM)
    see risk management
environmental codes 309
environmental movement 161
Environmental Protection Agency 16;
    Chemical Emergency Preparedness
    Plan 40–1
equilibrium, restoration of 13–14
equipment maintenance 138, 217
Estonia 190–1
ethical codes 310
ethics 209–12; absence in the financial
    crisis 268–9; biological crises and
    advance decisions on 127; lapses at
    Enron 257; reinforcing organizational
    culture with 294–5
evacuation 98–9
evacuation plans 97
evasion of responsibility 62
executives *see* chief executive officers
    (CEOs), top management
exercises, crisis 39
exposure: public 15–17; reducing
    144–5, 178, 200–1
extractive industries 36
Exxon Corp 10, 250
Exxon Valdez oil spill 10, 55, 78, 134, 207,
    236–7, 248, 249

fact-finding 54
Fannie Mae 259–60
fatalistic attitudes 3
Febreze 196–7
Federal Aviation Administration
    (FAA) 226
Federal Emergency Management
    Administration *see* FEMA
Federal Energy Regulatory Commission
    (FERC) 149, 150
Federal Housing Finance Agency
    (FHFA) 260
Federal Reserve 267
federal review 170
FEMA Emergency Management
    Strategies 90–105
Fernandez, F. 228
Ferrier, A. 290–1
field crisis communication center 38–9,
    54
financial crisis of 2008 5, 6, 27, 199,
    258–70; apologies by bankers 64–6;
    bubble bursts 261; deception 262–5;
    enabling factors 265–9; evolution
    of 258–62; government bailout
    261–2; other aspects of management
    failure 269–70; and the response
    strategies to crises of management
    failure 270–7
financial industry 6
financial information infrastructure
    255–7
financial media 267–8
financial models 269
financial reporting, fraudulent 255
financial rumors 198–9
Firestone tires 67–72
First Energy Corp. 141
Flextronics 118
flooding: Pakistan 89–90, 98;
    Queensland 89
Folino, P. 198–9
Fombrun, C.J. 9–10
Fonterra Co-operative Goup 290–1
Food and Drug Administration
    (FDA) 128, 223, 232, 245, 246
food industry: food safety oversight
    231–2; recalls 221–3; varying quality
    assurance standards 227
Ford: Firestone tires 67–72; Pinto
    case 304
foreign aid 106–8
foreign ownership 70–1

forestalling the initiating event 142,
   143–4
Foundation for Public Affairs *Public
   Interest Profiles* 20
France 173–4
fraud 287–9
Freddie Mac 259–60
free-market system, pressures of 6
freedom of the press 50–1
Fremont-Smith, M. 282–3
Friedman, Milton 312
Friedman, Monroe 176
Friehling, D. 294
Fritz, L. 109
frustrations, defusing 202
Fukushima Daiichi nuclear facility
   150–1
Fuld, R. 260, 262, 268

Gardberg, N.A. 9–10
Garvin, D.A. 307–8
General Motors 249
genetic modification 133, 333
Genoa G8 meeting 180
Geoghan, J.J. 47–8, 321
Georgia Power Company 311
Gibbs, S. 48–9
Gilmartin, R.V. 242, 246
Giuliani, R. 40
Glass Steagall Act 266
GlaxoSmithKline (GSK) 220, 226–7
Global Pandemic Initiative 129
global warming 19, 301; and renaissance
   of nuclear power 150–1
globalization 6–7, 113; anti-globalization
   protests 161–2, 167–8, 175–6, 178,
   181
Glovis Co. 282
Goldstein, S.Z. 32
Goodman, R.S. 66–7
Goodpaster, K.E. 212
goodwill 9
government: information sources 15;
   interference in relief efforts 107–8;
   laissez faire 265–7; officials and
   responsibility in natural disasters
   105–6; oversight 230–2, 275–6, 296–
   7; regulation *see* regulation; role of 312
government bailout 261–2
Graham, D.J. 243, 245
Grant Thornton 288, 295
Greenpeace 164
Greenspan, A. 265–6

Grocery Manufacturers Association 231
Guardian 136–7
guerrilla marketing 238
Guillain-Barre Syndrome (GBS) 126
Gulf of Mexico oil spill 131, 134–9,
   145–8, 216–19, 228–30
Gulfstream 225
gun controls 195

Haiti earthquake 87–8; relief 103–5
Halliburton 217–18
Hallmark/Westland Meat Co. 222
hard engineering 91, 92
Hayek, F. 312
Hayward, T. 136, 218–19, 230, 238
hazard information hot line 96
hazard management strategies 90–105,
   105–6; BP's poor application of
   145–8; mitigation 90, 91–2; phases
   of 142–5; preparedness 90, 91, 92–8;
   recovery 91, 92, 99–105; response 90,
   91, 98–9; technological crises 141–50
hazardous substances 16, 79
HBOS 65, 66
health infrastructure 124
healthcare workers (HCWs) 127
Hearit, K. 61, 62, 63
heparin 220, 297
herd instinct 280
Hershman, M.J. 286
high credibility people 41
high-signal accidents 82–3
Hilton Hotels Corp. 101
HIV/AIDS 113, 124
Holland 92
Hollek, D. 136
Holloway, C. 217
honesty 56–7
Hong, H. 261
Hong Kong 116
house prices, falling 258–9
Hu Jintao 98
Hubbard, D.W. 25, 26, 27
human climate, crises of 20–1,
   155–7, 302; application of issues
   management 156–7; *see also*
   confrontation crises; malevolence,
   crises of
human error 140–1
human intervention, degree of 77–8
Humane Society 222
humility 272
Huntingdon Life Sciences (HLS) 171–2

Hurricane Ike 37
Hurricane Katrina 5, 18, 86–7, 93, 94,
    98–9; relief efforts 100–2
hurricanes 19
Hyundai Motor Co. 282

Iacocca, L. 67
ideology 248
ignorance 263
Ike, Hurricane 37
image restoration strategies 61–75;
    accommodative strategies 62–3,
    67, 68–9, 181–2; analyzing crisis
    types 66–7; apologies see apologies;
    Archbishop Cardinal Law 73–4;
    defensive strategies 62–3, 66, 67,
    68–9, 205–6; Firestone/Ford tire
    recall 67–72; limits of 74
immorality 209–10
incentive systems 6
incompetence 263
India: Mumbai terrorist attacks 186;
    water problems for Pepsi Cola and
    Coca-Cola 166–7
Indian Ocean tsunami 5, 18, 86, 94–5,
    108; relief effort 102–3
industrial agriculture 112
IndyMac 260
ingratiation 63
innovative learning 307
inspection of products 247–8
Institute for Crisis Management 33
intelligence gathering 175–6, 202–3
Interfauna 173
Interim Haiti Recovery Commission
    105
International Accounting Standards
    Board 296
international cyberspying 188–9, 190–1
International Monetary Fund (IMF),
    protests against 161–2, 168
Internet: activist groups and 163;
    biological crises 130; rumors on
    197–8, 203
Internet Wire 198
investment bankers 255, 256
Iran earthquake 108, 110
issues, identification by activist
    groups 160, 161–2
issues management systems 11, 304;
    application of 156–7
Ivester, D. 224
Ivins, B. 205

J.P. Stevens boycott 177–8
Jack-in-the-Box 44
Jackson, J. 93
Jakob, M. 198–9
James, E.H. 14
Janis, I. 4, 308
Japan: Kobe earthquake 106–7; nuclear
    accidents 139–40, 148–9, 150–1
Jarvis, J. 45
JCO 139–40, 148–9
JetBlue 63–4
Jobs, S. 197
Johnson & Johnson 9–10, 226, 244;
    recalls 219; Tylenol 9, 10, 38, 54, 58,
    201, 205
justification 62–3
Jyllands-Posten cartoons 50–1, 159,
    164–6, 176

Kahneman, D. 43, 278–80
Kaizaki, Y. 70–1, 72
Kaluza, R. 217
Kaminski, V. 254
Kansai Electric Power Company
    (Kepco) 139–40
Kansas City Hyatt Regency floating
    walkways 131–2
Kashmir earthquake 110
Katrina, Hurricane see Hurricane
    Katrina
Kellerman, B. 70
Kellogg 227
Kelo v. New London 36
Ketchum 71
KHOU-TV 69
Kleinfeld, K. 286, 293
Kobe earthquake 106–7
Krol, J. 31
Kursk Russian submarine 46–7
Kurzweil, R. 133, 151

labor disputes 173–4
labor unions 173–4, 175
Lagadec, P. 11, 12–13
Lahart, J. 261
laissez faire government 265–7
Lampe, J. 68, 70, 71, 72
land use policies 92
Landrieu, M. 101
Law, Cardinal B.F. 48, 49; image
    restoration strategies 73–4
law enforcement 179–80, 205
lawyers 255, 256

Lay, K. 255, 257, 258
Lazare, A. 63
leaded paint 238–42, 247–8
learning 301–13; assessment
    of vulnerability 303;
    communications 305–6; decision-
    making process 306–8; developing
    relationships 306; from failures 43–4;
    organizational culture 309–10;
    organizational renewal 310–13;
    reducing vulnerability 303–4; variable
    time perspective 308–9; vigilance and
    monitoring systems 304
learning organizations 307–8
Lee, R. 171–2
legal action 170, 179–80
Lehman Brothers 258, 260, 262, 268
Lesly, P. 180–1, 307
levees 101
Li Changjiang 241
Liddy, E. 270, 274
Liechtenstein Affair 281–2
Liu Jianlun 116
lobbying 275–6
local knowledge 148
local media 93–4, 326
local planning committees 79
log, keeping a 42–3
logistics, relief and 110
Logue, D. 63
Lombardo, K. 48
Long-Term Capital Management
    (LTCM) 269
long-term perspective 309
Loscher, P. 293
loss aversion 279
low-probability events 11–12
Lukaszewski, J. 45, 51, 59
Lunar New Year snow storm 87, 95

mad cow disease 122–4, 128
Madoff, B.I. 5, 283–5, 294, 296
Magara, M. 39
maintenance, equipment 138, 217
maintenance learning 307
major incidents 34
malevolence, crises of 5, 21, 155–7,
    185–206, 302; bioterrorism 168–70,
    187–8; Boston University rape
    case 192–3; cybercrime 188–91;
    defamation by blogging 191;
    rumors 196–200, 203; strategies
    200–6; terrorism see terrorism; Virginia

Tech shooting 29, 193–6, 204–5;
    workplace violence 191–2, 200
Malthus, T. 1
management failure, crises of 5,
    21–2, 207–13, 302; central role
    of ethics 209–12; damaged
    relationships 208–9; measuring the
    degree of success 212–13; see also
    deception, crises of, misconduct,
    mismanagement, skewed values,
    crises of
Maple Leaf Foods 206
Marcus, A.A. 66–7
Marine Well Containment Co. 147–8
market, type of 177
marketplace rumors 199–200
Marriott Hotels Corp. 101, 103
Marsh, A. 180
massacres 29, 193–6, 204–5
Mattel toy recall 238–42, 247–8
McCubbin, I. 226–7
McDonald's 172
McIntyre, T. 27, 28
McKinnell, H. 109–10
Means, G.C. 35
media 15, 69; activist groups and 160,
    163–4, 179; background press
    materials 41–2; confrontation crises
    and taking the initiative 178–9; crisis
    media list 41; Danish newspaper
    cartoons 50–1, 159, 164–6, 176;
    escorting journalists/camera crews on
    the emergency site 57; financial
    267–8; local 93–4, 326; preparation
    through public education and 96–8;
    and reputational damage 45–6
media relations, application of basic rules
    of 52–3
meeting with reasonable activist
    groups 180–1
melamine 239, 289, 290
Merck 242–6, 247
Merkl, P. 344
Merrill Lynch 260–1, 270
Metabolife 345 diet pill 57–8
meteorological responses 92
Metropole Hotel, Hong Kong 116
Metropolitan Edison 55–6
Mexico 120–1
Middle East 50–1, 164–6
Minerals Management Service
    (MMS) 217, 232
minimization 62–3

minor incidents 34
Minow, N. 273
misconduct 21–2, 207–13, 281–97;
    financial crisis 270; Madoff swindle 5,
    283–5, 294, 296; Parmalat 287–9,
    295; Sanlu baby formula scandal 289–
    92, 293, 296–7; Satyam Computer
    Services 286–7, 292–3, 294, 295;
    Siemens 285–6, 293–4; strategies for
    handling 292–7
mismanagement 21, 207–13, 215–34;
    airlines 225–6; BP Deepwater
    Horizon oil spill 216–19; food
    recalls 221–3; pharmaceutical
    companies and quality control 219–
    20; strategies for handling 226–33;
    tainted Coca-Cola 223–5
mitigation 90, 91–2; crises of
    malevolence 200–2
Mitroff, I.I. 8, 34, 235
monitoring: activist groups 175–6;
    systems 304
Moody, J. 264–5, 268–9
Moody's 264–5, 274
Moore, P. 66
morality see ethics
Morris, K. 64–5
mortgages, subprime 259, 260, 263–4
mortification 63, 73
Motorola 10
Mozilo, A. 260
MRSA 112
Muhammad, cartoon depictions of 50–1,
    159, 164–6, 176
Mumbai terrorist attacks 186
Munn v. People 35–6, 270
Muslims 50–1, 159, 164–6
Myanmar 107–8
Myers, K.M. 26

Nader, R. 249
names of victims 57
nanotechnology 131, 152–3
Narain, S. 166–7
NASA 190
Nasser, J. 71
National Biocontainment
    Laboratory 168–70
National Rifle Association (NRA) 195
natural disasters 5, 18–19, 77–83,
    85–110, 301–2; hazard management
    strategies 90–105; major issues in
    relief efforts 106–10; major natural

disasters 85–90; relief and recovery
    efforts 99–105; similarities with
    biological diseases 113–14
naturalistic syndrome 3
Nebraska Beef 222
necessity 36
needs and wants, modification of 142–3,
    145
Neeleman, D. 64
negative affect 208–9
negative exchange 208–9
negotiation with activist groups 181–2
Neiman Marcus 181
Nelson, C. 10, 11
Nestle 227, 292
New America Media (NAM) 129–30
New Century Financial Corp. 31–2
New Orleans 86–7, 92, 93, 94; bungled
    evacuation 98–9; relief efforts 100–2;
    see also Hurricane Katrina
New York Society of Security
    Analysts 17
New York State Emergency
    Management Office 40
news conference 56
Nicolazzo, R. 28
Nieuwoudt, G. 284–5
Nike 159
NIMBY attitude 82
9/11 terrorist attack 161–2, 185
Nixon, W.B. 200
non-governmental organizations
    (NGOs) 160
nonprofit organizations 7, 250;
    misconduct 282–3
Nooyi, A.K. 167
North American Electric Reliability
    Council 150
Northern Illinois University 194–5
Northwest Airlines 226
nuclear accidents: Chernobyl 78, 132;
    Japan 139–40, 148–9, 150–1; Three
    Mile Island 55–6, 57, 83, 317
nuclear power 36; global warming and
    renaissance of 150–1
Nuclear Regulatory Commission 55

Ocean Spray 29
Office of Patient Protection 246
oil spills 236–7; Exxon Valdez 10, 55, 78,
    134, 207, 236–7, 248, 249; Gulf of
    Mexico 131, 134–9, 145–8, 216–19,
    228–30

Olympic Games 201
online newsrooms 41–2
Ono, M. 70, 72
openness 32, 56–7, 215–16; China and
    the SARS crisis 117
opportunity, crisis as 14
order and priority sequence 51
Organisation for Economic Cooperation
    and Development (OECD) 181
organizational change 4, 13–14
organizational culture 32; learning from
    crises 309–10; reforming 248–9,
    274–5; reinforcing with ethics 294–5
organizational development (OD)
    310–11
organizational learning 307–8
organizational renewal 310–13
organizations: activist groups and
    selection of a vulnerable target
    organization 160, 162; assessing
    vulnerability of 176–8, 303;
    preparedness for biological crises 126;
    as vulnerable terrorist targets 186
O'Toole, J. 215–16
outsourcing 228
overconfidence 279
oversight, public 230–2, 275–6, 296–7

Pakistan, flooding in 89–90, 98
Palepu, K. 286
pandemics 112–13; preparedness
    for 124–30
Paquette, S. 103
Parker, E. 239–40
Parmalat 287–9, 295
participation 182–3, 307
Partners in Health 104
Pauchant, T.C. 8, 235
Paulson, H. 259, 260, 261
Peanut Corporation of America
    (PCA) 221–2, 227; dysfunctional
    board 231
Pearson, C.M. 13, 212–13, 236
Pegan, F. 85
People for the Ethical Treatment of
    Animals (PETA) 171, 172
Pepsi Cola 10, 166–7
perceived risks 80–3
Perrow, C. 20, 132
personal vulnerability 303
Pfizer 36, 244, 246, 247
pharmaceutical companies 219–20
Phuket 103

physical environment, crises of 18–20,
    77–83, 301–2; coping with risk 78–83;
    similarities and differences 77–8; see
    also biological crises, natural disasters,
    technological crises
physical infrastructure, reinforcing 91–2
physical preparedness 93
Podmolik, M.E. 271–2
police 180
Ponzi scheme 283
population growth 1, 18
pork 121–2
Port-au-Prince 87–8
post-crisis analysis 43
post-crisis phase 26–7
power of activist groups 174–5
power blackouts 140–1, 149–50
precautionary principle 141, 146, 151
pre-crisis phase 26
preemptive strategies 57–8
pre-existing technology, insufficient
    137–8
"pre-mortem" 34–5
preparedness 26–32, 90, 91,
    92–8; building a supporting crisis
    preparedness infrastructure 32;
    components of crisis preparedness
    30–2; crises of malevolence 203–5;
    early warning systems 92, 93–5;
    examples of crisis preparedness 28–9;
    pandemics 124–30; physical 92, 93;
    public education 92, 96–8; state of
    crisis preparedness 26–8; surveys on
    state of crisis preparedness 29–30
preventive measures 143, 146
PricewaterhouseCoopers 295
priests, sexual abuse by 47–50, 73–4
privacy vs safety 195–6
private property 35–6, 270
private sector aid 108–9
Procter & Gamble (P&G) 177, 181,
    196–7
product recalls 205–6; Coca-Cola
    223–4; food 221–3; Firestone/Ford
    tires 67–72; Johnson & Johnson 219;
    Mattel toys 238–42, 247–8; Sanlu
    baby formula 291–2
product safety incidents 67
product tampering 58, 205–6;
    Tylenol 9, 10, 38, 54, 58, 201, 205
professional associations 17, 312
property rights 35–6, 270
psychoanalytic theory 13

public affairs 313
public confidence, restoring 276–7
public corporations 35, 36, 303
public education 96–8; biological
    crises 128–9
public exposure 15–17
public interest 35–6, 270
public interest groups 16, 20, 157; *see also*
    confrontation crises
public nature of an organization 35–6
public oversight 230–2, 275–6, 296–7
public policies 304
public policy committees 249–50
public relations 313; experts 16, 271–2;
    support after a crisis of deception
    276–7
public utilities 35
publics to be informed 40–1
Puerto Rico GSK plant 220
Putin, V.V. 47

quality assurance 226–8
quality control, neglect of 219–20
Queensland flooding 89

Raju, B. Rama 286, 287
Raju, B. Ramalinga 286, 287
rape case 192–3
Rasmussen, A.F. 50, 164, 165
rating agencies, failure of 264–5
rational behavior 278
Rawl, L.G. 55, 248
rebuilding 101–2
recalls *see* product recalls
recovery 91, 92, 99–105
regional transmission organizations
    (RTOs) 149
regulation 36; absence in the financial
    sector 265–7; failure of regulators
    and Parmalat fraud 288–9; financial
    sector's need to accept 275–6; food
    safety 231–2; fragmented and power
    blackouts 140–1; self-regulation 14
relationships: damaged 208–9;
    developing 306; fear of disrupting
    3–4; repair of damaged 292–3
Relenza 125
relief 91, 92, 99–105, 145; adequacy
    of pledges 108; major issues in relief
    efforts 106–10
remedial action 240–1, 293
reputational damage 9–10; caused by
    media 45–6; repairing 228–30

Research in Motion Ltd (RIM) 56
reserve requirements 266
response 90, 91, 98–9; quick and
    decisive in biological crises 130
reward/compensation system 257,
    273–4, 310
Reynolds American Inc. 31
risk: behavioral economics 278–80;
    connection between crisis management
    and 2–4; crises of the physical
    environment and coping with 78–83;
    obstacles facing risk recognition 3–4
risk analysis 78–9; reevaluation in crises
    of skewed values 247–8; relevance and
    technological crises 133–4
risk aversion 2
risk communication 78–9
risk management 25–44, 273;
    contingency planning 26, 33–42, 44;
    crisis preparedness 26–32; keeping a
    log 42–3; learning from failures 43–4
risk-management committees 31
risk perception 80–3; principles 81–3
Royal Bank of Scotland (RBS) 65
Rubin, R. 271, 274
rumors 196–200, 203; financial
    198–9; Internet 197–8, 203; in the
    marketplace 199–200
Russia: *Kursk* submarine 46–7;
    wildfires 89

safety: vs privacy 195–6; toys made in
    China 239–40
safety authorities 58
safety devices 146; implementing use of
    safety gear 145
safety testing 216–17
salmonella 188, 221, 222
Salvation Army 100
Samsung Electronics 282
Samsung Group 197
San Diego University business school 7
Sanlu baby formula scandal 289–92,
    293, 296–7
Satyam Computer Services 286–7,
    292–3, 294, 295
Schwab, K. 112
SARS (severe acute respiratory
    syndrome) crisis 6–7, 114–19
scandals 66–7, 281; *see also* misconduct
Schaubroeck, J. 43
science 1–2
Scott Paper Co. 350

Seattle protests 167–8, 175–6, 178, 181
secrecy 115–17, 119
Securities and Exchange Commission
   (SEC) 255, 257, 266, 270, 275, 296
securitization 263–4, 269
security analysts 255, 256
security measures 205;
   cybersecurity 201–2;
   strengthening 201–2
selective perception 307
self-regulation 14
September 11 terrorist attack 161–2,
   185
Sepulvado, R. 217
serious incidents 34
Sethi, S.P. 250
severity of a crisis 8, 34
sexual abuse scandal of the Catholic
   Church 47–50, 73–4
Sherrill, P. 192
shock learning 307
short-termism 279, 308–9
Sichuan earthquake 5, 87, 95, 98
Siemens 285–6, 293–4
Silbergeld, E. 112
silicon breast implants 207
simmering crisis 246
simulations 39
sincere apology, criteria for 70
single-loop learning 43
size, organizational 176–7
skewed values, crises of 21, 207–13,
   235–51; BP oil spill 137, 237–8; *Exxon
   Valdez* 236–7; financial crisis 269–70;
   Mattel's toy recall 238–42; Merck and
   the withdrawal of Vioxx 242–6, 247;
   strategies for crisis management
   246–50; Turner Broadcasting
   System 238
Skilling, J. 255
Slovic, P. 80
smallpox 188
smouldering crises 10
Snow Brand 63
social accounting 250
social audit 250
social media 15, 41, 197; BP's
   use of 229–30; Domino's Pizza
   video prank 27–8; and the Haiti
   earthquake 103–4
social performance 177–8
social reports 250
social responsibility: absence in the

financial crisis 268–9; acceptance
   of 211–12; corporate 235, 313
society, harmonizing business and
   312–13
soft engineering 91, 92
Sony 45
specialization 306–7
spokespersons: designation and
   training 42; speaking with a single
   voice 55–6
spying (cyberspying) 188–9, 190–1
stakeholder management 156–7
stakeholder symmetry/asymmetry 235,
   302
stakeholders 32, 161;
   communicating with 305–6;
   developing relationships 306;
   direct communication with key
   stakeholders 58–9
standards, in the food industry 227
static kill procedure 138
Steele, J.M. 249
Stiglitz, J. 264
stock exchanges 255, 256
stock options 257; backdating of 294
Stop Huntingdon Animal Cruelty
   (SHAC) 171–2
stress 12–13
subprime mortgages 259, 260, 263–4
successful outcomes, criteria for 212–13
suddenness 10–11
Sullenberger, C. 225
Sullivan, M. 268
Superfund Amendments and
   Reauthorization Act (SARA) 16, 79
supply chain disruption 7
supporting crisis preparedness
   infrastructure 32
suppression of information 115
surprise, avoiding 175–6
swine flu (H1N1) 112–13, 120–2, 125–6,
   128

tactics, crisis-provoking 160, 162–3
Tamiflu 125
Tanzi, C. 287, 288, 289
technological crises 19–20, 77–83,
   131–53, 301–2; BP oil spill 131,
   134–9, 145–8, 216–19, 228–30;
   hazard management strategies 141–50;
   nuclear accidents 139–40, 148–9,
   150–1; power blackouts 140–1, 149–50;
   relevance of risk analysis 133–4

technology 1–2; the future for
  dangerous technologies 150–1;
  nanotechnology 131, 152–3; rapid
  pace of growth of 132–3; supporting
  crisis preparedness infrastructure 32
temporary shelter 99–100
terrorism 185–6, 202–3, 204, 205, 341,
  344; bioterrorism 168–70, 187–8;
  Mumbai attacks 186; 9/11 161–2,
  185
Thain, J. 269–70, 273
Three Mile Island accident 55–6, 57,
  83, 317
tiger teams 204
time compression 12–13
time perspective 279; variable 308–9
TJX 189–90, 200
Tokyo Electric Power Co. (Tepco)
  139–40, 150–1
Tonna, F. 289
top management: alerting 53–4;
  replacement of 274, 293–4;
  willingness to recognize risks 30–1;
  see also chief executive officers (CEOs)
Top Taste 206
Topol, E.J. 243
Topps Meat Co. 5, 221
Toronto University Joint Centre for
  Bioethics 127
Toshiba 316
tourism 102–3
toy recall 238–42, 247–8
trade associations 227
trade publications 59
training 39, 203–4
transactions 211
transformational development
  (TD) 310–11
transparency 127, 128–9, 215–16, 270–2
trauma theory 13
Troubled Assets Recovery Plan
  (TARP) 262
trust 208, 262
tsunami 150–1; Indian Ocean 5, 18, 86,
  94–5, 102–3, 108; Padang 110
Turner Broadcasting System 238
TWA Flight 800 40–1
Twitter 41
Tyco 31
Tylenol 9, 10, 38, 54, 58, 201, 205
typologies of crises 17–22, 66–7

UBS AG 270

uncertainty 11–12
unified authority structure 147
Union Bancaire Privee (UBP) 284–5
Union Carbide 67
unions 173–4, 175
United Kingdom (UK): apologies by
  British bankers 64–5, 66; mad cow
  disease 122–3, 124
United States (US): adequacy of
  relief pledges 108; apologies by
  bankers 65–6; Coast Guard 41;
  Department of Agriculture
  (USDA) 223; Postal Service 192;
  power blackout 140–1
universal banking model 273–4
unknown risks 82
Upshaw, L. 272
upstream hazard control measures
  142–3; BP's poor application 145–6
USA Today 69
USAir Flight 427 322

vaccination 125–6
Vatican 48, 49
vertical integration 7
video activists 179
vigilant problem solving 308
violence: Boston University
  rape case 192–3; massacre at
  Virginia Tech 29, 193–6, 204–5;
  workplace 191–2, 200
Vioxx 242–6, 247
Virginia Tech shootings 29, 193–6,
  204–5
viruses 114
visibility 176–7; reducing 200–1
Vorhaus, R. 218
vulnerability 33–6; assessing
  organizational 176–8, 303; assessing
  personal 303; based on organization's
  public nature 35–6; business as
  a vulnerable terrorist target 186;
  reducing 200–2, 303–4; selection of
  a vulnerable target organization 160,
  162; specific vulnerabilities 33–5

Wagner, J. 102
Wallach, L. 168
Wal-Mart 93, 100–1
wants and needs, modification of 142–3,
  145
warning signal 11, 69, 216, 224, 237,
  256

Washington Mutual (WaMu) 260
water problems 166–7
Waugh, W.L. 91–2
Weldon, W. 226, 244
Wen Jiabao 87
Wenhua, T. 296
whistle-blowing 16
Whitman, C. 193
wildfires: Australia 88–9, 97–8, 99; Russia 89
Wilson Group Communications 16–17
Witt, J.L. 90, 99
workplace violence 191–2, 200
World Bank: involving public interest groups in decision making 182–3; protests against 161–2, 168
World Economic Forum 178, 180

World Health Organization (WHO): legitimacy crisis 118–19; pandemic scale 129–30; SARS crisis 114, 115, 116, 117, 118–19
World Trade Center terrorist attacks 161–2, 185
World Trade Organization (WTO), protests against 168
worst case scenarios 34
Wright County Egg Co. 222–3

Yamaguchi-gumi 107
Yates, D. 103
YouTube 27–8

Zimbardo, P. 210
Zumwinkel, K. 282